*Estate Planning Strategie*

# A Lawyer's Guide to Retirement and Lifetime Planning

*Jay A. Soled*

**Senior Lawyers Division**
**American Bar Association**

Cover design by Cathy Zaccarine.

The materials contained herein represent the opinions of the authors and editors and should not be construed to be the action of either the American Bar Association or the Senior Lawyers Division unless adopted pursuant to the bylaws of the Association.

Nothing contained in this book is to be considered as the rendering of legal advice for specific cases, and readers are responsible for obtaining such advice from their own legal counsel. This book and any forms and agreements herein are intended for educational and informational purposes only.

06                  5 4 3 2

### Library of Congress Cataloging-in-Publication Data

   Estate planning strategies: a lawyer's guide to retirement and lifetime planning / Jay Soled, editor.
        p.  cm.
     Includes bibliographic references and index.
     ISBN 1-59031-094-2
        1. Lawyers—Retirement—United States. 2. Practice of law—Economic aspects—United States. 3. Estate planning—United States. 4. Lawyers—Taxation—United States. 5. Lawyers—Medical care—United States.  I. Soled, Jay A.

KF315 .E84 2002
332.024'344—dc21

                                    2002007864

Discounts are available for books ordered in bulk. Special consideration is given to state bars, CLE programs, and other bar-related organizations. Inquire at Book Publishing, ABA Publishing, American Bar Association, 750 North Lake Shore Drive, Chicago, Illinois 60611.

www.ababooks.org

*To my wife, Amy*

# SUMMARY OF CONTENTS

# CONTENTS

## Chapter 3
## Minimum Distribution Requirements   21
*Louis A. Mezzullo*

## Chapter 4
## The Simplified Retirement Plan Alternative   37
*David L. Higgs*

## *Chapter 5*
## The New Individual Retirement Account   45
*Stephen P. Magowan*

## **PART II: Inter Vivos Gifts   53**

## *Chapter 6*
## Lifetime Tax Planning   55
*Allan C. Bell*

*Chapter 7*
**The Charitable Remainder Trust   73**
*Michael V. Bourland and Jeffrey N. Myers*

*Chapter 8*
**Charitable Lead Trusts  87**
*Santo Bisignano, Jr. and Toby M. Eisenberg*

*Chapter 12*
**Family Foundation: The Legacy Continues   175**
*Stephen A. Frost*

## Chapter 13
## Qualified Personal Residence Trusts   193
*Carmela T. Montesano*

## Chapter 14
## Grantor-Retained Annuity Trusts and Grantor-Retained Unitrusts   203
*Zeb Law*

*Chapter 18*
**The Living (Revocable) Trust: An Estate-Planning Tool   253**
*Sarah M. Linsley*

## Chapter 19
## Joint Accounts: Dangers and Alternatives 263
*Richard V. Wellman*

## Chapter 20
## Jointly Owned Property 271
*Robert T. Danforth*

## Chapter 21
## Estate Planning Malpractice and Ethical Issues 281
*Isabel Miranda*

# INTRODUCTION

JAY A. SOLED

On June 7, 2001, President Bush signed into law the Economic Growth and Tax Relief Reconciliation Act of 2001 (EGTRRA). Among other things, EGTRRA fundamentally alters and reshapes the nation's transfer tax system (that is, estate, gift, and generation-skipping transfer tax(es)) and ushers in a new era in estate planning.

This book is designed as a guide to help circumnavigate the estate-planning world and specific changes EGTRRA has brought. To assist in the navigation process, the book is divided into three parts.

The first part of the book summarizes the estate-planning strategies lawyers should develop regarding clients' retirement assets. All too often retirement assets comprise the bulk of a client's net worth. Unfortunately, all too often lawyers pay too little attention to the proper disposition of these assets and their concomitant tax burden. Dedication of the first section of this book to the estate planning do's and don'ts for retirement assets testifies to the importance of this area of the law.

The second part of the book reviews lifetime planning strategies that assist clients in minimizing their transfer tax burdens. Although EGTRRA reduces transfer tax rates, increases the applicable exclusion amount, and (for a one-year period) eliminates the estate tax (see summary of EGTRRA, following), these changes are gradual—and, as a practical matter, it is far from certain that these changes will ever be fully instituted. To the contrary, given looming budget shortfalls and the coming Social Security solvency crisis, the majority of commentators share the view that EGTRRA's historic changes to the transfer tax system may never come to pass. Circumspection is therefore the lawyers' watchword. This section of the book presents a menu of various lifetime estate-planning options for lawyers and their clients to consider.

The third part of the book focuses upon the importance of proper testamentary planning. Its chapters discuss how clients should plan for the disposition of their estates in ways that fulfill their testamentary intent while simultaneously being tax-efficacious. It concludes with a chapter on estate-planning malpractice, highlighting the consequences associated with a lawyer's failure to meet professional responsibilities.

Having discussed the arrangement of this book, a short overview of the changes associated with EGTRRA is now in order. While EGTRRA's changes are generally pro-taxpayer, they form a landscape akin to that of a Monet, which is striking and colorful, but not very clear or sharp in focus. It is upon this landscape, however, that lawyers and their clients must now traverse.

## A. Structural Changes to the Transfer Tax System

EGTRRA makes four major changes to the transfer tax system. First, the Act gradually reduces the maximum estate and gift-tax rate from 55 percent to 45 percent. Second, the Act gradually increases the applicable exclusion amount (generally, the amount taxpayers can transfer tax-free during lifetime and/or at death to nonspouse beneficiaries) from $675,000 (for 2001) to $3.5 million (for 2009). (The chart at the end of the introduction illustrates on a year-by-year basis how EGTRRA phases in these rate reductions and increases in the applicable exclusion amount.) Third, EGTRRA gradually increases the generation–skipping transfer tax exemption to mirror the increase in the applicable exclusion amount. Lastly, EGTRRA completely phases out federal estate and generation-skipping transfer taxes effective January 1, 2010, only to reinstate them again (in the form they existed in 2002) after December 31 of that year, when EGTRRA is scheduled to expire.

## B. The Gift Tax

EGTRRA does not call for repeal of the gift tax. Apparently, Congress was concerned that this would encourage taxpayers to structure arrangements with the intent to reduce their income tax obligations. That is, absent a gift tax, taxpayers might transfer as gifts income-generating assets to related taxpayers in lower income tax brackets.

The tax rate on taxable gifts through 2009 will gradually decline. In 2010, the maximum gift-tax rate will be further reduced to the top individual income tax rate which, at that time, is scheduled to be 35 percent. The lifetime gift-tax exclusion is not, however, scheduled to exceed $1 million. On January 1, 2011, the maximum gift-tax rate is scheduled to increase to 55 percent because EGTRRA expires on December 31, 2010.

## C. Carryover Basis

Effective January 1, 2010, EGTRRA also repeals the basis-equals-fair-market-value rule. By way of background, when a taxpayer dies, the Internal Revenue Code currently adjusts the tax basis of any property included in a taxpayer's gross estate to fair market value. For example, if A had purchased land in 1990 for $100,000 and died in 2000 when the land was worth $7 million, A's beneficiaries would have had a $7 million tax basis in the land received by inheritance. This rule can, upon sale of the inherited property, significantly reduce the capital gain and income tax liability of estate beneficiaries.

In lieu of the basis equals fair market value rule, EGTRRA institutes a carryover basis rule beginning in 2010. Under the new rule, subject to several exceptions, recipients of property transferred at a decedent's death will receive a tax basis in the property equal to the lesser of the decedent's adjusted basis or the fair market value of the property on the date of the decedent's death. In addition to the decedent's existing tax basis in the property, nonspouse beneficiaries will be able to add up to $1.3 million to the bases of inherited assets; furthermore, a surviving spouse will be able to add up to an additional $3 million. Using the prior example with A as the decedent, a nonspouse beneficiary would have a $1.4 million ($100,000 + $1.3 million) tax basis in the land, while a surviving spouse would have a $4.4 million tax basis ($100,000 + $1.3 million + $3 million).

## D. Our Expert Navigators

The purpose of this book is to sensitize lawyers to the estate-planning needs of their clients in a legal environment that is in transition. Planning in the area of estate planning has always been a painstaking task; EGTRRA now makes this an even more daunting task.

To assist in the navigation process, many of the nation's top estate-planning experts and practitioners have been assembled to participate in the production of this book. EGTRRA may have affected the directional tide of estate planning, but using the wisdom of those who participated in this book should lead to your smooth sailing.

Applicable Exclusion Amounts and Highest Estate and Gift Tax Rates

| Calendar Year | Estate and GST Tax Death-Time Transfer Exemption | Highest Estate and Gift Tax Rates |
|---|---|---|
| 2002 | $1.0 million | 50% |
| 2003 | $1.0 million | 49% |
| 2004 | $1.5 million | 48% |
| 2005 | $1.5 million | 47% |
| 2006 | $2.0 million | 46% |
| 2007 | $2.0 million | 45% |
| 2008 | $2.0 million | 45% |
| 2009 | $3.5 million | 45% |
| 2010 | N/A (taxes repealed) | 35% |
| 2011 | $1.0 million | 55% |

# PART I

*Social Security, Pensions, and IRAs*

# CHAPTER 1

# The Social Security Cash Machine

JONATHAN BARRY FORMAN

As a theoretical model of social planning and reward for hard work, the Social Security system's Old-Age and Survivors' Insurance (OASI) program is a thing of beauty. In this largest U.S. social welfare program, which collected $396 billion in payroll taxes in 1999 and distributed $334 billion in benefits that same year,[1] workers pay taxes with the assurance that, when they retire or die, they or their families will receive their just rewards.

If only reality fit the model. The truth is that the OASI's outflow of benefits is based on calculations that unfairly favor some workers and their families over others: Low earners fare comparatively better than high earners, married couples fare better than singles, single-earner couples fare better than dual-earner couples, and elderly retirees fare better than elderly workers.

## I. Cash In, Benefits Out

OASI benefits are overwhelmingly financed through payroll taxes imposed on workers covered by the Social Security system.

### A. Financing OASI

In 2002, for example, employees and employers each pay a Social Security payroll tax equal to 7.65 percent on up to $84,900 of wages earned in covered employment, and 1.45 percent of wages over that amount.[2] Similarly, self-employed workers pay an equivalent Social Security tax of 15.3 percent on the first $84,900 of self-employment earnings, and 2.9 percent of self-employment earnings over that amount. The lion's share of these payroll taxes is used to finance the OASI program (the rest pay for disability insurance and Medicare). For 2002, employees and employers each pay an OASI tax of 5.3 percent on the first $84,900 of wages earned in covered employment, and self-employed workers pay an equivalent OASI tax of 10.6 percent on up to $84,900 of net earnings.

In addition, Social Security benefits are subject to income taxation. A complicated two-tier formula determines the actual amount. Basically, single taxpayers with incomes over $25,000 and married couples with incomes over $32,000 must include as much as half of their Social Security benefits in income, and single taxpayers with incomes over $34,000 and married couples with incomes over $44,000 must include as much as 85 percent of their Social Security benefits in income. These taxes provide additional financing for the OASI program.

3

### B.  Reaping Benefits

*1.  Worker Beneficiaries*

Workers over age 62 generally are entitled to OASI benefits if they have worked in covered employment for at least ten years. Benefits are based on a measure of the worker's earnings history in covered employment known as the average indexed monthly earnings (AIME). Basically, the AIME measures the worker's career-average monthly earnings in covered employment.

The AIME is linked by a formula to the monthly retirement benefit payable to a worker at full retirement age, a benefit known as the primary insurance amount (PIA). For a worker turning 62 in 2002, the PIA is equal to 90 percent of the first $592 of the worker's AIME plus 32 percent of the next $2,975 plus 15 percent of AIME over $3,567 (if any).[3] It is worth noting that, on its face, the benefit formula is progressive, meaning it is designed to favor workers with relatively low career-average earnings.

A worker's benefits may be increased or decreased for several reasons. Benefits are indexed each year for inflation (as measured by the increase in the Consumer Price Index). Also, benefits payable to workers who choose to retire later than their normal retirement age are actuarially increased through a mechanism known as the delayed retirement credit. On the other hand, workers who retire earlier than their normal retirement age have their benefits actuarially reduced. Moreover, the retirement earnings test can reduce the benefits of individuals ages 62 to 64 who continue to work after retirement. In 2002, these workers lose $1 of benefits for every $2 of annual earnings over $11,280.[4]

*2.  Auxiliary Beneficiaries*

Retired workers are not the only beneficiaries of OASI. Dependents and survivors of the worker may also receive additional monthly benefits. These auxiliary benefit amounts are also based on the worker's PIA. (For convenience, worker and auxiliary benefits are generally combined into a single monthly check.)

For example, a 65-year-old spouse of a retired worker is entitled to a monthly spousal benefit equal to 50 percent of that worker's PIA. Consequently, a retired worker and spouse generally can claim a monthly benefit equal to 150 percent of what that retired worker alone could claim. Furthermore, a sixty-five-year-old widow or widower of the worker is entitled to a monthly surviving-spouse benefit equal to 100 percent of a worker's PIA. Auxiliary beneficiaries can begin receiving actuarially reduced benefits before age 65.

These auxiliary benefit amounts are subject to a variety of limitations. For example, the retirement earnings test also limits the benefits paid to auxiliary beneficiaries who continue to work, unless they have reached full retirement age. Also, the maximum monthly benefit that can be paid any worker is limited to between 150 and 188 percent of the worker's PIA. Moreover, under the dual entitlement rule, when someone is entitled both to a worker's benefit and also to a benefit as an auxiliary of another worker, only the larger of the two benefits is paid.

## II.  Your Money's Worth?

So how well do workers who have paid into the Social Security system fare when the time comes for them to be on the receiving end? The best way to understand OASI's distributional features is to evaluate the program's impact over the course of a worker's lifetime. This lifetime perspective leads to a comparison between the OASI taxes paid by a worker and the expected benefits.

For example, one might compare the expected value at age 65 of the OASI taxes that a worker paid over a career, together with interest at a market rate on those tax payments, with the expected value at age 65 of the stream of OASI benefits that the worker can expect to receive for life. The worker will receive his or her money's worth if the expected value of benefits to be received equals the expected value of all taxes paid. If the expected value of taxes paid exceeds the expected value of benefits, then the worker would in effect be financing other program participants. But if the expected value of benefits exceeds the expected value of the taxes paid, then the worker would reap extra benefits from other participants.

Numerous studies have made just such comparisons. Their results clearly show that the link between the OASI taxes paid by a worker and the expected benefits is quite loose and can vary dramatically depending on such factors as family status, income, and age.[5] If we compare the current OASI program to a model in which each worker earned an actuarially fair rate of return on taxes paid, the current program clearly allows significant transfers that favor some workers over others.

In short, not everyone gets his or her money's worth. In particular, the current OASI program favors early generations of retirees over later generations, low earners over high earners, married couples over singles, larger families over smaller families, single-earner couples over dual-earner couples, and elderly retirees over elderly workers. We'll discuss these in turn.

### A. Early Generations versus Later Generations

Early generations of OASI beneficiaries receive disproportionately greater benefits than their meager tax contributions might otherwise justify. Their rich rewards are the inevitable consequence of two facts: (1) Early participants paid relatively low taxes over relatively short coverage periods, yet (2) they received relatively generous benefits over relatively long benefit periods. Thus, the OASI program favors early generations of beneficiaries over later generations.

Fortunately, the OASI program is close to maturity, with most workers having been in covered employment or self-employment throughout their careers. Additionally, both the OASI tax rate and tax base have been increased for actuarial soundness. Studies project that by the time the baby boomers retire (starting around 2010), the value of the OASI benefits they will receive should roughly equal the value of the OASI taxes they paid.[6] Generations retiring prior to 2010 will receive more favorable treatment, but the size of these intergenerational transfers will diminish over time.

### B. Low Earners versus High Earners

Because of the progressive formula used to compute OASI benefits, workers with low earnings over their careers tend to receive disproportionately greater benefits than workers with high earnings. Note, however, that this redistribution occurs only within the limited range of covered earnings (up to $84,900 in 2002); above this cap, earnings are not redistributed. For example, a worker earning $1 million a year pays no more OASI tax than a worker earning $84,900 a year does. Also, the progressive redistribution (from high-income to low-income workers) may be offset by the longer life expectancies of high-income workers and their spouses and by the greater likelihood that spousal and surviving-spouse benefits will be paid to spouses of high earners.

### C. Married Couples versus Singles; Larger Families versus Smaller Families

Because of spousal and surviving-spouse benefits, married couples tend to receive relatively more benefits than singles. To illustrate this dichotomy, consider that a single worker with no dependents will receive a benefit at normal retirement age of just 100 percent of the worker's PIA, while a worker with a spouse will receive 150 percent of the worker's PIA, and a surviving spouse can receive 100 percent of a worker's benefit long after that worker's death.

Furthermore, providing auxiliary benefits for other dependents favors larger families over smaller families and singles. A worker with a spouse and additional dependents could receive a monthly benefit of as high as 188 percent of the worker's PIA, yet a worker with a spouse and no other dependents would receive a monthly benefit of just 150 percent of the PIA. In contrast, a single worker would receive a monthly benefit of just 100 percent of the PIA.

### D. Single-Earner versus Dual-Earner Couples

Two additional problems result from providing spousal and surviving-spouse benefits based on the earnings of a retired worker. First, two-earner couples generally receive lower total benefits than one-earner couples with the same earnings. Second, because married women with earnings might earn less and work a shorter time than their husbands, they could receive little or no additional OASI benefits from their OASI tax payments.

As more and more women enter the workforce, these two inequities will become increasingly important. In 1950, only about one-third of women were in the workforce, yet by 1998 they had nearly doubled their presence: Nearly 60 percent of women age 20 and older were in the workforce.[7] Also, of the 13.5 million retired women who received Social Security benefits in December 1999, about 5.8 million were dually entitled.[8]

Let's examine these two inequities.

#### 1. The Penalty on Dual-Earner Couples

The individual income tax is based on individual income, but married couples may file jointly and enjoy preferential tax rates. In contrast, the OASI tax is based on individual filing units (workers), but OASI benefits are paid based on certain family-unit relationships (workers and their auxiliaries). Consequently, the OASI tax and benefit structure can result in significant penalties on dual-earner couples as opposed to single-earner couples.

Figure 1.1 compares the OASI benefit entitlement of four hypothetical couples with various average annual lifetime earnings. All of the couples reached age 65 in 1992.

Even though the Cleavers, Bunkers, and Keatons all had the same average annual lifetime earnings and so paid the same total OASI taxes, their respective OASI worker and spousal benefits vary dramatically, depending upon the relative earnings of the two spouses.

**FIGURE 1.1**

Average Annual Lifetime Earnings and 1992 Monthly Social Security Retirement Benefits[a]

|  | Cleavers | Bunkers | Keatons | Seavers |
|---|---|---|---|---|
| EARNINGS |  |  |  |  |
| Husband | $24,000 | $16,000 | $12,000 | $24,000 |
| Wife | $ 0 | $ 8,000 | $12,000 | $ 8,000 |
| Family Total | $24,000 | $24,000 | $24,000 | $32,000 |
| BENEFITS |  |  |  |  |
| Husband | $ 957 WB[b] | $ 712 WB | $ 591 WB | $ 957 WB |
| Wife | $ 478 SB[b] | $ 468 WB | $ 591 WB | $ 478 SB |
| Family Total | $ 1,435 | $ 1,180 | $ 1,182 | $ 1,435 |
| SURVIVOR BENEFITS |  |  |  |  |
| Amounts | $ 957 | $ 712 | $ 591[c] | $ 957 |
| Percent of Couple's Benefit | 67% | 60% | 50% | 67% |

**Notes**
[a] For workers retiring at age 65 in 1992.
[b] WB = Workers Benefit; SB = Spousal Benefit.
[c] Spouse continues to collect on her own benefit. Survivor benefit does not apply.

The Cleavers, a single-earner couple, end up with the highest combined worker and spousal benefit ($1,435 per month). That's $250 a month more than either the Bunkers or the Keatons, the dual-earner couples with identical family earnings ($24,000 per year). Moreover, the Seavers receive no family benefit over the Cleavers, even though the Seavers consistently earned and paid OASI taxes on another $8,000 a year in family earnings.

Similar inequities can be observed when surviving-spouse benefits are considered. The table shows surviving-spouse benefits that each wife could claim if she survived her husband. There again, even though the Cleavers, Bunkers, and Keatons all had the same average annual lifetime earnings, the Cleaver widow, of the single-earner couple, ends up with the highest surviving-spouse benefit ($957). Moreover, the Seaver widow gains no additional surviving-spouse benefit over the Cleaver widow, even though the Seavers consistently paid OASI taxes on $8,000 a year more in family earnings.

### 2. The Penalty on Secondary Workers

The inequity really falls on the secondary workers—those married individuals who earn less than their spouses do. When a secondary worker is entitled to OASI benefits both as a retired worker and as a spouse (or surviving spouse) of a primary worker, the dual entitlement rule prevents the secondary worker from receiving both the full worker's benefit and the full spousal (or surviving-spouse) benefit. Instead, only the larger of the two benefits is paid. Thus the secondary worker gets no return on OASI taxes paid unless his or her worker benefit exceeds the spousal (or surviving-spouse) benefit based on the primary worker's earnings record.

Indeed, for many secondary workers in dual-earner couples, the additional OASI taxes they paid will produce no more OASI benefits than if they had not worked at all and paid no OASI taxes. This inequity will occur any time the worker benefit earned by one spouse is more than twice the worker benefit earned by the other. He or she would then receive a greater OASI benefit as a spouse than as a retired worker.

For example, compare the Cleavers to the Seavers in the table. The Seavers' combined worker and spousal benefit is no larger than the total received by the Cleavers. In effect, the Seaver wife received no OASI benefit from the OASI taxes she paid on her $8,000 a year of earnings.

Surviving spouses fare even worse. A surviving spouse will receive no OASI benefit from the OASI taxes she paid unless her earnings were greater than her husband's. Clearly substantial penalties are imposed upon dual-earner couples in general and on secondary workers in particular.

### E. Elderly Retirees versus Elderly Workers

Monthly OASI benefits are paid as a matter of right to anyone covered who retires at age 62 or older. Should a person continue to work, his or her OASI benefits may be reduced by the OASI earnings test. Further, continuing to work means continuing to pay Social Security and income taxes on those subsequent earnings—on top of income tax on a portion of the OASI benefits. With these tax provisions and the earnings test, some elderly are socked with such high effective marginal tax rates that they are discouraged from working. For example, a worker who faces the 27.5-percent income tax rate, the inclusion of 85 percent of his or her OASI benefits in income, and the 7.65 percent Social Security tax rate will face an effective marginal tax rate of almost 60 percent. If also subject to the Social Security retirement earnings test, their effective marginal tax rates are even higher.

## III. Moving toward an Individual Account System

Such problems have made Social Security reform a hot topic for the past few years. Many analysts have called for replacing all (or part) of the current Social Security system with a system of individual retirement savings accounts (IRSAs). These would operate pretty much like today's employer-sponsored 401(k) plans or Individual Retirement Accounts (IRAs).[9]

For example, the 1994–1996 Social Security Advisory Council issued a report on how to reform the Social Security system.[10] The Council members were unable to achieve a consensus, but a majority agreed that at least a portion of Social Security payroll tax contributions should be redirected into IRSAs that would invest in the stock market. Under the Individual Accounts (IA) approach, these individual accounts would be held by the government, invested in secure equity funds, and annuitized on retirement.

Alternatively, under the Personal Security Accounts (PSA) approach, these individual accounts would be held by financial institutions, and individual workers would direct their investment.[11] Reallocating 5 percentage points of the employee's share of Social Security payroll taxes would finance these PSAs. Workers under age 55 (at the time of adoption of the proposal) would participate in the 5-percent payroll reallocation and receive PSA benefits based on their accumulations plus interest. Workers could begin withdrawing funds from their PSAs at age 62, and any funds remaining in their accounts at death could be passed on to their heirs.

These days, it is common for proponents of individual accounts to talk about adding or "carving out" 2 or 3 percent of payroll to fund individual accounts. For example, the Committee for Economic Development advocated leaving the basic Social Security system intact but creating a second tier of privately owned personal retirement accounts (PRAs). Both employers and employees would be required to contribute 1.5 percent of payroll to these PRAs, and the self-employed would be required to contribute the entire 3 percent. Similarly, the National Commission on Retirement Policy offered a proposal to allocate 2 percentage points of the current payroll tax into Social Security Individual Savings Accounts.

Unlike the current defined-benefit Social Security system, an individual account system would be a defined contribution plan; there would be no redistribution at all. Payroll contributions and the earnings on those contributions would remain in individual accounts, and no money would ever be taken from a worker's account to provide benefits for other workers or other workers' families.

Moreover, unlike the current Social Security system, which tends to push older workers into early retirement, an individual account system would be retirement-neutral insofar as timing is concerned. Whoever worked past normal retirement age would continue to have additional contributions made to their accounts and would continue to earn income on the balances in those accounts—eliminating financial penalties for staying in the workforce.

## *IV. Conclusion*

This chapter raises some serious questions about the fairness of Social Security's OASI program. The current program seems unfair to single workers, dual-earner couples, and elderly workers. It is time to reform the OASI program.

### *Endnotes*

1. SOCIAL SECURITY ADMINISTRATION, ANNUAL STATISTICAL SUPPLEMENT, 2000 (TO THE SOCIAL SECURITY BULLETIN 136 (2001).

2. Social Security Administration, *Cost-of-Living Increase and Other Determinations for 2002*, 66 Fed. Reg. 54,047 (October 25, 2001).

3. *Id.*

4. *Id.*

5. See, e.g., Jonathan B. Forman, *Promoting Fairness in the Social Security Retirement Program: Partial Integration and a Credit for Dual-earner Couples*, 45 TAX LAW. 915 (1992).

6. *Id.*

7. Howard N. Fullerton, Jr., *Labor Force Participation: 75 Years of Change, 1950–98 and 1998–2025*, 122, 12 MONTHLY LAB. REV. 3, 4 (December 1999).

8. SOCIAL SECURITY ADMINISTRATION, ANNUAL STATISTICAL SUPPLEMENT, 2000 (TO THE SOCIAL SECURITY BULLETIN) 159–160, 208 (2001).

9. *See, e.g.,* Jonathan Barry Forman, *Universal Pensions*, 2 CHAPMAN L. REV. 95, 110–14 (1999).

10. *Id.* at 110–11.

11. *Id.*

# CHAPTER 2

# Social Security

HAROLD G. WREN

## I. Introduction

Social Security is a term used to describe benefits paid monthly to the beneficiaries under the Old-Age, Survivors', and Disability Insurance Act (OASDI). While Social Security is sometimes used as a generic term to include several different solutions to social problems, such as unemployment or disability insurance, we use it here to refer to the benefits paid by the United States to those persons who have paid the OASDI tax throughout their working lives with a view to receiving back an annuity for the rest of their lives upon retirement. Most lawyers today will receive the maximum Social Security benefit ($1,536 per month in 2001) when they retire. This monthly payment of their annuity then becomes the base of all their retirement income.

Everyone thinking about retirement must think about Social Security. Sometimes an estate planner may overlook the significance of Social Security in the overall estate plan. For most people, this is unsound. For example, if your annual income will be $320,000, then your Social Security income of $16,000 a year (or 5 percent) may seem relatively unimportant. If your retirement income is going to be around $64,000, then the $16,000 a year that you receive from Social Security amounts to 25 percent of your retirement income; it is now much more significant. Most lawyers will find that we are in the latter category. Give some serious thought to your financial planning using Social Security as the base of your retirement program.

## II. Payment of Social Security Tax

### A. Tax Rate

In 2001, the tax rate for Social Security taxes was 7.65 percent on the first $80,400 of earnings, or a maximum Social Security of $6,150.60. The maximum taxable amount increases each year, based on increases in the average wages and salaries of all employees in the country.

In legal theory, there are two Social Security taxes: (1) Old-Age, Survivors', and Disability Insurance (OASDI) and (2) Hospital Insurance (HI). OASDI pays for the typical Social Security benefits, and HI pays for Part A of Medicare—that is, hospital benefits for those who are covered. These two separate payroll taxes are added together and withheld from employees' wages. Since 1990, the tax rate for OASDI has been 6.20 percent on a maximum taxable amount, which reached $80,400 in 2001.[1] For HI, the tax rate has been 1.45 percent on earnings with no limit on the taxable amount. Employers match both the OASDI of 6.20 percent and the HI for 1.45 percent.

Self-employed persons pay at a tax rate double that of employed persons: 12.4 percent for OASDI and 2.9 percent for HI, or a total of 15.3 percent. But the self-employed are permitted to reduce their adjusted gross income by one-half of this tax on their income tax returns. This equalizes the tax effect on the self-employed with that of the employee.

### B. What Is Taxed?

What constitutes earnings for purposes of the Social Security taxes is roughly the same as what constitutes earned income for purposes of the federal income tax. Thus, meals and lodging provided by the employer are included unless provided for the convenience of the employer. Similarly, tips, if they are $20 or more a month, are treated as regular wages. If you have two or more employers during a calendar year, each employer must withhold the Social Security taxes up to the maximum earnings: for example, $80,400 in 2001. If your total earnings from all employers exceed this amount, you typically will overpay your taxes. Any amount over the maximum annual tax may be applied against the payment of your income taxes on Form 1040, or you may file a claim for a refund.

## III. Who Is Eligible for Benefits?

Few people in our society today are not covered by Social Security. The three most common groups that are ineligible for Social Security are (1) federal government employees hired prior to 1984, (2) about 25 percent of state and local government employees, and (3) railroad workers.[2] Anyone else age 62 or over is eligible to apply for Social Security benefits.

In large law firms, it is not unusual to have elaborate pension plans along with a gradual phasing-out of the retiring partner's responsibilities and income. However, lawyers in small firms and solo practitioners are much less likely to have pension plans. Partners in large firms also often become Of Counsel to supplement their pension plans.

## IV. What Benefits Are Available?

### A. Retirement Benefits

As of this writing you are entitled to the full benefit at age 65, the present full retirement age (FRA). However, current law allows you to take an early retirement, beginning at age 62, with a decreased benefit, or to delay your retirement until age 70 with an increased benefit.[3]

FRA will increase by two-month increments for each of the five years from 2004 through 2008, reaching 66 in 2009. The FRA will remain at that level through 2020, at which time it will begin another increase by two-month increments until it reaches 67 in 2026.

In 2001, the maximum monthly benefit for a 65-year-old retiree was $1,536 ($18,432 annually). If you were married, your total monthly benefit would be 150 percent of this amount, or $2,304 ($27,648 annually).

If you elected to retire at 62, you would receive a monthly benefit of $1,307 ($15,684 annually). If you were married, your benefit would be $1,307 plus 37.5 percent of your FRA primary insurance amount (PIA), $520, for a total monthly benefit of $1,629 ($19,548 annually).

If you retired at age 70 in 2001, your monthly benefit would increase by 6 percent for each year over 65. Thus, your annual benefit would be increased by 30 percent, and you would receive a monthly benefit of $1,996.80 ($23,961.60 annually). If you were married and your spouse also reached 70 in 2001, your benefit would be $2,994.75 monthly ($35,937 annually).

## B. Spouse's Benefits

While retirement benefits are the most important part of Social Security, you should be familiar with other benefits. If both spouses have worked all their lives and both retired at age 65 in 2001, their benefits would be $3,072 monthly and $36,864 annually. These figures would be reduced to $2,614 monthly and $31,368 annually if both retired at age 62, and increased to $3,993.60 monthly and $47,923.20 annually if their retirement was at age 70.

In the event of your death, your surviving spouse will continue to receive the Social Security to which you are entitled. If your spouse continues to care for a child under 16 (or any age if the child was disabled prior to age 21), your spouse will be entitled to an additional 50 percent of your entitlement.

The FRA for a surviving spouse's benefits will also progress two years after the changes in the normal retirement age for worker benefits. Thus, the first two-month increment will be in 2006; the normal retirement age will reach 66 in 2011 and 67 in 2028.

Your divorced spouse may be entitled to benefits as early as age 62 if your spouse was married to you for at least ten years. Divorced spouses are normally entitled to the same benefits as spouses. Ironically, the divorced spouse may receive more financial protection than the spouse may because the benefits for divorced spouses are not subject to the maximum family benefit.[4] This benefit will terminate if the divorced spouse should remarry. Your divorced spouse can receive benefits if you are at least 62, whether retired or not, or if you are receiving Social Security disability benefits. If you are 62 but not retired, then you must have been divorced at least two years earlier before the divorced spouse can receive benefits.

## C. Child's Benefits

The Social Security law is very liberal in its definition of "child." The term includes both legitimate and illegitimate natural children, adopted children, stepchildren, and dependent grandchildren (if their parents are deceased or disabled). To be eligible, a child must be under 18, under 19 if in high school, or any age if disabled before age 22. Each child is entitled to 50 percent of your PAI ($768 per month in 2001 if the worker was entitled to the monthly maximum benefit of $1,536).

## D. Other Benefits

There is also a lump-sum death benefit of $255, payable to the surviving spouse who was living with a retiree at the time of his death. If no such person survives the decedent, payment may be made to certain other qualified persons.

### E. Disability Benefits: Supplemental Security Income (SSI)

Up to this point, we have been dealing with Social Security benefits that accompany retirement or death. Someone might be disabled even before becoming eligible for retirement. "Disability" means that you are so severely impaired, either mentally or physically, that you are incapable of performing any substantial gainful work. The impairment must be expected to either last at least 12 months or result in an earlier death.

To qualify for disability benefits, you must have earned a minimum number of quarters of coverage, and some of these must have been earned in recent years. The number of quarters required ranges from 40 for those born in 1936–39 to six for those born after 1977. Disability benefits begin after a waiting period of five months. To qualify, you must have been disabled throughout this period. Benefits can be paid retroactively for up to 12 months, not including the five-month waiting period. If a disabled person dies before filing a claim, the family can apply for the disability benefits within three months of the death. The amount of the disability benefit is the same as the normal retirement benefit at age 65 unless the person is already receiving a benefit reduced by having taken early retirement. SSI benefits normally terminate at age 65 when Social Security benefits begin.

## V. Calculating the Amount of Your Social Security Benefits

### A. Importance of the Earnings Record

Retiring lawyers must determine exactly what their entitlements will be upon retirement. Your earnings record becomes the prime factor in calculating your entitlement. Once you are 55 or older, the Social Security Administration (SSA) will figure your benefits before your retirement. You simply fill out a Request for Earnings and Benefit Estimate Statement Form (Form SSA–7004–SM) (SPEC) (6-98). A copy of the form appears on page 14 as Figure 2.1. This form can also be filled out online at http://www.ssa.gov/online/ssa-7004.html (last visited May 26, 2002). Within six weeks you will receive a statement telling you how much your monthly benefit check will be when you retire and how much Social Security will pay you and/or members of your family should you become disabled or die. With this knowledge, you will be better able to determine your investment strategy to prepare for those years when you will be living on a fixed income.

All monthly benefits are based on the PIA. To determine this figure, you need to know your average indexed monthly earnings (AIME). Your area SSA office staff will be of immense help not only by giving you all of your past earnings history, but also by computing your AIME and PIA. The SSA also has an online program, known as a "Retirement Planner," which can be used to calculate your future benefits: http://www.ssa.gov/retire2/index.htm.

### B. Effect of Early Retirement

As indicated earlier, you can take early retirement at any time between ages 62 and 65. For each month that you retire early, your PIA will be reduced by five-ninths of 1 percent for each of the first 36 months that entitlement is prior to your FRA, plus five-twelfths of each month in excess of 36 months. Keep in mind that the FRA goes to 66 in 2009 through 2026, and to 67 in 2027. For those who retire at 62 in those years, the reduction will be to 75 percent and 70 percent of the PIA, respectively.

**FIGURE 2.1**

Request for Earnings and Benefit Estimate

Form Approved
OMB No. 0960-0466

[ ] SP

## Request for Earnings and Benefit Estimate Statement

[ ] Please check this box if you want to get your statement in Spanish instead of English.

Please print or type your answers. When you have completed the form, fold it and mail it to us. (If you prefer to send your request using the Internet, contact us at http://www.ssa.gov)

1. Name shown on your Social Security card:

_____  _____
First Name                      Middle Initial

_____
Last Name Only

2. Your Social Security number as shown on your card:

[ ][ ][ ] – [ ][ ] – [ ][ ][ ][ ]

3. Your date of birth (Mo.-Day-Yr.)

[ ][ ] – [ ][ ] – [ ][ ]

4. Other Social Security numbers you have used:

[ ][ ][ ] – [ ][ ] – [ ][ ][ ][ ]
[ ][ ][ ] – [ ][ ] – [ ][ ][ ][ ]

5. Your sex:  [ ] Male   [ ] Female

**For items 6 and 8 show only earnings covered by Social Security.** Do NOT include wages from State, local or Federal Government employment that are NOT covered for Social Security or that are covered ONLY by Medicare.

6. Show your actual earnings (wages and/or net self-employment income) for last year and your estimated earnings for this year.

A. Last year's actual earnings: *(Dollars Only)*

$ [ ][ ][ ] , [ ][ ][ ] . [0][0]

B. This year's estimated earnings: *(Dollars Only)*

$ [ ][ ][ ] , [ ][ ][ ] . [0][0]

7. Show the age at which you plan to stop working.

[ ][ ]  *(Show only one age)*

8. Below, show the average yearly amount (not your total future lifetime earnings) that you think you will earn between now and when you plan to stop working. Include performance or scheduled pay increases or bonuses, but not cost-of-living increases.

If you expect to earn significantly more or less in the future due to promotions, job changes, part-time work, or an absence from the work force, enter the amount that most closely reflects your future average yearly earnings.

**If you don't expect any significant changes, show the same amount you are earning now (the amount in 6B).**

Future average yearly earnings:  *(Dollars Only)*

$ [ ][ ][ ] , [ ][ ][ ] . [0][0]

9. Do you want us to send the statement:
   To you? Enter your name and mailing address.
   To someone else (your accountant, pension plan, etc.)? Enter your name with "c/o" and the name and address of that person or organization.

_____
Name

_____
Street Address (Include Apt. No., P.O. Box, or Rural Route)

_____  _____  _____
City              State    Zip Code

**Notice:**
I am asking for information about my own Social Security record or the record of a person I am authorized to represent. I understand that if I deliberately request information under false pretenses, I may be guilty of a Federal crime and could be fined and/or imprisoned. I authorize you to use a contractor to send the statement of earnings and benefit estimates to the person named in item 9.

▲

**Please sign your name (Do Not Print)**

_____

_____  _____
Date              (Area Code) Daytime Telephone No.

Form SSA-7004-SM Internet (6-98) Destroy prior editions    ♻ Printed on recycled paper

## C. Delayed Retirement Credits

As noted earlier, you can increase your benefits by delaying your retirement to age 70. For those who reached 65 in 2000 or 2001, the amount of the delayed retirement credit (DRC) is an additional 6 percent. It then increases at the rate of one-half of 1 percent for every two-year period (6.5 percent for 2002–03, 7 percent for 2004–05, 7.5 percent for 2006–07) until it reaches 8 percent for 2008.

A lawyer who reached 65 in 2001 and retired would have a monthly benefit of $1,536. Delaying retirement for five years until age 70 will increase the monthly benefit by 35.5 percent,[5] or a total of $2,081 per month ($24,972 annually). If both spouses were 65 in 2001 and they continue to work and then retire at 70, their total annual income from Social Security for the family will be $49,944. As more and more people live beyond traditional life expectancies, more workers will opt for later retirement—consistent with the increase of the full retirement age to 66 in 2009 and to 67 in 2027.

## D. Earnings Limitations

To avoid earnings limitations on social security payments prior to 2000, a taxpayer had to wait until age 70 to retire. In that year, Congress enacted the Senior Citizens Freedom to Work Act, eliminating all earnings limitations for those 65 or older. Once you reach 65, you need not worry that some portion of your Social Security benefit might be withheld because of your earnings.

Nevertheless, Congress retained some limitations on earnings for those under 65. If you are under 65 all year, you are permitted to earn $10,680 with no reduction of benefits. Above that amount, $1 of benefits will be withheld for every $2 of earnings. If you attained age 65 during 2001, you were allowed to earn $25,000 during that year with no reduction of benefits. Above that amount, $1 of benefits was withheld for every $3 of earnings.

## E. Effect of the Other Pensions

In industrial America, corporations often integrate their pension plans with Social Security. This is less likely within law firms. The primary problem of planning your estate will be the coordination of your Social Security with your other forms of retirement income and investment program. For example, a beneficiary may be drawing a pension from the military. This, along with Social Security and sometimes a portion of your pension income, cannot be changed. The beneficiary will continue to draw these amounts as long as you live, and your survivor will continue to draw a reduced benefit.

Some lawyers or their spouses may have worked for federal, state, or local government and were not covered by Social Security when that employment ended. In that event, two-thirds of the pension benefits from the government employment of your spouse will be offset against any Social Security benefit for which you are eligible as a spouse, widow, or widower.

Once you have learned how much you and your spouse will need to live on in retirement, you are free to budget any excess for investment purposes. Typically, you will have 90 days from the time you retire to roll over tax-free any portion of your pension. During this period, you should determine how much you or you and your spouse will need to live on, and combine your Social Security benefits, your military pension, your investment income, and a portion of your pension income to provide annuities for yourself and your spouse. You can then convert any portion of your pension that is not needed into a nest egg for future investments or emergencies, remembering that you may have to pay income tax for any portion of your nest egg on which the tax was deferred until after your retirement.

## *VI. Applying for Benefits*

### A. When to File

Once you have decided that you are going to retire, how do you apply for benefits? Suppose you expect to reach age 65 on May 19 of next year, and retire sometime thereafter. You should contact the SSA no later than three months before your sixty-fifth birthday, that is, February 19. Better yet, file in January of that year.

### B. Where to File

Normally, you will file your application for Social Security benefits with the office of the SSA that handles your particular ZIP code. The toll-free telephone service of the SSA is now fully automated, and you can call 1-800-772-1213 for help. The SSA will often have one of its employees listening in on your conversation to guarantee that you receive prompt and courteous service. The district office, based on your ZIP code, will give you precise instructions about what to bring when you file your application. Schedule the earliest possible application date.

You can also file online at http://www.ssa.gov/online/#claims for regular or SSI benefits if you are disabled prior to age 65. You can find a lot more information on the SSA's Web site: Form SS–5 can be downloaded, and the SSA's locator service will give you the location of the office nearest you, their hours of operation, and directions to get there.

### C. Evidence Required in Support of Application

As an applicant for Social Security benefits, you must submit evidence to prove your identity and fulfillment of all benefit requirements. This usually means proving your age and any family relationship of those you seek benefits for (that is, your spouse or child). You should have little difficulty proving these facts. While the SSA prefers original records, it will accept certified copies. Birth certificates, religious birth records, marriage licenses and/or certificates, divorce decrees, and death certificates are examples. Call your district office to find out what documents will be required.

If you are filing for disability benefits under the SSI program, you will have to present more complicated proof. All medical impairments are listed on Form SSA–3368–F8. Use the earliest possible date of initial disability. Give full details about any medical treatment, including the names of providers. If gathering all this information is time-consuming, give the SSA clerk a written statement of intent to file so that the application will be dated earlier than the fully completed form.

Although SSA administers the payment of disability payments, SSI is a separate program. SSI is funded out of the General Treasury, which reimburses SSA for expenses incurred in the administration of SSI. In 2001, the maximum payment available to an eligible individual was $540 per month ($796 for an eligible couple).

## D.  Time Limits

Although it is wise to file well in advance of your entitlement, applications may be filed after you have become entitled or even ceased to be entitled. Doing this may cause the person who is filing or members of the family to lose some benefits. For example, if you file for old-age and survivors' benefits after the first month of entitlement, you will receive benefits only for a maximum of six months preceding the filing. Applications for disability benefits are accepted up to 12 months after the disability is ended. If the delay is because of the applicant's physical or mental condition, such applications may be accepted up to 36 months after the disability has ended if the disabled person is still alive.

## E.  Your Right to Appeal

The law provides a series of steps to appeal the determination your SSA entitlement. You may request a reconsideration of filing Form SSA–561 within 60 days after the initial determination (within ten days to request continuation of benefits, and 30 days in the case of overpayment). You may appoint a representative (who need not be a lawyer) to help you review the case file and/or present additional evidence. The SSA reviews your case file and evidence and then issues a decision.

Within 60 days thereafter, you may file on Form HA–501 a request for a hearing before an administrative law judge (ALJ). At the hearing, you and/or your representative may review the case file, provide new evidence, and present, subpoena, and cross-examine witnesses. Within 60 days after receiving the ALJ's decision, you may request (on Form HA–520) that the SSA Appeals Council review your case. This is the central review body with the SSA, which will normally reverse an ALJ only if it finds an abuse of discretion, error of law, a finding unsupported by evidence, or a broad policy issue affecting the public interest. Neither you nor your representative is present at this appellate review within the agency, but you may obtain copies of documents in the record and a copy of the transcript of oral evidence at the hearing. You may also file and/or provide new evidence. All of the proceedings on this review go into your file.

Within 60 days after receipt of the Appeals Council decision, a claimant may seek judicial review in the federal district court. The court reviews the entire case file and reaches a decision as in other cases of judicial review of actions of administrative agencies. In one scenario, a claimant may obtain an expedited appeal to the federal district court following a reconsideration determination, an ALJ decision, or the filing of a request for appeals council review that resulted in no final decision. This occurs when the claimant and the SSA agree that the only factor against the claim is a provision of the law that the claimant believes is unconstitutional. The claimant may then file an action in the federal district court within 60 days after receiving notice that such an agreement has been signed.

A lawyer who represents a client before the SSA in administrative proceedings may charge a fee with the approval of the SSA. If there should be litigation in the federal court, the prevailing party may recover lawyers' fees, expenses, and costs of litigation, under the Equal Access to Justice Act (EAJA).

Claims for SSI benefits are often denied on the original application. The SSA will conduct an internal review, which could be cursory in nature. At this point, you should apply to the Disability Review Board, a state agency that reviews the denial of claims by the SSA. If the board should deny the claim, you may then appeal to an ALJ; there will be a full hearing, and appeals are often successful. Petitioners before the ALJ need not be represented by lawyers, although they often are. A lawyer licensed in some state need not be a member of the local bar to represent a claimant.

## VII. *Taxes after Retirement*

A portion of your Social Security benefits (SSB) may be included in your gross income after you retire. Benefits include any social security payments plus any amounts withheld for Part A of Medicare. To place the burden of this tax on those best able to pay it, Congress provided that above certain thresholds, as much as 85 percent of Social Security benefits would be included in the adjusted gross income of a recipient beneficiary.

The initial base amount for single persons (or married persons living apart for the entire year) is $25,000, and for married persons filing a joint return, $32,000. Taxpayers include 50 percent of the excess over these thresholds in adjusted gross income. Since 1944, single persons also include in gross income an *additional* 35 percent of SSB above $34,000; married persons filing a joint return include an *additional* 35 percent above $44,000. In other words, a total of 85 percent of Social Security benefits above these thresholds will be included in adjusted gross income.

## VIII. *The Future of Social Security*

During the 2000 presidential campaign, both sides promised that the Social Security trust funds would never be distributed. There was much talk about lock boxes and the integrity of these funds. Any lawyer would recognize that what the candidates call "trust funds" could never constitute a true trust because there has never been a segregation of the res.

The good intentions of the Bush administration to keep Social Security inviolate had to be placed aside when our nation was attacked on September 11, 2001. Since that date and up to this writing, the administration has focused on our nation's security, not Social Security. When the initial trauma of the Twin Towers and the Pentagon attacks has abated and terrorism is behind us, Congress and the administration may turn to serious consideration of the problems of Social Security.

Those interested in Social Security will continue to debate whether Social Security is on the brink of financial disaster. One view is that Social Security should be completely overhauled to avoid a crisis. Those who hold this view believe that the payments into the Treasury will be unable to meet the Social Security program's commitments owing to the large number if baby boomers who will be retiring in the near future.[6] Others argue that the 1983 Social Security Commission made a deliberate decision to build up trust fund reserves to accommodate the baby-boom bulge. Social Security's trustees have reported that the system will to able to pay full benefits only until 2038, after which benefits will shrink to 70 percent. This can be fixed easily by modest adjustments, such as raising the maximum earnings base.

Some of the debate centers around whether the trust funds are an asset of the government or merely promises that future taxpayers will have to redeem. The present trust fund surplus, by one view, consists of Treasury securities of a trillion dollars that are as real as similar Treasury securities in the hands of pension funds or individuals. These funds are not merely government IOUs, but surpluses in a lockbox to pay future benefits.

Some critics claim that a program for national savings is essential, and Social Security does nothing to save or invest for the future. Counterarguments claim we have had lower taxes than we would have had otherwise, and the system has also helped to reduce the national debt and keep interest rates low.

Some argue that Social Security should not end with the life of the beneficiary, but should give the individual a means of accumulating wealth. This view favors the use of private accounts, much like a pension. But others note that this was never intended to be the purpose of Social Security; rather, the purpose was to provide workers (along with their survivors) income protection and a floor for financial security.

## IX.  Conclusion

The shape and, perhaps, the solvency of Social Security are not certain. Nevertheless Social Security is currently—and undoubtedly will be in the future—a cornerstone of estate planning.

### Endnotes

1. For 2002, the Social Security wage base is $84,900. There will be no change in the tax rate.

2. Railroad workers are covered under the Federal Railroad Retirement System. To the extent that they are covered under both Railroad Retirement and Social Security, their benefits are coordinated.

3. See discussion of the delayed retirement credit, *infra,* p. 11.

4. The maximum family benefit (MFB) is a cap on what a family may receive when the benefits are based on the earnings record of one worker. For example, if a lawyer should die leaving a spouse and one dependent child, the MFB would be 188 percent of the monthly benefit of $1,536 or $2,887.68. But if the same lawyer should die leaving a divorced spouse and a dependent child, the surviving family would be entitled to a monthly benefit of $3,072.

5. Delayed retirement credits (DRCs) are earned for each of the years from 2001 through 2005. These are 6.0 percent in 2001, 6.5 percent in 2002 and 2003, and 7.0 percent in 2004 and 2005 for a total of 35.5 percent.

6. Just who the baby boomers are is a matter of debate. We identify them as that part of the population born during the 15-year period between 1946 and 1961. They will reach age 65 between 2011 and 2026.

# CHAPTER 3

# Minimum Distribution Requirements

LOUIS A. MEZZULLO

## I. Introduction

To discourage indefinite deferrals, a qualified retirement plan or Individual Retirement Account (IRA)—other than a Roth IRA—must stipulate that the entire interest of a participant—whether he or she is in active status, retired, or terminated with a vested benefit—be distributed or begin to be distributed on or before the required beginning date (RBD), generally April 1 of the calendar year following the calendar year in which the participant reaches age $70^1/2$. In the case of a participant in a qualified retirement plan who does not own more than five percent of the sponsoring employer, the deadline is April 1 of the calendar year following the later of: the calendar year in which the participant reaches age $70^1/2$, or the calendar year in which the participant retires.[1] A 50-percent penalty is imposed on the excess of the amount required to be distributed under these rules over the amount actually distributed.[2] A required minimum distribution may not be rolled into an IRA, because the purpose of the minimum distribution rules is to subject the minimum distribution to current income tax.[3]

On January 17, 2001, the Internal Revenue Service (I.R.S.) published new proposed regulations dealing with the required minimum distribution rules that apply to benefits held in qualified retirement plans and individual retirement accounts—replacing the proposed regulations published on July 27, 1987.[4] The original proposed regulations (hereinafter the "1987 proposed regulations") were amended on December 30, 1987, in response to concerns over the use of trusts as beneficiaries. In addition, Notices 88-38, 96-67, and 97-75, which provided additional guidance on the required minimum distribution rules, are incorporated in the new proposed regulations with modifications (hereinafter the "2001 proposed regulations"). The preamble to the 2001 proposed regulations contained a model amendment that could be adopted by a plan to apply the 2001 proposed regulations to distributions in 2001. If a participant received a distribution in 2001 from a qualified retirement plan that has not adopted the model amendment, the participant may roll over the excess of the required minimum distribution (under the 1987 proposed regulations) over the required minimum distribution under the 2001 proposed regulations to an IRA. Distributions made to a participant before his or her RBD are not considered credits against future required distributions, although they will reduce the account balance used for determining the minimum distribution after the participant reaches his or her RBD.[5] If the participant dies after beginning to receive benefits under a plan but before his or her RBD, the participant will be deemed to have died before his or her RBD for purposes of the minimum distribution rules. One set of rules applies to the payment of benefits if the participant dies before his or her RBD, another set if after.

A participant who dies after he or she has begun receiving payments under an irrevocable annuity that began before the participant's RBD and that satisfies the minimum distribution rules will be treated as dying after his or her RBD even if the participant has not reached age 70$^{1}/_{2}$.[6] To satisfy the minimum distribution rules, the annuity must be payable over the life of the participant or the lifetimes of the participant and the participant's designated beneficiary, and the minimum distribution incidental death benefit rule must be satisfied.

## II. TEFRA Transition Rule

Tax Equity and Fiscal Responsibility Act (TEFRA), which first established minimum distribution rules for plan benefits and IRAs, contained a transition rule that permits distributions of benefits from qualified retirement plans to begin at a later date and to be paid out over a longer period than permitted under the minimum distribution rules for a participant who signed a written designation of the form of payment before 1984.[7] To satisfy this transition rule, the Internal Revenue Service (I.R.S.) requires that the form of payment and the beneficiary designation must have satisfied the law in effect before January 1, 1984, including the incidental death benefit rule as it existed at that time.[8] The incidental death benefit rule formerly required that the actuarial value of the benefits payable to the participant during the participant's lifetime had to exceed 50 percent of the value of the total benefits, unless the only other beneficiary entitled to benefits was the participant's spouse.[9]

Because this transition rule allows a participant to defer the receipt of benefits until the participant actually retires, it should be determined whether an individual who was a participant in a plan before January 1, 1984 has made such an election. If the form of payment is changed or the payout period is increased, the transition rule no longer applies and, under the proposed regulations, the participant must receive by the end of the calendar year following the calendar year in which the change occurred not only the current year's required distribution, but the amount of all distributions that would have been required in earlier years if the transition rule had not applied.[10] Consequently, such a participant may be required to receive such a large distribution in one year that the participant's income is pushed into a higher income-tax bracket.

Because a valid spousal consent to a waiver of a nonparticipant spouse's rights under the Retirement Equity Act (REA) to a survivor annuity or death benefit was not possible before August 23, 1984, a married participant must obtain his or her spouse's consent if the designation does not name the spouse as the beneficiary—or, in the case of a plan subject to the qualified annuity rules, the form of payment is not a qualified joint and survivor annuity. Because any form of payment signed before January 1, 1984, would not satisfy REA, the spouse's consent probably will be required to validate the form of payment under REA. Fortunately, a spousal consent to a waiver of REA rights does not invalidate the application of the transition rule.[11]

The transition rule will no longer apply if the benefits covered by the rule are transferred to another plan by the voluntary action of the participant.[12] For example, if the participant receives a distribution of benefits from a plan covered by the transition rule, and transfers the distribution tax-free to another qualified retirement plan, the transition rule will no longer apply to the transferred benefits—even if the benefits of the other plan also are covered by the transition rule.

## A. Calculating the Required Distribution

Starting at the RBD, payments must be made over the life of the participant or over the joint lives of the participant and designated beneficiary, or over a period not extending beyond the life expectancy of the participant or the joint and last survivor expectancies of the participant and designated beneficiary.[13]

If the participant's benefit is in the form of an individual account (for example, a profit-sharing plan or a money-purchase pension plan), the minimum amount to be distributed during each distribution calendar year is determined by dividing the participant's benefit by the applicable distribution period.[14] The first distribution calendar year is generally the year in which the participant reaches age $70^1/_2$, unless the participant owned less than five percent of the sponsoring employer and has not retired. In that case, the first distribution calendar year is the year in which the participant retires. The calendar year during which the RBD occurs will have two required distributions if the participant waits to receive the first distribution until after the end of the first distribution calendar year. The first distribution, which must occur by April 1, is attributable to the first distribution calendar year. The second distribution, which must occur by December 31 of the same year, is attributable to the second distribution calendar year (which coincides with the RBD).[15] For example, a participant who reached age $70^1/_2$ in 2001 must receive one distribution by April 1, 2002, and another distribution by December 31, 2002. Distributions for subsequent distribution calendar years must be made on or before December 31 of the distribution calendar year.

A participant may not want to wait until his or her RBD to receive the first distribution just to avoid having two distributions in the same year. Two distributions may push the participant's income into a higher income tax bracket. In the case of an individual account, the benefit used to determine the minimum distribution amount is the account balance (whether or not vested) as of the last valuation date in the calendar year immediately preceding the distribution calendar year. However, if the required minimum distribution exceeds the vested account balance, only the vested account balance need be distributed. This amount is increased by contributions or forfeitures added to the account after the valuation date during the valuation year or made after the valuation year but allocated as of a date in the valuation year. The account balance is reduced by distributions from the account made after the valuation date during the valuation year. In the case of the second distribution calendar year, the account is also reduced by any amount distributed on or before April 1 of that year to meet the minimum distribution requirement for the first distribution calendar year.[16]

For example, assume that the annual valuation date in a particular qualified retirement plan is November 30. Also assume that the qualified retirement plan has adopted the model amendment applying the new required minimum distribution rules for distributions in 2001. Lastly, assume that the participant's account balance as of November 30, 2001, is $262,000, the participant's RBD is April 1, 2002, the designated beneficiary is the participant's brother, and there are no forfeitures or additional contributions added to the participant's account before the end of 2001. Because the applicable distribution period under the uniform distribution period table is 26.2, the required minimum distribution that must be distributed by April 1, 2003, is $10,000. The applicable distribution period for the second distribution year (2003) will be 25.3 under the uniform distribution period table. If the participant's account balance on November 30, 2002, was $263,000, the account balance for purposes of determining the required minimum distribution that must be paid on or before December 31, 2003, is $253,000, because the $10,000 distributed before April 1, 2003, is deducted from the account balance as of November 30, 2002, for purposes of determining the account balance to be used for the 2003 distribution year. Consequently, an additional $10,000 must be distributed by December 31, 2003.

To determine the minimum distribution for a particular distribution calendar year, the account balance is not reduced by distributions made pursuant to a QDRO after December 31 of the valuation year.[17] For example, using the above assumptions—and assuming a distribution was made to the participant's former spouse under a QDRO on March 1, 2003, of $20,000—the distribution required to be made to the participant by April 1, 2003, and by December 31, 2003, is not reduced by the amount distributed to the former spouse.

### B. Life Expectancies

Under the 2001 proposed regulations, life expectancies are relevant at the participant's RBD only if the participant's sole designated beneficiary is the participant's spouse who is more than ten years younger than the participant. In this case, the applicable distribution period is the joint and last survivor expectancy of the participant and spouse, determined each year. In all other cases, the applicable distribution period is determined under the uniform distribution period table, which is based on the joint and last survivor expectancy of the participant and a hypothetical beneficiary ten years younger than the participant, recalculated each year.[18] This table was the minimum distribution incidental death benefit table under the 1987 proposed regulations. If the participant dies after his or her RBD, the applicable distribution period after the participant's death will not be affected by whether the applicable distribution period was determined under the uniform distribution period table or the joint and last survivor expectancy of the participant and his or her spouse.

## III. Defined Benefit Plans

For defined benefit plans, distributions in the form of an annuity must be made in periodic payments at intervals of not longer than one year[19] under most plans, monthly. Payments must begin on the RBD and, as long as the payments are made according to the scheduled intervals (at least annually), the minimum distribution rules should be met.[20] The 2001 proposed regulations eliminated any difference between an annuity with a period certain of 20 years or less and a life annuity with a period certain exceeding 20 years. However, the period certain must not exceed the shorter of the applicable distribution period or the joint and last survivor expectancy of the participant and the participant's beneficiary.[21]

### A. Minimum Distribution Incidental Death Benefit Rule

Distributions from qualified retirement plans and IRAs also must satisfy the minimum distribution incidental death benefit (MDIB) rule.[22] This rule is designed to prevent a participant from extending the payout period by designating a very young person to be his or her beneficiary. Before 1989, the I.R.S. had imposed a similar rule pursuant to published revenue rulings.[23] The pre-1989 rule required that more than 50 percent of the actuarial value of the benefit had to be payable to the participant over his or her life expectancy, unless the spouse was the only beneficiary after the death of the participant. The new MDIB rule first applied in 1989 to qualified retirement plans and was based on tables in the 1987 proposed regulations.

If the designated beneficiary of a joint and last survivor annuity is not the spouse, the benefit payable to the designated beneficiary after the death of the participant must be a reduced percentage of the benefit payable to the participant if the participant is more than ten years older than the designated beneficiary is.[24] For example, if the beneficiary is 25 years younger than the participant, the beneficiary's payment amount cannot exceed 66 percent of the benefit payable to the participant. If the spouse is the designated beneficiary, the MDIB rule is satisfied as long as the general minimum distribution rules are satisfied.[25] The 2001 proposed regulations treat the use of the uniform distribution period table as satisfying the MDIB rule for individual account plans.[26]

## IV. Distributions after the Death of the Participant

### A. Death on or after the RBD

Under the 2001 proposed regulations, if the participant dies after his or her RBD and has a designated beneficiary, and the spouse is not the sole designated beneficiary, the applicable distribution period is the designated beneficiary's life expectancy determined in the calendar year following the calendar year of the participant's death, reduced by one year for each year thereafter.[27] If the participant's sole designated beneficiary is the spouse, the applicable distribution period is the spouse's life expectancy determined in the calendar year following the calendar year of the participant's death, and redetermined each subsequent year until the spouse dies. At that point the applicable distribution period becomes the spouse's life expectancy determined in the calendar year of the spouse's death, reduced by one year for each year following the calendar year after the calendar year of the spouse's death.[28] If the participant does not have a designated beneficiary, the applicable distribution period is the participant's life expectancy, determined in the year of the participant's death, reduced by one year for each year thereafter.[29]

### B. Death before the RBD

Under the 2001 proposed regulations, if a participant dies before reaching his or her RBD and he or she has a designated beneficiary as of December 31 of the calendar year following the calendar year of his or her death (the beneficiary determination date), the deceased participant's plan benefits and IRAs must be distributed over the designated beneficiary's life expectancy, beginning no later than the end of the calendar year after the calendar year of the participant's death.[30] If the participant's sole designated beneficiary is his or her surviving spouse, the distribution must begin by the end of the calendar year in which the participant would have reached age $70^{1}/_{2}$, or, if later, December 31 of the calendar year following the calendar year of the participant's death (that is, should the participant die during the year in which he or she turns $70^{1}/_{2}$).[31] A surviving spouse may have relied on an interpretation of the 1987 proposed regulations (expressed in several private letter rulings) that implied that a spouse who was the oldest beneficiary of a trust, but not necessarily entitled to receive all distributions made to the trust, could wait until the participant would have reached age 70$^{1}/_{2}$ to begin receiving required minimum distributions. Some commentators have suggested that such a spouse should be able to continue to rely on this interpretation of the 1987 proposed regulations after the 2001 proposed regulations became effective.

Unless the surviving spouse is the participant's sole designated beneficiary, the life expectancy of the designated beneficiary is determined in the calendar year following the calendar year of the participant's death, and is reduced by one year for each year thereafter.[32] If the surviving spouse is the participant's sole designated beneficiary, while the spouse is alive the applicable distribution period is the spouse's life expectancy determined each year.[33] Once the spouse dies, the remaining applicable distribution period is the spouse's life expectancy in the calendar year of his or her death, reduced by one for each calendar year since the year immediately following the calendar year of the participant's death.[34] The life expectancy of a designated beneficiary, including a spouse who is the participant's sole designated beneficiary, is determined under Treas. Reg. Section 1.72-9, Table V.[35]

If the participant does not have a designated beneficiary by the beneficiary determination date, the participant's plan benefits or IRAs must be distributed by the end of the fifth calendar year following the calendar year of the participant's death.[36] Note that this five-year rule was the default rule under the 1987 proposed regulations unless the spouse was the participant's designated beneficiary. Consequently, unless the designated beneficiary elected to receive the deceased participant's account over the beneficiary's life expectancy or the plan provided for such a distribution, the five-year rule applied. Under the 2001 proposed regulations, the life expectancy rule applies unless there is no designated beneficiary or the plan provides that the five-year rule shall apply, unless the designated beneficiary elects otherwise. Depending upon the terms of the plan, a designated beneficiary may elect to have the five-year rule apply[37]—perhaps advisable if the designated beneficiary's remaining life expectancy is less than five years.

If the participant's sole designated beneficiary fails to take the required minimum distributions in any of the first four calendar years following the calendar year of the participant's death, the regulations provide for an automatic waiver of the 50-percent excise tax if the designated beneficiary receives the entire remaining plan benefit or IRA by the end of the fifth year following the calendar year of the participant's death.[38] A plan may provide that the five-year rule always applies to certain types of distributions or all of them, and can apply different methods of distribution to different employees.[39]

A designated beneficiary being determined as of the beneficiary determination date presents a potential problem if the person who is the designated beneficiary of the participant at the participant's death dies before the beneficiary determination date, and the participant has not named a contingent beneficiary who would qualify as a designated beneficiary. Commentators have suggested that the final regulations should provide that the individual or individuals who are entitled to the plan benefit or IRA as of the beneficiary determination date would be treated as the participant's designated beneficiary or beneficiaries.

## V.  Designated Beneficiary Rules

A designated beneficiary must be an individual.[40] An individual beneficiary of a trust may be treated as a designated beneficiary if the trust meets the requirements discussed below.[41] A participant's designated beneficiary after his or her death is determined as of the beneficiary determination date (December 31 of the calendar year following the calendar year of the participant's death).[42] If there are two or more beneficiaries, only the oldest beneficiary will be treated as a designated beneficiary unless each beneficiary is entitled to a separate share or account.[43] If there are two or more beneficiaries and one of the beneficiaries is not an individual, the participant will be treated as not having any designated beneficiary unless the nonindividual beneficiary is entitled to a separate share or account.[44]

A separate account in an individual account plan or IRA is a portion of a participant's benefit determined by an acceptable separate accounting including allocating investment gains and losses, and contributions and forfeitures, pro rata in a reasonable and consistent manner between such portion and any other benefits.[45] Further, the amounts of each such portion of the benefit will be separately determined as the respective amounts of the required minimum distribution.[46] A benefit in a defined benefit plan is separated into segregated shares if it consists of separate identifiable components that may be separately distributed.[47]

To be treated as a designated beneficiary, an individual must be designated under the terms of the plan, including an affirmative election by the participant per the terms of the plan.[48] An individual who becomes entitled to the benefit under applicable state law is not a designated beneficiary.[49] Although not free from doubt, the proposed regulations suggest that a participant will not have a designated beneficiary if his or her estate is the named beneficiary, even though an individual becomes entitled to receive the benefit by the beneficiary determination date.[50] It is hoped that the final regulations permit such an individual or individuals to be treated as a designated beneficiary or designated beneficiaries.

There are three ways that the identity of the designated beneficiary can be changed after the participant's death but before the beneficiary determination date. First, one or more beneficiaries may be cashed out, that is, they receive the entire amount of the plan benefit or IRA to which they are entitled.[51] For example, if a participant has named a charitable organization as the beneficiary of the first $100,000 of his or her plan benefit or IRA and an individual as the beneficiary of the remaining portion, the participant would not be treated as having a designated beneficiary after his or her death under the old rules because the charity's right would not be treated as a separate account. However, under the new rules, if $100,000 is paid to the charity before the beneficiary determination date, the charity will no longer be considered in determining whether the participant has a designated beneficiary.

Second, one or more beneficiaries may disclaim their right to receive the plan benefit or IRA.[52] Although the disclaimer must be made before the beneficiary determination date in order to eliminate the disclaiming beneficiary for purposes of determining the oldest beneficiary, if the disclaimer is made more than nine months after the participant's death, the disclaimer will not be a qualified disclaimer under Internal Revenue Code (I.R.C.) Section 2518, resulting in the disclaiming beneficiary being treated as making a taxable gift to the beneficiary or beneficiaries who become entitled to receive the plan benefit or IRA as a result of the disclaimer.

Third, separate accounts may be created for each beneficiary before the beneficiary determination date.[53] For example, if the benefits are payable in equal shares to the participant's three children and to a grandchild of a predeceased child, and separate accounts were created before the beneficiary determination date, each child and the grandchild could take distributions from his or her separate account based on his or her life expectancy, rather than the life expectancy of the oldest child. Because of language in the 2001 proposed regulations, there is some question whether the creation of separate accounts if the participant dies after the participant's RBD will be effective for allowing the beneficiaries of each separate account to be treated as designated beneficiaries of that account.[54] The final regulations are likely to clarify that separate accounts may be created when the participant dies after the RBD.

The 2001 proposed regulations provide that if a beneficiary's entitlement to a participant's benefit or IRA is contingent on an event other than the participant's death or the death of another beneficiary, the contingent beneficiary is considered in determining which designated beneficiary has the shortest life expectancy.[55] However, if a subsequent beneficiary is entitled to a portion of a participant's benefit or IRA only if another beneficiary dies before the entire benefit to which the other beneficiary is entitled has been distributed by the plan or IRA, the subsequent beneficiary will not be considered a beneficiary when it comes to determining who is the designated beneficiary with the shortest life expectancy or whether a beneficiary who is not an individual is a beneficiary. This rule does not apply if the other beneficiary dies before the beneficiary determination date—wherein the subsequent beneficiary would be treated as the designated beneficiary.[56]

If the designated beneficiary whose life expectancy is being used to calculate the distribution period dies after the beneficiary determination date, this same beneficiary's remaining life expectancy will be used to determine the distribution period, whether or not a beneficiary with a shorter life expectancy is entitled to receive the plan benefit or IRA.[57] A participant will not be treated as having a designated beneficiary if the plan or IRA provides or allows the participant to specify that, after the end of the calendar year following the calendar year in which the participant dies, any person or persons have the discretion to change the participant's beneficiaries. However, a beneficiary who is treated as the designated beneficiary may have the right to designate a subsequent beneficiary for distributions of any portion of the participant's benefit or IRA after the designated beneficiary dies.[58]

The 2001 proposed regulations provide two examples of how these rules operate. In the first example, an unmarried participant dies in calendar year 2001 at age 30. As of December 31, 2002, the participant's sister is the beneficiary of the participant's account balance under the plan. Prior to the participant's death, the participant designated that, if his sister died before the participant's entire account balance had been distributed to the sister, the participant's mother would be the beneficiary of the account balance. Because the mother is entitled to receive some of the participant's plan benefit only if the sister dies before the entire benefit has been distributed, the mother is disregarded in determining the participant's designated beneficiary. Accordingly, even after the sister's death, the sister's life expectancy will continue to be used to determine the distribution period, although the payments are being made to the mother.[59]

In the second example, the facts are the same except that the sister, rather than the participant, designates the mother as the beneficiary of any amount remaining after the sister's death. The mother is still disregarded in determining the participant's designated beneficiary.[60]

## A. Trusts as Beneficiaries

The 2001 proposed regulations do not change the requirements under the 1987 proposed regulations, as amended in 1997, that a trust must satisfy in order to have the oldest individual beneficiary of the trust treated as a participant's designated beneficiary. However, the uniform distribution period table has affected the time by which these requirements must be satisfied. In addition, the regulations clarify when a spouse will be treated as the sole beneficiary of a trust.

In order for an individual who is the beneficiary of a trust to be treated as the participant's designated beneficiary, the trust must satisfy the following four requirements during any period during which required minimum distributions are being determined by taking into account the designated beneficiary's life expectancy:[61]

1. The trust must be a valid trust or would be a valid trust under state law if it had a corpus;
2. The beneficiaries of the trust entitled to the plan benefits or IRA must be identifiable;
3. The trust must be either irrevocable or, by its terms, will become irrevocable at the participant's death; and
4. Certain documentation requirements must be satisfied.

Unless the participant's sole designated beneficiary is his or her spouse and the spouse is more than ten years younger than the participant, these requirements (including the documentation requirements) must be satisfied by the beneficiary determination date. In this case, the uniform distribution period table is used for determining the required minimum distribution, and the life expectancy of a designated beneficiary is irrelevant. However, if the spouse is the participant's sole designated beneficiary and is more than ten years younger than the participant, these requirements must be satisfied at the RBD if the participant wishes to use the joint and last survivor expectancy of the husband and wife rather than the uniform distribution period table. In this case, the spouse's life expectancy is relevant in determining the joint and last survivor expectancy of the participant and his or her spouse each year.

The requirement that the trust beneficiaries entitled to the plan benefits or IRAs be identifiable is necessary because the age of the oldest beneficiary is required to calculate the minimum distribution after the participant's death (or after the RBD if the participant's sole beneficiary is his or her spouse and is more than ten years younger than the participant). If there are any beneficiaries of the trust entitled to the plan benefits or IRAs which do not qualify as designated beneficiaries for purposes of calculating minimum distributions, such as charities or creditors (for example, funeral expenses), the participant may be treated as not having a designated beneficiary.[62] Unfortunately, the I.R.S. has taken the position that separate accounts must be established in the beneficiary designation form. Simply naming a trust that has separate shares for different beneficiaries will not create separate accounts for purposes of the minimum distribution rules.[63]

To satisfy the documentation requirements, the participant or trustee must furnish to the plan administrator by the beneficiary determination date either the trust instrument or a list of beneficiaries, including contingent and remainder beneficiaries, and the conditions on their entitlement. In addition, the participant or trustee must certify that the list is complete and agree to furnish a copy of the trust instrument if requested by the plan administrator. If the spouse is the sole designated beneficiary and is more than ten years younger than the participant, these requirements apply at the beginning of the year in which such a spouse becomes the participant's sole designated beneficiary, if the participant wants to use the joint and last survivor expectancy of the participant and the spouse redetermined each year in lieu of the uniform distribution period table. In this case, if the trust agreement is amended during the participant's lifetime, a copy of the amendment or corrected certification (if the amendment changes the information certified) must be furnished to the plan administrator within a reasonable time.[64]

The documentation requirements are overbroad, because in many cases there will be numerous contingent and remainder beneficiaries that will have to be listed, as well as a description of how they will become entitled to receive a benefit. Only the name and age of the oldest beneficiary of each separate share of the trust that is a beneficiary of the trust with respect to a plan benefit or IRA is needed by the plan administrator to determine the required minimum distribution. A plan administrator will not usually be qualified to interpret the terms of a trust agreement. However, the proposed regulations now require the IRA trustee to report to the I.R.S. and the account holder the amount required to be distributed from the IRA for each calendar year and to inform the account holder that he or she may take the minimum distribution required from all IRAs from any one or more of his or her IRAs.[65] This information may be beneficial to the account holder or the beneficiary of the IRA. However, this requirement may be difficult to administer, especially in the first calendar year after the calendar year of the participant's death, because the designated beneficiary will not be determined until December 31 of that year.

No documentation should be required to be provided to the financial institution sponsoring an IRA, because IRA sponsors are not responsible for determining required minimum distributions and the account holder may take the total of the required minimum distributions calculated separately for each of his or her IRAs from any one or more of his or her IRAs.[66] For example, assume that a participant has four IRAs and that each IRA has an account balance as of the end of the previous calendar year of $500,000, for a total amount in all four IRAs of $2 million. Assume also that the applicable distribution period is ten years, so the required minimum distribution will be $200,000 (10 percent of $2 million). Although each IRA sponsor would be required to notify the participant that he or she had a required minimum distribution from each IRA of $50,000 (10 percent of the $500,000 value of each IRA as of the end of the preceding calendar year), the participant could take the aggregate required minimum distribution of $200,000 (10 percent of $2 million) from one IRA, $50,000 from each IRA, or any variation thereof. Consequently, each IRA sponsor may never know whether the account holder was taking his or her required minimum distribution in any given year. If a trust is the beneficiary of a qualified plan benefit or IRA, questions arise over which beneficiaries of the trust must be considered in determining who is the oldest beneficiary and whether any beneficiary is not an individual. If at least one beneficiary of the trust that must be considered for this purpose is not an individual, such as a charitable organization, then the participant will be treated as not having a designated beneficiary. Apparently, any potential beneficiary of the trust, including a nonindividual beneficiary or a beneficiary who is older than the apparent designated beneficiary, must be taken into account in determining whether there is a designated beneficiary under the minimum distribution rules, unless such beneficiary would become entitled to receive distributions from the plan or IRA only if one or more prior individual beneficiaries have died prematurely. Consequently, the only beneficiary of a trust who can be disregarded is one entitled to receive some of the plan benefit or IRA only by surviving another beneficiary who would receive the balance of the plan benefit or IRA if he or she were alive at the relevant event (such as the death of the individual who was the original designated beneficiary). Absent that, all distributions from the plan or IRA made to the trust must be redistributed to individual beneficiaries while they are alive.

For example, if a participant names a trust as his or her beneficiary, and under the terms of the trust the oldest beneficiary is the participant's spouse, and following the spouse's death the assets of the trust, including the right to receive the remaining plan benefit or IRA, are payable in equal shares to the participant's children who survive the spouse, and if there are no children then living, to a charitable organization, the charitable organization would not be considered in determining whether the participant had a designated beneficiary, because its entitlement to receive some of the plan benefit or IRA depends on none of the participant's children surviving the spouse. On the other hand, if the trust agreement provided that the trust continued in existence after the spouse's death, and at the death of the last child to die the assets were payable to the charitable organization, the charitable organization would be considered in determining whether the participant had a designated beneficiary unless all distributions from the plan or IRA were required to be distributed to individual beneficiaries of the trust when received by the trust.[67] In addition, the terms of the trust should not direct that plan benefits or IRAs distributed to the trust be used to pay debts or expenses of the participant's estate, including federal and state estate and death taxes; otherwise the participant may not be treated as having a designated beneficiary because the participant's estate could be treated as a beneficiary of the plan benefit or IRA.

None of these rules imposed by the I.R.S. seem to make any policy sense, because the distributions to the trust always will have been subject to income tax—more than likely at a higher rate than if paid to an individual beneficiary because it will have been taxable to a trust (usually in a higher federal income tax bracket than an individual). In addition, if an individual had been named as the beneficiary instead of a trust, the balance of the plan benefit or IRA held by the individual, plus any remaining plan benefit or IRA not yet distributed, could be payable to either an older beneficiary or a nonindividual beneficiary without affecting the status of the individual as the designated beneficiary. Note that some of these unfavorable consequences can be eliminated before the beneficiary determination date by cashing out certain beneficiaries, by having certain beneficiaries disclaim their interests, and by segregating plan benefits or account balances into separate accounts.[68]

## B. Two Examples

The 2001 proposed regulations provide two examples that confirm the I.R.S.'s position taken in Rev. Rul. 2000-2,[69] relating to the qualification for the marital deduction of a plan benefit or IRA payable to a qualified terminable interest property (QTIP) trust, and clarify when a surviving spouse will be treated as the participant's sole designated beneficiary when the spouse is a beneficiary of a trust to which the plan benefit or IRA is payable.

In the first example, the participant dies in 2001 at the age of 55, survived by the participant's spouse, who is 50 years old. The participant has named the trustee of a testamentary trust established under the participant's will as the beneficiary of all amounts payable from the participant's account in a defined contribution plan. It is stated that the participant's account balance is invested only in productive assets. Further, by the end of the calendar year following the calendar year of the participant's death, a copy of the trust agreement and a list of the trust beneficiaries are provided to the plan administrator. At the date of the participant's death, the trust was irrevocable and was a valid trust under the laws of the state of the participant's domicile. The participant's account balance was includable in the participant's gross estate under I.R.C. Section 2039.

Under the terms of the trust, all trust income is payable annually to the spouse, and no one has the power to appoint the trust principal to any person other than the spouse. The participant's children, who are all younger than the spouse, are the sole remainder beneficiaries of the trust. No other person has a beneficial interest in the trust. Under the terms of the trust, the spouse has the power, exercisable annually, to compel the trustee to withdraw from the participant's account balance an amount equal to the income earned on the assets in the account during the calendar year and to distribute that amount through the trust to the spouse. The plan contains no prohibition on withdrawals from the participant's account of amounts in excess of the annual required minimum distributions. In accordance with the terms of the plan, the trustee of the trust elects to receive annual required minimum distributions using the life expectancy rule for distributions over a distribution period equal to the spouse's life expectancy. If the spouse exercises the withdrawal power, the trustee must withdraw from the participant's account the greater of the amount of income earned in the account during the calendar year or the required minimum distribution. However, under the terms of the trust, as well as applicable state law, only the portion of the plan distribution received by the trustee equal to the income earned by the assets in the account is required to be distributed to the spouse, along with any other trust income.

Because some amounts distributed from the plan to the trust may be accumulated in the trust during the spouse's lifetime for the benefit of the children, as remainder beneficiaries of the trust, even though access to those amounts is delayed until after the spouse's death, the children are treated as beneficiaries of the participant's plan benefit in addition to the spouse, and the spouse, therefore, is not the sole beneficiary. Although the spouse's life expectancy, determined in the calendar year following the participant's death, will be used for purposes of determining the required minimum distributions to the trust, the spouse's life expectancy will not be redetermined each year as it would have been had the spouse been the participant's sole designated beneficiary. Instead, the spouse's life expectancy will be reduced by one for each year that elapses. In addition, the distributions to the spouse must begin by the end of the calendar year following the calendar year of the participant's death, rather than by the end of the year in which the participant would have reached age $70^1/_2$.[70]

In the second example, the assumptions are the same, except that the trust requires that all amounts distributed from the plan to the trustee while the spouse is alive be paid directly to the spouse upon receipt by the trustee. In this case, the spouse is the sole beneficiary of the participant's plan benefit for purposes of determining the designated beneficiary, because no amounts distributed from the plan to the trust are accumulated in the trust during the spouse's lifetime for the benefit of any other beneficiary. Consequently, the annual required minimum distributions may be postponed until the end of the calendar year in which the participant would have reached age $70^1/_2$. Note that because the spouse is the sole designated beneficiary, the spouse's life expectancy may be redetermined each year for purposes of determining the required minimum distribution to the trust while the spouse is alive.[71]

## VI. Spousal Rollovers

Regardless of whether the participant dies before or after his or her RBD, if the spouse is the beneficiary of all or part of the participant's plan benefit or IRA, he or she may roll the plan benefit (if permitted under the plan) or IRA, or the part of which he or she is beneficiary, into his or her own IRA, or, in the case of an IRA, elect to treat the decedent's IRA as his or her own.[72]

If the participant dies after his or her RBD without receiving the required minimum, it will have to be paid to the surviving spouse before the end of the year.[73] If the surviving spouse has already reached his or her RBD, he or she must also begin receiving required minimum distributions in the year the rollover occurs.

Because of the technical language of the 2002 proposed regulations, two required minimum distributions may be required in the same year if the spouse has already reached his or her RBD and elects to treat the decedent's IRA as his or her own or rolls the decedent's IRA or plan benefit into his or her own IRA in the calendar year of the decedent's death.[74] The final regulations should clarify that only one required minimum distribution must be made in such event. Unless clarified, this result may be avoided if the surviving spouse waits until at least the calendar year following the calendar year of the decedent's death, when it is clear that it would only be the spouse's required minimum distribution that would have to be made if the spouse has already reached his or her RBD and the spouse elects to treat the decedent's IRA as his or her own or rolls over the decedent's plan benefit or IRA into his or her own IRA.

## VII. Conclusion

The 2001 proposed regulations are certainly a vast improvement over the 1987 proposed regulations and have eliminated most of the traps for the unwary. Of course, the I.R.S. and Treasury still need to clarify some issues, such as whether an individual who becomes a beneficiary of the participant's plan benefit or IRA under a deceased participant's will (or by intestacy) can be treated as a designated beneficiary; whether a surviving spouse who elects to treat the deceased participant's IRA as his or her own or rolls it into his or her own IRA in the year of the participant's death must take two required distributions in the same year; and whether a separate account may be created for different beneficiaries if the participant dies after the RBD. There is also the practical problem of determining who may be treated as the designated beneficiary when the original beneficiary dies after the participant but before December 31 of the calendar year following the participant's death and the participant has not named (or the plan or IRA document does not designate) a successor beneficiary.

### Endnotes

1. I.R.C. § 401(a)(9)(A), (C), as amended by § 1404(a) of the Small Business Act. The meaning of the term "retires" under the new definition of required beginning date is uncertain. For example, must the participant work full-time or will merely working part-time allow the participant to defer the commencement of required minimum distributions after reaching age $70^1/_2$? What if the participant had always been a part-time employee? Will a participant be required to take distributions from plans in which he or she participated that are sponsored by employers for whom the participant no longer works, although the participant continues to work for another employer after reaching age $70^1/_2$? Will a participant be required to begin receiving benefits after reaching age $70^1/_2$ from a plan sponsored by a prior employer with respect to which he or she was a more-than-five-percent owner, although he or she is now working for an employer with respect to which he or she is not a more-than-five-percent owner?

On the other hand, will a participant reaching age $70^1/_2$ who is a more-than-five-percent owner of the employer for whom he or she is currently working, but was not a more-than-five-percent owner of a prior employer who sponsored a plan in which the participant has an accrued benefit, be required to begin receiving the accrued benefit from the former employer's plan? Finally, can a participant in a plan sponsored by an employer with respect to which the participant was a more-than-five-percent owner roll his or her accrued benefit into the plan of a new employer with respect to which the participant is not a more-than-five-percent owner and thereby defer the payment of the accrued benefit until he or she retires from the new employer?

2. I.R.C. § 4974(a).
3. I.R.C. § 402(c)(4)(B).
4. 66 Fed. Reg. 3928-01.
5. 2001 Prop. Reg. § 1.401(a)(9)-2, Q&A 6.
6. 2001 Prop. Reg. §§ 1.401(a)(9)-2, Q&A 5, 1.401(a)(9)-6, Q&A 10.
7. TEFRA § 242(b)(2); TRA 86 § 1121(d)(4)(A).
8. I.R.S. Notice 83-23, 1983-2 C.B. 418.
9. Rev. Rul. 72-240, 1972-1 C.B. 108; Rev. Rul. 72-241, 1972-1 C.B. 108.
10. 2001 Prop. Reg. § 1.401(a)(9)-8, Q&A 16.
11. 2001 Prop. Reg. § 1.401(a)(9)-8, Q&A 13.
12. 2001 Prop. Reg. § 1.401(a)(9)-8, Q&A 14, 15.
13. I.R.C. § 401(a)(9)(A).
14. 2001 Prop. Reg. § 1.401(a)(9)-5, Q&A 1(a).
15. 2001 Prop. Reg. § 1.402(a)(9)-5, Q&A 1(b), (c).
16. 2001 Prop. Reg. § 1.401(a)(9)-5, Q&A 3.
17. Priv. Ltr. Rul. 9011031.
18. 2001 Prop. Reg. § 1.401(a)(9)-5, Q&A 4.
19. 2001 Prop. Reg. § 1.401(a)(9)-6, Q&A 1(a).
20. 2001 Prop. Reg. § 1.401(a)(9)-6, Q&A 1(d).
21. 2001 Prop. Reg. § 1.401(a)(9)-6, Q&A 3.
22. I.R.C. § 401(a)(9)(G).
23. Rev. Rul. 72-240, 1972-1 C.B. 108; Rev. Rul. 72-241, 1972-1 C.B. 108.
24. 2001 Prop. Reg. § 1.401(a)(9)-6, Q&A 2(c).
25. 2001 Prop. Reg. § 1.401(a)(9)-6, Q&A 2(b).
26. 2001 Prop. Reg. §§ 1.401(a)(9)-5, Q&A 1(d), 1.401(a)(9)-6, Q&A 2.
27. 2001 Prop. Reg. § 1.401(a)(9)-5, Q&A 5(a)(1), (c)(1).
28. 2001 Prop. Reg. § 1.401(a)(9)-5, Q&A 5(a)(1), (c)(2).
29. 2001 Prop. Reg. § 1.401(a)(9)-5, Q&A 5, Appendix G.
30. 2001 Prop. Reg. § 1.401(a)(9)-3, Q&A 3(a).
31. 2001 Prop. Reg. § 1.401(a)(9)-3, Q&A 3(b).
32. 2001 Prop. Reg. § 1.401(a)(9)-5, Q&A 5(c)(1).
33. 2001 Prop. Reg. § 1.401(a)(9)-5, Q&A 5(c)(2).
34. *Id.*
35. 2001 Prop. Reg. § 1.401(a)(9)-5, Q&A 6(a).
36. I.R.C. § 401(a)(9)(B)(ii).
37. 2001 Prop. Reg. § 1.401(a)(9)-3, Q&A 4(c).
38. 2001 Prop. Reg. § 54.4974-2, Q&A 8(b).
39. 2001 Prop. Reg. § 1.401(a)(9)-3, Q&A 4(b).
40. 2001 Prop. Reg. § 1.401(a)(9)-4, Q&A 1.
41. 2001 Prop. Reg. § 1.401(a)(9)-4, Q&A 5.
42. 2001 Prop. Reg. § 1.401(a)(9)-4, Q&A 4(a).
43. 2001 Prop. Reg. § 1.401(a)(9)-5, Q&A 7(a)(1).
44. *Id.*
45. 2001 Prop. Reg. § 1.401(a)(9)-8, Q&A 3(a).
46. *Id.*
47. 2001 Prop. Reg. § 1.401(a)(9)-8, Q&A 3(b).
48. 2001 Prop. Reg. § 1.401(a)(9)-4, Q&A 1.
49. *Id.*
50. 2001 Prop. Reg. § 1.401(a)(9)-4, Q&A 3(a).

51. 2001 Prop. Reg. § 1.401(a)(9)-4, Q&A 4(a).
52. *Id.*
53. *See* 2001 Prop. Reg. § 1.401(a)(9)-8, Q&A 2(b).
54. See, however, PLRs 200052042, 200052043, and 200052044, in which the I.R.S. took the position that separate accounts were established if the participant named two or more persons as beneficiaries of equal shares of his or her remaining IRA.
55. 2001 Prop. Reg. § 1.401(a)(9)-5, Q&A 7(b).
56. 2001 Prop. Reg. § 1.401(a)(9)-5, Q&A 7(c)(1).
57. 2001 Prop. Reg. § 1.401(a)(9)-5, Q&A 7(c)(2).
58. 2001 Prop. Reg. § 1.401(a)(9)-5, Q&A 7(d).
59. 2001 Prop. Reg. § 1.401(a)(9)-5, Q&A 7(c)(3), *Example 1.*
60. 2001 Prop. Reg. § 1.401(a)(9)-5, Q&A 7(d)(2).
61. 2001 Prop. Reg. § 1.401(a)(9)-4, Q&A 5.
62. Priv. Ltr. Rul. 9820021.
63. Priv. Ltr. Rul. 199903050.
64. 2001 Prop. Reg. § 1.401(a)(9)-4, Q&A 6.
65. 2001 Prop. Reg. § 1.408-8, Q&A 10.
66. 2001 Prop. Reg. § 1.408-8, Q&A 9.
67. *See* 2001 Prop. Reg. § 1.401(a)(9)-5, Q&A 7(c)(3), *Examples 2, 3.*
68. 2001 Prop. Reg. §§ 1.401(a)(9)-4, Q&A 4(a), 1.401(a)(9)-8, Q&A 3(a).
69. I.R.B. 2000-3.
70. 2001 Prop. Reg. § 1.401(a)(9)-5, Q&A 7(c)(3), *Example 2.*
71. 2001 Prop. Reg. § 1.401(a)(9)-5, Q&A 7(c)(3), *Example 3.*
72. I.R.C. § 402(c)(9); 2001 Prop. Reg. § 1.408(a)-8, Q&A 5(a). See Section VI of this chapter for a discussion of rollovers.
73. 2001 Prop. Reg. § 1.408-8, Q&A 5(a).
74. *See id.*

# CHAPTER 4

# The Simplified Retirement Plan Alternative

DAVID L. HIGGS

## I. Introduction

"Our life is frittered away by detail. . . . Simplify, simplify."[1] Few of us seem able—or willing—to follow Henry David Thoreau's advice and adopt a simple lifestyle. Perhaps the best we can hope for is to simplify some of the more complex tasks before us. Given increased technological requirements and governmental red tape, Thoreau's advice can be profitably applied to retirement plans in the new millenium.

The simplified employee pension (SEP) is indeed a simplified retirement plan alternative. A SEP operates like a traditional profit-sharing plan but with substantially reduced administrative time and expense. A SEP may be easily adopted (normally by using a preprinted government form), requires neither submission to nor advance approval by the Internal Revenue Service, requires no annual tax return, and eliminates fiduciary responsibility. A SEP permits deductible contributions by an employer like a traditional profit-sharing plan, and benefits accumulate tax-deferred for participants. A SEP allows an employer to substantially eliminate administrative expenses while maintaining a retirement plan for its employees.

Some requirements associated with SEPs, such as expanded coverage and vesting requirements, may make SEPs less desirable for some employers. However, a SEP *is* a simplified retirement plan alternative worth considering—especially for small employers.

## II. Accumulation of Wealth

A SEP permits the tax-deferred accumulation of benefits for each participant like a traditional retirement plan. Contributions to the SEP by the employer are not included in the income of participants when contributions are made. Employer contributions are made to the individual retirement account (IRA) of each SEP participant. The participant does not count the contribution amount toward income until a withdrawal is made from the IRA—which need not occur until the participant attains age $70^1/_2$.[2]

Earnings on investments in any IRA are not subject to current income taxation until the participant receives an actual distribution from the IRA. The SEP/IRA permits tax-deferred growth of investments, which can accumulate substantial wealth for a participant. Figure 4.1 illustrates such potential for accumulation of wealth within a

SEP/IRA, assuming a regular annual contribution and a consistent annual rate of return of 10 percent.

**FIGURE 4.1**

SEP/IRA Potential Accumulation of Wealth

| Annual Contribution | 10 Years | 20 Years | 30 Years |
| --- | --- | --- | --- |
| $ 5,000 | $ 79,687 | $ 286,375 | $ 822,470 |
| $10,000 | $159,374 | $ 572,750 | $1,644,940 |
| $20,000 | $319,468 | $1,145,500 | $3,289,880 |
| $30,000 | $479,202 | $1,718,250 | $4,934,820 |

Even if contributions are made for only ten years and then left to accumulate tax-deferred, the IRA growth will be substantial. For example, if the $159,374 (amount accumulated after ten years of an annual $10,000 contribution) continues to grow for twenty more years (without further contributions) at 10 percent per year, the IRA value increases to over $1 million.

The benefits of compounding interest and tax-deferred growth, while not peculiar to a SEP, are principal reasons for establishing and maintaining any retirement plan. By adopting a retirement plan and making consistent annual contributions, an employer can provide some retirement security for its employees and thereby a significant employee benefit.[3]

## III.  SEP Advantages

The tax-deferred growth within the SEP/IRA is not unlike the growth permitted in a participant's account in a traditional retirement plan, such as profit-sharing. However, there are distinct advantages of a SEP as compared to other tax-qualified retirement plans.

### A.  Simplified Adoption

For most employers, a SEP may be adopted by execution of a preprinted IRS (IRS) form.[4] The form is only 15 lines—*not pages*—long! The IRS has approved the form to qualify a plan as a SEP.

A SEP may be adopted by an employer at any time on or before the due date of the employer's income tax return for the year involved.[5] For example, if the employer is a sole proprietor who files income tax returns on a calendar-year basis, the employer could adopt a SEP for any given year until April 15 of the following year. A traditional retirement plan, by comparison, must be in writing and executed on or before the end of the plan year to which it relates. (Funding of the traditional retirement plan need not be made before the end of the plan year, however.)

Because adopting the SEP document may be so simple, the employer may save money that might otherwise be spent for professional services in adopting a traditional retirement plan. The IRS form is free, so there may be no need to pay a lawyer or benefit consultant to draft a specific plan or to pay anyone for a plan document. The SEP form is preapproved by the IRS and no user fees[6] will be paid to the IRS. Compared to a traditional retirement plan, adopting a SEP is easier and less expensive.

## B. Simplified Administration

Once the SEP is adopted, its administration is also simpler than for a traditional retirement plan. A SEP is funded through each participant's IRA; that is, the employer contribution is allocated and contributed to each IRA. There is no single trust that holds all the assets for the benefit of all plan participants. In a SEP, each participant—not the employer—has responsibility for investing his or her IRA account. In fact, once the employer determines the annual contribution amount and contributes it to each participant's IRA for the year, the employer has no further administrative responsibility for the SEP.

## C. Simplified Reporting and Disclosure

For a traditional retirement plan, a summary plan description (SPD) must be prepared, which summarizes the plan's content. The SPD must be furnished to each participant.[7] No SPD is required for a SEP. A SEP participant need only be furnished a copy of the preprinted IRS form and the corresponding information on the back of the form.[8]

For a traditional retirement plan, employers must prepare and file an annual information return with the IRS on Form 5500 series. No such annual return is required for SEP.[9]

Under traditional retirement plans, an employer is obliged to furnish an annual statement to each participant of the participant's account balance, earnings and losses, and contributions. An employer that maintains a SEP is required only to furnish an annual statement to each active participant of the amount of the SEP contribution, if any, paid to the participant's IRA.[10]

## D. Simplified Fiduciary Duties

A traditional retirement plan is administered by a plan administrator (often the employer), and plan assets are invested by a trustee (generally either a commercial trustee or an individual, such as the principal owner of the employer). Because of the discretion vested in these persons, they are considered fiduciaries of the plan. As fiduciaries, they owe specific legal duties to plan participants, including the prudent investment of the plan assets.[11]

Because a SEP is funded through participant IRAs, the employer is in no way responsible for investing a participant's assets. Participants have complete responsibility for their own investing. The employer simply has no fiduciary duty with respect to investing assets.[12]

## *IV. Technical Requirements for a SEP*

A SEP is statutorily authorized by Internal Revenue Code I.R.C. Section 408(k). As compared to a traditional retirement plan, few technical requirements must be satisfied by a SEP.

## A. Written Plan

To establish a SEP, an employer must adopt and execute a written SEP document on or before the due date of the employer's income tax return for the year involved.[13] The written document should specify the manner in which the contributions are to be made, the eligibility requirements for participation, and the manner in which contributions are to be allocated to participants.

## B. Participation

The eligibility requirements for a SEP are simpler and more liberal than are those for a traditional retirement plan. Each employee who has attained age 21, has performed service for the employer during at least three of the preceding five years, and receives at least $300 (as indexed) in compensation from the employer during the year must participate in the SEP.[14] Part-time employees may not be excluded from participation unless their compensation is below the threshold amount. The expansive coverage requirements for a SEP are a price of simplicity.

Leased employees are treated as employees for purposes of the participation requirement and may not be excluded from the SEP coverage.[15] Further, the term "employer" includes all corporations in a controlled group of corporations,[16] all commonly controlled trades or businesses,[17] and all members of an affiliated service group.[18] Each employee of the employer, as that term is defined in the aggregate, must be permitted to participate in the SEP.

Still, certain employees may be specifically excluded from participation in the SEP.[19] Employees who are covered by a collective bargaining agreement in which retirement benefits were the subject of good-faith bargaining, and certain nonresident aliens are not required to participate in the SEP. Employees who have not met the minimum age, service, and compensation requirements may also be excluded from participation until those requirements are satisfied.

## C. Contributions and Allocation Method

As with a traditional profit-sharing plan, employer contributions to a SEP are made at the discretion of the employer. The contribution amount may vary from year to year, and in some years the employer may elect to make no contribution at all. Contributions that are made to the SEP may not discriminate in favor of any highly compensated employee.[20] The allocation method for employer contributions must be specified in the SEP document.[21]

In general, employer allocation of contributions to a SEP must bear a uniform relation to compensation: Compensation in excess of $200,000 (as indexed) may not be considered.[22] Each participant receives the same percentage of compensation as a contribution to the participant's SEP/IRA. This basic allocation method is illustrated in Figure 4.2:

### FIGURE 4.2

Sample SEP Uniform Employer-Allocation Method

| Name | Compensation | Contribution Allocated |
|------|------|------|
| Craig | $200,000 | $30,000 |
| Carolyn | $ 40,000 | $ 6,000 |
| Scott | $ 20,000 | $ 3,000 |

In this example, because each of the three participants receives the same percentage compensation—15 percent—this allocation method meets the SEP requirements.

As an alternative allocation method, a SEP may allocate contributions per Social Security-permitted disparity rules.[23] Under an integrated SEP, the more highly compensated employees will receive a greater percentage of the employer's contribution. Generally, integration is accomplished by allowing one contribution percentage for compensation in excess of the Social Security wage base and a different percentage for all other compensation.[24] An example of a permissible integration allocation is shown in Figure 4.3:

**FIGURE 4.3**

Sample SEP Integrated Employer-Allocation Method

| Name | Compensation | Contribution Allocated |
|------|--------------|------------------------|
| Craig | $150,000 | $22,500 |
| Carolyn | $ 40,000 | $ 4,673 |
| Scott | $ 20,000 | $ 2,336 |

As the example[25] illustrates, the more highly compensated employee, Craig, receives a disproportionate percentage of the contribution (15 percent) as compared to the lowest-paid employee, Scott (11.68 percent).[26] The integrated allocation method will allow an employer to provide a greater benefit to highly compensated employees than to rank-and-file employees.

### D. Funding through an IRA

A SEP must be funded through the IRA of each participant.[27] Each participant must establish a separate IRA into which the employer contributions are made each year.

Because contributions are made to a participant's IRA, the participant is in effect fully and immediately vested in the contribution, that is, the participant is entitled to the entire amount in the IRA whenever the participant desires. The distribution and taxation rules of an IRA apply, and the employer may not prevent a participant from withdrawing contributions from the IRA at any time.[28]

This full-vesting requirement of a SEP is another liberalization of the rules that might otherwise be applied in the traditional profit-sharing plan. A traditional retirement plan may impose a graduated vesting schedule such that if an employee prematurely terminates service with the employer, the employee may forfeit all or portions of the employee's plan benefit.

## V. Federal Income-Tax Consequences of a SEP

### A. Employer

An employer is allowed a deduction for federal income-tax purposes for contributions made to a SEP. An employer may deduct SEP contributions in an amount up to 25 percent of the aggregate compensation paid to SEP participants during the year involved.[29] This is the same deduction limitation imposed on contributions to a traditional profit-sharing plan.

## B. Employee

As with a traditional retirement plan, an employee is not required to include in income the employer contributions to the participant's SEP/IRA. An employee may exclude from income the employer contributions to the SEP/IRA in an amount equal to the lesser of 15 percent of compensation or $40,000 in any year.[30]

The normal rules of taxation of distributions from an IRA apply to the SEP/IRA. As such, the participant must include in income any distribution from the SEP/IRA in the year in which it is received. Distributions prior to age 59½ will normally be subject to an additional 10 percent early-distribution penalty.[31]

## VI. The SIMPLE IRA Alternative

Prior to 1997, employees could include a salary-reduction feature as part of a SEP. The salary-reduction SEP allowed participating employees to elect to have a portion of their compensation contributed to the SEP on their behalf. After 1996, the salary-reduction SEP was replaced with another simplified salary-reduction arrangement: the SIMPLE IRA.[32] The SIMPLE IRA allows each eligible employee, along with the employer, to make contributions to the employee's IRA and accumulate tax-advantaged funds for retirement.

### A. Participants

A SIMPLE IRA is an option for an employer with 100 or fewer employees who each receive at least $5,000 in compensation. In a SIMPLE IRA, all employees who receive at least $5,000 of compensation from the employer during any two preceding calendar years and who are expected to receive at least $5,000 of compensation in the current year must be eligible to participate. (Employees covered by a collective-bargaining agreement and certain nonresident aliens may be excluded from coverage in the SIMPLE IRA.)

### B. Contributions

An employee participating in the SIMPLE IRA could make salary reduction contributions of up to $6,500 per year in 2001, and increasing thereafter until the limit becomes $10,000 in 2005.Unlike a 401(k) plan, there are no special nondiscrimination tests to be satisfied. The employer must satisfy one of the following contribution formulas: (a) match employee contributions on a dollar-for-dollar basis up to 3 percent of compensation, or (b) 2 percent of compensation contribution for each eligible employee, whether or not the employee makes elective deferrals. (An employer may reduce the 3-percent matching contribution to 1 percent for limited time periods.)[33] Other discretionary contributions by the employer are not permitted. Contributions to the SIMPLE IRA are excluded from employees' income for federal income-tax purposes and are deductible by the employer. All contributions are fully vested.

### C. Distributions

Distributions from a SIMPLE IRA are generally taxed in the same manner as distributions from IRAs. A SIMPLE IRA may be rolled over to an IRA after the employee has participated for at least two years. During the first two years of participation, distributions subject to the additional early-distribution tax are taxed at 25 percent rather than 10 percent.[34]

## D. Adoption

The SIMPLE IRA may be adopted by using a model form issued by the IRS.[35] As with the model SEP, the model SIMPLE IRA is not filed with the IRS. An employer may require that all contributions under the SIMPLE IRA be made to a particular financial institution, though there must be procedures in place to allow each participant to transfer the participant's account to another SIMPLE IRA or regular IRA selected by the participant.

## E. Administration

The SIMPLE IRA also has simplified reporting requirements for both the trustee and sponsoring employer. The normal ERISA rules, such as filing the annual report with the IRS, do not apply. Neither does fiduciary responsibility for investment performance apply to an employer to the extent the participant exercises control over the assets in the account.[36]

# VII. Conclusion

An employer considering any retirement plan must give the matter thorough investigation and careful thought. For an employer, particularly a small employer, looking to simplify its retirement plan, the SEP or SIMPLE IRA presents a viable and simplified alternative. A SEP or SIMPLE IRA offers the tax benefits of a traditional retirement plan but with a simplified administrative process. Keep Thoreau's directive in mind: Simplify![37]

## Endnotes

1. Henry David Thoreau, Walden 66 (Signet Classic ed. 1854).

2. 26 USC §§ 408(a)(6) and 401(a)(9). Distributions from an IRA must begin by April 15 of the year following the calendar year in which the participant attains age $70^1/_2$. (Hereafter, the Internal Revenue Code of 1986 (chapter 26 of the USC) will simply be referred to as "Code.") Regulations promulgated in 2001 simplify the minimum distribution process and generally extend the period of time over which distributions may be made. These simplified distribution rules apply to tax-qualified plans, IRAs, and SEPs.

3. An employer must consider the direct cost of providing the retirement benefit for all employees and weigh that cost against the tax benefits for owners and the value of the employee benefit in attracting and retaining employees. An additional benefit to owners is that contributions to a retirement plan will generally not be subject to employment taxes.

4. I.R.S. Form 5305-SEP. This form may not be used if the sponsoring employer maintains any other tax-qualified plan or has ever maintained a defined-benefit pension plan. This form may not be used if the employer utilizes the services of leased employees as that term is defined in I.R.C. § 414(n). An employer not permitted to use the preprinted government form may be able to adopt a prototype SEP document from a brokerage firm or financial institution or may adopt an individually designed SEP.

5. Prop. Reg. § 1.408-7(b).

6. On ruling requests submitted to the IRS, a user fee is required. For plans with fewer than 100 participants, the fee may be as much as $700. See I.R.S. Form 8717.

7. ERISA Reg. § 2520.104b-2(a).

8. I.R.S. Form 5305-SEP. If the employer adopts a nonmodel SEP, the employer should furnish employees with a copy of Notice 81-1, 1981-1 C.B. 610.

9. I.R.S. Form 5305-SEP; ERISA Reg. § 2520.104.48.

10. I.R.S. Form 5305-SEP.

11. ERISA Reg. §404(a).

12. An employer that maintains an individual account plan, such as a profit-sharing plan, may reduce its fiduciary responsibility for plan investments if it allows for participant-directed accounts in accordance with ERISA §404(c).

13. I.R.C. § 408(k)(5); Prop Reg. §1.408-7(b).

14. I.R.C. § 408(k)(2).

15. I.R.C. § 414(n)(3). A leased employee is defined in I.R.C. § 414(n) and may be generally described as a person, other than an employee, who provides services to the recipient employer pursuant to an agreement with a third party and does so on a substantially full-time basis and at the primary direction of the recipient.

16. I.R.C. § 414(b).

17. I.R.C. § 414(c).

18. I.R.C. § 414(m).

19. I.R.C. § 408(k)(2).

20. I.R.C. § 408(k)(3). Highly compensated employee is defined at I.R.C. § 414(q).

21. I.R.C. § 408(k)(5).

22. The compensation limit is increased to $200,000 beginning in 2002, a change made by the Economic Growth and Tax Relief Reconciliation Act of 2001 (EGTRRA).

23. I.R.C. § 408(k)(3)(D).

24. I.R.C. § 401(l).

25. The example is based on an integration level at the 1996 taxable wage base and an integration rate of 5.7 percent.

26. A preprinted government form may not be used if the SEP utilizes an integrated allocation formula. In addition, if an integration formula is used and the SEP is top-heavy, certain minimum contributions may be required. I.R.C. § 408(k)(1)(B).

27. I.R.C. § 408(k)(1).

28. I.R.C. § 408(k)(4).

29. I.R.C. § 404(h). EGTRRA increased the deduction limit beginning in 2002.

30. I.R.C. § 402(h). While EGTRRA increased the employer limit for deduction purposes to 25 percent of covered compensation, EGTRRA did not increase the 15-percent limit for exclusion purposes on an individual basis. A contribution in excess of 15 percent of an employee's compensation would not be excluded from the employee's income. This apparent inconsistency could be corrected by technical correction legislation.

31. I.R.C. § 72(t). There are exceptions to the early distribution penalty, including distributions that are part of a series of substantially equal periodic payments. *See* I.R.C. § 72(t)(2)(A)(iv).

32. The SIMPLE 401(k) is also similar to the SIMPLE IRA but is not discussed herein.

33. I.R.C. § 408(p)(2)(C)(ii).

34. I.R.C. § 72(t)(6).

35. I.R.S. Form 5305-SIMPLE or I.R.S. Form 5304-SIMPLE.

36. ERISA §101(g).

37. 66 THOREAU, *supra* n.1.

# CHAPTER 5

# The New Individual Retirement Account

STEPHEN P. MAGOWAN

## I. Introduction

Within the past generation, the life expectancy of Americans has increased significantly—while the manner of providing income for retired seniors has changed dramatically. The classic pension promise—work for $x$ years, generally 30 or more, and you will receive a pension equal to a percentage, frequently 60 percent, of your highest three or five years salary average—has largely disappeared or diminished. In its place, employers have created a system whereby employees invest their own retirement money plus, in some instances, a portion of employer-provided funds on a tax-favored basis in mutual funds. To state this more simply, defined contribution plans have replaced defined benefit plans as the retirement vehicle of choice.

At the center of this change is the individual retirement account (IRA). The growth of retirement assets in qualified defined-contribution plans and individual retirement accounts has been well documented. IRAs serve as important savings vehicles in their own right, but most wealth in IRAs comes from rollover contributions made by participants from their qualified plans, such as 401(k) plans, profit-sharing plans, and the like. Because working couples are commonplace, estate and financial planners frequently must deal with multiple retirement accounts valued at hundreds of thousands of dollars. The introduction in the Taxpayer Relief Act of 1997 of a new nondeductible IRA—the Roth IRA—made planning in this area both more interesting and more complicated.

In 2001, the Internal Revenue Service (IRS) and Congress made significant changes to IRAs in ways that impacted the life cycle of IRAs from initial contributions to minimum distributions. In early 2001, the I.R.S. proposed new minimum distribution rules for IRAs and qualified plans. These new minimum distribution rules are covered in Chapter 3. Later in 2001, Congress in the Economic Growth and Tax Relief Reconciliation Act of 2001 (EGTRRA) introduced significant changes to the contributions rules relating to IRAs and added a short-term tax credit for contributions to IRAs while permitting IRAs to be rolled over liberally into qualified plans. Understanding the complexity of the new IRA the I.R.S. and Congress have created is a must for estate planners.

## II. Overview of Roth and Traditional IRAs

Roth IRAs and Traditional IRAs differ from each other in many important respects.[1] The key differences between the Roth and Traditional IRAs are:

(a) Contributions to a Roth IRA are not tax-deductible although certain taxpayers may be entitled under EGTRRA to a tax credit for a portion of their Roth IRA contributions. Contributions to a Traditional IRA can be tax-deductible, depending on a number of factors, including a taxpayer's income and whether the taxpayer participates in a qualified plan.

(b) Distributions from a Roth IRA are not taxed if the account holder keeps the funds in the account for the period required under the statute and receives only qualified distributions from the account. Distributions from a Traditional IRA are generally subject to income tax, unless the taxpayer has made any nondeductible contributions.

Contributing to a Traditional IRA results in an immediate tax savings to many taxpayers each year. How much depends on the taxpayer's bracket. If the taxpayer is in the 27.5-percent income-tax bracket, a $2,000 deductible Traditional IRA contribution would result in a $550 reduction in the taxpayer's federal income taxes ($2,000 times 27.5 percent). By contrast, a contribution to a Roth IRA produces no immediate tax savings. However, the assets in the Roth IRA grow tax-free; furthermore, qualifying distributions from a Roth IRA are not subject to income tax.[2]

## III. Contribution Rules for Roth and Traditional IRAs

The rules governing contributions for Roth and Traditional IRAs work in tandem.

### A. Combined Contribution Limitation Rules

Until the calendar year beginning January 1, 2002, the aggregate nonrollover contributions an account owner could make for any taxable year to Roth and Traditional IRAs was $2,000. Thus, the owner could mix and match contributions with, say, $1,000 to a Traditional IRA and $1,000 to a Roth IRA.[3] Rollover contributions from, for instance, an employer's 401(k) plan did not count against this limitation.

Under EGTTRA, beginning January 1, 2002, the specific reference in the Internal Revenue Code (I.R.C.) to the $2,000 figure is replaced with a reference to the defined term "deductible amount."[4] The deductible amount is determined under the following figure:

**FIGURE 5.1**

EGTTRA Deductible Amount

| Taxable Years | Deductible Amount |
| --- | --- |
| 2002 to 2004 | $3,000 |
| 2005 to 2007 | $4,000 |
| 2008 and thereafter | $5,000 |

After 2008, the $5,000 amount will be indexed for a cost of living adjustment in increments of $500 with a base year of 2007.

EGTTRA also allows individuals who have reached the age of 50 before the close of a tax year to have an increased deductible in accordance with Figure 5.2:

**FIGURE 5.2**

EGTTRA Deductible Amount for Taxpayers Over 50

| Taxable Years | Additional Amount |
| --- | --- |
| 2002–2005 | $ 500 |
| 2006 and thereafter | $1,000 |

These amounts are in addition to the regular deductible amount limits.[5]

## B. Special Roth Contribution Limits

There are other special Roth IRA contribution rules. The maximum amount that an account owner can contribute to a Roth IRA is phased out for joint taxpayers at incomes from $150,000 to $160,000 and for single taxpayers with incomes from $95,000 to $110,000.[6] However, there are no additional restrictions for taxpayers who participate in other qualified plans. Thus, if an account owner and her spouse earn jointly $130,000 a year, and are both active participants in a qualified plan (that is, a 401(k) plan), they could still contribute the maximum amount to a Roth IRA.[7]

## C. Tax-Deductible Contributions to a Traditional IRA

If a taxpayer and taxpayer's spouse do not actively participate in a qualified pension plan, they may each contribute the maximum deductible amount to a Traditional IRA, up to the lesser of (a) the deductible amount for the given tax year or (b) their combined compensation. If the taxpayer and the taxpayer's spouse participate in a qualified pension or profit-sharing plan, the amount they can contribute to a Traditional IRA on a tax-deductible basis is restricted depending on adjusted gross income. Under the rules existing prior to the Taxpayer Relief Act of 1997, deductible contributions were phased out for joint taxpayers with income from $40,000 to $50,000 and for single taxpayers with income between $35,000 and $45,000. The Taxpayer Relief Act of 1997 liberalized these rules by increasing the dollar amounts taxpayers can earn while participating in the plan. This enables such workers to contribute more on a deductible basis into a Traditional IRA.

Under these rules, a taxpayer's deductible contribution is phased out over the ranges shown in Figures 5.3 and 5.4:

**FIGURE 5.3**

Phase-Out Income Ranges for Joint Returns

| For Taxable Years Beginning In: | The Phase-Out Income Ranges Are: |
| --- | --- |
| 2001 | $53,000–63,000 |
| 2002 | $54,000–64,000 |
| 2003 | $60,000–70,000 |
| 2004 | $65,000–75,000 |
| 2005 | $70,000–80,000 |
| 2006 | $75,000–85,000 |
| 2007 and thereafter | $80,000–100,000 |

**FIGURE 5.4**

Phase-Out Income Ranges for Single Returns

| For Taxable Years Beginning In: | The Phase-Out Income Ranges Are: |
|---|---|
| 2001 | $33,000 to 43,000 |
| 2002 | $34,000 to 44,000 |
| 2003 | $40,000 to 50,000 |
| 2004 | $45,000 to 55,000 |
| 2005 and thereafter | $50,000 to 60,000 |

The Taxpayer Relief Act of 1997 also made an important change for working and nonworking spouses. For many years if one spouse was participating in a qualified plan, the rule deemed the other spouse also participated, which restricted the contributions of the other spouse to a Traditional IRA. Thus, if the couple's joint income was too high, the nonworking spouse could not contribute to an IRA. The Taxpayer Relief Act of 1997 provided that if one spouse participated in a qualified plan, and the other did not, the nonparticipant could make a contribution of up to the deductible amount to a Traditional IRA or a Roth IRA—even if he or she did not work. The nonparticipant did not need to have earned income in order to be able to contribute to the IRA. The deductible amount limit stepped down to zero for taxpayers with joint incomes from $150,000 to $160,000.

## IV. More EGTRRA Changes

EGTRRA included other items that enhance the flexibility of IRAs and encourage contributions.

### A. Rollovers from IRAs to Qualified Plans

Effective January 1, 2002, EGTRRA permitted taxpayers to roll over distributions from an IRA into a qualified plan even if the IRA was not a conduit IRA.[8] Under pre-EGTRRA law, a distribution from an IRA could not be rolled over if there was any amount in the IRA not attributable to a rollover from a qualified plan. IRA owners may want to consider rolling over into their employer's plan in order to consolidate their retirement assets and also to lower their annual account fees. By rolling into an employer's plan, an IRA owner also may obtain access to mutual funds that would otherwise carry high broker's fees to access.

### B. Nonrefundable Tax Credit

For tax years after December 31, 2001, and before January 1, 2007, certain taxpayers may be able to obtain a nonrefundable tax credit for a portion of their Roth or Traditional IRA contribution.[9] The credit equals a percentage (50 percent, 20 percent, or 10 percent) of up to $2,000 of contributions and is in addition to a deduction or exclusion available for the contribution. The percentage of the contribution permitted as a credit is determined by the taxpayer's income as in Figure 5.5:

**FIGURE 5.5**

Permitted Percentage of IRA Contribution

| Joint Returns | | Head of Household | | All Others | | Applicable Percentage |
|---|---|---|---|---|---|---|
| Over | Not over | Over | Not over | Over | Not over | |
| 0 | $30,000 | $ 0 | $22,500 | $ 0 | $15,000 | 50 |
| 30,000 | $32,500 | 22,500 | 24,375 | 15,000 | 16,250 | 20 |
| 32,500 | 50,000 | 24,375 | 37,500 | 16,250 | 25,000 | 10 |
| 50,000 | | 37,500 | | 25,000 | | 0 |

The credit can offset both regular income tax and alternative minimum tax. It is available to taxpayers meeting the foregoing income requirements who are at least 18 years old as of the close of the tax year and who are neither claimed as a dependent nor a student (as defined in I.R.C. Section 151(c)(4)).

## V. Distribution Rules for Traditional IRAs

Most individuals intend that the monies they transfer into an IRA will stay there as long as possible so that they can take advantage of tax-deferred growth. However, with Traditional IRAs a taxpayer must begin to receive distributions from his or her account by no later than his or her required beginning date, which is April 1 of the calendar year following the calendar year the owner turned $70^1/_2$. This requirement is imposed by the minimum distribution rules of I.R.C. Section 401(a)(9) and proposed Treasury Regulations promulgated thereunder. Owners of Roth IRAs are not subject to the minimum distribution rules. Chapter 3 deals with the minimum distribution provisions in detail.

## VI. Taxation of Distributions from Roth IRAs

### A. Qualified Distributions

If the taxpayer or the taxpayer's successors receive a qualified distribution from a Roth IRA, they pay no tax on the distribution.[10] Under the statute a qualified distribution is defined as any payment or distribution:

(a) made on or after the date on which the owner reaches age $59^1/_2$;

(b) made to a beneficiary (or to the estate of the individual) on or after the death of the owner;

(c) attributable to the individual's being disabled (In a sense, a Roth IRA could serve as a supplement in disability-protection planning, which is helpful, as almost anyone working has a far more likely chance of being disabled in a given year than of dying.); or

(d) that is a qualified special-purpose distribution.[11]

### B. Certain Distributions within Five Years

A payment or distribution is not treated as a qualified distribution if it is made within the five-taxable-year period beginning with the first taxable year for which the individual made a contribution to a Roth IRA. Nevertheless, the taxpayer is treated as having first withdrawn his or her contributions, which were already taxed. Thus, taxpayers can always withdraw an amount equal to their contributions tax-free.

## C.  Retirement Planning with a Roth IRA

Using a Roth IRA to supplement retirement savings can be a powerful tool. For instance, assume a 35-year-old taxpayer saves $2,000 in a Roth IRA for five years, and then contributes $1,000 a year for five more years. Assuming an 8-percent return, at age 70 this taxpayer would have $202,207 in the Roth IRA, from which the taxpayer could then draw down $26,000 a year, *tax-free*, for 13 years. This is an after-tax equivalent of approximately $43,000 at 40 percent. A taxpayer who saved $2,000 a year from ages 30 through 55, under the same return assumptions, could receive $77,000 a year *tax-free*, for 13 years: the after-tax equivalent of $128,000. Using the same assumptions in a Traditional IRA, the owner could withdraw the same amounts, but they would be subject to income tax.

## VII.  *The Magic of an Inherited Roth IRA*

From an income and estate-tax perspective, the Traditional IRA can be a difficult asset with which to plan. A Traditional IRA is considered an item of "income in respect of a decedent."[12] This is a complicated way of saying that the account can be subject to both estate tax and income tax. How does this happen?

Let's say a taxpayer bequeathed 100 shares of IBM stock to the taxpayer's daughter. The taxpayer bought these shares for $1.00 apiece, so the taxpayer's total basis in the shares equals $100. Assume further that at the taxpayer's death the shares are trading at $100, and that the daughter then sells the shares for $100 apiece 12 months after the taxpayer's death. Under income tax rules, the daughter's basis for calculating gain on the sale would be the value of the shares at her mother's death, that is, $10,000.[13] Thus, the daughter would pay no income tax when she sold the shares. If she sold the shares at $110, she would pay capital gains tax on the difference between $110 and $100, not between $110 and $1.

The Traditional IRA does not enjoy this benefit of the stepped-up basis. Assume that instead of leaving IBM shares, the taxpayer designated her daughter as beneficiary of a $10,000 Traditional IRA and that, 12 months after the taxpayer's death, the daughter withdrew all the funds from the Traditional IRA to pay for funeral and related expenses. In this instance, the daughter would have to pay ordinary income tax on the full $10,000.[14] Thus, a Traditional IRA that is subject to both estate and income tax can be greatly reduced.

The Roth IRA is different. The Roth IRA is subject to estate tax, but there is no income tax when qualifying distributions are made out of a Roth IRA. This seems to place the Roth IRA on the same playing level as capital assets, but the Roth IRA is even better. The post-death appreciation in the Roth IRA is also not taxable, while post-death appreciation in stocks and other capital assets *is* taxable, albeit at lower capital-gains tax rates.

## VIII.  *Conversions of Traditional IRAs to Roth IRAs*

Married and single taxpayers whose adjusted gross income does not exceed $100,000 (and who are not married individuals filing a separate return) are permitted under the I.R.C. to convert a Traditional IRA to a Roth IRA.[15] This can eliminate decedent tax liability and also create an income-tax-free investment for the taxpayer's heirs. When a taxpayer does this conversion, however, the transfer is treated as taxable. Thus, if a taxpayer converts a $100,000 Traditional IRA to a Roth IRA, the taxpayer would have to pay income tax on $100,000.

Retirees with substantial assets could consider converting all or part of their Traditional IRAs to Roth IRAs. This would prepay income tax the descendants would be subject to in any case and reduce the size of the taxable estate by taking the income tax out of the estate for estate-tax purposes. This would leave the beneficiaries a nontaxable savings account from which to draw for college expenses, home-buying, and other anticipated expenses.

## IX. Conclusion

The rules governing Roth and Traditional IRAs are complicated. Working with an estate planner and a financial advisor who understand the rules can help taxpayers and their families take advantage of the planning opportunities available. It is important that any planning be integrated with the taxpayer's estate plan as a whole.

### Endnotes

1. Traditional IRAs are generally governed by Code Section 408 and Roth IRAs are generally governed by Code Section 408A. All "Code Section" references herein are to the Internal Revenue Code of 1986, as amended by EGTRRA, unless otherwise noted.

2. *Compare* I.R.C. § 408A(d)(1) *with* I.R.C. § 408(d).

3. I.R.C. § 219(b) prior to amendment by EGTRRA.

4. I.R.C. § 219(b)(1)(A) as amended by EGTRRA.

5. I.R.C. § 219(b)(5)(B) as amended by EGTRRA.

6. I.R.C. § 408A(c)(2). The reduction is accomplished in the following manner for married taxpayers or a married individual filing a separate return: The maximum contribution amount cannot exceed an amount equal to the statutory amount, that is, for 2002, $3,000, reduced by an amount that bears the same ratio to the statutory amount as the taxpayer's joint income subtracted by $150,000 bears to $10,000. In the case of a single taxpayer, $150,000 is replaced with $95,000 and $10,000 with $15,000.

7. Under EGTRRA, in 2006, each could also potentially contribute $20,000 to a 401(k) Plan account.

8. I.R.C. § 408(d)(3)(A).

9. *See generally* I.R.C. § 25B.

10. I.R.C. § 408A(d).

11. I.R.C. § 408A(d)(2).

12. *See* I.R.C. § 691.

13. I.R.C. § 1014.

14. In this instance, if the mother's estate were subject to estate tax, the daughter would be entitled to a deduction, generally, for the portion of the estate tax attributable to the IRA. I.R.C. § 691(c).

15. I.R.C. § 408A(c)(3)(B). It is one of the great oddities of the I.R.C. that the income limitation for Traditional to Roth conversions is the same for married and single taxpayers.

# PART II

*Inter Vivos Gifts*

# CHAPTER 6

# Lifetime Tax Planning

ALLAN C. BELL

## I. Introduction

The principal purpose of the gift tax is to limit avoidance of the estate tax: Making lifetime gifts removes from an estate property otherwise subject to estate tax. The gift tax, then, complements the estate tax. Accordingly, the taxes are integrated: Rates for lifetime transfers and transfers upon death are identical, at least through 2009.[1] At death, the estate tax is determined by applying the rate schedule to cumulative lifetime gifts and death transfers to arrive at a tentative tax, and then by subtracting the gift taxes payable on the lifetime transfers.

## II. Unified Credit

Consistent with the integration of the rates, the law through 2001 allowed a unified credit against the estate and gift taxes. Like an income tax credit, the unified credit is a dollar-for-dollar reduction in the tax. The maximum credit prior to the Taxpayer Relief Act of 1997 (the 1997 Act) was $192,800, which is equivalent to an exemption of $600,000. In other words, the estate or gift tax upon the transfer of property worth $600,000 would be $192,800, which would be fully absorbed by the unified credit. The estate and gift-tax rates for U.S. citizens and residents prior to the 1997 Act began at 37 percent for the first dollar above $600,000 and then rose quickly in a compressed structure to a 55 percent maximum at transfers over $3 million. The benefit of both the unified credit and the lower estate-tax brackets began to be phased out once the taxable estate exceeded $10 million.[2]

The 1997 Act gradually increased the unified credit over nine years, resulting in the following exemption schedule:

**FIGURE 6.1**

Unified Credit Exemption Schedule

| Year | Exemption |
|------|-----------|
| 1998 | $ 625,000 |
| 1999 | $ 650,000 |
| 2000 and 2001 | $ 675,000 |
| 2002 and 2003 | $ 700,000 |
| 2004 | $ 850,000 |
| 2005 | $ 950,000 |
| 2006 and after | $1,000,000 |

Because the increases in the unified credit were phased in very slowly (considering inflation), the tax savings would have been modest even when the law took full effect.

## III.  EGTRRA

The Economic Growth and Tax Relief Reconciliation Act of 2001 (EGTRRA) unlinks the integration or unification of the gift- and estate-tax structure. Effective January 1, 2010, EGTRRA repeals the estate tax but not the gift tax, albeit only for one year under the sunset provision with current transfer-tax law returning on January 1, 2011. Until scheduled estate-tax repeal in 2010, EGTRRA reduces the maximum estate and gift-tax rates and increases the estate and gift-tax exemption equivalents as follows:

### FIGURE  6.2

EGTRRA Maximum Estate and Gift Taxes

| Year | Estate Tax | | Gift Tax | |
|------|-----------|--------------|-----------|--------------|
| | Exemption | Maximum Rate | Exemption | Maximum Rate |
| 2001 | $  675,000 | 55% | $  675,000 | 55% |
| 2002 | $1,000,000 | 50% | $1,000,000 | 50% |
| 2003 | $1,000,000 | 49% | $1,000,000 | 49% |
| 2004 | $1,500,000 | 48% | $1,000,000 | 48% |
| 2005 | $1,500,000 | 47% | $1,000,000 | 47% |
| 2006 | $2,000,000 | 46% | $1,000,000 | 46% |
| 2007 | $2,000,000 | 45% | $1,000,000 | 45% |
| 2008 | $2,000,000 | 45% | $1,000,000 | 45% |
| 2009 | $3,500,000 | 45% | $1,000,000 | 45% |
| 2010 | Unlimited | 0% | $1,000,000 | 35% |

In 2011 and thereafter, the estate and gift-tax law in effect in 2001 will be reinstated with an estate and gift-tax exemption of $1 million.

The maximum gift-tax rate, then, is reduced according to the same schedule as the maximum estate-tax rate; however, in 2010, while the estate tax is scheduled to be eliminated, the maximum gift-tax rate will be identical to the projected maximum individual income-tax rate (35 percent in 2010). Furthermore, while the estate-tax exemption will increase from $1 million to $3.5 million over the 2002 to 2009 repeal phase-in period, the gift-tax exemption increased to $1 million in 2002 and remain at that amount indefinitely.[3]

This unlinking of the estate and gift taxes means that children and grandchildren who receive gifts from their parents and grandparents could pay as much as 35 percent in taxes on sums that they receive as gifts—even though they could ultimately inherit the same amounts tax-free.

In line with political reasons and budget constraints, the gift tax is retained to prevent income and estate-tax avoidance. For example, in the absence of gift tax, you could make a gift to someone in a lower income-tax bracket than you—such as a child or a citizen of another country—with no income tax. This lower-bracket taxpayer could sell the asset, pay little or no tax, and then gift the income or capital gains proceeds back to you. Furthermore, without gift tax, you could take advantage of the one-year estate-tax elimination in 2010 to make significant gifts and establish a dynasty trust of unlimited size and duration that would escape the estate tax upon its scheduled return in 2011 and thereafter.

The retention of the gift-tax structure then coupled with the EGTRRA sunset provision leads many to believe that the estate tax will never be completely repealed. By the time full repeal would be instituted in 2010, there will have been two presidential and four congressional elections since passage of EGTRRA. Tax legislation that phases in over such an extended budget horizon is the most vulnerable to revision, particularly when the projected surplus is far from certain. Because of this uncertainty created by the extended phase-in, temporary repeal may never occur. Obviously, many changes in the tax law are likely before 2011, making it difficult, if not impossible, to accurately predict what the transfer taxes will be then.

Until passage of EGTRRA, making lifetime gifts was good planning from a transfer-tax perspective. EGTRRA may make the advantages less clear. You do not want to pay a gift tax on a lifetime transfer that you could otherwise make estate-tax-free at death. However, if the estate tax is not repealed, or if it is phased out and then reinstated before any significant reductions occur (as scheduled under EGTRRA), the traditional advantages of transferring wealth during life will still apply.

Let us assume that the advantages of making gifts outweigh the advantages of not doing so, even in light of the mixed messages wrought by EGTRRA.

## *IV. Gift-Taxation Terminology*

Any transfer for less than full consideration is a taxable gift as long as the person making the transfer completely parts with control over the subject matter of the gift. Thus, if you transfer property to a revocable trust, you have not made a taxable gift because you can revoke the trust and get the property back. Understanding the following terms will guide you through the intricacies of gift taxation.

### A. Annual Exclusion

The amount of gift tax you will have to pay depends upon the available deductions and exclusions, and whether you can split the gift with your spouse. The annual exclusion permits an infinite number of annual gifts of present interests of up to $10,000 per donee to be made gift-tax-free. The 1997 Act indexes the $10,000 exclusion annually for inflation after 1998 rounded to the next-lowest multiple of $1,000. The annual exclusion is allowed only for a gift of a present interest, not for a gift of a future interest.

To illustrate, suppose that a father irrevocably transfers $50,000 in trust. The trust accumulates the income until the father's 20-year-old son turns 30, at which time the trust pays the principal to the son. If the son dies before age 30, the trust pays the principal and accumulated income to the son's estate. The gift to the son is a gift of a future interest for purposes of the gift tax, and no part of the gift qualifies for the annual exclusion. On the other hand, suppose that the father irrevocably transfers $50,000 in trust: The trust pays the net income to the son for life and the principal to the son's estate at the son's death. The father has made two gifts to son: (1) a gift of income that is a present interest and, thus, qualifies for the annual exclusion; and (2) a gift of principal that is a future interest and does not so qualify. In sections VII and VIII you will read more about other ways to obtain the annual exclusion.

## B.  Gift-Splitting

Gift-splitting means your spouse consents to being treated as the donor of one-half of any taxable gift made by you to a third person. This allows a married couple to use two annual exclusions and lifetime exemptions with respect to a single gift. For example, suppose a mother gives $20,000 in cash to her daughter. The mother gets only one $10,000 annual exclusion and so makes a $10,000 taxable gift, requiring her to absorb part of her lifetime exemption. However, if the father consents to gift-split, the father and mother will get two $10,000 annual exclusions, or $20,000, and the gift passes completely gift-tax-free to daughter. Likewise, suppose the mother gifted $1,370,000 in cash to daughter in 2001. The mother got one $10,000 annual exclusion and, assuming she had not previously used any of her lifetime exemption, fully absorbed her lifetime exemption equivalent of $675,000, thereby making a taxable gift of $685,000 to her daughter. However, if the father consented to gift-split, the father and mother would use two annual exclusions and lifetime exemptions, and the gift would have passed completely gift-tax-free to the daughter.

## C.  Charitable Deduction

The law allows a gift-tax charitable deduction for the value of a gift to charity. For outright distributions, there is no limit on the amount of this deduction—as there is on the income-tax charitable deduction.

A partial gift must be in one of several forms in order to qualify for the deduction. Charitable gifts of income interests and remainder interests in trust not only allow property to be passed on to the next generation at a reduced gift- and estate-tax cost, but also permit income-tax savings.

## D.  Marital Deduction

A U.S. citizen or resident has an unlimited marital deduction for qualified gifts made to a spouse who is a U.S. citizen. For 2001, there is a $106,000 annual exclusion (indexed annually for inflation) for qualified gifts to alien spouses. The marital deduction, the requirements and uses of which are dealt with in Chapter 18, is an important estate planning device for the married donor.

## E.  Compliance

Every taxpayer who makes a gift must file a gift-tax return, Form 709 (U.S. Gift and Generation-Skipping Transfer Tax Return), even if the lifetime exemption otherwise shelters the transfer from gift tax—unless the gift qualifies for the available exclusions and deductions so that no current gift tax is due (for example, a birthday gift not exceeding $10,000). Even when no tax is due because a married couple gift-splits $20,000 or less, a shorter return, Form 709-A (U.S. Short Form Gift-tax Return), must still be filed to report the gift-splitting election. To avoid filing such a return, the donor spouse could transfer $10,000 of the intended $20,000 gift to his or her spouse, who, in turn, would complete the gift to the donee.

Gift-tax returns must be filed on or before April 15 of the year following the calendar year in which the gifts are made. An automatic extension is granted if the taxpayer extends his or her income-tax return filing date for gifts made in the same year. Gift tax must be paid on the original due date of the return, regardless of any extension of time for filing the return. In order to avoid late-payment penalties, an extension should be requested.

# V. Generation-Skipping Transfer Tax

Without careful planning, a gift to, or for the benefit of, a grandchild could be subject to generation-skipping transfer (GST) tax in addition to gift tax.

## A. GST Tax Origins

Assume a father establishes a trust for his son's benefit that provides income paid to the son for the son's life and, at father's death, the trust property is distributed to son's children (father's grandchildren). Prior to 1976, father was subject to gift tax upon the establishment of the trust, but no estate tax was ever due when son's interest terminated upon son's death. Thus, son's generation was "skipped" for gift- and estate-tax purposes when the corpus of the trust was distributed to son's children. The GST tax rules of 1976 were imposed to make up for the absence of estate or gift tax being levied in the son's generation.

The introduction of this new tax in 1976, however, did little to deter capable taxpayers. In wealthy families, the grandparent would often transfer assets, outright or in trust, to his grandchildren. In this way, no GST taxes would ever be imposed. The Tax Reform Act of 1986 established a new GST tax and repealed the prior tax.

The new law continues to cover the first scenario, in which the middle generation has some interest in the GST trust, and also subjects the direct skip of the second example to the tax. Now there is a transfer tax levied upon the passage of wealth between each and every generation. The GST tax rate is a flat rate equal to the maximum gift- and estate-tax rate.

## B. Exemptions and Exceptions

There are three important exemptions and exceptions to the imposition of the GST tax. First, for 2001, each transferor had a $1.06-million exemption (indexed annually for inflation) that applied at the time of transfer. For example, a father could transfer $1.06 million to a trust for the benefit of his son and eventually his grandchild, applying his exemption to the transfer; this exempted the trust from GST tax even if the trust corpus appreciates to $2 million at the date of termination.

Second, there was a predeceased-child rule that negated the imposition of the GST tax. This occurred when the middle-generation member (transferor's son or transferee's parent) died before the first-generation donor.

Third, any outright transfer of property was not subject to the GST tax if not treated as a taxable gift because of the annual gift-tax exclusion or because of the gift-tax exclusion for transfers for educational and medical expenses (see section VI.B.).

## C. GST Tax Rate/Exemption under EGTRRA

EGTRRA reduces the maximum GST tax rate and increases the GST exemption as follows:[4]

### FIGURE 6.3

EGTRRA Impact on GST

| Year | Exemption | Maximum Rate |
|------|-----------|--------------|
| 2001 | $1,060,000 | 55% |
| 2002 | $1,060,000 (adjusted for inflation) | 50% |
| 2003 | $1,060,000 (adjusted for inflation) | 49% |
| 2004 | $1,500,000 | 48% |
| 2005 | $1,500,000 | 47% |
| 2006 | $2,000,000 | 46% |
| 2007 | $2,000,000 | 45% |
| 2008 | $2,000,000 | 45% |
| 2009 | $3,500,000 | 45% |
| 2010 | Unlimited | 0% |

In 2011 and thereafter, the GST tax law in effect in 2001 will be reinstated with an exemption of $1.06 million as adjusted for inflation.

## VI. Outright Gifts

There are several ways to make outright gifts while promoting your tax-planning goals.

### A. Uniform Gifts to Minors Act and Uniform Transfers to Minors Act

Every state (and the District of Columbia) has, in one form or another, laws simplifying the making of gifts to minors; these laws make unnecessary the appointment of a guardian or the establishment of a trust. Under the Uniform Gifts to Minors Act, cash, securities, life insurance policies, and cash equivalents (certificates of deposit, bank accounts, and so forth) may be transferred to a custodian and invested under a prudent man standard provided in the law. The majority of states have now adopted the Uniform Transfers to Minors Act as a successor to the Uniform Gifts to Minors Act. The Uniform Transfers to Minors Act expands the types of property that can be given to minors to include all types of property (money, securities, life insurance, real property, tangible personal property, and partnership and limited liability company interests) and permits the broad use of custodial transfers by trustees and executors.

A gift made under either uniform act is irrevocable. The custodian is under legal obligation to hold and manage the custodial property, and is authorized to apply as much of the income and principal of the property for the benefit of the minor as he or she deems appropriate. All property must be distributed outright to the minor at the age of majority or to the minor's estate in the event of prior death. Although state law sets the age of majority, the distribution age under a uniform act may be different.

The chief advantage of a gift under the uniform acts is its simplicity. Such gifts also qualify for the $10,000 gift-tax annual exclusion. Thus, no gift-tax return is required, and no gift tax is due on transfers of up to $10,000 a year. (If you and your spouse elect to gift-split, no tax is due on transfers of up to $20,000 under the uniform acts.) Furthermore, since a custodianship is not a trust for income-tax purposes, no trust income-tax returns are required. Rather, the minor donee reports all custodial income, whether or not distributed, directly on his or her individual income-tax return.

If you, as a parent, are legally obligated under state law to support your child, you will be taxed on any custodianship income used for support of the minor child. An increasing number of states consider a college education part of the parental support obligation. Using custodial funds to pay for luxuries not covered by the parents' legal support obligation will eliminate this potential income-tax problem.

The uniform laws permit you to serve as custodian of your own gift, but this would not be wise: The value of the property is included in your gross estate for estate-tax purposes if you die while serving in that capacity and before your child attains the majority age for distributions. In contrast to establishing a trust, a grandparent or parent usually will incur less expense by establishing and maintaining an account under either one of the uniform acts.

There is often a price to be paid for this administrative savings, however: One must consider the ability of the minor to manage the property when distributed. A trustee may control property transferred in trust beyond the required age of distribution under the uniform acts and without the loss of the gift-tax annual exclusion. Many grandparents and parents are unwilling to let large sums of money come under the control of an 18- or 21-year-old and will use a trust rather than one of the uniform acts for large gifts. The advantages and disadvantages of a trust versus a transfer under a uniform act should be carefully weighed before deciding which transfer is most appropriate for a particular beneficiary.

## B. Educational and Medical Expenses

In addition to the annual exclusion, transfers of any amounts for educational and medical expenses are not considered gifts for gift-tax purposes. The amounts must be paid directly to the provider of certain medical or educational services to the donee. The exclusion does not apply to payments that reimburse the donee for medical care payments, nor to amounts reimbursed by insurance.

The unlimited exclusion applies to tuition payments to foreign or domestic educational organizations and to payments for medical care. The exclusion does not cover the purchase of books, materials, and supplies, nor the payment of laboratory fees, room and board, and other related expenses.

For example, assume a father pays more than $30,000 a year for his son's medical school tuition, and son is an adult or father's support obligation under state law does not encompass medical school tuition. The tuition payments constitute gifts from father to son that qualify for the unlimited gift-tax exclusion. Likewise, if son pays $50,000 a year in medical bills to a doctor and a hospital for father, the medical payments are gifts from son to father, but they also qualify for the unlimited medical exclusion.

For educational expenses, applicable state-sponsored qualified tuition programs or an Internal Revenue Code (I.R.C.) Section 529 college savings program should be explored. This investment grows free from income tax. Distributions for qualified higher-education expenses (including tuition, fees, room and board, books, and other supplies needed to attend an institution of higher education) made after December 31, 2001, are federal income-tax-free. A 10-percent penalty applies on any earnings withdrawn for nonqualified expenses. For gift-tax purposes, contributions are a completed gift to the beneficiary and eligible for the $10,000 (or $20,0000 for married couples) annual gift-tax exclusion. Furthermore, the contributor may gift $50,000 to the account and elect to average the gift over a five-year period beginning with the year of contribution.

## VII.  Gifts in Trust

Using trusts to bestow gifts will further your tax-planning goals. There are numerous types of trusts from which to choose.

### A.  Irrevocable Minor's Trust

If you create a trust for your child or grandchild in which the trustee has the discretion to distribute both income and principal for the child's or grandchild's benefit before he or she reaches age 21, at which time any unused income and principal must be completely distributed to him or her, the gift-tax annual exclusion will be available for gifts to the trust. Such a trust will shift the income on the corpus away from you, remove the corpus from your estate, and at the same time take maximum advantage of the $10,000 gift-tax annual exclusion—or, if you gift-split with your spouse, $20,000.

You should neither designate yourself as trustee nor retain the power to remove and appoint a trustee and substitute yourself because either action would cause the trust assets to be included in your estate if you die prior to the trust's termination. Discharge of support obligations must be considered here as well.

The same nontax factors that are considered when implementing a custodial account are present here: You must be willing to permit the beneficiary to obtain possession of the trust corpus at age 21. If you think you can sufficiently influence the beneficiary after he or she turns 21, you may be able to persuade the beneficiary to voluntarily extend the trust.

### B.  Current-Income Trust

If you wish property held for the benefit of your child or grandchild to remain in trust beyond his 21st birthday, you might consider a current-income trust. Such a trust does not have to terminate when the minor beneficiary turns 18 or 21 as under the Uniform Gifts to Minors Act or Uniform Transfers to Minors Act, nor does the minor beneficiary have any power to terminate the trust upon turning 21 as in an irrevocable minor's trust.

As its name applies, a current-income trust beneficiary must have an income interest for a fixed number of years or for life; that is, all ordinary income must be distributed to the beneficiary currently during the term of the trust. Gifts to such a trust qualify for the gift-tax annual exclusion only up to the actuarial value of the beneficiary's income interest. The remainder interest is a gift of a future interest, which requires the filing of a gift-tax return and the payment of gift tax or absorption of your unified credit. Thus, a $20,000 gift in trust for the life of a five-year-old is a present interest (tax-free gift) regarding $19,414 and a future interest (taxable gift) regarding $586 (based upon Internal Revenue Service (IRS) actuarial valuation tables assuming a 6-percent interest rate—a rate that fluctuates monthly).

Because all trust income must be paid currently to the beneficiary, the trust must invest in income-producing assets. Gifts to a trust that allow the trustee to invest in nonincome-producing property, even if the trustee never makes such an investment, do not qualify for the annual exclusion. The trustee can have wide discretion concerning principal distributions to the beneficiary. However, no other beneficiary can receive principal.

As with other situations, you can be taxed on any trust income actually used to discharge any legal support obligations you have to the beneficiary. You should be able to avoid such a tax if the trustee pays the income directly to the beneficiary—not to a third-party service provider for the beneficiary's benefit—and the beneficiary then makes the payment to the third party.

Unlike the irrevocable minor's trust, you may serve as trustee if you distribute principal only for the "health, education, support, and maintenance" of the beneficiary. Such an "ascertainable standard," as the law refers to it, prevents trust income from being taxed to you or the property being included in your estate if you predecease the beneficiary.

## C. Irrevocable Crummey Support Trust

If the current-income trust inhibits your dispositive intentions by requiring you to give all the property to the beneficiary at age 21 or to distribute all income currently to the beneficiary, you should consider the use of a Crummey trust. Named for a landmark case, this trust is probably the most advantageous method of creating a present interest for purposes of the annual gift-tax exclusion, and it is superior to the two other methods.

In a Crummey trust the beneficiary is given a withdrawal power over the annual contribution to the trust. The withdrawal power gives the beneficiary a present interest in the trust, thus qualifying transfers to the trust for the annual gift-tax exclusion. The Internal Revenue Service (I.R.S.) requires that proper notice be given so the beneficiary has actual knowledge of the legal right to withdraw, and that the beneficiary must be capable, or have a guardian capable, of exercising the withdrawal power.

To increase the number of available annual exclusions, you may use several Crummey power holders. Each trust beneficiary would have the right to withdraw his or her pro rata share of the transfer. As long as they have some contingent beneficial interest in the trust, there can be several Crummey power holders (for example, the primary beneficiary and his or her children) possessing withdrawal rights when a trust really has only one intended beneficiary. (The I.R.S. has taken a contrary position that has been restricted by the courts.)[5] This would allow you to exceed the $10,000 or $20,000 per donee exclusion. Of course, you should be certain that the power holders will not exercise their rights, or your purpose will be defeated. If every power holder has a beneficial interest in the trust, you can probably attain your goal simply by informing the power holders that no more gifts to the trust would be made if they exercised their withdrawal powers.

Nonetheless, assume you intend to gift-split with your spouse and contribute $20,000 per beneficiary per year to the trust. You would probably want each beneficiary's withdrawal power to lapse after a certain period, typically 30 to 60 days, following each annual contribution. Otherwise, the beneficiary would have a cumulative withdrawal power over ever-increasing amounts, which would do little to limit the temptation to exercise that power. However, the lapse of the withdrawal power, which is a general power of appointment, may cause adverse gift- and estate-tax consequences to the beneficiary. The law deems a lapse of a general power of appointment in excess of the greater of $5,000 or 5 percent of the trust corpus (commonly referred to as a five-or-five exemption) to be a taxable gift made by the beneficiary to the other remaindermen of the trust.

Thus, if a beneficiary's noncumulative demand power is limited to the greater of $5,000 or 5 percent of the trust corpus, no such adverse consequences will result.

For example, assume you and your spouse establish a Crummey trust for your son and daughter and contribute $40,000 ($20,000 per beneficiary to take advantage of the double annual exclusion). Upon the lapse of each child's right to exercise withdrawal power, each will be deemed to have made a $15,000 ($20,000 minus $5,000) gift to the other. For this reason, many Crummey trusts limit the beneficiary's withdrawal right to a five-or-five power. However, this restriction prohibits you from taking full advantage of the $10,000 annual gift-tax exclusion or the $20,000 exclusion if you gift-split with your spouse.

Two methods may be used to avoid this problem. First, the power holder could be given a "hanging" power, which lapses only to the extent of the five-or-five limitation. The excess (if any) is carried over to the next year when it lapses again only to the extent of the five-or-five exemption, taking into account any contribution to the trust during that year. Or, as discussed in section IV, for a gift to be complete, the donor must give up sufficient dominion and control over the property. If a Crummey power holder is given a testamentary power of appointment over his interest in the trust corpus, control is retained even after the lapse of the annual withdrawal power, and the gift is then incomplete for gift-tax purposes.

## D.  Estate Preservation Insurance / Dynasty Asset Protection / GST Trust

An irrevocable life insurance trust is one of the most important means of providing immediate liquidity for the nonliquid estate, and of providing for the needs of the insured's survivors at no estate-, and little or no gift-tax cost. Properly structured, life-insurance proceeds can provide liquidity to permit an estate to pay federal and state death taxes, administrative expenses incurred in probate, and/or debts owed by the decedent. In the estate planning context, life insurance allows the avoidance of the forced sale of estate assets at a depressed price and provides an estate with the ability to meet the immediate and future needs of the surviving family members. The irrevocable life insurance trust ensures this liquidity by permitting the trustees to purchase assets from the estate at estate-tax values, or loan money to the estate even though the insurance proceeds are excluded from the taxable estate.

For an irrevocable life insurance trust, you would gift sufficient cash each year to the trustees to enable the trust to purchase and maintain insurance on the lives of you and your spouse. Second-to-die life insurance is particularly cost-effective. A second-to-die life insurance policy insures both your life and your spouse's life but pays only upon the survivor's death. Because the actuarial probability that both of you will die in any particular year is so much lower than the probability that only one of you will die, premiums are generally significantly lower for a second-to-die policy than for a policy insuring either of you.

At the time of the surviving spouse's death, the trustees would collect the policy proceeds and administer the funds, together with any assets from your estates, for your beneficiaries. Crummey withdrawal rights regarding cash contributions to the trust (to cover insurance policy premiums) are included to obtain the gift-tax annual exclusions. The insurance proceeds should not be taxed in either spouse's estate, but the proceeds will provide the surviving spouse's estate liquidity by permitting the trustees to purchase assets from the estate and the predeceasing spouse's testamentary trusts or to loan money thereto.

Only the trustees of a specifically prepared irrevocable trust should be the initial applicants, owners, and beneficiaries of such insurance. Upon the surviving spouse's death, lifetime trusts for your descendants' benefit should be created for the following asset-protection and GST reasons.

Retaining property in trust for each generation's lifetime accomplishes at least two significant purposes. First, it insulates such assets from a potential matrimonial equitable distribution or other creditor proceeding. Second, it allows a significant portion of property to pass from each generation's respective estates to the next generation without any estate or GST tax. Any transfer to, or for the benefit of, grandchildren, whether directly or indirectly through a trust continuing beyond the children's respective lifetimes, is subject to a federal GST tax. However, each of you and your spouse could allocate the necessary portion of your respective GST tax exemption to the trust contributions. This allows the property (plus any appreciation) to bypass your children's estates free of any applicable estate and GST taxes for your grandchildren's benefit.

Such a trust, while skipping each of your children's taxable estates, is still quite available for their benefit. Income and principal distributions to, or for the benefit of, your child and that child's children could be made in the trustees' discretion. Each of your children could even be a trustee of his or her own trust. In addition, each of your children could annually withdraw the greater of 5 percent or $5,000 of that child's trust principal for no matter what purpose without anyone's consent. Lastly, each child could have the power, during lifetime and/or upon death, to appoint undistributed trust assets among any person or entity, including charity, other than that child, that child's creditors, that child's estate, and the creditors of that child's estate.

## E. Charitable Remainder Trust

In a charitable remainder trust, a specified sum is paid annually to one or more designated noncharitable beneficiaries. At the end of the trust term, the principal is paid to charity. A charitable remainder trust containing low- or no-income-producing and highly appreciated property, such as publicly traded securities, can allow you to (1) dispose of such property free of an immediate large capital gains tax; (2) maintain a generally tax-exempt income stream until your death or until the death of the survivor of you and your spouse; (3) obtain a current charitable income-tax deduction in the year of the trust creation; and (4) satisfy any philanthropic urge.

In order to take the income, gift, or estate tax deduction, a charitable remainder trust must be in one of two forms: a unitrust or an annuity trust. In a unitrust, a fixed percentage of not less than 5 percent of the net value of trust assets valued annually is payable to the noncharitable beneficiary or beneficiaries for life or for a term of 20 years or less. In an annuity trust, a sum certain, not less than 5 percent of the initial fair-market value of the trust corpus, is payable annually either for the life or lives of persons in being at the creation of the trust or for a term of 20 years or less, unless shortened by a stated contingency. The annuity payment is thus a constant amount. No additional contributions may be made to a charitable remainder annuity trust.

Funding a charitable remainder annuity trust entitles you to a charitable income-tax deduction equal to the present value (discounted by the actuarial valuation tables) of the charitable remainder interest in the trust. Distributions from the trust are taxed to the noncharitable beneficiary or beneficiaries retaining the character they had in the trust. Each payment is treated in four ways: first, as ordinary income to the extent of the trust ordinary income for the year and undistributed ordinary income for prior years;

second, as capital gain to the extent of the trust capital gains for the year and undistributed capital gains for prior years; third, as other income (for example, tax-exempt income) to the extent of the trust's other income for the year and undistributed income for prior years; and fourth, as a tax-free distribution of principal.

In general, the charitable remainder trust is exempt from federal income tax. However, the exemption is lost if the trust has any unrelated business income, including debt-finance income. The I.R.S. has published guidelines and sample language for drafting charitable remainder trusts that require technical compliance.

For example, assume you are age 70 and transfer $100,000 in appreciated common stocks to a charitable remainder annuity trust, providing for a $7,000 annual payout to you for your life with the remainder going to charity. You would receive an immediate income-tax deduction of approximately $40,508 (based upon I.R.S. actuarial valuation tables assuming a 6-percent interest rate, a rate that fluctuates monthly). The deduction is limited to 30 percent of your adjusted gross income, if the property is ultimately passing to "public" charities, with a five-year carryover for any amount in excess of this threshold. Assuming you are in the 35.5-percent income-tax bracket, the tax savings would be $14,380.

Should the trust property not be producing a high-enough income yield, the trustees may sell the property at no income-tax cost since the trust is tax-exempt. In contrast, if you had sold the property while you owned it, you would, under present law, have capital gains income tax on the sale.

After your death, the charity receives the remaining balance of trust assets. The charitable beneficiary or beneficiaries do not have to be irrevocably designated by you at the trust's inception. They can be designated by you and your spouse later during your lifetimes, by your wills at death, or by individuals appointed by you. Finally, the assets would not be taxed in your estate at your death.

The 1997 Act imposes two restrictions on charitable remainder trusts. The Act requires that (1) a charitable remainder trust not have a maximum payout percentage in excess of 50 percent of the trust's fair market value, and (2) the value of the charitable remainder be at least 10 percent of the net fair-market value of property transferred in trust on the date of contribution to the trust.

### F. Grantor Charitable Annuity Lead Trust

If you have followed an annual charitable giving program, you might consider the establishment of a grantor charitable annuity lead trust. This trust involves a transfer in trust of property that generates income for a fixed period. Each year the trust is required to pay such income to the designated charities. When the trust terminates, you get the property back. The trust allows you to take a large, up-front charitable deduction in the year you fund the trust for donations that are made in later years.

To illustrate, suppose that in a given year you have an unusually high income. In such a year, you may wish to accelerate your charitable giving plans for the next few years to offset some of the high income tax. The creation of the trust entitles you to an income-tax charitable deduction of the actuarial value of the charitable income interest in trust on the date of the transfer. For example, suppose you contribute $50,000 worth of property to a charitable lead trust with payments of income of $10,000 a year to charity for five years. This will produce an immediate deduction of $42,124 (based upon I.R.S. actuarial valuation tables assuming a 6-percent interest rate, a rate that fluctuates monthly). The deduction is limited to 30 percent (20 percent if the trust is funded with long-term capital gains property) of your adjusted gross income with a five-year carryover.

During the term of the trust, the income earned will be fully taxable to you with no offsetting charitable deduction, even though all or most of the income will be paid out to charity. This disadvantage can be avoided by transferring tax-exempt municipal bonds to the trust. Even though you are obligated to report all of the trust's income, none of it is taxable to you because it consists entirely of tax-exempt interest.

The creation of the trust involves a gift of the income interest to the charitable beneficiaries. As the income interest is a qualified annuity interest, it will qualify for the gift-tax charitable deduction. Consequently, the establishment of the trust does not result in any taxable gift. Nonetheless, you still must file a gift-tax return.

Because you retained a reversionary interest in the trust, the assets of the trust will be included in your estate if you should die prior to the expiration of the trust term. The value of the income interest remaining at your death, however, will qualify for the estate-tax charitable deduction because it is in the form of a qualified annuity.

## G. Grantor-Retained Annuity Trust

A grantor-retained annuity trust (GRAT) is a way of saving estate tax at a small gift-tax cost. You, as grantor, retain the right to receive an annuity from trust property for a fixed term. If you survive the annuity term, the trust principal passes to your descendants, and that trust principal, including all its appreciation, is excluded from your estate for federal estate-tax purposes.

Because you retain a right to an annuity from the trust property, you are treated as making a gift only of the present value of the right to receive the property at the end of the annuity term. You offset your available lifetime exemption in the amount of the discounted gift and, thus, do not pay any current gift tax. In the event you die during the term of the trust, all or a portion of the value of the trust property is included in your estate as if you never created the GRAT. However, special trust provisions would minimize or eliminate the estate-tax inclusion.

For example, assume at age 50 in 2001, you created a three-year GRAT with property currently worth $1 million. You reserved an annuity of $313,077 at the end of the first year and 20 percent more than the prior year's payment in each succeeding year for two more years. Your surviving children (or a trust for their benefit) are the remaindermen. If you die during the three-year term, the remaining annuity payments would be made to your estate, and the balance of property, if any, can pass to your spouse. At the end of three years, the property may be worth $1.5 million. You have made a gift equal to only $8,144 (based upon I.R.S. actuarial valuation tables assuming a 6-percent interest rate, a rate that fluctuates monthly). Since a gift in that amount is covered by your available lifetime gift exemption, there is no current gift tax. Assuming you survive three years, assets worth $360,401 ($1.5 million less annuity payments of $313,077 in the first year, $375,692 in the second year, and $450,830 in the third year) are removed from your estate with a lifetime exemption cost of only $8,144, saving additional estate taxes of approximately $172,992, assuming a 48-percent estate-tax rate.

The $1 million figure is only an example. You may transfer a substantially smaller amount to a GRAT and obtain the same 99-percent discount. Because all your rights in the GRAT expire after the annuity term, you never should transfer any amount that would leave you uncomfortable psychologically or economically. To avoid this financial loss, with proper planning you may give your spouse an interest in the GRAT property after termination of your annuity interest, thus retaining the beneficial interests of the GRAT property for your spouse's lifetime.

### H.  Qualified Personal-Residence Trust

A qualified personal-residence trust (QPRT) is based upon concepts similar to the GRAT. Personal residences are not limited to primary residences and may include vacation residences.

For example, assume you own your residence with a $500,000 value. You are age 60 and create a trust that always provides you or your spouse the opportunity to use the trust property—whether as the initial trust beneficiary (for the greater of eight years, if you, as the grantor, survive such term, or the lifetime of your spouse, if your spouse survives you) or as a fair rent-paying tenant (if your spouse does not survive the term, or if your spouse predeceases you).

At the surviving spouse's death, the real estate may be worth $750,000. The gift- and estate-tax consequences would be as follows: You have made a gift equal to only $274,720, a 45-percent discount off the $500,000 value of the real estate (based upon I.R.S. actuarial valuation tables assuming a 6-percent interest rate, a rate which fluctuates monthly). Since such a gift is covered by your lifetime gift exemption, there is no current gift tax. Assuming you survive eight years, assets worth $750,000 are removed from the surviving spouse's estate with a lifetime exemption cost of only $274,720, which saves additional federal estate taxes of approximately $337,500, assuming a 45-percent estate-tax rate.

If you die prior to the expiration of the eight-year term, the then-current value of the trust assets will be fully includable in your gross estate for federal estate-tax purposes. However, in such an event, the amount of the $274,720 lifetime exemption initially offset on the trust's creation will be restored. If your spouse survives you, the trust property will qualify for the estate-tax marital deduction, thus creating no current estate-tax liability. Thus, there is no gift- or estate-tax downside as a result of your death prior to the expiration of the eight-year term.

If you outlive your spouse and survive the eight-year term, you will have to pay a fair-market rent to continue using the residence. If this represents any risk to your security, do not implement a QPRT. However, the payment of rent to the trust can present an extraordinary planning opportunity. Assuming you can afford to pay market rent, substantial amounts will be transferred (in the form of rental payments) to your ultimate beneficiaries without gift- or estate-tax consequences because the QPRT is a grantor trust for income-tax purposes. Be sure it is characterized as rent and not as a gift or bequest.

## VIII.  Other Techniques

In addition to making outright gifts and gifting via trusts, there are several ways to transfer wealth and still meet your tax-planning goals.

### A.  Private Foundation

The establishment of a private foundation permits you and your family to make sizable charitable gifts while still retaining a degree of control over the gifted cash or other property. Gifts to a private foundation also provide significant income-tax benefits.

You may establish a private foundation by forming a charitable nonprofit corporation. Forms and other documents are then filed with the I.R.S. to obtain a ruling that the organization is treated as a tax-exempt private foundation. Once you have the I.R.S. ruling, contributions to the private foundation retroactive to its inception are deductible for income-tax purposes within the normal limitations.

The private foundation itself does not perform a direct charitable function; rather, its resources are channeled to one or more public charities that directly carry out the charitable purpose. Generally, the private foundation is required to distribute annually an amount equal to at least 5 percent of its assets.

The foundation's directors may receive compensation for serving, provided it is reasonable under the circumstances. Similarly, private foundation expenditures for executives' travel expenses (to attend foundation meetings and other legitimate activities) are also permissible. Finally, the private foundation may be the recipient of distributions from the charitable remainder trust and/or charitable lead trust described in sections VII. E. and F.

## B. Delaware Family Limited Liability Company

This form of ownership allows you to transfer significant amounts of wealth for the benefit of your children and grandchildren (or qualifying trusts for their benefit) without relinquishing control. The company permits you to discount the value of gifts, retain control over the gifted assets, and protect the interests from potential claims of creditors.

You (and/or your spouse) contribute a portion of your respective investment portfolio to a newly formed limited liability company in exchange for majority membership interest(s). You name yourself as the manager of the company. You children and/or grandchildren (or qualifying trusts for their benefit) contribute cash in exchange for modest membership interests.

As manager, you have complete management control of the company: You make all decisions regarding the company assets: if and when distributions are made, how company assets are invested, and whether you are paid management fees or a salary. Gifts of the company interests can be made, but asset control is not lost.

The company also offers limited liability. If a judgment is brought against you, your assets will be in the company, thereby limiting your liability. Also, gifts of company interests are considered personal property and out of creditors' reach.

All company interests have pro rata rights concerning income and capital distributions only after the manager's management fee is paid. You could then gift a portion of the membership interests (instead of the underlying assets) to your children and/or grandchildren (or their trusts).

Gifts of such interests are nonmarketable and may represent a minority interest; therefore, they can usually be discounted for gift- and estate-tax purposes. These discounts can range anywhere from 10 percent to 50 percent, depending upon the nature of the company's underlying assets and other factors.

Absence of marketability discount reflects the company operating agreement and underlying applicable state law that restricts the sale or transfer of the interest so that there is no ready market for that interest. A minority discount reflects the inability of the company member to compel company distributions or to compel liquidation to obtain his or her share of the assets that the company owns. It also reflects the inability of the company member to control company investments. As a result, the value of the underlying assets is discounted because the gift now consists of an assignee interest in the company that owns the property instead of the property itself.

Thus, because such interests are generally subject to significant valuation discounts for lack of marketability and control, you can transfer substantial interests in the company for the benefit of your children and/or grandchildren (or their trusts) at a reduced gift-tax cost. Assuming a 20-percent valuation discount would allow you to transfer 25 percent more than you otherwise would have been able to so transfer. For example, you could transfer a $12,500 interest per donee within your $10,000 annual exclusion. Together with your spouse, then, you could transfer a $25,000 interest per donee within your $20,000 combined annual exclusions. Similarly, you and your spouse could each make current use of your available lifetime exemptions, allowing you the same leverage: giving away 25 percent more than you would have otherwise been able to transfer within your lifetime exemption. For example, you and your spouse could, collectively, transfer $2.5 million of company interests within your $2-million combined lifetime exemptions. Of course, the same valuation discounts are applicable at your death, thereby reducing the value of your taxable estate and resulting estate taxes due and payable.

### C. Sale to Grantor Trust

As an alternative to gifting your company interests, you could sell such interests to the asset protection/generation-skipping trust for the benefit of your descendants. The difference between the gross value of the company assets and the discounted company interests are removed from your taxable estate.

Furthermore, if the company interests sold to the trust outperform the interest payable to you on the promissory note, then this excess appreciation passes transfer-tax-free to your children and/or grandchildren. At your death, only the remaining unpaid principal balance on the note should be included in your taxable estate. By exchanging an asset with substantial potential growth (the company interest) for a no-growth asset (the promissory note), you are freezing the value of property at its current value for estate-tax purposes.

In addition, since the trust is a grantor trust for income-tax purposes, you continue to pay the income tax attributable to the trust's company interest. This income-tax liability results in an estate-tax benefit because the income tax you pay on behalf of the trust reduces your taxable estate, but is not treated as an additional taxable gift to the trust. For the same reason the sale of the company interest is not treated as a capital gains transaction, and the payment of interest is not treated as taxable income to you.

## IX.  Conclusion

Lifetime gifts provide many estate-planning opportunities. Implementing the techniques appropriate for your personal family and financial circumstances allows you to (1) significantly reduce estate-tax consequences; (2) provide continuity of direction in management of assets; (3) increase the asset holdings of your descendants in a tax-advantageous manner; and/or (4) provide the means to pay any estate taxes incurred.

## *Endnotes*

1. I.R.C. § 2001(c), § 2502(a).
2. Taxpayer Relief Act of 1997 § 501(a)(1)(A), PL 105-34, 8/5/97.
3. EGTRRA § 511, § 521(a)-(b), PL 107-16, 6/7/2001.
4. EGTRRA § 521(c), PL 107-16, 6/7/2001.
5. TAM 9141008, 9045002, 8727003, Estate of Cristofani v. Comr., 97 T.C. 74 (1991).

# CHAPTER 7

# The Charitable Remainder Trust

MICHAEL V. BOURLAND
JEFFREY N. MYERS

## I. Introduction

Used correctly, an Internal Revenue Code (I.R.C.) Section 664 charitable remainder trust (CRT) can accomplish a donor's donative goals and tax goals. (All references to Sections are to the I.R.C. of 1986, as amended, unless otherwise stated.)

## II. Charitable Remainder Trusts

A charitable remainder trust (CRT) is an irrevocable trust valid under applicable state law. An amount of income and/or principal from the CRT is payable to noncharitable beneficiaries, usually the grantor of the CRT and the grantor's spouse. The remainder interest is irrevocably payable to charity. The CRT pays no income tax; therefore, the CRT is not taxed on any gain it realizes upon selling appreciated property, whether the grantor donates the appreciated property or the appreciation occurs after donation. The grantor of an inter vivos CRT is entitled to an immediate income- and gift-tax charitable deduction in the amount of the present value of the remainder interest passing to charity. The estate of the decedent who created a testamentary CRT is entitled to an estate-tax charitable deduction for the present value of the remainder interest passing to charity.

## III. Legislative History

In 1969, Congress reacted to the abuse it perceived regarding charitable deductions resulting from gifts of remainder interests to charity. Congress believed that donors were taking income-, gift-, and estate-tax charitable deductions based on values not ultimately passing to the charity. Prior to 1969, the tests to obtain such charitable deductions were liberal. A gift to a split-interest trust (that is, in which the present interest is held by a noncharitable beneficiary and the remainder interest is held by the charitable beneficiary) enabled the donor to receive these charitable deductions if the interest passing to charity was presently ascertainable.[1] Further, as long as the ability of the trustee to invade corpus for the noncharitable beneficiary was subject to an ascertainable standard, the donor was entitled to the deduction.[2] Congress amended the charitable deduction sections (170, 2055, and 2522) to deny charitable deductions for gifts of remainder interests in split-interest trusts unless the gift of the remainder interest was made through a trust that qualified under the newly enacted Section 664, which provides the definitional scheme for a CRT.

## IV. Requirements of a CRT

### A. Definitions

A CRT provides for a specified distribution to one or more beneficiaries, at least one of which is not a charity, for life or for a term (not to exceed 20 years), or a combination of a life and term of years with an irrevocable remainder interest paid to charity.[3] The following definitions will be used in this chapter as they are used in the regulations:[4]

1. **Annuity amount:** The amount distributed to the noncharitable beneficiary of a charitable remainder annuity trust.
2. **Unitrust amount:** The amount distributed to the noncharitable beneficiary of a charitable remainder unitrust.
3. **Recipient:** The beneficiary who receives the annuity amount or unitrust amount.
4. **Charitable Remainder Annuity Trust (CRAT):** The annuity amount paid to the recipient is set when the trust is created. The annuity amount is a fixed percentage or dollar amount of the *initial* fair-market value of the trust assets. Thus, the annuity amount paid to the recipient does not change from year to year.[5]
5. **Charitable Remainder Unitrust (CRUT):** The unitrust amount paid to the recipient is a fixed percentage of the fair market value of the trust's assets *valued annually.* Thus, the unitrust amount fluctuates from year to year. There are four types of CRUTs:
   a. *Fixed-percentage (fixed-percentage unitrust or flat unitrust):* The recipient receives a fixed percentage of the trust assets valued annually.[6]
   b. *Lesser of income or fixed-percentage without makeup (NICRUT):* The recipient receives the lesser of the trust's net income for that year or the fixed percentage of the trust assets valued annually.[7]
   c. *Lesser of income or fixed percentage with makeup (NIMCRUT):* The recipient receives the lesser of the trust's net income for that year or the fixed percentage—but in a year in which the trust's net income exceeds the fixed percentage, such excess is used to make up for past deficiencies in years when the net income was less than the fixed percentage.[8] Typically, under state trust-law accounting, income excludes capital gains (that is, capital gains are allocated to principle).[9] However, a trust may allocate post-contribution capital gains to income. An example is a contribution of $500,000 in stock with a zero basis. If the stock is subsequently sold for $800,000, the first $500,000 must be allocated to principal, but the next $300,000 can be allocated to income for purposes of determining that year's income.

d. *FLIP CRUT:* The FLIP CRUT is a CRUT (1) in which the initial unitrust amount to the recipient is the lesser of income or the fixed percentage, and (2) in which after a triggering event, the unitrust amount changes (flips) to the fixed percentage. These requirements must be satisfied to use the FLIP CRUT:

   (i) The change (FLIP) from the NIMCRUT (NICRUT) to the fixed percentage CRUT is triggered on a specific date or by a single event whose occurrence is not discretionary with, or within the control of, the trustee or any other person;

   (ii) The FLIP occurs at the beginning of the taxable year that immediately follows the taxable year during which the triggering event or date occurs;

   (iii) Following the flip, the CRT becomes a fixed percentage CRT (and any makeup account is forfeited).[10]

A triggering event based on the sale of unmarketable assets or the marriage, divorce, death, or birth of a child will not be considered discretionary with, or within the control of, the trustees or any other person.[11] For purposes of a FLIP CRUT, unmarketable assets are assets that are not cash, cash equivalents, or other assets that can be readily sold or exchanged for cash or cash equivalents. For example, unmarketable assets include real property, closely held stocks, and an unregistered security for which there is no available exemption permitting public sale.[12]

The FLIP CRUT is useful to create a retirement account or a deferred income stream: The donor can fund the FLIP CRUT with cash or securities and pick a date certain in the future as the triggering event. Prior to the triggering event, the trustee invests the trust assets in growth, nonincome-producing assets with the intent to enlarge the trust corpus. Upon the date certain (that is, retirement or date donor wants the payment stream to become fixed), the CRUT flips. To make the unitrust payment the trustee will either sell sufficient assets to satisfy the payment or distribute the assets in-kind to the unitrust beneficiary, who in turn can sell the assets. Ordinarily, unless there is undistributed ordinary income, the unitrust amount would be taxed to the unitrust beneficiary at capital gains rates. The FLIP CRUT is also useful when the assets used to fund the CRUT are unmarketable assets (real property or closely held stock) and the unitrust beneficiary of the CRUT desires a payout equal to a fixed percentage of the value of the assets. The Internal Revenue Code (I.R.C.) specifically states that the triggering event may be the sale of those unmarketable assets. During the period the trust holds the unmarketable assets, the CRT is either a NIMCRUT or NICRUT so that the trustee is not required to distribute undivided interests in the unmarketable assets. When the unmarketable assets are sold the CRUT flips and then the unitrust amount is a fixed percentage.

## B. No Hybrids

The trust must either be a CRAT or a CRUT—not a combination.[13] Additional contributions cannot be made to a CRAT because the annuity amount is based only on the value of the assets at creation. Additional contributions *can* be made to a CRUT as long as the governing instrument provides a formula that takes into account the additional contribution when figuring the unitrust amount.[14]

## C.  Annuity Amount and Unitrust Amount[15]

There are certain statutory requirements that must be satisfied within the trust document. The governing instrument must provide that the fixed percentage be at least 5 percent but no more than 50 percent.[16]

The governing instrument must contain language regarding proration of the unitrust or annuity amount in the event of a short taxable year (less than 12 months). The annuity or unitrust amount shall be the amount otherwise payable multiplied by a fraction, the numerator of which is the number of days in the taxable year of the trust and the denominator of which is 365 (366 if February 29 is a day included in the numerator). The governing instrument of the CRT must also include language providing that if the CRAT or CRUT is terminated in a trust-taxable year, the annuity or unitrust amount that must be distributed shall be the amount otherwise determined multiplied by a fraction, the numerator of which is the number of days in the period beginning on the first day of such taxable year and ending on the day that the CRT terminates and the denominator of which is 365 (366 if February 29 is a day included in the numerator).[17]

The governing instrument must require that the trustee pay to the recipient (if an undervaluation) or receive from the recipient (if an overvaluation) an amount equal to the difference between the annuity amount or unitrust amount that the trustee should have paid and the annuity amount or unitrust amount that was actually paid to the recipient.[18]

Generally, the unitrust or annuity amount must be fixed. However, a trust may provide for a reduction in the unitrust or annuity amount upon the death of a recipient or the expiration of the term—as long as the governing instrument of the CRT provides that (1) the distribution of the excess annuity or unitrust amount is made to a charity and (2) the total of the unitrust or annuity amount payable after the distribution to the charity is not less than five percent.[19]

The CRT must function exclusively as a CRT from inception.[20] Therefore, the payment of the unitrust or annuity amount must be due for the year the CRT was created. However, a CRT will not fail to function exclusively as a CRT merely because payment of the unitrust or annuity amount is made after the close of the taxable year—provided that the payment is made within a reasonable time thereafter.[21] With testamentary CRTs, the CRT is deemed created in the year of the decedent's death.[22] In this case, the governing instrument of the CRT should also include a provision allowing the executor of the decedent's estate to defer such payment for a reasonable time to allow administration of the decedent's estate.[23] In that event, the governing instrument may include a requirement to defer the payment of the annuity or unitrust amount until the end of the taxable year in which the CRT is completely funded.[24] If such a deferment provision is made, the governing instrument must provide that within a reasonable time after such funding, the trustee will pay to the recipient (in the case of underpayment) or must receive from the recipient (in the case of overpayment) the difference between the annuity or unitrust amount actually paid and required to be paid, plus interest compounded.[25]

## D.  Term of Payment of Annuity Amount and Unitrust Amount

The governing instrument must specify the term of the annuity and unitrust amount and the term may continue for a term not to exceed 20 years, the life or lives of a named individual or individuals, or the combination of a life or lives and a fixed term of years.[26]

The governing instrument of the CRT may provide that the acceleration of the term will cause the assets to be distributed to charity. However, this possibility is not taken into account in valuing the remainder interest.[27]

## E. Recipient of Annuity Amount and Unitrust Amount[28]

The recipient requirements of the CRAT and the CRUT are the same. The trust document must specifically name a person(s) as recipient(s) of the annuity or unitrust amount. The donor may name more than one recipient (either successively or concurrently) as long as the trust otherwise satisfies its 10-percent charitable-deduction factor. Additionally, charity may be named as one of the annuity- or unitrust-amount beneficiaries; however, the donor will not receive an additional income-tax charitable deduction.

To minimize the gift-tax consequences of naming an individual other than the donor or the donor's spouse as a successive recipient of the unitrust or annuity amount, the grantor may retain the right to revoke by will any recipient's interest (other than charity), leaving no completed gift to this successive recipient. However, the power to revoke is a retention of a power includable in the grantor's estate for federal estate-tax purposes.

The grantor may name multiple concurrent annuity- and unitrust-amount beneficiaries with the power in the trustee to sprinkle such amount among the recipients. However, if the grantor chooses to be trustee, he or she may not retain the power to sprinkle among the recipients because the trust would become a grantor trust and disqualify it as a charitable remainder trust.

## F. Charitable Remainderman[29]

The governing instrument must provide that at end of the term, the entire corpus of the CRT will pass to charity. Such charitable interest can pass outright or it can continue in trust for the benefit of the charity. The governing instrument may provide for more than one charitable remainderman, who can be concurrent or successive. The governing instrument also must provide that if the named charitable remainderman is not a qualified charity under the Code at the time of the distribution, then the distribution must go to an alternate charitable remainderman that is a qualified charity under the Code at the time of the distribution. The governing instrument must provide the means to select the alternate charity; the grantor may substitute an alternate charity as the remainderman.[30]

The present value of the remainder interest ultimately passing to the charitable remainderman must equal at least 10 percent of the net fair-market value of the property transferred to the CRT on the date of the contribution to the CRT.[31] CRATs must also meet the not-so-remote-as-to-be-negligible-5-percent-probability test of Rev. Rul. 77-374. This ruling provides that a CRAT does not qualify for a charitable deduction (and by implication is not a qualified trust) unless the possibility that the charitable transfer will not occur is so remote as to be negligible. If there is more than a 5-percent probability that the noncharitable income beneficiary will survive the exhaustion of the trust assets, that probability is not negligible.[32]

The governing instrument may permit the trustee of a CRT to make an early distribution of corpus to charity as long as, in the case of distributions in-kind, assets distributed have adjusted bases fairly representative of the adjusted bases of all assets available. Further, it may provide that the grantor reserves the right to terminate the trust, resulting in the acceleration of the distribution to the charity.[33]

## G. Private-Foundation Restrictions

### 1. Self-Dealing

The CRT is a tax-exempt entity, treated as a private foundation in certain circumstances and must preclude self-dealing. Self-dealing includes any direct or indirect

(a) sale or exchange or leasing of property between a trust and a disqualified person;

(b) lending of money or extension of credit between a trust and a disqualified person;

(c) furnishing of goods, services, or facilities between a trust and a disqualified person, unless such goods, services, or facilities are made available to the general public on at least as favorable a basis as they are made to the disqualified person;[34]

(d) transfer to, or use by or for the benefit of, a disqualified person of the income or assets of a private foundation;[35]

(e) agreement by a private foundation to make any payment of money or other property to a government official (as defined in Section 4946[c]) other than an agreement to employ such individual for any period after the termination of his or her government service (if terminating within 90 days);[36] and

(f) payment of compensation (or payment or reimbursement of expenses) by a trust to a disqualified person, unless (i) for personal services; (ii) reasonable and not excessive; and (iii) necessary to carry out the exempt purpose.[37] The trustee, who is also the grantor, may be entitled to reasonable compensation as trustee as long as the compensation is not paid out of the grantor's annuity or unitrust amount and the compensation is reasonable and not excessive.[38]

A disqualified person is a substantial contributor to the CRT (an individual, trust, estate, corporation, or partnership that contributes an aggregate amount in excess of $5,000 to the CRT, if its total contributions are more than 2 percent of the total contributions received); a family member of a substantial contributor (spouse, descendants, and spouses of descendants); or a person owning more than 20 percent of either an entity that is a substantial contributor to the CRT or an entity in which a disqualified person (considering the attribution rules of Code Section 4946[a][4]) owns more than 35 percent.

Any disqualified person who engages in self-dealing is assessed an excise tax of 5 percent of the amount involved in the transaction for each year that the transaction is uncorrected. Additionally, a foundation manager (CRT trustee) who knows the act is prohibited but approves it may also be subject to a tax of 2.5 percent of the amount involved (up to $10,000 for each such act) for each year that the transaction is uncorrected. If the transaction is not promptly corrected and the 5 percent was initially assessed, the disqualified person may be assessed an additional tax of 200 percent of the amount involved. Any foundation manager who does not correct the transaction may also be subject to an additional assessment of 50 percent of the amount involved (up to $10,000 for each occurrence.)

## 2. *Unrelated Business-Taxable Income*

A CRT which has unrelated business-taxable income in excess of $1,000 will be taxed on all of its income—not just the tainted income: all of it—in the trust-tax year in which the trust has unrelated business-taxable income.[39] Unrelated business-taxable income is defined as income derived by an organization from any unrelated trade or business regularly carried on by the organization in excess of $1,000.[40] The conduct of an unrelated trade or business is not substantially related to the exercise of the organization's charitable functions.[41] The sale or disposition of inventory or property held primarily for sale to customers in the ordinary course of business will create unrelated business-taxable income on any proceeds over $1,000.[42] Although the sale or disposition of any other property will not create unrelated business-taxable income,[43] any income from debt-financed property will.[44] A CRT has debt-financed income if the CRT acquires realty subject to a mortgage. The CRT will not have unrelated business-taxable income for a period of ten years following the gift as long as:

    a. it does not assume the debt; or[45]

    b. the debt was placed on the property more than five years before the date of the gift,[46] the property was held by the donor for more than five years before making the gift, and the CRT does not assume the debt.[47]

## H. Estate Tax

Estate tax cannot be paid from a CRT. If this were so, the CRT would not exclusively operate as a CRT from inception. The governing instrument must contain provisions for the payment of estate taxes from sources other than the trust itself. The life interest of a survivor-income beneficiary can take effect only if the survivor beneficiary furnished funds for payment of federal estate taxes or state death taxes for which the trust was liable.[48] Be careful in defining death taxes. The term "death taxes" does not necessarily include estate taxes.[49]

The governing instrument must not permit the debts and expenses of a decedent's estate to be made from the assets of a testamentary CRT.[50]

## I. Asset Valuation

The legislative history of Section 664 indicates that Congress contemplated denying the charitable deduction when a grantor of a CRT, who was also trustee, transferred hard-to-value assets (that is, all assets other than cash, cash equivalents, and marketable securities) to a CRT unless an independent trustee valued those assets.[51] Thus, if the grantor is the trustee of a CRT, the governing instrument must provide that the annual valuation of such assets be prepared by an independent valuation trustee or by a qualified appraiser.[52] An independent trustee is a person other than the grantor, the grantor's spouse, a noncharitable beneficiary, or a party related or subordinate to either of them.[53] A cotrustee who is independent may value the trust's unmarketable assets.

## J. Trustee

The grantor, noncharitable beneficiary, and/or charitable remainderman may serve as trustee(s). Check applicable state law to ensure the charity has trustee powers. Under

Texas law, a charity can be the trustee of a CRT of which it is a beneficiary.[54] The governing instrument of a CRT may permit the grantor to remove, replace, and self-appoint the trustee.[55]

### K. Annuity Amount and Unitrust Amount

Although the CRT is tax-exempt, receipt of the annuity or unitrust amount will be included in the recipient's gross income and taxable to the recipient. When determining the tax character of the annuity or unitrust amount received by the recipient, a four-tier system is used. The distributions to the recipient are made on a worst-in-first-out philosophy. Under the first tier, a distribution is ordinary income to the extent of the CRT's ordinary income for that year and any undistributed ordinary income from prior years. Under the second tier, absent current or prior year's ordinary income, the distribution is treated as capital gains to the extent of the CRT's capital gains for that year and undistributed capital gains from prior years. Under the third tier, absent current or prior year's capital gains, the distribution is treated as other income to the extent of the CRT's other income for that year and prior years. Finally, under the fourth tier, after all the ordinary income, capital gains, and other income (current year and former years), the distribution to the recipient is treated as a distribution of corpus.

Here is an example of how the tier system works in a NIMCRUT: Assume a NIMCRUT received $7,500 of income in its third year, all of which was tax-exempt bond interest. It had no undistributed ordinary income or capital gain, except for $30,000 in undistributed capital gain from prior taxable years, and its unitrust amount for the third year was $9,000. The amount distributable for the third year was $7,500. Under the four-tier system, this amount will be characterized as capital gain rather than tax-exempt income, even though it actually arose in the third year from tax-exempt sources. This is because no tax-exempt income will be deemed distributed until all undistributed capital gain for the current year and all prior years is deemed distributed. Thus, the trust's undistributed capital gain income goes down by $7,500, and its undistributed tax-exempt income goes up by the same amount for purposes of characterizing the fourth-year and later distributions.[56]

Making a distribution of property other than cash may satisfy the unitrust or annuity amount. This could happen with a CRAT or a fixed-percentage CRUT in which the recipient is entitled to the fixed percentage. If the annuity or unitrust amount is satisfied by making a distribution in-kind, such is deemed to be a sale of the property resulting in realization of gain by the CRT.[57] For example, if a donor funds a fixed-percentage CRUT with closely held stock of a C corporation and then the stock cannot be sold, the trustee will be obligated to distribute enough stock to the donor to meet the annual fixed percentage. The CRUT will realize the capital gain on that stock even though it was not sold; the capital gain will be passed through to the recipient under the income-tax characterization rules causing the recipient to recognize gain.

## V. Tax Attributes of Charitable Remainder Trusts

### A. Donor's Income Tax Deduction

The donor is entitled to a federal income-tax charitable deduction for the fair-market value of the remainder interest passing to charity. The value of the donor's federal income-tax charitable deduction is a function of (1) the type of charitable remainder-man; (2) the type of property contributed to the CRT; and (3) whether, at the end of the noncharitable term, the assets are distributed outright to the charitable remainderman or held in trust for his or her benefit.[58]

There are two types of charitable remaindermen: (1) public charity (and those private foundations treated as public charity for tax purposes) and (2) private-family foundations. Public charity includes churches, educational institutions, hospitals and medical institutions, university endowment funds, governmental units, publicly supported organizations under Sections 170(c)(2) and 509(a)(2) (museums, drama companies, ballet companies, and so forth), supporting organizations under Section 509(a)(3), private operating foundations, and two types of private foundations: distributing foundations and foundations that maintain a common fund. There are two types of property: appreciated property and nonappreciated property. Both include cash, securities (publicly traded and nonpublicly traded), and real and personal property. Finally, while most CRTs distribute their assets directly to the charitable remainderman upon the termination of the trust, it is possible to hold the assets in trust for the charity's benefit.

Once the type of charitable remainderman, property, and distribution scheme is determined, the applicable adjusted-gross-income limitations are applied. When the donor contributes either cash or nonappreciated property to the CRT and the charitable remainderman is public charity, the donor's fair-market-value income-tax charitable deduction is limited to 50 percent of his or her adjusted gross income (AGI) with a five-year carryforward[59] (limited to 30 percent of AGI if the assets are held in trust for the charity). When the donor contributes appreciated property to the CRT and the charitable remainderman is public charity, the donor's fair-market-value income-tax charitable deduction is limited to 30 percent of AGI with a five-year carryforward[60] (limited to 20 percent of AGI if the assets are held in trust for the charity). When the charitable remainderman is a private foundation, the AGI limit is reduced to 30 percent for cash and appreciated public securities and 20 percent for gifts of all other appreciated property; however, the donor is entitled only to an income-tax charitable deduction of the adjusted basis on the property, not the property's fair-market value.

Finally, regardless of charity or property type, for an individual whose AGI exceeds the threshold amount for itemized deductions, the charitable deduction for that year is reduced by the lesser of 3 percent of AGI in excess of the threshold amount or 80 percent of the total amount otherwise allowed as itemized deductions.

## B. Federal Return Filings Required for a CRT

There are two one-time filing requirements of a CRT's donor, one one-time filing requirement of a CRT's trustee, and two annual filing requirements of a CRT's trustee. The donor of the CRT must file Form 709 (Federal Gift and Generation-Skipping Transfer Tax Return). Form 709 must be filed on April 15 of the year following the gift; there is no gift tax due because a gift to a CRT qualifies for the gift-tax charitable deduction. For all noncash gifts, the donor must file Form 8283 (Noncash Charitable Contribution) with the donor's federal income-tax return. In order to prepare Form 8283 for unmarketable assets, the donor must obtain a qualified appraisal. Unmarketable assets are defined as not cash, cash equivalents, or other assets that can be readily sold or exchanged for cash or cash equivalents. For example, unmarketable assets include real property, closely held stock, and an unregistered security for which there is no available exemption permitting public sale.

If the CRT receives assets other than cash, and sells, exchanges, or otherwise disposes of such assets within two years of the date of contribution, the trustee of the CRT must file Form 8282 (Donee Information Return). If the CRT receives cash or the assets received are not sold within two years, no such filing is required.

The trustee of the CRT must annually file Form 5227 (Split Interest Trust Informational Return) and Form 1041-A (Trust Federal Income Tax Return) (if the CRT has gross income in excess of $600).

## C. Gift-Tax Consequences

The gift-tax consequences to the donee of a CRT gift are dependent upon the recipient of the annuity or unitrust amount. When the donor is the sole recipient of the annuity or unitrust amount, there is no taxable gift. If the donor's spouse is the only other recipient of the annuity or unitrust amount, although the donor has made a gift to his or her spouse of the value of same, it is shielded by the marital deduction.

Gift tax becomes an issue when others (besides the donor and donor's spouse) are recipients of the annuity or unitrust amount. For example, if the CRT is for the benefit of donor and then his or her spouse and then their children, then donor has made a gift to his or her spouse that does not qualify for the marital deduction.[61] Further, donor has made a gift to his or her children. However, donor can retain the right to revoke by will donor's spouse's and children's rights to the annuity or unitrust amount without disqualifying the trust as a CRT; if donor retains this right, the gifts are incomplete.[62] If donor retains the right to revoke, the CRT assets will be included in donor's estate at his or her death.[63]

## D. Estate-Tax Consequences

The estate-tax consequences to the donor who holds a CRT interest at his or her death are similar to the gift-tax consequences. If donor was sole recipient, the value of the CRT assets is includable in donor's estate, but the inclusion is shielded by the estate-tax charitable deduction for the value of the assets passing to charity at donor's death. When a surviving spouse is the sole succeeding recipient of the annuity or unitrust amount, the value of the CRT assets is includable in donor's estate, but the inclusion is shielded by (1) the marital deduction for the value of the annuity or unitrust amount going to the spouse and (2) the charitable deduction for the value of the remainder interest going to charity.

Estate tax, like gift tax, becomes an issue when others (besides the donor's spouse) are succeeding recipients of the annuity or unitrust amount. For example, if the CRT is for the benefit of donor's spouse and then their children, donor has made a gift to his or her spouse that does not qualify for the marital deduction.[64] Further, donor has made a gift to his or her children. In this instance, the value of the annuity or unitrust amount going to all recipients is included in donor's estate for federal estate-tax purposes.

## E. Estate-Tax Consequences of Testamentary CRT

The estate-tax consequences of the testamentary CRT are also similar to gift-tax consequences. If the donor's spouse is the sole recipient of the CRT, the value of the annuity or unitrust amount is entirely shielded by the marital deduction and the remainder interest is shielded by the charitable deduction.[65] If the spouse and others are the recipients of the CRT, the value of the annuity and unitrust amount passing to the spouse and other recipient(s) is not shielded by the marital estate-tax deduction, but the value of the remainder interest passing to charity is shielded by the charitable estate-tax deduction.[66]

## VI. CRT Advantages and Disadvantages

The CRT has several advantages that can benefit a donor in satisfying his or her income tax, estate, and charitable gift-planning goals. In addition to the income-tax charitable deduction, the CRT minimizes the income tax consequences from the sale of capital gain property. Because the CRT is a tax-exempt entity, it realizes no gain upon the sale of an asset, capital or otherwise. Donor can contribute highly appreciated property to a CRT and benefit from the appreciated value of the asset because donor's annuity or unitrust amount will be greater thanks to the asset's high value not being reduced by income tax on the appreciation. The donor benefits from the appreciation while avoiding payment of the tax from the appreciation.

The key is to make sure that as of the date of the funding—not just creation—of the CRT, the trustee is under no legal obligation to sell the asset. The courts will collapse separate transactions if, when the first step was undertaken, there was a binding commitment to undertake the later steps.[67] The courts will also collapse a series of transactions if they were so interdependent that the "legal relations created by one transaction would have been fruitless without the completion of the series."[68] If appreciated property is contributed to a CRUT or CRAT and if the trustee of the trust is obligated, as of the date of the contribution, to sell such property, the IRS will ignore the CRUT or CRAT as the seller of the property. Instead the donor will be deemed the seller and will realize the gain.[69] The court stated that "once the right to receive income has 'ripened' for tax purposes, the taxpayer who earned or otherwise created that right, will be taxed on any gain realized from it, notwithstanding that the taxpayer has transferred the right before actually receiving the income . . . [T]o determine whether a right has 'ripened' for tax purposes, a court must consider the realities and substances of events to determine whether the receipt of income was practically certain to occur."[70]

The CRT can also work as a retirement vehicle. Because the CRT is a tax-exempt entity, the value of CRT assets can grow at a faster rate: gain realized on the sale of CRT assets is not recognized for income-tax purposes in the CRT. The recipient of the unitrust amount from a CRUT gets the benefit from such growth because the fixed percentage is applied to a larger capital base.

The disadvantages are few, but the chief disadvantage of a CRT is that charity, not the donor's family, ultimately gets the assets in the CRT. One way to curtail this disadvantage is to set up a nonestate-taxable side fund for the donor's family with, among other options, an irrevocable life insurance trust. The death benefits paid to a properly structured irrevocable life insurance trust are excludable from the insured's estate and, thus, the death benefits can be used as a nonestate-taxable way to replace those assets going to charity in the CRT. The insured normally will pay the premium on the insurance policy through gifts to the irrevocable life insurance trust.

## VII. Conclusion

This chapter is an overview of the charitable remainder trust, its technical requirements, and its tax attributes. The charitable remainder trust is a useful estate and charitable gift-planning tool that should not be overlooked if one has charitable gift-planning goals; however, as with all estate and charitable gift planning techniques, it is important to review your individual goals and objectives when considering the charitable remainder trust.

## Endnotes

1. Treas. Reg. § 20.2055(a).

2. Treas. Reg. § 20.2055-2(b); Estate of Sternberger v. Commissioner, 348 U.S. 187, 194 (1955); Rev. Rul. 54-285, 1954-2 C.B. 302.

3. Treas. Reg. § 1.664-1(a)(1)(i).

4. Treas. Reg. § 1.664-1(a)(1)(iii).

5. I.R.C. § 664(d)(1).

6. I.R.C. § 664(d)(2).

7. I.R.C. § 664(d)(2), (d)(3).

8. *Id.*

9. Tex. Prop. Code Ann. § 113.102(b)(1) (2001).

10. Treas. Reg. § 1.664-3(a)(l)(i)(c).

11. Treas. Reg. § 1.664-3(a)(1)(i)(d).

12. Treas. Reg. § 1.664-1(a)(7)(ii).

13. Treas. Reg. § 1.664-1(a)(2).

14. Treas. Reg. § 1.664-2(b), -3(b).

15. I.R.C. § 664(d)(1)(A), (d)(2)(A).

16. *Id.*

17. Treas. Reg. § 1.664-2(a)(1)(v)(a), (b); 1.664-3(a)(1)(v)(a), (b).

18. Treas. Reg. § 1.664-2(a)(1)(iii), -3(a)(1)(iii).

19. Treas. Reg. § 1.664-2(a)(2)(ii), -3(a)(2)(ii).

20. Treas. Reg. § 1.664-2(a)(5)(i), -3(a)(5)(i).

21. Treas. Reg. § 1.664-2(a)(1)(i)(a), 1.664-3(a)(1)(i)(a).

22. Treas. Reg. § 1.664-1(a)(5).

23. *Id.*

24. *Id.*

25. Rev. Rul. 92-57, 1992-2 C.B. 123 (modifying the interest computation in Rev. Rul. 88-81, 1988-2 C.B. 127 and Rev. Rul. 82-165, 1982-1 C.B. 117); Rev. Rul. 88-81, *supra* note 25 (requiring such provision to be mandatory if the trustee can defer payment of the annuity amount or unitrust amount). *See also* Rev. Rul. 80-123, 1980-1 C.B. 205.

26. Treas. Reg. § 1.664-2(a)(5), 1.664-3(a)(5); I.R.C. § 664(d)(1)(A), 664(d)(2)(A).

27. Treas. Reg. § 1.664-2(a)(5), 1.664-3(a)(5); I.R.C. § 664(d)(1)(A), 664(d)(2)(A); Priv. Ltr. Rul. 91-38-024 (June 19, 1991).

28. I.R.C. § 664(d)(1)(A), (d)(2)(A); Treas. Reg. § 1.664-2(a)(3), -3(a)(3).

29. I.R.C. § 664(d)(1)(C), (d)(2)(C); Treas. Reg. § 1.664-2(a)(6), -3(a)(6).

30. Rev. Rul. 76-8, 1976-1 C.B. 179.

31. I.R.C. § 664(d)(1)(D), (d)(2)(D).

32. Rev. Rul. 77-374, 1977-2 C.B. 329.

33. Treas. Reg. § 1.664-2(a)(4), -3(a)(4); Priv. Ltr. Rul. 91-38-024 (September 20, 1991).

34. Treas. Reg. § 53.4941(d)(3)(b)(1).

35. *Id.*

36. I.R.C. § 4941(d).

37. *Id.*

38. Rev. Rul. 74-19, 1974-1 C.B. 155; Treas. Reg. § 53.4941(d)-3(c)(1).

39. Treas. Reg. § 1.664-1(c); I.R.C. § 512(b)(12).

40. I.R.C. § 512(a)(1).

41. I.R.C. § 513(a).

42. I.R.C. § 512(b)(5), (b)(12).

43. I.R.C. § 512(b)(5), (b)(12).

44. I.R.C. § 514(a).

45. I.R.C. § 514(c)(2)(B); Treas. Reg. § 1.514(c)-1(b)(3).

46. *Id.*

47. *Id.;* See Priv. Ltr. Rul. 95-33-014 (May 15, 1995) (wherein the donor remained liable on the nonrecourse debt qualifying for the exception). *But see* Priv. Ltr. Rul. 90-15-049 (January 16, 1990) (wherein the grantor remained personally liable on the debt causing the CRT to disqualify because it was a grantor trust).

48. Priv. Ltr. Rul. 88-19-021, May 13, 1988; Rev. Rul. 82-128, 1982-C.B. 71.

49. Priv. Ltr. Rul. 92-25-026 (March 23, 1992).

50. Treas. Reg. § 1.664-1(a)(6) (ex. 3).

51. H.R. REP. NO. 91-413, at 60 (1969), 1969-3 C.B. 200, 239.

52. Treas. Reg. § 1.664-1(a)(7).

53. Treas. Reg. § 1.664-1(a)(7)(iii).

54. Texas Nonprofit Corporation Act art. 1396-2.31 (2001).

55. Rev. Rul. 77-285, 1977-2 C.B. 213.

56. Treas. Reg. § 1.664-1(d)(l)(iii).

57. Treas. Reg. § 1.664-1(d)(5).

58. I.R.C. § 170.

59. I.R.C. § 170(b)(1)(A); Treas. Reg. § 1.170A-8(a)(2).

60. I.R.C. § 170(b)(1)(C)(i); Treas. Reg. § 1.170A-8(a)(2).

61. I.R.C. § 2523(g).

62. Treas. Reg. § 1.664-2(a)(4), 1.664-3(a)(4); Priv. Ltr. Rul. 95-17-020 (January 26, 1995); Priv. Ltr. Rul. 93-26-049 (April 5, 1993).

63. Rev. Rul. 79-243, 1979-2 C.B. 343; IRC § 2038(a)(1); PLR 9326049.

64. I.R.C. § 2523(g).

65. I.R.C. §§ 2055(c), 2036(a), 2056(b)(8).

66. *Id.*

67. Maine Foods, Inc. v. Commissioner, 93 T.C. 181 (1989).

68. *Id.* at 199.

69. Palmer v. Commissioner, 62 T.C. 684 (1974).

70. Ferguson v. Commissioner, Nos. 21808-03, 18250-94 (9th Cir. T.C. April 28, 1997).

# CHAPTER 8

# Charitable Lead Trusts

SANTO BISIGNANO, JR.
TOBY M. EISENBERG

## I. Introduction

A charitable lead trust (CLT) is a split-interest trust under which a lead income interest (in the form of a guaranteed annual payment) is paid to one or more charities for a term of years, or for the life or lives of individuals who are alive at the inception of the trust. A remainder interest is paid to one or more private individuals (or trusts for their benefit) upon termination of the trust. These trusts must take the form of a charitable lead annuity trust or charitable lead unitrust if they are to qualify for certain tax advantages. They can be irrevocable living trusts or testamentary trusts, and they can be grantor trusts (where the grantor is taxed on trust income) or nongrantor complex trusts.

A charitable lead annuity trust (CLAT) is a split-interest trust that pays an income interest in the form of a guaranteed annuity to charity(ies) for the term of the trust with the remainder interest passing to one or more noncharitable beneficiaries upon conclusion of the charitable term. A charitable lead unitrust (CLUT) is generally structured like a CLAT except the lead income interest is paid in the form of a guaranteed unitrust payment: an annual payment recalculated each year based on a fixed percentage rate and on the fair market value of the trust assets in that year. CLTs are valuable estate-planning tools because they allow charitable and noncharitable gift-giving at substantial tax savings.

## II. Economic Growth and Tax Relief Reconciliation Act of 2001

Does passage of the Economic Growth and Tax Relief Reconciliation Act of 2001 (EGTRRA) render an analysis of CLTs obsolete? For those clients who believe they will live to see, and die to take advantage of, the repeal of the federal estate tax and generation-skipping transfer (GST) tax, the use of CLTs purely as an estate-tax- and/or GST-tax-avoidance technique may seem misplaced. However, the authors believe that despite the hype surrounding repeal of the "death tax," the CLT will continue to be a very useful estate planning technique for the wealthy, charitably minded client.

## A. Repeal May Not Be a Reality

As a result of EGTRRA, true repeal of the estate tax and GST tax only occurs if a decedent dies in 2010. Unless EGTRRA, or at least that portion relating to estate tax and GST tax, is extended or repealed, the laws in effect prior to EGTRRA will be reinstated in 2011. Thus, the leverage effect of the CLT may still make sense to those clients who believe outliving the estate tax and GST tax is an elusive goal.

## B. Leveraging the Gift-Tax Exemption with CLTs

CLTs allow for leveraging the gift-tax exemption and perhaps passing considerable amounts to a donor's descendants without the imposition of a gift tax. EGTRRA did not repeal the federal gift tax. It merely increased the applicable exclusion to $1 million. Clients who are charitably inclined should consider using an intervivos CLT to transfer considerable wealth to children and/or more remote descendants with few or no gift-tax consequences. Leveraging techniques are discussed in section VI.

## C. Taxpayers Who Have Maxed Out Charitable Deductions

CLTs are still viable for taxpayers whose ability to utilize federal income-tax charitable deductions is impaired because of limitations imposed by the size of adjusted gross income or the reduction in itemized deductions imposed by Internal Revenue Code (I.R.C.) Section 68. CLTs can be seen as a way to obtain an unlimited federal income-tax charitable deduction.

## D. Grantor CLTs for One-Time Income Payment

Taxpayers who receive extraordinary income in a given year (winning a lottery, for example) may resort to grantor CLTs to obtain a one-time federal income-tax deduction to offset the extraordinary income.

# III. Overview of CLTs

## A. CLTs in General

Unless otherwise indicated, whenever the terms "charitable lead annuity trust," "charitable lead unitrust," or "charitable lead trust" (and their acronyms) are used in this chapter, they shall mean tax-qualified CLTs and shall include both nongrantor and grantor charitable lead trusts.

The general requirements for the CLAT and the CLUT are as follows:

### 1. Valid Trust

The trust must be a valid trust under applicable state law.[1]

### 2. Annual Payments

a. GENERAL
The annual payments to charity must be made either (a) for a period certain or (b) for a period measured by the life (or lives) of one or more individuals, each of whom must be alive at the creation of the trust (or must be alive at the date of the decedent's death

if a testamentary CLT).[2] However, in an effort to eliminate the perceived abuses of Vulture Trusts, in which a taxpayer selects a charitable term for the CLT based on the lifetime of an individual who was not expected to live to actuarial life expectancy, the Treasury issued final regulations limiting the class of individuals who can be used as measuring lives for a CLT. That class shall be limited to the donor's or decedent's spouse or an individual who is either a lineal ancestor of a noncharitable remainder beneficiary or a spouse of such ancestor.[3]

Subject to the limitation on measuring lives described above, the guaranteed annuity will meet the payment requirement if it is paid for the life of a specified individual plus a specified term.[4] The guaranteed annuity may also be paid for a period measured by more than one measuring life; for example, for the joint lifetime of A and B. A guaranteed annuity for a term of years plus lives-in-being will also work.[5]

b. NO MAXIMUM-PAYMENT PERIOD

A term-of-years CLT may last for any number of years selected by the donor and is not subject to a 20-year maximum term as required for charitable remainder trusts.

### 3. *Annual Income Payments to One or More Qualified Charities*

As a general rule, the annual income payments must be paid to a charitable organization as described in I.R.C. Section 170(c).[6] However, commentators recommend that the trust be drafted so the charities qualify under I.R.C. Sections 170(c), 2055(a), *and* 2522(a) to minimize any uncertainty regarding the tax attributes of the CLT. This drafting will also permit private nonoperating foundations to be beneficiaries of the annuity payment.

Indeed, a donor's private nonoperating foundation may be an ideal lead beneficiary of a CLT. However, before selecting the private foundation as the lead beneficiary, consider the following issues:

If the donor to an intervivos CLT is a director, trustee, or member of a governing body of the private foundation, the I.R.S. may claim that the trust property should be includable in the donor's gross estate under I.R.C. Section 2036 because of the donor's power to control the distributions from the charitable entity.[7] This is a rather harsh and anomalous result that overlooks that the donor cannot personally benefit from foundation distributions and must act in a fiduciary capacity.

The I.R.S.'s position has been that 100 percent of a contribution to a private nonoperating foundation from a split-interest trust must be considered in the calculation of the foundation's minimum distribution requirement for the year in which the CLT payment is made.[8] In effect, the foundation becomes nothing more than a conduit to receive and quickly distribute payments it receives from the split-interest trust. However, in *Ann Jackson Family Foundation v. C.I.R.*,[9] the Ninth Circuit Court of Appeals held that this result is unwarranted and therefore such contributions from split-interest trusts may be added to principal with only 5 percent of that contribution distributed by the foundation each year. In light of this Ninth Circuit holding, the I.R.S. seems to have backed off its position.

Even if the amount contributed to the charitable foundation from the CLT need not be distributed immediately, the trustee of the CLT must, in fact, exercise expenditure responsibility over such distribution to ensure that it is ultimately used for charitable purposes.[10] The scope of this requirement is unclear, but the administrative burden might be significant. (See discussion in Section IV.A.17.)

### 4. No Payment for Private Purposes

The trustee may not make any payments for noncharitable (private) purposes during the charitable term.[11] The only exception is for payment for those private purposes paid by the trustee from a separate, noncharitable portion of the trust. Such payments must not take preference over payment of the charitable interest.[12]

### 5. Excess Income

The trust may provide that income in excess of the guaranteed annual payment shall be paid to or for the use of charity(ies). However, any income-, gift-, or estate-tax deduction to the donor or decedent shall still be limited to the initial deduction amount.[13]

### 6. Private Foundation Restrictions

a. GENERAL

The governing trust instrument must meet the same requirements for the governing instruments of private foundations outlined under I.R.C. Section 508(e)(1).[14] Accordingly, the trust must include provisions that

> (i) require trust income for each taxable year to be distributed at such time and in such manner as not to subject the trust to tax under I.R.C. Section 4942;
>
> (ii) prohibit the trust from engaging in any act of self-dealing (as defined in I.R.C. Section 4941(d));
>
> (iii) prohibit the trust from retaining any excess business holdings (as defined in I.R.C. Section 4943(c));
>
> (iv) prohibit the trust from making any investments in such a manner as to subject the trust to tax under I.R.C. Section 4944; and
>
> (v) prohibit the trust from making any taxable expenditures (as defined in I.R.C. Section 4945(d)).

b. EXCEPTION FOR 60-PERCENT-OR-LESS CHARITABLE DEDUCTIONS

If the charitable interest upon inception of the trust does not exceed 60 percent of the value of the property transferred to the trust, the prohibitions against excess business holdings and jeopardy investments need not be included in the governing instrument.[15]

### 7. Private Beneficiary

By definition, upon expiration of the charitable term, at least one of the beneficiaries must be a noncharitable beneficiary.

## B. CLATs

### 1. General

The trust must require the payment of a guaranteed annuity payable at least annually to one or more charitable beneficiaries.[16]

### 2. Irrevocable Right

An income interest will be considered a guaranteed annuity *only if* the interest constitutes an irrevocable right, pursuant to the terms of the trust, to receive the guaranteed annuity.[17]

### 3. Readily Determinable upon Date of Transfer

In addition, the value of the guaranteed annuity amount must also be readily determinable upon the date of transfer to the trust in the case of an intervivos CLAT or the date of the decedent's death (or alternate valuation date) in the case of a testamentary CLAT.[18] An amount is determinable if the exact amount that must be paid under the trust can be ascertained as of the date of transfer.[19]

This readily determinable requirement can be satisfied by a variety of annuity payments, such as (i) a stated sum, (ii) an annuity amount based on a fixed percentage of the fair market value of the property initially contributed to the trust, or (iii) a formula amount that defines the level annuity amount in terms of a given level of tax savings (for example, that annuity amount that, if payable over the term of the trust and given the applicable federal midterm rate, would produce a federal estate-tax charitable deduction equal to the decedent's adjusted gross estate).[20]

### 4. No Minimum Payment

The annuity amount provided under a CLAT can be any fixed amount, unlike the 5-percent minimum payout requirement for a charitable remainder annuity trust.

## C. CLUTs

### 1. General

The trust must require the payment of a unitrust interest payable at least annually to one or more charitable beneficiaries.[21]

### 2. Irrevocable Right

An income interest is a unitrust interest only if it is an irrevocable right, pursuant to the trust, to receive payment not less often than annually of a fixed percentage of the net fair market value of the trust assets determined annually.[22]

### 3. Assets and Liabilities Count

In determining the net fair market value of the trust property, all assets and liabilities of the trust must be taken into account, whether an item of income or principal.[23]

## IV. Basic Tax Consequences

### A. Income-Tax Consequences to Donor of Gifts to Intervivos CLTs

#### 1. Income Tax Deduction Availability for Gifts to Intervivos Tax-Qualified Grantor CLTs

A donor to an intervivos CLAT or CLUT will be entitled to a *one-time* federal income-tax charitable deduction in the year of the creation and funding of the trust *if and only if* the trust is a grantor trust within the meaning of I.R.C. Sections 671–677.[24] This means that the donor must be taxed on trust income during the charitable term of the trust.

#### 2. Limits on Income Tax Deduction

Because the gift to the CLT is considered a gift "for the use of" rather than "to" a charity, the donor's income tax deduction for a cash gift is generally limited to 30 percent of the donor's adjusted gross income for the taxable year with a five-year carryover of the excess.[25] The donor's income tax deduction for a gift of publicly traded marketable securities will be limited to 20 percent of the donor's adjusted gross income.[26]

### 3. Consequences If Donor Ceases to Be Owner

If during the charitable term the donor ceases to be treated as the owner of the trust under I.R.C. Sections 671–677, the donor must recapture, as income, any charitable deduction received, reduced by the discounted present value of the amounts of trust income previously taxed.[27]

### 4. Excess Income of Grantor CLT

Because the donor to a grantor CLT received a one-time federal income tax charitable deduction for the donor's charitable contribution to the trust, the donor is not entitled to any additional deduction during the term of the trust for the trustee's payment of the required annuity amounts or unitrust payments to the charitable beneficiary(ies). However, the donor is permitted an annual income-tax charitable deduction for items of gross income paid by the trust to charitable beneficiaries if (i) such amounts are in excess of the required annuity amounts or unitrust payments and (ii) if the trust authorizes the payment of same to charities.[28]

### 5. No Federal Income Tax Deduction to Nongrantor CLT

A donor's gift to a nongrantor CLT will *never* entitle the donor to a federal income tax charitable deduction.

## B. Gift-Tax Consequences to Donor for Intervivos Gifts to CLTs

### 1. No Discretion by Donor in Selection of Charities

A gift to an intervivos CLT under which the donor retains no discretion over selection of charities will entitle the donor to the unlimited federal gift-tax charitable deduction for the present actuarial value of the income interest required to be paid to the charitable beneficiary(ies).[29] This is true even if the grantor is not treated as owner of the trust under the grantor trust rules.[30]

If donor, as a trustee or otherwise, retains the power to select or change the identity of the charitable beneficiaries, then the gift of the income interest will be considered to be incomplete for gift-tax purposes because donor has retained dominion and control over that portion of the transferred property.[31] If donor serves as a board member or officer of the charitable lead beneficiary, he or she should be officially precluded from having any say over how such lead payments shall be used.[32]

### 2. Gift-Tax Consequences of Gift of Remainder Interest

If the remainder interest is not payable to the donor, then upon transfer to the CLT, the donor will be deemed to have made a gift of a future interest of the present value of the remainder interest in the trust.[33] This gift will not qualify for the annual gift-tax exclusion.

## C. Estate-Tax Consequences to Donor

### 1. No Power to Select Charitable Beneficiary(ies), No Reversionary Interest

If the donor of an intervivos CLT does *not* retain the power, as trustee or otherwise, to select the identity of the charitable beneficiary(ies) and does not retain a reversionary interest in the trust, then no portion of the trust shall be includable in the donor's estate for federal estate-tax purposes.[34]

This same result can be obtained even if the trust is a grantor CLT if the additional provisions causing it to be a grantor trust would not cause the trust to be includable in the grantor's estate for federal estate-tax purposes. A power that can be retained by the grantor that would cause the trust to attain "grantor trust status" but not cause inclusion in the grantor's estate is the power to acquire trust assets by substituting property of equivalent value without the approval or consent of a fiduciary.[35]

### 2. Donor Retains Power to Select Charitable Beneficiaries

On the other hand, if the donor directly or indirectly retains the power under the CLT to select or change the identity of the charitable beneficiary(ies), the entire trust will be includable in the donor's estate for federal estate-tax purposes.[36] Furthermore, if the grantor of an intervivos CLT is a member, director, or officer of the charity that is the income beneficiary of the lead trust, the I.R.S. holds that the entire corpus of the CLT is includable in the grantor's estate pursuant to I.R.C. Section 2036(a)(2).[37]

### 3. Unlimited Charitable Deduction for Testamentary Gifts to CLTs

If a decedent makes a testamentary gift to a CLT, the decedent's estate will be entitled to an unlimited federal estate-tax charitable deduction for the value of the income interest payable to the charity(ies).[38]

### 4. Donor Retains Reversionary Interest

An intervivos CLT will be includable in donor's gross estate if immediately before donor's death donor has retained a reversionary interest in the trust worth more than 5 percent of the then-current net value of the trust.[39] However, with inclusion donor will get a federal estate-tax charitable deduction for the value of the unexpired charitable term of the CLT.[40]

## D. GST Tax Consequences

### 1. Inclusion Ratio and Applicable Fraction

The amount of GST tax payable in connection with distributions from a CLT is determined by the inclusion ratio of that trust. If it is zero, no distribution from that trust will be subject to the GST tax. However, if the inclusion ratio is one, all distributions from that trust to skip-persons will be subject to the GST tax. If a trust has an inclusion ratio of more than zero but less than one (for example, 0.5), then a distribution from the trust to a skip-person will be subject to the GST tax in an amount equal to the amount of distribution multiplied by the applicable maximum estate-tax rate, multiplied by the inclusion ratio.

The trust inclusion ratio is determined by subtracting the applicable fraction from the number one. With any transfer of property subject to the GST tax, the numerator of the applicable fraction is the amount of exemption allocated to the transfer, and the denominator of the applicable fraction is the amount of the trust contribution minus the sum of (a) administration expenses attributable to the transfer, (b) debts attributable to the transfer, and (c) the gift- or estate-tax charitable deduction attributable to the transfer.

The inclusion ratio for any trust can be expressed by the following formula:

$$\text{Inclusion Ratio} \ = \ 1 - \text{Applicable Fraction}$$

The applicable fraction for *testamentary* transfers can be expressed by the following formula:

$$\text{Applicable Fraction} = \frac{\text{Amt. of Allocated GST Tax Exemption}}{\text{Amt. of Transfer } minus \text{ I.R.C. Sections 2053, 2054, and 2055 Deductions Attributable to Transfer}}$$

The applicable fraction for *lifetime* transfers can be expressed by the following formula:

$$\text{Applicable Fraction} = \frac{\text{Amt. of Allocated GST Tax Exemption}}{\text{Amt. of Transfer } minus \text{ Charitable Deduction Attributable to Transfer}}$$

### 2. Applicable Fraction Redefined for CLATs

Any CLT seems an ideal vehicle for effective generation-skipping transfers. Because the amount of the charitable deduction attributable to the gift to the CLT reduces the size of the denominator of the applicable fraction, judicious allocation of the exemption amount would result in an applicable fraction equal to one and an inclusion ratio of zero. Unfortunately, in 1988 Congress amended Section 2642(e) by redefining the applicable fraction for transfers to CLATs. Accordingly, under I.R.C. Section 2642(e), the numerator of the fraction is the allocated portion of the GST exemption increased each year by an interest rate determined at the rate used for valuing the charitable interest, compounded annually, for the term of the charitable interest. The denominator is the actual value of the property in the trust immediately after the termination of the charitable lead interest minus the applicable deductions described above. Thus, if the property grows at a rate higher than the interest rate used in determining the charitable deduction, the applicable fraction will never be equal to one. Because of this redefinition of the applicable fraction for CLATs, they are no longer useful for generation-skipping transfers.

### 3. Applicable Fraction Redefined for CLUTs

The good news is that the redefinition of I.R.C. Section 2642(e) does not apply in transfers to CLUTs. Those types of trusts should continue to be useful as GST tax devices (see discussion in section IV.B.).

## E. Valuation of Charitable (and Remainder) Interest

The value of income-, gift-, and estate-tax deductions attributable to any gift to a CLT is equal to the present actuarial value of the future stream of annuity amounts or unitrust payments over the term of the trust, determined by using the rate corresponding to 120 percent of the I.R.C. Section 1274(d)(1) federal midterm rate for the month in which the valuation of the interest is made. The rate for a given month is formally announced on or about the 20th of the preceding month (for example, rates for June are announced on May 20).The taxpayer can make the valuation of the income interest based on the month in which the transfer occurs or on either of the two preceding months.[41] By waiting until the end of the month to make the transfer, the taxpayer will have rates from four months to choose from: the current month's rate, the two preceding months' rates, and the next month's rate.

## F. Income-Tax Consequences to Charitable Beneficiaries

Because charitable beneficiaries are generally exempt from federal income tax, all distributions to charity are not subject to taxation in the hands of the charity.

## G. Taxation of Nongrantor CLTs

### 1. Taxation as a Complex Trust

Unlike a charitable remainder trust (CRT), which is exempt from income tax, a nongrantor tax-qualified CLT is taxed as a complex trust and therefore subject to the rules of complex trusts as provided under I.R.C. Sections 661–663.[42] Any undistributed income will be taxed to the trust.[43]

### 2. Unlimited Charitable Income Tax Deduction with Lookback Option

A nongrantor CLT is also entitled to a federal income-tax charitable deduction for items of gross income that, pursuant to the terms of the trust, are paid during the taxable year to one or more charities.[44] Furthermore, I.R.C. Section 642(c)(1) provides for a lookback option: Amounts that are paid to qualified charities within one year after the close of the taxable year can be treated as having been paid during the prior taxable year.[45]

### 3. No Percentage Limitations on Charitable Deductions

Unlike the percentage limitations imposed on the federal income-tax charitable deduction for gifts by individuals, the deduction provided under I.R.C. Section 642(c) does not impose any such percentage limitations on distributions out of items of gross income of a CLT. However, the deduction is allowed only in connection with distributions payable out of items of gross income. If the trust has no gross income, no such deduction can be taken.

### 4. In-Kind Distributions

As a general rule, no I.R.C. Section 642(c) charitable deduction will be allowed for distributions in kind from a CLT. The deduction is available only for distributions of items of gross income.[46] However, a deduction will be available when a distribution of appreciated property causes the trust to recognize capital gain.[47]

### 5. No Statutory Tier System

Unlike a CRT, no statutory tier system is available for distributions from a CLT to its charitable beneficiaries. Thus, distributions are not presumed to carry out ordinary income, then capital gain, then nontaxable income, then principal. The character of the income distributed to charity is dependent upon local law or the governing instrument.[48] If neither local law nor the governing instrument is helpful, the character of the income distributed shall consist of an appropriate proportion of each class of the items of trust income.[49] (According to Gen. Couns. Mem. 39,161 and Priv. Ltr. Rul. 87-27-072, the I.R.S. has argued that it will not recognize a governing instrument tier system unless it has a "substantive economic effect independent of tax consequences.")[50]

### 6. Allocation of Depreciation, Amortization, and Depletion

Unless the instrument provides otherwise, deductions attributable to depreciation, amortization, and depletion shall be allocated between the trust and the charitable beneficiary on the bases of the income distributed to each.[51]

### 7. Governing Instrument Requirements

CLTs are generally subject to the private foundation provisions imposing a tax on self-dealing,[52] excess business holdings,[53] jeopardy investments,[54] and certain taxable expenditures.[55] Accordingly, no income-, gift-, or estate-tax charitable deduction shall be allowable to a donor for gifts made to a CLT unless the governing trust instrument (i) requires the distribution of income in such a way as to avoid the excise tax imposed on undistributed income under I.R.C. Section 4942, (ii) prohibits the trustee from engaging in any act of self-dealing, (iii) prohibits the trustee from retaining any excess business holdings, (iv) prohibits the trustee from making any jeopardy investments, and (v) prohibits the trustee from making any prohibited taxable expenditures.[56]

### 8. Special Exception from Excess Business Holdings and Jeopardy Investments Restrictions for 60-Percent-or-Less CLTs

If the charitable interest upon inception of the trust does not exceed 60 percent of the value of the property transferred to the trust, the prohibitions against excess business holdings and jeopardy investments need not be included in the governing instrument, and such holdings and investments are permitted.[57]

### 9. No I.R.C. Section 642(c) Deduction for Distributions of Unrelated Business Taxable Income

No charitable deduction will be allowed by a CLT for charitable distribution of unrelated business taxable income.[58]

### 10. Alternative Minimum Tax Not Applicable

The income earned by CLTs is not subject to alternative minimum tax.

## V. Drafting CLTs

### A. General Requirements Applicable to All CLTs

Unless otherwise noted below, drafters of CLTs should incorporate the following provisions:

### 1. No Hybrid Trusts

The trust must be drafted to be either a CLAT in every respect or a CLUT in every respect.[59] Thus, a trust which provides for the payment each year to a charity of the *lesser* of a sum certain or a fixed percentage of the annual net value of the trust assets is not a CLT because it is neither entirely a CLAT nor entirely a CLUT.[60]

### 2. Prohibited Transactions

The trustee must be required to make distributions at such time and in such a manner as not to subject the CLT to tax under I.R.C. Section 4942. Furthermore, except as noted below, the trustee must be prohibited from (a) engaging in self-dealing as defined in I.R.C. Section 4941(d); (b) making taxable expenditures as defined in I.R.C. Section 4945(d); (c) making jeopardy investments as defined in I.R.C. Section 4944; or (d) retaining any excess business holdings as defined in I.R.C. Section 4943(c).[61] However, the trust need not prohibit jeopardy investments or excess business holdings if, upon creation of the trust, the actuarial value of the charitable interest does not exceed 60 percent of the value of the transfer to the trust.[62]

### 3. Distributions in Cash or Kind

The trust instrument may permit the trustee to pay the annuity amount or unitrust payment in cash or in kind. However, if a distribution in kind is made in satisfaction of the required charitable distribution, the amount paid, credited, or required to be distributed shall be considered as an amount realized by the trust from the sale or other disposition of property. Therefore, the trust will recognize short-term or long-term capital gain, as applicable, in an amount equal to the excess of the fair market value of the property transferred over the cost basis of that property.[63]

### 4. Short Taxable Year

The CLT should also include language providing that in the case of a taxable year, which is for a period of less than 12 months, the annuity amount or unitrust payment shall be the amount otherwise payable multiplied by a fraction, the numerator of which is the number of days in the taxable year of the trust and the denominator of which is 365 (366 if February 29 is a day included in the numerator). The trust should also include language providing that in the case of a trust taxable year in which occurs the termination of the CLAT or CLUT, the annuity amount or unitrust payment that must be distributed shall be the amount otherwise determined multiplied by a fraction, the numerator of which is the number of days in the period beginning on the first day of such taxable year and ending on the day the CLT terminates and the denominator of which is 365 (366 if February 29 is a day included in the numerator).[64]

### 5. Required Charitable Beneficiaries

The required annuity amount or unitrust payment must be payable to a qualified charity or charities.[65] However, it is recommended that the trust be drafted so that each charity qualifies under I.R.C. Sections 170(c), 2055(a), and 2522(a). This will allow the donor's private nonoperating foundation to be a lead beneficiary.

### 6. Alternate Charity(ies) as Beneficiary(ies)

The trust should also stipulate that if an organization that is to receive a charitable distribution is not an organization qualified under I.R.C. Sections 170(c), 2055(a), and

2522(a), then the required charitable distribution shall be to one or more alternative organizations that are described in each of those I.R.C. sections. The trust should state how those alternate charities are to be selected.

### 7. Taxable Year

The taxable year of the CLT must be a calendar year.

### 8. Complete Gift

If the CLT is to be removed from the grantor's estate for federal estate-tax purposes, the trust should be structured so that the gift to it is complete for gift-tax purposes. Accordingly, the donor should not retain a power, as trustee or otherwise, to select charities.

### 9. Tier System for Distributions

Unlike I.R.C. Section 664(b) dealing with the character of distributions from a CRT, the character of payments made to charities under a CLT is not governed by a statutory tier system. If there are no provisions in the trust instrument attempting to identify the character of charitable distributions, local law may characterize the payments. If neither the trust instrument nor local law addresses the issue, the annuity amounts and unitrust payments will be deemed to consist of a pro rata portion of all the items of the trust's income.[66] To maximize the trust's charitable deduction and minimize the trust's income, the trust should provide that a charitable distribution shall first carry out ordinary income until exhausted, then capital gains until exhausted, then unrelated business taxable income until exhausted, then tax-exempt income until exhausted, and then trust corpus. Be mindful that, despite clear indication that a tier system imposed within the trust instrument will go into effect,[67] the I.R.S. position as of this writing is that such a provision will be ignored unless it has a "substantive economic effect" independent of tax consequences.[68]

### 10. Allocation of Depreciation, Amortization, and Depletion

To minimize the tax consequences to the CLT, the trust instrument should allocate all depreciation, amortization, and depletion deductions to the trust. Otherwise, those deductions will be allocated between the charitable beneficiary(ies) and the trust, based on income distributed to each.[69]

### 11. Allocation of Capital Gains

The trustee should be given the power to allocate capital gains either to trust income or to trust corpus. An allocation to income may ensure that distribution of such gain to charities will qualify for the I.R.C. Section 642(c) deduction.

### 12. Allocation of Trustee Fees

Under the trust, fiduciary fees should be allocated to income rather than corpus. This will ensure they are deductible. However, do not charge such payments against the annuity amount or unitrust payment: Treat them as deductions in computing trust taxable income.

### 13. No Prepayment Provisions

Do not allow the trustee to prepay (or commute) the required annuity amounts or unitrust payments. The current I.R.S. position is that this will disqualify the CLT.[70]

### 14. Power in Trustee to Amend Trust to Maintain Qualification

A power should be granted to the trustee to amend the trust solely for the purposes of maintaining its tax-qualified status as a qualified CLT.

### 15. Valuation of Unmarketable Assets

The CLT should require unmarketable assets transferred to the trust to be valued in compliance with the rules under Treas. Reg. Section 1.664-1(a)(7); that is, the valuation should be (a) performed exclusively by an independent trustee or pursuant to a qualified appraisal, as defined in Treas. Reg. Section 1.170A-13(c)(3); or (b) undertaken by a qualified appraiser, as defined in Treas. Reg. Section 1.170A-13(c)(5). Unmarketable assets include assets that are not cash, cash equivalents, or other assets that can be readily sold or exchanged for cash or cash equivalents.[71] The nonexclusive examples provided by the regulations include real property, closely held stock, and an unregistered security for which there is no available exemption permitting public sale.[72] The term "independent trustee" is defined as a person who is not the (a) grantor of the trust, (b) a noncharitable beneficiary, or (c) a related or subordinate party to the grantor, the grantor's spouse, or a noncharitable beneficiary (within the meaning of I.R.C. Section 672[c] and the applicable regulations).[73]

### 16. Violation of Grantor Trust Rules to Achieve Income Tax Deduction and Estate-Tax Exclusion

As noted earlier, an individual will be entitled to a federal income-tax deduction for the charitable portion of a gift to a CLT if and only if the grantor is treated as the owner of the trust (and therefore taxable on trust income) under the grantor trust rules of I.R.C. Sections 671–678. A way to achieve this and benefit from estate-tax exclusion is to permit the grantor to have a power, exercisable in a nonfiduciary capacity without the approval or consent of the trustee, to reacquire trust corpus by substituting other property of equivalent value. This will violate the grantor trust rules under I.R.C. Section 675(4)(C) but is a power that, if held by the grantor, will not cause inclusion of the trust in the grantor's estate for federal estate-tax purposes.

### 17. Private Foundation as Lead Beneficiary

It is arguable, but not yet certain, that if a private foundation is the beneficiary of a CLT, then the trustee will have to exercise expenditure responsibility over the required charitable distributions.[74] In Priv. Ltr. Rul. 98-26-031 (March 27, 1998), the I.R.S. held that a CLUT's distribution to a private foundation will not be a taxable expenditure under I.R.C. Section 4945(d) if the trustees of the CLUT exercise expenditure responsibly. However, in Priv. Ltr. Rul. 1999-52-093 (October 7, 1999), the I.R.S. held that a CLAT was not subject to the expenditure responsibility requirement. The difference in rulings may be based on the discretion granted to the trustees. In the 1998 ruling, the selection of the lead charities was left to the discretion of the trustees. In the 1999 ruling, the CLAT mandated a distribution of the annuity amount to the lead private foundation.

### 18. Designation of Charitable Beneficiaries

The identity of the charitable beneficiaries need not be stated within the trust document, and anyone may be given the power to designate qualified charitable beneficiaries. The only requirement is that the required lead distribution be made to a qualified charity.[75]

### 19. Identity of Trustee

Anyone other than the donor can serve as a trustee of the CLT without adverse tax consequences to the donor. If the identity of the charitable beneficiary has been predetermined and the trustee has no discretion other than to distribute the required guaranteed annuity amounts or unitrust payments to the predetermined charitable beneficiary, then there is no reason why the donor could not be the trustee. The only exception to this rule is if the assets transferred to the trust consisted of voting stock in a closely held business, whereupon care should be taken to avoid application of I.R.C. Section 2036(b). Under that I.R.C. section, the donor's retained power to vote stock in a closely held corporation (for example, as trustee of a CLT) is a retained benefit that would cause the stock to be includable in the donor's estate for federal estate-tax purposes.

## B. Special Drafting Requirements Applicable Only to CLATs

In addition to the general requirements above applicable to all CLTs, the CLAT shall also include the following requirements:

### 1. Guaranteed Annuity

The trust must provide for the payment of a guaranteed sum certain, payable not less often than annually, to qualified charities.[76] The amount of the guaranteed payment(s) must be determinable at the creation of the trust. Furthermore, unlike a CRT, there is no minimum charitable amount.

This guaranteed annuity amount can be expressed in a number of ways, such as a fixed percentage of the fair market value of the assets initially contributed to the CLT, a specific dollar amount, or a formula designed to achieve a predetermined level of tax savings.

### 2. No Additional Contributions

CLATs should specifically prohibit additional contributions.[77]

### 3. Makeup Provision

The CLAT should include a makeup provision if the formula establishes the guaranteed annuity amount on the basis of a fixed percentage of the initial net fair market value of the trust. In that case, the governing instrument should require that the trustee pay to the charity(ies) in the case of an undervaluation (or receive from the charity(ies) in the case of an overvaluation) an amount equal to the difference between the annuity amount that the trustee should have paid to the charitable recipient(s) had the correct fair market value been used and the annuity amount that the trustee actually paid to the recipient(s). Such payments or repayments should be required within a reasonable time after the correct fair market value is determined.

## C. Special Drafting Requirements Applicable Only to CLUTs

The CLUT must include the following requirements:

### 1. Fixed Percentage Payable at Least Annually

The CLUT must include language requiring the trustee to pay to the charitable beneficiary(ies), not less often than annually, a fixed percentage of the net fair market value of the trust assets determined annually over the period required under the instrument.[78]

### 2. Valuation Date

For purposes of valuing the unitrust interest, the trustee may use (a) the value on the valuation date prescribed in the trust instrument; (b) a value on any one date during the trust year (as long as that valuation date does not change); or (c) a value determined by taking the average valuations on one or more dates during the year (as long as those valuation dates do not change).

### 3. Additional Contributions Permitted

Unlike the CLAT, a CLUT may permit additional contributions.[79]

### 4. Makeup or Payback for Incorrect Valuations

The governing instrument of the unitrust should also provide for either a makeup or payback provision if the value used in calculating the unitrust payment turns out to be incorrect. The trustee should be required to pay to the charitable recipient(s) in the case of an undervaluation (or to be repaid by the charitable recipient(s) in the case of an overvaluation) an amount equal to the difference between the unitrust payment(s) that the trustee should have paid to the charitable recipient(s) if the correct value had been used, and the unitrust payment(s) that the trustee paid to the charitable recipient(s). These payments or repayments must occur within a reasonable time after the final determination is made.

## D. Special Drafting Requirements Applicable Only to Testamentary CLATs and CLUTs

The drafting requirements for testamentary CLTs are generally the same as those for intervivos CLTs. However, there are important provisions that should be included in such testamentary instruments:

### 1. Apportionment of Debts, Expenses, and Taxes

The will or other testamentary instruments should not be drafted to apportion debts, expenses, and taxes out of the assets of the CLT after the funding of the trust. Otherwise, those payments would be deemed to have been made for noncharitable purposes and would disqualify the trust. The will should provide for payment prior to funding.

### 2. Obligation to Begin Payments at Date of Death

For a CLT created upon the death of the decedent (including those created pursuant to a trust includable in the decedent's estate for federal estate-tax purposes, such as a revocable management trust), the trust should provide that the obligation to pay the annuity amount or the unitrust payment must begin at the date of the decedent's death. If this is included, the CLT shall be deemed to have been created as of the date of the decedent's death. However, another provision should be added allowing the executor of the decedent's estate, or the trustee in the case of a revocable trust, to defer such payment for a reasonable period of time to enable the decedent's executor to complete the administration of decedent's estate. In that event, the governing instrument should include a requirement to defer paying required annuity amounts or unitrust payments until the end of the CLT's taxable year in which the complete funding of the trust occurs. Within a reasonable time thereafter, the trustee must pay to the charitable recipient(s) (in the case of an underpayment) or must receive from the charitable recipient(s) (in the case of an overpayment) the difference between the annuity amount(s) or unitrust payment(s) actually paid and the annuity amount(s) or unitrust payment(s) payable, with each such amount compounding at the same rate used in determining the initial charitable deduction.

### 3. No-Contest Clauses

No contest (in terrorem) clauses are often inserted in wills and trusts to prevent a beneficiary from contesting or questioning the terms of the trust or the activities of the executor or trustee. However, such clauses are not recommended for CLTs. While there is no specific authority dealing with CLTs, Priv. Ltr. Rul. 79-42-073 (July 20, 1979) and Priv. Ltr. Rul. 77-32-011 (May 10, 1977) hold that the use of a no-contest clause in a CRT disqualifies the trust and thereby disallows the estate-tax charitable deduction. The I.R.S. reasoned that if a beneficiary contests the will and thereby loses the beneficial interest in the CRT, the requirement that the identity of the beneficiaries (in all cases) and the income payments (in the case of a guaranteed annuity) be ascertainable at the creation of the trust is violated. By analogy, if all remainder beneficiaries in a CLT unsuccessfully contest the trust, thereby forfeiting their remainder interest, the trust might become disqualified as failing to have at least one private-remainder beneficiary.

### E.  Need for Advanced Ruling(s)

There are no I.R.S.–approved forms for CLTs. Consequently, if the stakes are high enough, it is wise to request an advance ruling from the I.R.S. before execution of a CLT.

## VI.  Appropriate Assets

If one is considering establishing a CLT, appropriateness of certain types of gifts to that trust must be evaluated. Following are types of assets to be considered:

### A. Cash

The transfer of cash to a CLT is generally appropriate and quite flexible. The biggest advantage is that the cash can easily be converted into a portfolio of appreciating assets without adverse tax consequences to the grantor (in the case of a grantor CLT) or to the trust (in the case of a nongrantor CLT). The biggest disadvantage of using cash or equivalents in funding a CLT is that if the assets of the trust remain as cash or equivalents, the yield is not likely to keep pace with the required charitable distribution unless the annuity amount or unitrust payment is set very low. Then the trustee will be forced to dip into the corpus of the trust, thereby frustrating the goal of passing the remainder interest intact to the remainder beneficiaries.

## B. Marketable Securities

Because of their appreciation potential, marketable securities are good assets to transfer to or to be purchased by a CLT—especially if the objective is to generate an annual return for the trust that substantially exceeds the required charitable distribution. Another advantage is that ownership by the trust will not generally run afoul of the excess business holdings or jeopardy investment prohibitions.

## C. Closely Held Business Interests

Using an interest in a closely held business to fund a CLAT may be advantageous, especially if that closely held business interest can generate sufficient distributable income to satisfy the required charitable distributions. A gift to a CLT of a minority interest in a business could entitle the donor to a minority interest and lack of marketability discount, notwithstanding the high level of distributions. Such distributions enhance the trust's ability to pass wealth to the noncharitable remainder beneficiaries because a lower effective annuity, which is based on the fair market value (including discounts) of the initial assets, will be required (see discussion in Section VI.E.). The biggest problem with the transfer of this kind of asset is that the CLT is viewed as a private foundation, and ownership of closely held business interests could violate the excess business holdings and jeopardy investment rules. This could be avoided if the initial charitable deduction does not exceed 60 percent of the value of the assets transferred to the trust. Using closely held corporate stock and partnership interests as assets to fund a CLUT has the principal disadvantage of requiring annual valuations in order to determine the size of the unitrust amount, thereby adding to the cost of administering the trust.

## D. Unencumbered Real Estate Other Than a Personal Residence

The transfer of unencumbered real estate to a CLT will not, by itself, disqualify the trust. However, to avoid having to value the property each year, the transfer of unencumbered real estate to a CLAT seems more appropriate and practical than transferring the property to a CLUT. The major problem in using such property is that it must produce substantial current income to enable the trustee to make the required charitable distributions. If not, undivided interests in the property will need to be transferred to the charity to make up the difference. With a nongrantor CLT, such distributions of corpus will not likely qualify for the federal income-tax charitable deduction available to trusts because such payments will probably not have been paid out of gross income.

## E. Mortgaged Real Estate

As in the case of a charitable remainder trust, encumbered real estate should *not* be transferred to a CLT. The mere ownership of encumbered real estate could cause the trust to be deemed to have unrelated business income, including debt-financed income.[80] In general, a CLT will be deemed to have debt-financed income if it acquires realty subject to a mortgage, unless (a) the encumbered realty was acquired by testamentary transfer (although it must pay off the debt or get rid of the property within ten years); or (b) the mortgage was placed on the property more than five years before the transfer—although, again, the trustee must pay off the mortgage or get rid of the property within ten years.[81]

Even if the transfer of mortgaged real estate would not result in disqualification, the transfer could give rise to part-sale-part-gift treatment with the debt being treated as an amount realized in calculation of gain or loss.[82] This happens even if the CLT does not assume the debt, but not if the CLT is a grantor trust.

## VII. *Planning with CLATS and CLUTS*

CLTs are useful estate planning tools for charitably inclined taxpayers who wish to make charitable gifts and provide substantial residual benefits to or for the benefit of children, grandchildren, and other family members. Here are some ideas for anyone contemplating using a CLT in this way:

### A. Allowing Charitably Inclined Clients to Provide for Charities and Pass Property to Children at Little or No Gift- or Estate-Tax Cost

#### 1. *General Description*

If properly structured, the CLT allows a wealthy, charitably inclined client to pass substantial property to children at little or no gift- or estate-tax cost, especially with intervivos nongrantor CLTs. The general rule is, If you want to make substantial annual gifts to charity now and also want eventually to provide for your children or grandchildren, then consider the CLT.

2. *Example 1:* Geraldine Generous, age 50, is a wealthy single philanthropist who routinely gives $120,000 per year to charity. This gift is her only itemized deduction. She has a net worth of $20 million. This year her adjusted gross income from interest, dividends, and directorships was $500,000; and it is expected to stay at that level in the foreseeable future. Among her assets are $2 million of high-grade, long-term corporate bonds paying 6-percent annual interest.

Geraldine has two adult children, Gerald (28) and Ginny (24). Each child is mature, reliable, and independent. Geraldine would like to continue her charitable giving but eventually would also like to transfer $2 million to her two children as tax-efficiently as possible.

Geraldine establishes a 25-year nongrantor CLAT. The trust is required to pay $120,000 per year to the Geraldine Generous Advise and Consult Fund (Advise and Consult Fund), established by the local Communities Foundation. She transfers the $2 million of bonds to the trust. The optimum I.R.C. Section 7520 rate at the time of the gift is 6 percent. Here are the results:

    a. Geraldine will be entitled to a $1,534,008 federal gift-tax charitable deduction for the present value of the annual $120,000 guaranteed annuity amounts for the 25-year term.

    b. Geraldine will have made an adjusted taxable gift of $465,992. This equals the value of the remainder interest passing to Gerald and Ginny at the end of the 25-year period.

c. Geraldine will *not* be entitled to a federal income-tax charitable deduction because the trust is not a grantor trust. However, the trust will be entitled to fully deduct each $120,000 distribution to the Advise and Consult Fund paid from items of gross income.

The effect of the transfer to the CLAT is that, from an income-tax standpoint, less money goes to the I.R.S., leaving more for charity and/or children. Geraldine has shifted $120,000 of income each year to the CLAT (because the income-generating assets now belong to the CLAT), thereby reducing her own adjusted gross income. Furthermore, because the CLAT has an unlimited charitable deduction, the CLAT will receive a full $120,000 charitable deduction each year for its annuity payment to charity, whereas the same $120,000 gift to charity by Geraldine would be subject to limitations. Thus, even though Geraldine does not get to directly deduct the $120,000 in gifts to charity, her family is in a better position with a gift of the $2 million of bonds to the CLAT than if she had not made the gift, because less money passes to the I.R.S. This is summarized in Figures 8.1 and 8.2:

## FIGURE 8.1

### Taxable Income without CLAT

| | Geraldine | CLAT[83] | TOTAL |
|---|---|---|---|
| Adjusted Gross Income: | $500,000 | $0 | $500,000 |
| Less Charitable Deduction: | (108,000) | 0 | (108,000) |
| Taxable Income w/o CLAT | 392,000 | 0 | 392,000 |

## FIGURE 8.2

### Taxable Income with CLAT

| | Geraldine | CLAT | TOTAL |
|---|---|---|---|
| Adjusted Gross Income: | $380,000 | $120,000 | $500,000 |
| Less Charitable Deduction: | 0 | (120,000) | (120,000) |
| Taxable Income with CLAT | 380,000 | 0 | 380,000 |

If the trust does not decrease in value, at least $2 million passes to Gerald and Ginny in 25 years at the cost of using up $465,992 of the applicable exclusion.

## B. Using a Grantor CLT to Offset a Charitably Minded Client's Unusually High Income

### 1. General Description

A grantor CLT can be used to generate a one-time federal income tax deduction to offset a charitably minded client's unusually high income.

*2. Example 2:* Same fact pattern as Example 1, except in January of this year, Generous Family, Inc., was sold and Geraldine's share of the sale proceeds was $5 million—all of which will be taxable to Geraldine as long-term capital gain. Thus, without further planning, Geraldine expects this year's adjusted gross income to be $5,500,000.

Geraldine decides to set up the same 25-year, $120,000-per-year CLAT, but upon advice of counsel she has the trust drafted as a grantor trust. The results are:

a. Geraldine will receive a one-time federal income-tax charitable deduction of $1,534,008, which can be used to offset the $5,350,000 of adjusted gross income. Any excess can be carried forward for five years.[84]
b. Geraldine will be taxed on trust income during the entire term of the trust. However, this result can be minimized if the trustee changes the investment mix to municipal bonds and/or low-dividend stock.[85]
c. Geraldine will have made an adjusted taxable gift of $465,992.

If the trust does not decrease in value, at least $2 million will pass to Gerald and Ginny at the cost of $465,992 of unified credit.

## C. Using CLUTs to Leverage the GST Tax Exemption

### 1. General Description

One of the most useful applications of CLTs is the use of a CLUT to enable charitably minded clients to make leveraged GST gifts. In determining the applicable fraction for a GST gift to a CLUT, the value of the charitable deduction attributable to the GST gift reduces the denominator of the fraction without any further adjustment. This will enable tax efficient GST gifts with a minimum drain on available GST exemption.

2. *Example 3:* Geraldine Generous likes the notion of using a CLT to continue her $120,000-per-year charitable gifting plan but instead would like the remainder of the trust to pass in further trust for the benefit of her grandchildren and great-grandchildren. Accordingly, Geraldine transfers the $2 million of corporate bonds to a 25-year, 6-percent nongrantor CLUT with the remainder interest passing to a trust for her grandchildren and great-grandchildren. The results of this arrangement are:

a. Geraldine will be entitled to a federal gift-tax charitable deduction of $1,533,820. This is equal to the present value of the 6-percent annual unitrust payments over the 25-year term.
b. Geraldine will have made an adjusted taxable gift of $466,180. This is equal to the value of the remainder interest passing into the educational trust for Geraldine's grandchildren and great-grandchildren.

If Geraldine allocates $466,180 of her GST exemption to the CLUT, the trust will have an inclusion ratio of zero computed as follows:

$$\text{Applicable Fraction} = \frac{\text{Amount of GST Exemption Allocated to Transfer (\$466,180)}}{\text{Amount of Transfer (\$2 million) } minus \text{ Charitable Deduction Attributable to Transfer (\$1,533,820)}}$$

$$= \frac{\$466,180}{\$2,000,000 - \$1,533,820} = 1$$

Because the applicable fraction equals one, the inclusion ratio is equal to zero (one minus one).

Geraldine will not be entitled to a federal income-tax charitable deduction because the trust is not a grantor trust. However, the trust will be entitled to a deduction for each distribution to the Advise and Consult Fund, as long as the distribution is paid from gross income.

Even though Geraldine is unable to deduct the $120,000 of gifts to charity, the effect of the transfer to the CLUT is a similar (or better) tax position. If the trust does not decrease in value, at least $2 million will pass in trust to her grandchildren and great-grandchildren without a GST tax.

### D. Outperforming the Required Return by Transferring Appreciation to Children

#### 1. General Description

The fundamental advantages of using a CLT are to accomplish the client's charitable objectives while at the same time shifting all appreciation to the remainder beneficiaries. This can be accomplished only if the return on the CLT assets exceeds the required payout rate. If it does, the results can be dramatic.

*2. Example 4:* Geraldine Generous elects to establish a 25-year CLAT that pays an annual guaranteed annuity equal to 6 percent of the net fair market value of the assets initially transferred to the trust. However, instead of transferring $2 million of long-term 6-percent bonds to the trust, Geraldine transfers $2 million in cash and requests that the trustee hire Mike Moneymaker as investment manager with specific direction to invest in a manner that substantially outperforms the 6-percent rate of return the I.R.S. is then requiring in valuing the charitable gift of the guaranteed annuity payments (that is, the I.R.C. Section 7520 rate).

Over the 25-year history of the CLAT, Mike Moneymaker and his protégé son, Mike Moneymaker, Jr., produce an average annual net after-tax rate of return of 12 percent per year. The results are as follows:

a. Geraldine will be entitled to a $1,534,008 federal gift-tax charitable deduction for the present value of the annual $120,000 guaranteed annuity amounts for the 25-year term.

b. Geraldine will have made an adjusted taxable gift of $465,992 equal to the value of the remainder passing to Gerald and Ginny.

c. Geraldine will not be entitled to an income-tax charitable deduction because the trust is not a grantor trust. However, the trust will be entitled to fully deduct each $120,000 distribution to the Advise and Consult Fund paid from gross income. Because Mike Moneymaker and son are expected to select a portfolio of trust investments that emphasizes capital appreciation rather than current income, it is important for the trust to allocate capital gains to income (for trust-accounting purposes) so that distributions to the Advise and Consent Fund are considered paid out of gross income.

Even though Geraldine does not get to deduct the $120,000 of gifts to charity, the effect of the transfer to the CLAT may be that she closely approximates (or even improves) the tax position that she would have been in had she not made the gift. At the end of 25 years, $18,000,064 of trust property shall pass to Gerald and Ginny at the cost of only $465,992 of applicable exclusion!

## E. Leveraging the Leverage Via Discounted Gifts to CLTs

### 1. General Description

A donor's gift of a minority interest in a privately held corporation or partnership can entitle the donor to lack of marketability and/or minority interest discounts in determining the fair market value of the gifted property.[86] If the enterprise produces a steady and significant cash flow, a gift of a minority interest in it could produce a leverage-of-the-leveraging effect and allow for the charitably minded client to transfer substantial valuable assets to the remainder beneficiaries.

### 2. Example 5: Geraldine Generous establishes Generous Investments, Ltd. (GIL), a limited partnership. She also establishes Generous Management, Inc. (GMI), an S corporation, and capitalizes GMI with $25,000. Geraldine owns 100 percent of the common stock of GMI. GMI contributes $20,202 to GIL in return for a 1-percent general partnership interest. Geraldine contributes $2 million to GIL in return for a 99-percent limited-partnership interest. Geraldine sells 50 percent of GMI to Gerald for $12,500 and sells 50 percent of GMI to Ginny for $12,500.

Geraldine creates two identical 20-year CLATs: one under which Gerald is the remainder beneficiary and one under which Ginny is the remainder beneficiary. The trustee of each CLAT is Major Trust Company. At the end of each year, each CLAT is required to pay the Advise and Consult Fund a guaranteed annuity equal to 8 percent of the initial net fair market value of the assets contributed to the CLAT.

Geraldine gives a 49.5-percent limited-partnership interest to each CLAT. Although the pro rata net asset value of each 49.5-percent limited-partnership interest in GIL is $1 million ($2 million total), Reliable Valuation Services opines that the fair market value of each limited partnership interest is $650,000, which reflects a 35 percent combined lack of control and lack of marketability discount. The assets of the partnership grow at a net rate of return of 10 percent over the trust term. What has been accomplished:

  a.  Geraldine is entitled to a federal gift-tax charitable deduction of $1,192,870 in connection with her gifts of limited partnership interests. Remember, each gift is valued at $650,000, not $1 million.
  b.  Geraldine has made adjusted taxable gifts totaling $107,130.
  c.  At the end of each year, Geraldine's Advise and Consult Fund will receive a total distribution of $104,000: $52,000 from each CLAT. Each CLAT's guaranteed annuity payment is equal to 8 percent of the initial fair market value of the 49.5 percent limited partnership interest, that is, $0.08 \times \$650,000$, or $52,000.
  d.  GFI has to earn only 5.2 percent on its assets each year to meet this guaranteed annuity obligation.
  e.  At the end of twenty years, Gerald and Ginny will each receive one-half of $7,498,400, or $3,749,200 each.
  f.  Even if the net rate of return is only 8 percent, Gerald and Ginny will eventually receive one-half of $4,562,670, or $2,281,335.
  g.  At a 10-percent net rate of return, the leverage is nearly 70 to 1. At an 8-percent net rate of return, the leverage is nearly 43 to 1.

### 3. Also Useful in Transferring Family Businesses

With substantial discounts available with the transfer of closely held stock, a charitably minded client could use a CLT to transfer an interest in a family business to the children on a very favorable basis. The leverage concept described in Example 5 would also apply here.

## F. Using an Aggressive Technique: Transfer by the Sick-But-Not-Too-Sick Client

### 1. General Description

Another moderately aggressive planning idea is to transfer assets to a CLT for the life of the donor when the donor's health is bad enough to reasonably conclude that he or she will not live to normal actuarial life expectancy, but not bad enough to ignore the actuarial tables. For administrative consistency, I.R.C. Section 7520 requires taxpayers to use government-mandated actuarial tables to value life estates, interests for a term of years, and remainders and reversions following those term interests.[87] These actuarial tables are based on mortality statistics to reflect the 1990 census and will eventually reflect the 2000 census.[88] However, the taxpayer is prohibited from using the I.R.S. actuarial tables in valuing life estates, and remainders or reversionary interests following a life estate if the individual who is the measuring life is known to have an incurable illness or other deteriorating physical condition with at least a 50-percent probability that the individual will die within one year.[89] Should the individual survive for at least 18 months, he or she is presumed not to be terminally ill unless this is rebutted by clear and convincing evidence.[90] This sad state of affairs could provide a charitably minded client with a planning opportunity if that client has a better than 50-percent chance to live for more than one year.

### 2. Example 6:

John Doe, age 70, is suffering from a terminal illness, but his team of doctors believes he will live for three to five years. They also unanimously agree there is a greater-than-50-percent probability that he will live for more than a year. John transfers $3 million of cash and marketable securities to the CLAT that will pay an annuity to the University of Sky-High Tuition equal to 11 percent of the initial fair market value of the gift. The annuity will be paid at the end of each year of John's life. At John's death, the trust assets will be distributed in equal shares to John's four children. John retains no power over the trust that will cause the trust to be includable in John's estate for federal estate-tax purposes. The trust is a nongrantor trust; therefore, John will not be entitled to a federal income-tax deduction in connection with his gift to the CLAT.

The value of John's federal gift-tax charitable deduction is $2,418,012. That makes the value of John's adjusted taxable gift $581,988, which is the remainder interest using the I.R.S. exhaustion method based on John's actuarial life expectancy under the actuarial tables mandated by I.R.C. Section 7520.

John dies three years after creating and funding the trust. The trust grows at an annual rate of 8 percent. Total charitable lead payments are $990,000. At the time of John's death, the trust is worth $2,707,824. Thus, for an adjusted taxable gift of $581,988, John has transferred approximately $2.7 million to his children.

## VIII.  Sample Form of CLAT

Exhibit A contains one form of a CLAT. No guarantees are made regarding this form; however, it is hoped practitioners will be helped in drafting their own forms of CLAT.

## IX.  Conclusion

The CLT can be a powerful and exciting estate-planning tool for the client who wants to provide immediate benefits to one or more charities, while ultimately benefiting children, grandchildren, or more remote descendants. However, the use of such trusts requires precise drafting and the careful selection of assets. This chapter gives estate planning practitioner guidance in drafting and planning such trusts. Even in light of EGTRRA, CLTs should prove to be powerful wealth transfer vehicles.

# EXHIBIT A
# FORM OF CHARITABLE LEAD ANNUITY TRUST

Irrevocable Trust Agreement

Between

[Settlor]
Settlor

And

[Trustee]
Trustee

Creating A Charitable Lead Annuity Trust
To Be Known As The
[Trust Name] Charitable Trust
(No Discretion in Trustee to Select Charities)

> NOTE: THIS FORM IS NOT INTENDED TO AND CANNOT REPLACE THE INDEPENDENT JUDGMENT OF EACH ATTORNEY WITH RESPECT TO APPLICABILITY, ACCURACY, VALIDITY, AND TAX CONSEQUENCES IN PARTICULAR CIRCUMSTANCES AND IS, THEREFORE, SUBMITTED WITHOUT WARRANTY.

[Trust Name] Charitable Trust

THIS IS AN IRREVOCABLE AGREEMENT OF TRUST made and entered into by and between [Settlor] (the "Settlor") and [Trustee] (the "Trustee").

## ARTICLE I
*IDENTIFICATION AND DEFINITIONS*

1.1   *Settlor.* All references in this instrument to the "Settlor" mean [Settlor].

1.2   *Children.* All references in this instrument to "Children" or "Settlor's Children" mean [Children] and any child or children born to or legally adopted through court proceedings by Settlor. All references to a "Child" or "Settlor's Child" mean one (1) of Settlor's Children.

1.3   *Descendants.* All references in this instrument to a "descendant" or "descendants" of any person mean all lawful lineal descendants of all degrees of the designated person (whether or not such person is alive) including any adopted descendant but only if legally adopted through court proceedings when under the age of fourteen (14) years. Furthermore, all references in this instrument to "Settlor's descendants," "descendants of Settlor," or any substantially similar reference to any one (1) or more descendants of Settlor shall mean only Settlor's Children (as defined above) and the descendants of Settlor's Children. A child in gestation who is born alive shall be considered a child in being throughout the period of gestation.

1.4   *Distribution to Descendants.* Whenever this instrument requires the Trustee of any trust created hereunder to make distributions to the "descendants" of any person or to the "then living descendants" of any person, the property to be distributed shall be divided as follows: (a) one (1) share for each then living child of that person and (b) one (1) share for each deceased child of that person who leaves descendants then living. Each then living child of that person shall take one (1) share and the share of each deceased child of that person shall be divided among such deceased child's then living descendants in the same manner. This section is intended to avoid repeated use of the term "per stirpes"; however, it is intended to result in a per stirpes distribution among such descendants.

1.5   *Code.* All references in this instrument to the "Code" mean the Internal Revenue Code of 1986, as amended, and shall refer to corresponding provisions of any subsequent federal tax law.

1.6   *Texas Trust Code.* All references in this instrument to the "Texas Trust Code" mean the Texas Trust Code, including any amendments subsequent to the execution of this instrument.

1.7   *Trustee.* All references in this instrument to the "Trustee" are to those persons named under Article IV hereof while serving in such capacity hereunder and shall also include any successor Trustee or Trustees while serving in such capacity hereunder, unless another meaning is clearly indicated or required by context or circumstances. Further, use of the singular term "Trustee" shall include the plural term "Trustees" unless the context and circumstances clearly indicate otherwise.

1.8   *Disqualified Person.* All references in this instrument to a "Disqualified Person" shall mean any individual or entity who or which is a "disqualified person" with respect to this trust within the meaning of Section 4946 of the Code and Regulations thereunder.

1.9   *Charities.* All references in this instrument to "Charities" shall mean organizations described in each of Sections 170(c), 2055(a) and 2522(a) of the Code. All references in this instrument to a "Charity" mean one (1) of the Charities.

1.10   *The Charitable Beneficiary.* All references in this instrument to the "Charitable Beneficiary" shall mean [Charity].

## ARTICLE 2
*ASSETS*

Contemporaneously with the execution of this trust agreement, the property described in Schedule A annexed hereto has been transferred to the Trustee by Settlor. The Trustee shall hold, administer, and distribute the trust estate in accordance with the terms of this instrument.

## ARTICLE 3
*TERMS OF CHARITABLE LEAD ANNUITY TRUST*

3.1   *Purpose.* The purpose of this instrument is to establish a charitable lead annuity trust that provides a guaranteed annuity described under Sections 2055(e)(2)(B) and 2522(c)(2)(B) of the Code.

3.2   *Name of Trust.* This trust shall be known as the "[Trust Name] Charitable Trust."

3.3   *Guaranteed Annuity Payments.*

A. *Determination of Annuity Amount.* Subject to the provisions of Subsection 3.31), each year during the Annuity Period (hereinafter defined), the Trustee shall pay to the Charitable Beneficiary a guaranteed annuity amount equal to [percent] ([pct]%) of the initial fair market of the trust property (the "Annuity Amount").

B. *Annuity Period*. The Annuity Period (herein so-called) shall begin on the date this Trust Agreement is signed by the Settlor and the Trustee and shall end [term] ([no.]) years after that date.

C. *Payment of Annuity Amount and Source of Payment*. The Trustee may pay the Annuity Amount in cash, in kind, or partly in each. The Annuity Amount shall be paid in annual installments. The Charitable Beneficiary shall receive its first annual payment of the Annuity Amount on the day that is the last day of the first taxable year of the trust and shall thereafter receive such annual payment of the Annuity Amount on the last day of each taxable year of the trust until the expiration of the Annuity Period. Notwithstanding any existing or hereafter enacted state law, except on termination of the Annuity Period, no amount may be paid from this trust to or for the use of any person other than an organization described in each of Sections 170(c), 2055(a), and 2522(a) of the Code. An amount shall not be deemed to be paid to or for the use of any person other than an organization described in each of such Sections if the amount is transferred for full and adequate consideration.

D. *Payment Must Be to Qualified Charitable Organization(s)*. If the Charitable Beneficiary (or any other organization(s) designated by the Trustee to receive the Annuity Amount pursuant to this Subsection 3.3D) is not an organization described in each of Sections 170(c), 2055(a), and 2522(a) of the Code at the time when any principal or income of this trust is to be distributed to it, the principal or income that was to be distributed to that Charitable Beneficiary (or any other organization(s) designated by the Trustee to receive the Annuity Amount pursuant to this Subsection 3.3D) shall be distributed to such other organization or organizations described in each of Sections 170(c), 2055(a), and 2522(a) as the Trustee shall select. If the Trustee shall be unable to fulfill the Trustee's obligations under this subsection, a court of competent jurisdiction shall make any selection required by this subsection. In no event shall any portion of the principal or income of this trust be distributed during the Annuity Period of this trust to any organization that is not described in each of Sections 170(c), 2055(a), and 2522(a) of the Code.

E. *Incorrect Valuations*. If the initial fair market value of the trust property is incorrectly determined, then within a reasonable period after the value is finally determined for federal gift tax purposes, the Trustee shall pay to the Charitable Beneficiary (or any other organization(s) designated by the Trustee pursuant to Subsection 3.3D above), in the case of an undervaluation, or receive from such Charitable Beneficiary (or any other organization(s) designated by the Trustee pursuant to Subsection 3.3D above), in the case of an overvaluation, an amount equal to the difference between the Annuity Amount properly payable and the Annuity Amount actually paid.

F. *Undistributed Income*. Any income not distributed by the Trustee for the taxable year shall be accumulated and added to principal.

G. *Proration of the Annuity Amount for Short Taxable Years*. In the case of a taxable year which is for a period of less than twelve (12) months (other than the taxable year in which this charitable lead annuity trust terminates), the Annuity Amount which must be distributed hereunder shall be such amount multiplied by a fraction, the numerator of which is the number of days in that short taxable year, and the denominator of which is 365 (366 if February 29 is a day included in the numerator). In the case of the taxable year in which this charitable lead annuity trust terminates, the Annuity Amount shall be an amount multiplied by a fraction, the numerator of which is the number of days in the period beginning on the first day of such taxable year and ending on the date this charitable lead annuity trust terminates and the denominator of which is 365 (366 if February 29 is a day included in the numerator).

H. *Distributions of Property in Kind.* The adjusted basis for federal income tax purposes of any property which the Trustee shall distribute in kind to the Charitable Beneficiary (or any other organization(s) designated by the Trustee pursuant to Subsection 33D above) must be fairly representative of the adjusted basis for such purposes of all trust property available for distribution on the date of distribution.

I. *Termination and Distribution to Remainder Beneficiary(ies).* This trust shall terminate [term] ([no.]) years after the date this agreement was signed by the Settlor and the Trustee. Upon such termination, the Trustee shall divide the remaining trust estate into separate shares, equal in value, with one (1) share for each then living Child and one (1) share for the then living descendants, collectively, of each deceased Child. Each share for a then living Child shall be distributed by the Trustee to that Child. Each share for the then living descendants, collectively, of a deceased Child shall be distributed by the Trustee to that deceased Child's then living descendants. If upon termination of this Trust, none of the Settlor's descendants shall then be living, the then remaining trust estate shall be distributed to those persons other than creditors (the "Heirs-at-Law") who would have been entitled under Texas laws to inherit the Settlor's personal property had the Settlor died intestate, a single person without descendants, domiciled in and a resident of the State of Texas, and had the Settlor's death occurred at a point in time immediately after the termination of this trust, with the shares and proportions of inheritance by such Heirs-at-Law to be determined by Texas laws in force at the actual date of death of the Settlor.

J. *No Additional Contributions and No Prepayment.* No additional contribution shall be made to this trust after the initial contribution described on Schedule A is contributed to it. Furthermore, no portion of the Annuity Amount may be prepaid or commuted by the Trustee so as to disqualify the trust according to the Code and Regulations thereunder.

K. *Limitation of Trustee's Obligation.* The obligation of the Trustee to make payments hereunder is limited to the trust's assets.

L. *Prohibited Transactions.* If Section 4942 of the Code is at any time applicable to this trust, the Trustee shall make distributions at such time and in such manner as not to subject the trust to tax under Section 4942 of the Code. Except for the payment of the Annuity Amount to the Charitable Beneficiary, the Trustee shall not engage in any act of self-dealing, as defined in Section 4941(d) of the Code, and shall not make any taxable expenditures, as defined in Section 4945(d) of the Code. The Trustee shall not make any investments that jeopardize the charitable purpose of the trust, within the meaning of Section 4944 of the Code, or retain any excess business holdings, within the meaning of Section 4943(c) of the Code which would subject the trust to tax under Section 4943 of the Code.

[Alternative to above if charitable interest upon inception of trust does not exceed 60% of the value of the gift to the trust: L. *Prohibited Transactions.* If Section

4942 of the Code is at any time applicable to this trust, the Trustee shall make distributions at such time and in such manner as not to subject the trust to tax under Section 4942 of the Code. Except for the payment of the Annuity Amount to the Charity, the Trustee shall not engage in any act of self-dealing, as defined in Section 4941(d) of the Code, and shall not make any taxable expenditures, as defined in Section 4945(d) of the Code.]

M. *Death Taxes.* No estate, inheritance, or other death taxes shall be allocated to or recoverable from this charitable lead annuity trust.

N. *Taxable Year.* The first taxable year of the trust shall begin on the date this Trust Agreement is signed by the Settlor and Trustee and shall end on December 31 of the year of such signing. Subsequent taxable years of the trust shall be on a calendar-year basis.

O. *Governing Law.* The operation of the trust shall be governed by the laws of the State of Texas.

P. *Limited Power of Amendment.* This trust is irrevocable. However, the Trustee shall have the power, acting alone, to amend the trust in any manner required for the sole purpose of ensuring that the trust qualifies and continues to qualify as a charitable lead annuity trust that provides for a guaranteed annuity as described under Sections 2055(e)(2)(B) and 2522(c)(2)(B) of the Code.

Q. *Investment of Trust Assets.* Nothing in this trust instrument shall be construed to restrict the Trustee from investing the trust assets in a manner that could result in the annual realization of a reasonable amount of income or gain from the sale or disposition of trust assets.

R. *Valuation of Assets.* The assets gratuitously transferred to this charitable lead annuity trust shall be valued as finally determined for federal gift tax purposes. The Trustee, in the Trustee's sole discretion, shall appoint a Qualified Appraiser (hereinafter described) for the purpose of valuing unmarketable assets held by the charitable lead annuity trust. The Trustee shall report to the Qualified Appraiser the identity of all unmarketable assets of this trust. The Qualified Appraiser shall thereupon value such minimum-marketable assets as finally determined for federal gift tax purposes and report the value to the Trustee. Any asset other than cash, cash equivalents, or other assets that can be readily sold or exchanged for cash or cash equivalents (within the meaning of Section 1.664-1 (a)(7)(11) of the Treasury Regulations) shall, for the purposes of this subsection, be treated as an unmarketable asset.

    1.   *Qualified Appraiser; Appointment and Definition.*

        (a) The Qualified Appraiser for purposes of this subsection shall be appointed upon creation of the trust by the Trustee in a written instrument filed with the trust records for the purpose of valuing unmarketable assets held by the trust upon creation. If such appointed Qualified Appraiser should die, resign, or be unwilling or unable to serve for any reason, then the Trustee shall name a successor Qualified Appraiser in a written instrument filed with the trust records for purposes of valuing unmarketable assets held by this charitable lead annuity trust upon creation. The Qualified Appraiser shall have no powers, duties, or responsibilities with respect to the trust, except with respect to the matters described in this subsection and upon completion of such valuation and report to the Trustee, such Qualified Appraiser shall be discharged by the Trustee.

(b) A Qualified Appraiser is a person who meets the requirements outlined in Treasury Regulation Section 1. 170A-13(c)(5) and who performs a current qualified appraisal that meets the requirements outlined in Treasury Regulation Section 1. 170A-13 (c).

2. *Removal of Qualified Appraiser*. The Trustee shall have the power to remove a Qualified Appraiser, if and only if the Trustee:

(a) shall determine in good faith that sufficient cause exists that would justify the removal of the Qualified Appraiser by a court of competent jurisdiction in accordance with the laws of the State of Texas; and

(b) shall give such Qualified Appraiser thirty (30) days' written notice of such removal. Upon the expiration of thirty (30) days from the date of receipt of such notice, the Qualified Appraiser, as applicable, shall be deemed to have been removed.

3. *Resignation of Qualified Appraiser*. Any Qualified Appraiser named as described hereinabove, or any successor Qualified Appraiser may at any time resign upon giving the Trustee thirty (30) days' written notice of such resignation. Upon the expiration of thirty (30) days from the date of receipt of such notice, the Qualified Appraiser shall be deemed to have resigned.

3.4 *Contingent Trusts*. Upon termination of any trust created hereunder, if any share of the trust estate would be distributed, outright and free of trust, to (a) any person who is then under the age of twenty-one (21) years or (b) any person who is then incapacitated in the opinion of the Trustee by reason of legal incapacity or physical or mental illness or infirmity (any person described by the foregoing provisions (a) or (b) is hereinafter called the "Ward") and no other trust is then held under this instrument for such Ward's primary benefit, the Trustee is hereby directed to hold that Ward's share in a separate trust for the benefit of the Ward; and the Trustee shall distribute to the Ward, subject to the limitations of this section, so much of the trust net income or principal or both as will provide for the health, support, maintenance, or education of the Ward without the interposition of any guardian. The Ward's trust shall terminate when (1) the Ward is not under the age of twenty-one (21) years and (2) the Ward is, in the opinion of the Trustee, legally, mentally, and physically capable of receiving his share, whereupon all remaining trust property of that trust share shall be distributed to the Ward, outright and free of trust. If the Ward dies before the termination of his trust, his trust estate then remaining shall be distributed to the Ward's estate. Notwithstanding the foregoing, the Trustee may make a determination as to a Ward's incapacity in any reasonable manner, including, without limitation, seeking a court determination of incapacity or by utilizing the method for determining the incapacity of a Trustee under Section 4.13 hereof.

# ARTICLE 4
*THE TRUSTEE*

4.1 *Appointment of Trustee*. The Trustee of each trust created hereunder is [Trustee]. As used herein, unless another meaning is clearly indicated or required by context or circumstances, the term "Trustee" in the singular form and neuter gender shall refer collectively to all persons or entities who may at any time be serving as Trustee, whether original or successor, individual or corporate, or singular or plural in number. All powers and discretions conferred upon the original Trustee shall be vested in and exercisable by any successor Trustee or Trustees.

4.2 *Succession of Trustee.* If [Trustee] or any other Independent Trustee thereafter serving shall fail or cease to serve as a Trustee of any trust created hereunder, then the Trust Committee (hereinafter designated) shall appoint a successor Independent Trustee of that trust to serve as sole Trustee of that trust. If the Trust Committee shall fail to appoint such a successor Independent Trustee within one hundred twenty (120) days after receiving notice of the vacancy in trusteeship, then upon written request of any interested person, the judge of any statutory probate court or Texas district court located in [County] County, Texas, acting as an individual and not in any judicial capacity, and without liability for acting or failing to act, shall have the power to appoint such a successor Independent Trustee as sole Trustee.

4.3 *Resignation of Trustee.* Any Trustee may resign as to any trust created hereunder at any time (a) in any manner provided by law or (b) by filing written notice of resignation in the Deed Records of [County] County, Texas.

4.4 *Manner of Appointment.* Any appointment of a successor Trustee shall be by an instrument in writing signed by those making the appointment, acknowledged, and filed with the Trustee so appointed.

4.5 *Notice of Vacancy.* Whenever a vacancy in the office of a Trustee occurs, the Trustee of the trust or the Settlor (if no Trustee is then serving) shall forthwith notify the individual (or entity) who is next eligible to serve of his (or its) appointment or eligibility, and such individual (or entity) shall have thirty (30) days after receiving such notification in which to qualify. The individual (or entity) who is eligible to serve shall qualify by filing a written acceptance with the Trustee then acting, and if no Trustee is then acting, such written acceptance shall be filed in the Deed Records of [County] County, Texas.

4.6 *Succession of Corporate Trustee.* If any corporate Trustee before or after qualification changes its name, becomes consolidated or merged with another corporation, or otherwise reorganizes, any resulting corporation which succeeds to the fiduciary business of that corporate Trustee shall become a Trustee hereunder in lieu of that corporate Trustee.

4.7 *Trustee's Fees.* The Independent Trustee of each trust created hereunder shall be entitled to reasonable fees commensurate with its duties and responsibilities, taking into account the value and nature of the trust estate and the time and work involved. Each Independent Trustee hereunder shall also be entitled to reimbursement for out-of-pocket expenses it incurs in connection with the discharge of its fiduciary duties hereunder. No Disqualified Person shall be entitled to a fee for serving as a Trustee hereunder. However, each Disqualified Person shall be entitled to reimbursement of reasonable expenses incurred in connection with the performance of "personal services," as defined in Treasury Regulation Section 51.4942(d)-3(c), and such reimbursement of expenses shall not be excessive. Such fees shall be allocated between income and principal in accordance with Subsection 5.1T.

4.8 *No Bond.* No Trustee shall be required to furnish bond or other security except as herein expressly provided.

4.9 *Restriction on Who May Serve as Trustee and Definition of Independent Trustee.* Each Trustee hereunder must be an individual or entity that can possess the powers vested exclusively in a Trustee without (a) causing trust income or principal to be attributed to the Settlor, a Trustee, or a trust beneficiary for federal income, gift, or estate tax purposes prior to the distribution of the trust income or principal to the beneficiary if the presence of someone else in the office of Trustee would avoid that result, and (b) causing a Trustee, the Settlor, or a trust beneficiary to be treated as an owner of the trust for federal income, gift, or estate tax purposes if the presence of someone else in the office of Trustee would avoid that result. As used in this instrument, the term "Trustee" means a Trustee who meets the requirements of this section. The Settlor is absolutely prohibited from serving as a Trustee of any trust created hereunder. Furthermore, for all purposes of this instrument the term "Independent Trustee" shall mean either (a) a bank having banking and trust powers organized under the laws of the United States or any state and having trust assets under administration valued at not less than [Amount] Dollars ($[amt]) or (b) a private trust company having trust powers only organized under the laws of the United States or any state and having trust assets under administration valued at not less than [Amount] Dollars ($[amt]).

4.10  *Liability of Trustee.* No Trustee of any trust created hereunder shall be liable for any mistake or error in judgment but shall be liable only for willful default, willful misconduct, or gross negligence.

4.11  *Accounting to Successor Trustee.* Any successor Trustee is authorized to accept the accounts rendered and the property delivered by or for a predecessor Trustee without requiring an audit or other independent account of the acts of the predecessor Trustee. No successor Trustee shall have any duty, responsibility, obligation, or liability whatsoever for any acts or omissions of any predecessor Trustee; nor, unless in writing required to do so by a person having a present or future beneficial interest under a trust created by this instrument, shall any successor Trustee have by this instrument any duty to take action to obtain redress for breach of trust.

4.12  *Beneficiary under Disability.* A guardian or attorney-in-fact under a valid power of attorney of any beneficiary who is under any legal, physical, or mental disability may, in carrying out the provisions of this instrument, act and receive notice for the beneficiary and sign any instrument for the beneficiary.

4.13  *Incapacity of Individual Trustee.* If any individual Trustee becomes unable to discharge his duties as Trustee hereunder by reason of accident, physical or mental illness, progressive or intermittent physical or mental deterioration, or other similar cause and does not resign, then upon certification by two (2) board-certified doctors of medicine affirming that each has examined the Trustee and that each has concluded, based on his examination, that the Trustee is unable to discharge his duties as Trustee, that Trustee shall thereupon cease to be Trustee in the same manner as if he had resigned effective the date of the certification.

4.14  *Trust Committee.*

A.  *Appointment of Trust Committee.* The Settlor hereby appoints [Member-1], [Member- 2], and [Member-3] as members of a Trust Committee (herein so called) for each trust created hereunder. If membership in the Trust Committee is ever reduced to less than three (3) individuals, the remaining member or members of that committee shall appoint a sufficient number of individuals to bring the total membership of the committee to a total of three (3) individuals. If at any time there are no members serving under the Trust Committee, then a judge of any statutory probate court located in Dallas County, Texas, acting individually and not in any judicial capacity, and without liability for acting or failing to act, may appoint three (3) individuals to serve on such committee. Such appointment shall be by an acknowledged instrument in writing delivered to each individual so appointed. It is the Settlor's intention that there shall always be at least three (3) members serving on the Trust Committee for each trust created hereunder. Furthermore, the Settlor is absolutely prohibited from serving as a member of the Trust Committee for each trust created hereunder.

B. *Powers of Trust Committee.* In addition to other powers and discretions otherwise given to a Trust Committee by this instrument, the Trust Committee for each trust created hereunder, by majority vote, shall have the discretionary power by written instrument, acknowledged and signed by a majority of the members of the committee and delivered to the Trustee, (i) to remove a Trustee of any trust created hereunder at any time and for any reason and (ii) to appoint a successor Trustee as may be required under Section hereof. No Trustee or member of the Trust Committee shall be liable for the exercise of or failure to exercise such committee's discretionary powers granted hereunder. Furthermore, any successor Trustee so appointed must be an Independent Trustee.

## ARTICLE 5
*TRUST ADMINISTRATION*

5.1 *General Powers.* Subject to any limitations stated elsewhere in this instrument (including, without limitation, Article 111, Section 5. 10 and Article VII hereof), and in addition to all common law and statutory authority, the Trustee of each trust created hereunder shall have the following powers, such powers to be exercised only in good faith and in accordance with the Trustee's fiduciary obligations:

5.2 *Receive and Manage.* To receive, hold, manage, control, care for, and protect the trust estate; and to collect and receive all dividends, rents, profits, and income thereof.

5.3 *Sell and Exchange.* To sell any trust property for cash or on credit at public or private sales; to exchange any trust property for other property; to grant options to purchase or acquire any trust property; and to determine the prices and terms of sales, exchanges, and options.

5.4 *Lease.* To lease trust property for terms within or extending beyond the term of the trust for any purpose, including the exploration for and removal of oil, gas, and other minerals and entering into community oil leases, pooling, and unitization agreements.

5.5 *Real Estate.* To retain and invest in real property (including any land trust interest); to collect the rents and earnings; to keep the buildings and fixtures in repair; to employ agents and custodians; to make all reasonable expenditures to preserve the property; to insure the property, the Trustee, and any person having an interest in or responsibility for the care, management, or repair of the property against those risks identified by the Trustee; to sell and contract to sell, grant options to buy, convey, exchange, partition, dedicate, and mortgage; to lease and grant options to lease for any period of time; to grant or release easements; to improve and subdivide; to dedicate parks, streets, and alleys; to vacate any subdivision or alley; and to construct, remodel, and demolish or abandon buildings.

5.6 *Borrow.* Except as prohibited under the provisions of Subsection 3.3L, to borrow money for any purpose, either from the banking department of any corporate Trustee or from others, notwithstanding the fact any Trustee may have a financial interest in such source; to encumber or hypothecate trust property by mortgage, deed of trust, or otherwise; and to maintain, renew, or extend any indebtedness upon such terms as the Trustee shall deem appropriate. Furthermore, under no circumstances is a Trustee serving hereunder permitted to borrow money from any individual or entity who or which is a Disqualified Person.

5.7 *Loans.* To lend money to any person, other than to a Disqualified Person, including, without limitation, the Settlor, a Child, a descendant of a Child, or the estate of any of those persons; provided that any such loan shall be adequately secured and shall bear a reasonable rate of interest in light of the existing circumstances at the time of such loan.

5.8   *Conserve Estate.* To take any action with respect to conserving or realizing upon the value of any trust property and with respect to foreclosures, reorganizations, or other changes affecting the trust property.

5.9   *Abandon Property.* To abandon any property or interest in property belonging to the trust when, in the Trustee's discretion, such abandonment is in the best interest of the trust and its beneficiaries.

5.10   *Transactions Between Trusts.* Except as prohibited under the provisions of Subsection 3.3L, to purchase, sell, or exchange property between each of the trusts provided for herein and any other trust (other than a trust which is a Disqualified Person) of which any Trustee may be a Trustee as fully as they might deal with any third person.

5.11   *Agents.* To employ attorneys, accountants, investment advisors, depositaries, and agents, with or without discretionary powers, and to pay all expenses and fees so incurred.

5.12   *Investment Advisory Service.* To obtain professional investment advice in making decisions regarding the prudent investment of trust funds, including, without limitation, the power to retain professional investment managers (with or without discretionary powers), an investment advisory service or similar professional advisory group, and to pay all fees, commissions and/or expenses thus incurred from the trust estate.

5.13   *Investments.* To invest and reinvest the trust funds in every kind of property, real, personal, or mixed, and every kind of investment, specifically including, but not by way of limitation: corporate obligations of every kind; stocks, preferred or common; shares of investment trusts, investment companies, mutual funds, whether of the open-end or closed-end type; real estate or any interest in real estate; and interests in trusts, including common trust funds. The Trustee may make such investments without regard to diversification of risk or production of income.

5.14   *Interest in Assets.* To serve as a Trustee without increased liability or accountability, even if that Trustee has an interest of any nature whatsoever in any instrumentality in which assets of the trust may be invested.

5.15   *Securities.* To have all the rights, powers, and privileges of an owner with respect to the securities held in trust, including, but not limited to, the power to vote, give proxies, and pay assessments; to participate in voting trusts, pooling agreements, foreclosures, reorganizations, consolidations, mergers, and liquidations, and incident to such participation, to deposit securities with and transfer title to any protective or other committee (provided the Settlor is not a member of such protective or other committee) on such terms as the Trustee may deem advisable; and to exercise or sell stock subscription or conversion rights.

5.16   *Insurance.* To carry insurance of such kinds and in such amounts as the Trustee shall deem advisable to protect the trust estate and the Trustee against any hazard, using income or principal for such purpose.

5.17   *Documents.* To execute contracts, notes, conveyances, and other instruments containing covenants, representations, and warranties binding upon and creating a charge against the trust estate and containing provisions excluding personal liability; or to execute any other written instrument of any character appropriate to any of the powers or duties conferred upon the Trustee.

5.18 *Nominee.* To hold securities and other property in bearer form or in the name of a trustee or nominee with or without disclosure of any fiduciary relationship.

5.19 *Litigation.* To commence or defend at the expense of the trust such litigation with respect to the trust estate as the Trustee deems advisable; and to collect, pay, contest, compromise, settle, renew, or abandon any claims or demands of or against the trust estate without court authority on whatever terms the Trustee shall deem advisable. The Trustee's powers pursuant to this subsection shall apply during the term of the trust and after distribution of trust assets. However, the Trustee shall have no obligations or duties with respect to any litigation or claims occurring after distribution of trust assets unless the Trustee shall be adequately indemnified by the distributees for any loss in connection with such matters.

5.20 *Reliance.* To rely upon any notice, certificate, affidavit, letter, telegram, or other paper, document, or evidence believed by the Trustee to be genuine or sufficient in making any payment or distribution.

5.21 *Income and Principal.* To determine the allocation or apportionment of all receipts and disbursements between income and principal, including whether or not (and to what extent) to establish reserves for depreciation or depletion. In exercising this discretion, the Trustee may take into consideration the provisions of the Texas Trust Code but shall not be bound by those provisions. Notwithstanding the foregoing, the Trustee shall not exercise any power granted under this subsection in a manner that would jeopardize the qualification of the trust as a charitable lead annuity trust that provides for a guaranteed annuity amount as described under Sections 2055(e)(2)(B) and 2522(c)(2)(B) of the Code.

5.22 *Power to Deal With Environmental Hazards.* To (a) conduct environmental assessments, audits, and site monitoring to determine compliance with any environmental law or regulation thereunder; (b) take all appropriate remedial action to contain, clean up, or remove any environmental hazard including a spill, release, discharge, or contamination, either on its own accord or in response to an actual or threatened violation of any environmental law or regulation thereunder; (c) institute any legal proceedings concerning environmental hazards or contest or settle legal proceedings brought by any local, state, or federal agency concerned with environmental compliance, or by a private litigant; (d) comply with any local, state, or federal agency order or court order directing an assessment, abatement, or cleanup of any environmental hazards; and (e) employ agents, consultants, and legal counsel to assist or perform the above undertakings or actions. All reasonable and necessary expenses incurred in the Trustee's exercise of such powers shall be an expense of the trust estate.

5.23 *Retention of Corporate Trustee's Securities.* To retain any stock or other security received from any source and issued by any corporate Trustee in its individual capacity, by a bank holding company that owns stock of a Trustee bank, or by any related or affiliated corporation controlled by the bank holding company. This authority to retain includes stock dividends, securities issued in lieu thereof, and securities issued as a result of any recapitalization, consolidation, or merger of a Trustee. The Trustee shall have with respect to these stocks and securities the same powers that apply to other trust property.

5.24 *Purchase Property.* Except as prohibited under the provisions of Subsection 3.3L, to purchase property at its fair market value, as determined by the Trustee in the Trustee's discretion, from any person other than a Disqualified Person, including, without limitation, the Settlor, a Child, or a descendant of a Child.

5.25 *Distributions in Cash or Kind.* To make distributions hereunder in cash, in kind, or partly in each.

5.26 *Court Authority Not Required.* To exercise any and all of the powers, rights, and privileges contained herein and conferred hereby without obtaining the prior or subsequent authority, approval, or ratification by or from any court or judicial body.

5.27 *Miscellaneous Powers.* Generally to do and perform any and all acts, things, or deeds which in the judgment of the Trustee may be necessary or proper for the protection, preservation, and promotion of the interests of the trust properties and estate.

5.28 *Liability of Third Party.* No person dealing with the Trustee of any trust created hereunder shall be obligated to see to the application of any money paid or property transferred to or upon the order of the Trustee; nor shall any person be obligated to inquire into the propriety of any transaction or the authority of the Trustee to enter into and consummate the same.

5.29 *Fiduciary Capacity.* All discretionary powers vested in the Trustee of each trust created hereunder and its successors shall be exercised by the Trustee only in a fiduciary capacity.

5.30 *Change in Circumstances.* The Trustee of each trust created hereunder shall incur no liability for any payment or distribution made in good faith and without actual notice or knowledge of a changed condition or status affecting any distributee's interest in the trust.

5.31 *No Court Supervision.* No Trustee of any trust created hereunder shall be required to qualify before, be appointed by, or, in the absence of breach of trust, account to any court; nor shall any Trustee be required to obtain the order or approval of any court in the exercise of any power or discretion granted hereunder.

5.32 *Out-of-State Properties.* If at any time any trust property is situated in a jurisdiction in which a Trustee of any trust created hereunder is unable or unwilling to act, the Trustee of such trust may appoint an Ancillary Trustee (herein so-called) in that Jurisdiction and may confer upon the Ancillary Trustee any rights, powers, discretions, and duties to act solely with respect to those assets as the Trustee, in its discretion, deems necessary or expedient. The Ancillary Trustee shall be answerable to the Trustee for all assets which may be received by the Ancillary Trustee in connection with the administration of that property. The Trustee may pay to the Ancillary Trustee reasonable compensation for its services and may absolve it from any requirement that it furnish bond or other security.

5.33 *Maximum Duration of Trusts.* If not sooner terminated pursuant to the other provisions hereof, each trust created hereunder that has not theretofore vested in such a manner as to avoid application of the rule against perpetuities or any other law restricting the period of time for which property may validly be held in trust shall terminate twenty (20) years and eleven (11) months after the death of the last survivor of the following persons: Settlor and Settlor's descendants living at the date of execution of this agreement by Settlor. However, in no event shall any trust created herein extend beyond the maximum period of time permitted by the law of any jurisdiction which maybe applicable in determining the validity of that trust. The principal and undistributed income of a trust terminated pursuant to this section shall be distributed equally to the persons (or, if applicable, solely to the person) for whose primary benefit, in the Trustee's reasonable judgment, the trust is being held. [Comment: Make sure trust lasts at least as long as the Annuity Period].

5.34 *Permissible Distributions.* With respect to any sum or property, whether income or principal, which is required or permitted to be distributed out of any trust created hereunder to or for the benefit of any individual who at the time is a minor or is under a legal disability, the Trustee of such trust may properly make distributions in any one (1) or more of the following ways as such Trustee, from time to time, in its reasonable discretion, shall deem to be most expedient and in the best interests of such individual; namely, by paying, distributing, or applying such sum or property: (1) to such individual directly, (2) to the legal guardian of such individual with such distribution to be used for the exclusive benefit of such individual, (3) to a custodian for such individual under any Uniform Gifts or Transfers to Minors Act, (4) to the parent, spouse, or other individual having the care and custody of such individual who, as such individual's natural guardian, shall preserve the same for the immediate, exclusive, or ultimate benefit of such individual (or for such individual's estate), but who shall not be obligated to qualify as a legal guardian or account to any probate or like court therefore, (5) to the direct payment of any educational, medical, or other proper expense of such individual (including expenses, such as taxes, repairs, etc., reasonably appropriate to preserving any assets belonging to such individual), (6) to the purchase of stocks, bonds, insurance (the term "purchase" shall include any premium payment), or other properties of any kind, the ownership of which is registered in the sole name of such individual, or (7) to the making of a deposit into a bank, savings and loan association, brokerage, or other similar account in the sole name of such individual.

5.35 *Payments for Direct Benefit.* Even in the absence of minority or disability, distributions made in the manner described in (1) through (7) of subsection A above shall be conclusively deemed to have been made for the direct and exclusive benefit of such individual.

5.36 *Does Not Apply During Annuity Period.* Notwithstanding the foregoing, the provisions of this section shall not apply during the Annuity Period.

5.37 *Powers Cumulative.* Subject to the provisions of Article III, Section 5.10 and Article VII, the Trustee of each trust created hereunder shall have all of the rights, powers, and privileges and be subject to all of the duties, responsibilities, and conditions set forth in the Texas Trust Code (except to the extent those provisions are inconsistent with the provisions of this instrument, in which event the provisions of this instrument shall govern). Except as herein otherwise provided, the powers conferred upon the Trustee shall not be construed to limit any authority conferred by law but shall be in addition thereto.

5.38 *Delegation of Duties Among Trustees.* A Trustee of any trust created hereunder may at any time by an instrument in writing delegate to a Co-Trustee of such trust all or less than all of the powers conferred upon that Trustee, either for a specified time or until the delegation is revoked by a similar instrument.

5.39 *Spendthrift Trust Provision.* Each trust created hereunder is a spendthrift trust. Accordingly, prior to the actual receipt of property by any beneficiary under the terms of the trust, no property (income or principal) distributable under any trust created hereunder shall be subject to anticipation or assignment by any beneficiary, or to attachment by, or interference or control of, any creditor or assignee of any beneficiary, or be taken or reached by any legal or equitable process in satisfaction of any debt or liability of any beneficiary. Any attempted transfer or encumbrance of any interest in that property by any beneficiary hereunder prior to distribution shall be void.

5.40 *Charitable Lead Annuity Trust Savings Clause.* Notwithstanding any provision of this instrument to the contrary, all provisions of this instrument shall be construed and applied so the charitable trust created hereunder shall qualify as a charitable lead annuity trust that provides for a guaranteed annuity amount described under Sections

2055(e)(2)(B) and 2522(c)(2)(B) of the Code. The Trustee (a) shall not take any action or have any power that would disqualify and (b) shall have all additional powers necessary to qualify such trust as a charitable lead annuity trust that provides for a guaranteed annuity amount described under Sections 2055(e)(2)(B) and 2522(c)(2)(B) of the Code.

## ARTICLE 6
### RELEASE OF POWERS
Every power or interest (whether present or future) granted herein or implied by law to a Trustee of each trust created hereunder may be disclaimed, renounced, released, or restricted, in whole or in part, by the holder of that power or interest and may be reduced by the holder of that power or interest so as to reduce or limit the objects or persons in whose favor it would otherwise be exercisable. Any disclaimer, renunciation, release, or restriction of such a power or interest shall be by an acknowledged, written instrument executed by the holder of that power or interest and delivered to a Trustee or in any other manner permitted by law. As used in this section, the words "power" or "interest" include, without limiting the generality of their meanings, any power or interest granted to a Trustee which, by reason of a discretion granted to that Trustee, constitutes a power of appointment.

## ARTICLE 7
### LIMITATION OF POWER
Notwithstanding anything contained herein to the contrary, the following additional prohibitions shall apply:

7.1   *Deal with Trust Estate.* No individual or entity shall be authorized to purchase, exchange, or otherwise deal with or dispose of all or any part of the principal of any trust created hereunder or the income therefrom for less than an adequate consideration in money or money's worth.

7.2   *Vote Securities.* No individual or entity shall be authorized, without the written consent of the Trustee (acting in a fiduciary capacity), to exercise the power to vote or direct the voting of any stock or other securities of any trust created hereunder, or to control the investments or reinvestments of any such trust either by directing investments or by vetoing proposed investments or reinvestments.

7.3   *Insurance.* No assets or funds held in any trust created hereunder shall be applied to the payment of any premium on any policy of insurance on the life of the Settlor, any spouse of the Settlor, a Child, any spouse of a Child, any other descendant of a Child, any spouse of such other descendant, or any other Disqualified Person.

7.4   *No Commutation of Payments.* The commutation of the payment of annuity amounts is absolutely prohibited hereunder, it being the Settlor's express intention and direction that the payment of annuity amounts shall continue during the entire term of the charitable lead annuity trust created hereunder.

## ARTICLE 8
### IRREVOCABILITY OF TRUST
Subject to the provisions of Subsection 3.3P, each trust created hereunder shall be absolutely irrevocable and no person shall have any right or power to amend, modify, or revoke any such trust or any of its terms or provisions.

**ARTICLE 9**

*MISCELLANEOUS PROVISIONS*

   9.1   *Parties Bound.* Each trust created hereunder shall extend to and be binding upon the Trustee, the Settlor, the trust beneficiaries, and upon their respective heirs, executors, administrators, successors, assigns, and personal representatives.

   9.2   *Notices.* All notices provided for by this instrument shall be made in writing, (a) either by actual delivery of the notice to the person entitled thereto, or (b) by the mailing of the notice in the United States mail to the last known address of the person entitled thereto, postage prepaid. The notice shall be deemed to be received in case (a) on the date of its actual receipt by the person entitled thereto, and in case (b) on the date of deposit in the United States mail.

   9.3   *Use of Words.* As used in this instrument, the masculine, feminine, and neuter gender, and the singular or plural of any word each includes the others unless the context indicates otherwise.

   9.4   *Invalid Provisions.* If any provision of this trust instrument is unenforceable, the remaining provisions shall nevertheless be effective.

   9.5   *Titles, Headings, and Captions.* All titles, headings, and captions used in this trust instrument have been included for administrative convenience only and any conflict between the headings and text shall be resolved in favor of the text.

   IN WITNESS WHEREOF, the Settlor and the Trustee have hereunto set their hands in multiple originals on the dates set opposite their names, to be effective on the date signed by the Settlor.

_____              _____
              (Date)                                    [Settlor], Settlor
                                                         [Trustee], Trustee

                                        By:   _____
_____
              (Date)                                    [Trust Officer]
                                                         [Title]


STATE OF TEXAS                  §
                                §
COUNTY OF DALLAS                §


   BEFORE ME, the undersigned authority, on this day personally appeared [Settlor], Settlor, known to me to be the person whose name is subscribed to the foregoing instrument and acknowledged to me that he executed the same for the purposes and consideration therein expressed and in the capacity therein stated.

   GIVEN UNDER MY HAND AND SEAL OF OFFICE this _____ day of _____, 20____.


                                        _____
                                        Notary Public in and for the
                                        State of Texas
                                        My Commission Expires: _____

STATE OF TEXAS       §

§

COUNTY OF DALLAS     §

BEFORE ME, the undersigned authority, on this day personally appeared [Trust Officer], known to me to be the person and officer whose name is subscribed to the foregoing instrument and acknowledged to me that she executed the same for the purposes and consideration therein expressed as the act of [Trustee], a national banking association, and in the capacity therein expressed.

GIVEN under my hand and seal of office this _____ day of _____, 20___.

_____

Notary Public in and for the

State of Texas

My Commission Expires: _____

Schedule A

Attached to and made a part of the [Trust Name] Charitable Trust dated the _____ day of _____, 20___, by and between the undersigned Settlor and Trustee. The Trustee acknowledges receipt from the Settlor of the following-described assets which have been transferred to the Trustee in accordance with the foregoing Trust Agreement.

[Assets]

SIGNED FOR IDENTIFICATION:

_____

(Date)

_____

[Settlor], Settlor

[Trustee], Trustee

_____

(Date)

By: _____

[Trust Officer]

[Title]

## Endnotes

1. Treas. Reg. § 301.7701-1(c).
2. Treas. Reg. §§ 1.170A-6(c)(2)(i)(A), 20.2055-2(e)(2)(vi)(a), 25.2522(c)-3(c)(2)(vi)(a).
3. *Id.*
4. *Id.*
5. Rev. Rul. 85-49, 1985 C.B. 330.
6. I.R.C. § 170(c).
7. *See Estate of Revson,* 5 Ct. Cl. 362 (1984).
8. Treas. Reg. § 53.4942(a)-2(b)(1).
9. 15 F.3d 917 (9th Cir. 1994).
10. I.R.C. § 4945.
11. Rev. Rul. 88-82, 1988-2 C.B. 336.
12. Treas. Reg. §§ 1.170A-6(c)(2)(i)(E), 20.2055-2(e)(2)(vi)(f), 25.2522(c)-3(c)(2)(vi)(f).
13. Treas. Reg. §§ 1.170A-6(c)(2)(i)(C), 20.2055-2(e)(2)(vi)(d), 25.2522(c)-3(c)(2)(vi)(d).
14. I.R.C. § 4947(a)(2).
15. I.R.C. § 4947(b)(2)(A).
16. I.R.C. § 170(f)(2)(B), Treas. Reg. §§ 1.170A-6(c)(2)(i)(A), 20.2055-2(e)(2)(vi)(a), 25.2522(c)-3(c)(2)(vi)(a).
17. Treas. Reg. § 1.170A-6(c)(2)(i)(A).
18. Treas. Reg. §§ 1.170A-6(c)(2)(i)(A), 20.2055-2(e)(2)(vi)(a), 25.2522(c)-3(c)(2)(vi)(a).
19. Treas. Reg. §§ 1.170A-6(c)(2)(i)(A), 20.2055-2(e)(2)(vi)(a), 25.2522(c)-3(c)(2)(vi)(a).
20. *Id.; see also* Priv. Ltr. Rul. 2001-24-029 (March 22, 2001) (smallest annuity amount that would produce a 100-percent federal gift-tax charitable deduction); Priv. Ltr. Rul. 91-28-051 (April 17, 1991); Priv. Ltr. Rul. 91-18-040 (February 7, 1991).
21. I.R.C. §§ 170(f)(2)(B), 2055(e)(2)(B), 2522(c)(2)(B); Treas. Reg. §§ 1.170A-6(c)(2)(ii)(A), 20.2055-2(e)(2)(vii)(a), 25.2522(c)-3(c)(2)(vii)(a).
22. *Id.*
23. Treas. Reg. §§ 1.170A-6(c)(2)(ii)(A), 20.2055-2(e)(2)(vii)(a), 25.2522(c)-3(c)(2)(vii)(a).
24. I.R.C. § 170(f)(2)(B).
25. Treas. Reg. § 1.170A-8(a)(2); I.R.C. § 170(b)(1)(B), I.R.C. § 170(d)(1).
26. I.R.C. § 170(b)(1)(D).
27. I.R.C. § 170(f)(2)(B).
28. Rev. Rul. 88-82, 1988-2 C.B. 336.
29. I.R.C. §§ 2522(a), 2522(c)(2)(B).
30. *Id.*
31. Treas. Reg. § 25.2511-2(c).
32. *See, e.g.,* Priv. Ltr. Rul. 2001-08-032 (November 28, 2000).
33. Treas. Reg. § 25.2503-3(a).
34. I.R.C. §§ 2036, 2038.
35. *See e.g.,* Priv. Ltr. Rul 92-47-024 (August 24, 1992) (holding that the settlor's power to acquire trust assets by substituting property of an equivalent value, without the approval or consent of person acting in a fiduciary capacity, causes the trust to be a grantor trust and permits the grantor to take a federal income tax charitable deduction for the fair market value of the unitrust interest).
36. I.R.C. §§ 2036, 2038.
37. *See Estate of Revson,* 5 Ct. Cl. 362 (1984); Priv. Ltr. Rul. 2001-08-032 (November 28, 2000). Donor of a CLAT was a member of the board of directors of certain "lead" charities. Bylaws of charities were amended to prevent donor from exercising power of charities' assets. The I.R.S. ruled that the gift was complete for federal gift-tax purposes.
38. I.R.C. §§ 2055(a), 2055(e)(2)(B).
39. I.R.C. § 2037(a).
40. I.R.C. § 2055(e)(2)(B); Treas Reg. §§ 20.2055-2(e)(2)(vi)(d), -2(e)(2)(vii)(d).
41. I.R.C. § 7520(a).
42. *See* Priv. Ltr. Rul. 78-08-067 (November 28, 1977).

43. Treas. Reg. §§ 20.2055-2(e)(2)(v)(f), -2(e)(2)(vi)(e).

44. I.R.C. § 642(c).

45. Treas. Reg. § 1.642(c)-1(b).

46. *See e.g.,* Priv. Ltr. Rul. 89-31-029 (May 5, 1989).

47. Rev. Rul. 83-75, 1975-1 C.B. 114; see also Priv. Ltr. Rul. 92-01-029 (October 7, 1991).

48. Treas. Reg. § 1.642(c)-3(b)(2).

49. *Id.*

50. *See also* Priv. Ltr. Rul. 93-48-012 (August 31, 1993), Priv. Ltr. Rul. 92-33-038 (May 20, 1992), Priv. Ltr. Rul. 90-52-013 (September 27, 1990), Priv. Ltr. Rul. 90-48-044 (August 31, 1990).

51. I.R.C. §§ 642(c), 611(b)(3), 167(d); *see also* Treas. Reg. §§ 1.642(e)-1, 1.611-1(c)(4), 1.167(h)-1(b).

52. I.R.C. § 4941.

53. I.R.C. § 4943.

54. I.R.C. § 4944.

55. I.R.C. § 4945.

56. I.R.C. §§ 508(d)(2), 4947(a)(2).

57. I.R.C. § 4947(b)(2)(A).

58. I.R.C. § 681(a).

59. Treas. Reg. §§ 1.170A-6(c)(2)(i)(B)–6(c)(2)(ii)(B).

60. *See, e.g.,* Rev. Rul. 77-300, 1977-2 C.B. 352 (holding that a CLUT payment equal to the lesser of the trust's annual income and 6 percent of the annual fair market value would disqualify the trust).

61. *See* Priv. Ltr. Rul. 82-41-098 (July 19, 1982), Priv. Ltr. Rul. 80-06-029 (November 14, 1979), Priv. Ltr. Rul. 79-46-100 (August 20, 1979), Priv. Ltr. Rul. 79-46-057 (August 16, 1979).

62. I.R.C. §§ 4947(a)(2), 508(e). *See* Priv. Ltr. Rul. 91-28-051 (April 17, 1991) *but see* Priv. Ltr. Rul. 82-41-098 (July 19, 1982) (indicating that the "60-percent-or-less exception" is not applicable unless all income is paid to charity).

63. Rev. Rul. 83-75, 1983-1 C.B. 114.

64. *See* Priv. Ltr. Rul. 80-52-068 (September 30, 1980), Priv. Ltr. Rul. 79-38-099 (June 22, 1979) (suggesting that many of the charitable remainder trusts governing instrument requirements should be used in charitable lead trusts).

65. I.R.C. § 170(c).

66. Treas. Reg. §§ 1.643(a)-5(b), 1.662(b)-2; Rev. Rul. 71-285, 1971-12 C.B. 248; *see also* Priv. Ltr. Rul. 87-28-034 (April 13, 1987); Priv. Ltr. Rul. 80-21-095 (February 28, 1980); Priv. Ltr. Rul. 80-21-143 (February 29, 1980).

67. Treas. Reg. §§ 1.642(c)-3(b)(2), 1.643(a)-5(b).

68. *See* Gen. Couns. Mem. 39,161 (September 30, 1983); Priv. Ltr. Rul. 87-27-072 (February 8, 1987); *see also* Priv. Ltr. Rul. 93-48-012 (August 31, 1993); Priv. Ltr. Rul. 92-33-038 (May 20, 1992); Priv. Ltr. Rul. 90-52-013 (September 27, 1990); Priv. Ltr. Rul. 90-48-044 (August 31, 1990); Priv. Ltr. Rul. 88-28-047 (April 15, 1988); Priv. Ltr. Rul 88-23-022 (March 4, 1988); Priv. Ltr. Rul 89-31-029 (May 5, 1989).

69. I.R.C. §§ 642(c), 611(b)(3), 167(d); *see also* Treas. Reg. §§ 1.642(e)(i), 1.611-1(c)(4), 1.167(h)-1(b).

70. Rev. Rul. 88-27, 1988-1 C.B. 311; *see also* Priv. Ltr. Rul. 80-50-078 (September 19, 1980), Priv. Ltr. 80-43-129 (August 1, 1980) (supplementing Priv. Ltr. Rul. 80-28-087 [April 18, 1980]; Priv. Ltr. Rul. 80-04-054 [October 30, 1979]); Priv. Ltr. Rul. 87-45-002 (July 15, 1987).

71. Treas. Reg. § 1.664-1(a)(7)(ii).

72. *Id.*

73. Treas. Reg. § 1.664-1(a)(7)(iii).

74. *See* I.R.C. §§ 4942, 4945.

75. Rev. Rul. 79-101, 1979-1 C.B. 301; *see also* Priv. Ltr. Rul. 93-31-015 (May 6, 1993); Priv. Ltr. Rul. 81-16-043 (January 21, 1981); Priv. Ltr. Rul. 80-43-077 (July 29, 1980); Priv. Ltr. Rul. 79-30-079 (April 26, 1979).

76. Treas. Reg. §§ 1.170A-6(c)(2)(i)(A), 20.2055-2(e)(2)(vi)(a), 25.2522-3(c)(2)(vi)(a).

77. *See* Priv. Ltr. Rul. 80-34-093 (May 29, 1980); Priv. Ltr. Rul. 80-21-095 (February 28, 1980).

78. Treas. Reg. §§ 1.170A-6(c)(2)(ii)(A), 20.2055-2(e)(vii)(a), 25.2522(c)-3(c)(2)(vii)(a).

79. *See* Priv. Ltr. Rul. 80-52-068 (September 30, 1980), Priv. Ltr. Rul. 80-43-077 (July 29, 1980).

80. I.R.C. § 514.

81. I.R.C. § 514(c)(2)(B).

82. Treas. Reg. § 1.1011-2(a)(3).

83. The available federal income-tax charitable deduction is reduced by $12,000 (from $120,000 to $108,000) because under I.R.C. § 59, a taxpayer's itemized deductions must be reduced by 3 percent of adjusted gross income in excess of $100,000.

84. The ability to use the entire $1,534,008 will be partially limited by the I.R.C. Section 59 reduction in itemized deductions and by the charitable deduction being limited to 30 percent of Geraldine's adjusted gross income.

85. The danger of changing the investment mix is that the trustee, because of poor investment performance, may not be able to generate enough income to make the required annual payment.

86. *See, e.g.,* Rev. Rul. 93-12, 1993-1 C.B. 202, Kerr v. C.I.R., 113 T.C. 449 (1999), Estate of Nowell v. C.I.R., 77 T.C.M. 1239 (CCH 1999).

87. I.R.C. § 7520; Treas. Reg. § 20.7520-1; Treas. Reg. § 25.7520-1.

88. *See* Treas. Reg. §§ 20.7520-1(b)(2), 25.7520-1(b)(2).

89. Treas. Reg. §§ 1.7520-3(b)(3), 25.7520-3(b)(3).

90. *Id.*

# CHAPTER 9

# Annual Exclusion Gifts to Minors

BRADLEY E.S. FOGEL

## I. Introduction

One ubiquitous issue in estate planning is how to provide for young children—frequently, the client's children or grandchildren. If the client is willing to make lifetime gifts for the benefit of the child, then the client can make use of the federal gift-tax annual exclusion to transfer substantial sums to the child free of gift or estate tax. The federal gift-tax annual exclusion allows a donor to give up to $11,000 free of gift tax (as of calendar year 2002) to any individual in any calendar year.[1] If the donor is married and the spouse consents to splitting the gift, then $22,000 may be transferred free of gift tax each year.[2] The exclusion was $10,000 per year from 1982 until 2001.[3] The annual exclusion was indexed for inflation beginning in 1999.[4] In calendar year 2002, the exclusion increased to $11,000 because of such indexing.[5]

The Economic Growth and Tax Relief Reconciliation Act of 2001 (EGTRRA) made substantial changes and introduced great uncertainty into the federal transfer tax system. EGTRRA repealed the federal estate tax for decedents dying after December 31, 2009.[6] However, the changes to the Internal Revenue Code (I.R.C) made by EGTRRA, including repeal of the federal estate tax, are themselves repealed on December 31, 2010.[7] If no change is made, estate tax repeal will be effective only for decedents dying during calendar year 2010. It remains to be seen what form further legislative action will take.

EGTRRA did not repeal the federal gift tax. Instead, the gift tax is retained, even after estate tax repeal, to act as a backstop to the federal income tax. Nor did EGTRRA change the annual exclusion.[8] Of course, if the estate tax is repealed, the transfer tax motivation for making lifetime gifts (the possibility to exclude the assets from the donor's gross estate) is abrogated. On the other hand, it seems likely that many clients may delay estate planning because of their partially erroneous understanding that the estate tax is repealed. This may cause a flurry of estate planning if death becomes imminent. Because the annual exclusion may be used any time before death, it is an effective last-minute estate-planning tool. Thus, even greater use of the annual exclusion may be warranted.

The annual exclusion is a powerful technique. For example, if a donor and spouse transfer $22,000 to a child on the day the child was born and on every subsequent birthday until the child reached age 18, then at 18 the child would have about $750,000, assuming a 7-percent net annual return. At age 21, the child would have about $1 million.

A problem arises because the federal gift-tax annual exclusion is not available if the gift is of a future interest in property.[9] Thus, to make use of the annual exclusion, the donor must give the donee a present interest in property, such as outright owner-ship.[10] This is problematic when the gift is made to a minor. Most donors do not wish to give minors substantial outright gifts. Instead, donors prefer that the gifts be managed for the minor by a custodian or trustee.

This chapter describes three devices that allow such management and the rules associated with them:

(1) gifts to a custodian for a minor under a Uniform Gifts or Transfers to Minors Act;

(2) the 2503(c) trust, which is permitted by I.R.C. Section 2503(c);

(3) trusts with Crummey withdrawal powers (Crummey trusts).

The chapter concludes with a discussion of the generation-skipping transfer-tax issues potentially raised by each of these three techniques.

## II. Minors Acts

All states and the District of Columbia have some form of the Uniform Gifts to Minors Act (UGMA) or Uniform Transfers to Minors Act (UTMA), collectively referred to here as "Minors Acts." Gifts to a custodian under a Minors Act qualify for the federal gift-tax annual exclusion.[11]

### A. History

The forerunner of the Minors Acts was the Act Concerning Gifts of Securities to Minors, sponsored by the New York Stock Exchange and the Association of Stock Exchange firms in the 1950s. In 1965, the National Conference of Commissioners on Uniform State Laws (NCCUSL) adopted UGMA. UGMA broadened the earlier act by allowing custo-dial accounts to cover gifts of money as well as securities. In 1983, NCCUSL updated UGMA and renamed it UTMA. One of the most significant changes that NCCUSL made in UTMA was to expand the scope of property that a custodian could hold in a custodial account to include any property: real or personal, tangible or intangible.[12] In contrast, UGMA allowed custodial accounts only for securities, life insurance policies, annuity contracts, and cash.[13]

Minors Act custodial accounts are, in many ways, statutory trusts. The custodian of the account, who may be any person, including the donor or a trust company, holds property for the benefit of the minor. The custodian has the power to pay any property in the account (custodial property) to or for the benefit of the minor.[14] Neither UGMA nor UTMA distinguishes between income and corpus. Both UGMA and UTMA provide that a court may compel a custodian to distribute custodial property.

### B. Custodians

The class of eligible custodians is relatively broad. The donor, the minor's parents, another adult, or a trust company may act as custodian. If the donor acts as custodian, however, the custodial property will be included in the donor's gross estate for federal estate-tax purposes if the donor dies before termination of the custodianship.[15]

If the custodian has a legal obligation to support the minor (such as the minor's parent), the custodian's gross estate will include the custodial assets, if the custodian dies before termination of the custodianship.[16] Specifically, the Internal Revenue Service (I.R.S.) may argue that the parent, as custodian, has the power to use the custodial property to discharge the parent's legal obligation to support the child.[17] Thus, the parent has a general power of appointment over the custodial property and the property will be included in the parent's gross estate even though the parent is not the donor.[18] To avoid this problem, the donor should select a person other than the parent as custodian. Unfortunately, donors frequently create custodianships without the assistance of a lawyer; thus, the donor may be unaware of the estate tax ramifications of choice of custodian.

## C. Benefits and Disadvantages

An important benefit of a custodial gift is its simplicity. To create a custodial account, the donor simply transfers the property to a custodian under the applicable act.[19] The simplicity of a custodianship, however, has side effects. There is no substantial precedent concerning the legal rights and duties of a custodianship under a Minors Act, which may lead to uncertainty.[20] Moreover, some courts in custodianship cases have refused to draw analogies from the more developed body of precedent regarding trusts and trustees, which exacerbates the dearth of settled rules.[21] This uncertainty makes custodianships inappropriate for substantial gifts or gifts of property that may be more difficult to administer, such as partnership interests.

## D. Income Taxation Issues

A custodial gift indefeasibly vests the custodial property in the minor. In contrast, trust beneficiaries have only a beneficial interest in trust property. One significant result of this indefeasible ownership is that the custodial account is not recognized as a separate taxpayer. Thus, income from the custodial assets is taxed to the minor.[22] If the minor is under age 14, the kiddie-tax rules may tax income at the parent's marginal tax rates.[23]

Taxation of the income directly to the minor has both positive and negative aspects. The custodian does not need to file a separate tax return for the custodial property. By contrast, if a trustee held the property, the trustee would be required to file a federal income tax return in most instances. Further, considering the complexities of trust income taxation, a layperson probably would be unable to properly complete the necessary tax returns for the trust.

On balance, the lack of a requirement for a separate income tax return is a relatively minor benefit of a custodianship. However, if the value of the custodial property is small, the lack of a separate tax return may tip the balance in favor of the custodianship. An added advantage is that federal individual income tax rates are more progressive than the federal fiduciary income tax rates.[24] For this reason, taxing the income directly to the minor, as opposed to taxing it to a fiduciary with higher marginal rates, may provide income tax savings. Whether a custodianship results in income tax savings depends on the income earned, the minor's income tax bracket, the parents' income tax bracket, and the income tax bracket of the hypothetical trust.

### E. Termination and Other Terms of a Minors Act Account

Applicable state statutes set the terms of a custodianship, and donors generally cannot vary those terms. For example, Minors Acts dictate:

- the number of custodians that may serve (one);
- the mechanism of the appointment of successor custodians (the current custodian may appoint a successor);
- whether the custodian is required to give a bond (generally not);
- the permissible investments for the custodial property (generally very broad); and
- compensation to the custodian (UTMA provides for reasonable compensation).

For the most part, NCCUSL and state legislatures have drafted Minors Acts with terms that will be acceptable to most donors. The donor is unlikely to be interested in deviating from the terms of the Minors Act merely for the purpose of, for example, requiring the custodian to give a bond. However, some Minors Act provisions, such as the age at which the custodianship terminates, are likely to be quite distasteful to a donor.

The most significant drawback to a custodianship is that the custodian must distribute the custodial property to the minor at the age designated in the statute. Generally, the custodianship will terminate when the minor turns 18 or 21, depending on the state.[25] When the beneficiary reaches the designated age, the custodian must distribute the custodial assets outright to the beneficiary. If the beneficiary dies before reaching the designated age, the custodian must pay the property to the beneficiary's estate.

Mandatory distribution of custodial property to the minor at age 18 or 21 may be acceptable to a donor if the value of the custodial property at that time is expected to be relatively small. However, if the donor plans to make frequent annual exclusion gifts to a minor via a custodian, the value of custodial property distributed to the beneficiary when he reaches the age of majority may be significant. If so, the donor will likely be interested in a gift-giving device that will ensure that the minor will use such substantial sums to pay for college tuition, rather than for a Ferrari. A partial answer to this concern may be the use of a 2503(c) trust or a Crummey trust.

## III. 2503(c) Trusts

A 2503(c) trust allows a donor to make gifts to a minor in trust and receive the benefit of the federal gift-tax annual exclusion. The I.R.C. imposes three requirements for a 2503(c) trust.

### A. Requirement 1: Discretionary Distributions

First, the trust instrument must permit the trustee to expend trust assets for the benefit of the minor.[26] A trust will meet these requirements if the trust instrument allows the trustee to make wholly discretionary distributions to, or for the benefit of, the minor. If the trust instrument places substantial restrictions on the exercise of the trustee's discretion to make distributions, the trust will not qualify as a 2503(c) trust.[27] For example, in Rev. Rul. 69-345, 1969-1 C.B. 226, the I.R.S. ruled that a trust that required the trustee to consider other assets available to the minor in determining whether to make distributions did not qualify as a 2503(c) trust. The I.R.S. reasoned that the minor's parents as well as the minor had substantial other assets available, making distributions from the trust unlikely in light of the requirement to consider other assets. Some restrictions on the trustee's discretion will pass muster with the I.R.S. In Rev. Rul. 67-270, 1969-2 C.B. 349, the I.R.S. ruled that a 2503(c) trust may limit the trustee's discretion by a standard that is not an objective limitation; thus, standards such as welfare, happiness, or convenience should not run afoul of Section 2503(c). More limited standards, such as health or education, may be too restrictive. At the very least, use of a more restrictive standard engenders substantial risk of dispute with the I.R.S.[28]

## B. Requirement 2: Distribution to the Minor's Estate

The second requirement for a 2503(c) trust is that if the minor dies before age 21 (when the trust is required to terminate), the trustee must pay the trust assets to the minor's estate or as the minor appoints pursuant to a general power of appointment.[29] The purpose is to include the trust assets in the minor's gross estate if minor dies before trust termination.[30] The power of appointment may be exercisable either by will or inter vivos.[31] The trust instrument must place no restrictions of substance on the donee's exercise of the power. Just because a legal disability (such as minority) prevents the donee from exercising the power does not prevent the trust from qualifying as a 2503(c) trust.[32]

## C. Requirement 3: Distribution at Age 21

The third, and most problematic, requirement for a 2503(c) trust is that the principal and income of the trust must pass to the donee upon attaining age 21.[33] Clients may hesitate to transfer substantial assets to a trust if the corpus will be distributed to the beneficiary outright when turning 21. This is similar to the problem discussed in section II.C. for custodianships. When a minor reaches age 21, the assets of a 2503(c) trust may have considerable value. Consequently, the donor will likely be anxious to find a way to prevent the young donee from squandering the windfall.

A common way to address this problem is to provide in the trust instrument that the trust will continue unless the beneficiary elects to terminate it. The regulations expressly provide that a trust will not fail to qualify as a 2503(c) trust merely because "[t]he donee, upon reaching age twenty-one, has the right to extend the term of the trust."[34] The regulations do not address a trust that continues unless the beneficiary elects to terminate it. The difference is significant: Donors will probably not be satisfied with a trust that continues only if the beneficiary so elects. Instead, they generally prefer that the trust terminate only if the beneficiary affirmatively elects to do so.

In Rev. Rul. 74-43, 1974-1 C.B. 285, the I.R.S. revoked an earlier contrary ruling and held that a trust may qualify as a 2503(c) trust if the beneficiary, upon reaching age 21, has the right, even if only for a limited time, to terminate the trust. Similarly, the I.R.S. has privately approved a trust provision allowing a beneficiary to elect to terminate the trust within 60 days of his or her 21st birthday.[35] Drawing an analogy from the context of Crummey powers, discussed in section IV, a termination power that lasts only 30 days may also pass muster.[36]

A 2503(c) trust that gives the beneficiary only a temporary right to terminate the trust is likely to be much more attractive to the donor than a trust that requires outright distribution at age 21. A common concern of clients considering 2503(c) trusts or other devices for making gifts to minors is the risk that the beneficiary may squander the assets if the beneficiary receives the assets outright at an early age. A 2503(c) trust that continues unless the beneficiary elects to terminate it significantly alleviates that risk.

Even if the trust principal is substantial, it is likely that the donor and other members of the donee's family members will be able to exert subtle (or not-so-subtle) familial pressure on the beneficiary to prevent him or her from exercising the withdrawal power. Moreover, considering that the beneficiary must take the initiative and affirmatively act to terminate the trust, human nature and the laws of inertia make it likely that the beneficiary would allow the trust to continue beyond age 21.

Notwithstanding, the donor should be informed that for a period (probably at least 30 days) after the beneficiary reaches age 21, the beneficiary must have an unfettered opportunity to terminate the trust. The donor may decide to run that risk, assuming that the beneficiary will be unlikely to exercise this power, thus allowing annual exclusion gifts to remain in trust until the donee reaches a more suitable age. Nevertheless, the donor must realize that, if the trust assets are substantial, it may be difficult to persuade the beneficiary not to exercise the termination power. This is particularly true if there is family disharmony at the time. Further, the donor must decide whether to give the beneficiary a termination power when the donor establishes the trust, which may be when the donee is quite young. For these reasons, many donors are uncomfortable with the beneficiary having the right, upon turning age 21, to terminate the trust and receive a potentially substantial amount of assets outright.

No published authority requires a trustee to notify the beneficiary of his or her power to terminate the trust. If the trustee does not so notify the beneficiary, however, the I.R.S. may argue that the beneficiary's power of termination was illusory. It seems likely that the I.R.S. will take this position, considering that it takes an analogous position in the Crummey withdrawal power context.[37] Thus, the trust would not qualify as a 2503(c) trust and the I.R.S. may seek to deny the annual exclusion for gifts to the trust. Considering this potential cost, the trustee should provide the beneficiary with notice of the right to terminate the trust when the beneficiary attains age 21.

### D. Trustees

Transfer tax considerations tend to restrict the choice of trustee(s) of a 2503(c) trust in a manner similar to the restrictions on the choice of a custodian of a Minors Act account. If the donor serves as trustee of a 2503(c) trust and dies before termination of the trust, the donor's gross estate will include the trust assets because of the donor's ability to make discretionary distributions of trust assets.[38] Further, the I.R.S. will likely argue that the property should be included in the trustee's gross estate if the trustee is a parent or other individual with a legal obligation to support the beneficiary.[39] Thus, neither the parent of the beneficiary nor the donor should serve as trustee of a 2503(c) trust. The minor's parent could, however, serve as cotrustee, without adverse transfer-tax consequences, provided that the trust instrument gives the nonparent trustee the sole power to make distributions that might satisfy the parent's legal obligation. This option is not available in the context of custodianships since only one custodian may act and the custodian's power is delineated by the relevant Minors Act.

## IV. Crummey Trusts

### A. Crummey Powers

Gifts to a trust other than a 2503(c) trust generally do not qualify in full for the federal gift-tax annual exclusion.[40] However, if the beneficiary has a presently exercisable right to withdraw the property transferred to the trust, the I.R.S. will consider the gift to the trust to be a gift of a present interest and will allow an annual exclusion for the gift. These withdrawal powers are known as Crummey powers based on the seminal Ninth Circuit case that approved the use of a withdrawal power held by a minor to create a present interest that qualified for the annual exclusion.[41]

A Crummey power works simply. After a donor makes a gift to the trust, the beneficiary has a period of time, generally at least 30 days, to withdraw the assets of the trust with a value equal to the gift.[42] Although a shorter time might pass muster with the I.R.S.,[43] little seems to be gained. If the beneficiary does not withdraw the gift within the allotted time, the Crummey power lapses and the gift stays in the trust. The 30-day window makes the gift to the trust a present interest for gift-tax purposes, allowing the donor to take advantage of the federal gift-tax annual exclusion.

An important advantage of Crummey trusts over 2503(c) trusts or Minors Act accounts is their versatility. After the Crummey power lapses, the trust may continue as long as the donor wishes, subject only to the rule against perpetuities, if applicable. The donor also has great flexibility regarding the other terms of the trust. For example, the trust could provide that before age 35 the trustee may make distributions only for the beneficiary's school tuition. This flexibility comes at the cost of added administrative complexity of Crummey trusts—as compared to 2503(c) trusts or Minors Act accounts.

## B. Transfer-Tax Consequences to Power-Holder

If the donor is married, he or she may transfer up to $22,000 per beneficiary to the Crummey trust each year free of gift tax, provided the donor's spouse elects to split gifts with the donor on a timely filed federal gift-tax return.[44] In most cases, the beneficiaries will not exercise Crummey powers and will allow them to lapse. If a power to withdraw more than $5,000 (or 5 percent of the trust principal, if greater) lapses, then the excess is deemed a taxable gift made by the beneficiary to the other beneficiaries of the trust.[45] For example, if a beneficiary allows a $22,000 Crummey withdrawal power to lapse, he or she has likely made a $17,000 taxable gift.

Some lawyers simply ignore the potential taxable gift resulting from the lapse of a Crummey power. They reason that, although the taxable gift will use some of the beneficiary's unified credit,[46] gift and estate taxes are unlikely to become a serious issue for the beneficiary for many years. Thus, the argument goes, it is unwise to plan for the estate tax owed by the beneficiary's estate when it is possible that there may be no (or a very different) estate tax payable at that time. Further, if the minor beneficiary dies at a relatively young age, it is unlikely that the estate would owe any estate tax because of the unified credit. Moreover, the increases in the unified credit made by EGTRRA (that is, an exclusion of $3.5 million as of 2009), if made permanent, would render the transfer tax irrelevant for even more taxpayers.[47]

Rather than ignoring the issue, another approach is to prepare the trust instrument so that no person other than the particular beneficiary has an interest in the trust. Accordingly, when the beneficiary allows a Crummey power to lapse, no taxable gift results for want of a donee.[48] Similarly, if the beneficiary is given either a general or a limited power of appointment over the trust assets, the lapse of the withdrawal power will not be a completed gift.[49] Thus, lapse of the power would not be a taxable gift.

Even a Crummey trust drafted so that only a single beneficiary has an interest still gives the donor substantially more leeway to choose the terms than either a custodianship or a 2503(c) trust. Specifically, the requirement that the assets held in a 2503(c) trust be paid to the beneficiary's estate (if he or she dies before termination of a trust) or be expended for beneficiary's benefit during his or her lifetime, would alone eliminate any other party's interest in a Crummey trust. Thus, lapse of a Crummey power over such a trust bears no adverse gift consequences to the beneficiary. The Crummey trust has the added advantage of flexibility because it need not meet the other requirements of Section 2503(c).

If the potential taxable lapse of a Crummey power does not concern the donor (for example, if no gifts over $5,000 per beneficiary are planned), then a Crummey trust with a group of beneficiaries may be attractive. In this case, a donor may be able to, for example, create one Crummey trust for all of the donor's nieces and nephews, children, or grandchildren (subject to the generation-skipping transfer-tax issues discussed below). In contrast, if the donor used a 2503(c) trust, he or she would have to establish a separate trust for each beneficiary. The I.R.S. has privately ruled that in order to obtain the annual exclusion, the Crummey power-holder must have a substantial interest in the trust.[50] The courts have repeatedly rejected this position.[51] Nonetheless, giving Crummey powers to individuals with little or no interest in the trust engenders a substantial risk of litigation with the I.R.S.

## C. Income Taxation

For income tax purposes, the assets subject to a Crummey power are treated as owned by the power-holder since the power-holder has the power to vest these assets in him- or herself.[52] Once the power lapses, the (former) power-holder will continue to be taxed as the owner, assuming sufficient control over or access to trust assets.[53]

It is, however, possible to make a Crummey trust a grantor trust. This is done by giving the grantor a power or right listed in I.R.C. Sections 673 through 677. For example, the donor could be given the power to substitute trust assets with other assets of equal value.[54] Further, if the trust could be treated as owned by the power-holder or the donor, Section 678(b) provides that it will be treated as being owned only by the donor. Thus, for example, if the trustee uses trust income to pay the premiums on life insurance on the donor's life, then the trust will be taxed to the donor, even if the power-holder has powers that would otherwise make the trust taxable to the power-holder.[55]

During 2010 (between estate tax repeal and the sunset of EGTRRA), the federal gift tax is explicitly tied to the income taxation of trusts. Specifically, a transfer in trust is a "transfer of property by gift" unless the trust is treated as owned by the donor for income tax purposes, that is, a grantor trust.[56] Even after estate tax repeal, it should be possible to make effective use of Crummey powers. If the trust is treated as owned by the donor, rather than the power-holder, for income tax purposes, then transfers to it will not be taxed as gifts, regardless of whether the transfers qualify for the annual exclusion.[57] If the trust is not a grantor trust with respect to the donor, however, then transfer of a present interest to it should qualify for the annual exclusion.[58] Such a present interest could be obtained through the use of a Crummey power.

## D. Crummey Notices

The most significant drawback of a Crummey trust, compared to a 2503(c) trust or a Minors Act account, is its administrative complexity. An example is the requirement of Crummey notices. The I.R.S. requires that every time a donor makes a gift to a Crummey trust, the trustee must notify each power-holder of the gift and of the power-holder's right to withdraw his or her proportionate share of the gift from the trust.[59]

Courts have been more lax than the I.R.S. in requiring a trustee to send Crummey notices. For example, in *Crummey*, the court noted that it was "likely" that some, if not all, of the beneficiaries had no knowledge of their withdrawal rights or even when contributions were made to the trust.[60] The court nevertheless allowed the annual exclusions claimed by the taxpayer. Moreover, in *Holland v. Commissioner*, the Tax Court minimized the importance of Crummey notices and held, in any event, that written notice was unnecessary because the beneficiaries had actual notice of their power. Rulings by the I.R.S. leave little doubt that it believes the law requires a trustee to notify Crummey power-holders of their powers for the donor to receive an annual exclusion for the gift.[61]

A trustee typically sends Crummey notices to a beneficiary whenever a donor makes a gift to the trust. If the beneficiary is a minor, the trustee must send the notice to the minor's legally appointed guardian or to the minor's parents.[62] If the minor's guardian is also the trustee, the I.R.S. has privately ruled that the trustee need not self-notify of the minor's withdrawal right.[63]

If a Crummey notice is required, the beneficiary (or the guardian) may be asked to acknowledge receipt of the notice in writing. The trustee or the lawyer should retain these acknowledgments. The acknowledgments are important because the I.R.S., when auditing the donor's estate tax return, may seek proof that the notices were sent and, thus, that the annual exclusions were properly allowed.

The acknowledgments should be carefully drafted to prevent the beneficiary from releasing the withdrawal power by expressly declining to exercise it. Instead, the beneficiary should allow the power to lapse. If the beneficiary releases the power, then the $5,000 or 5-percent exclusion is not available and the entire unwithdrawn amount may be deemed a taxable gift by the beneficiary.[64]

## E. Other Complications: The Cost of Flexibility

The requirement that the trustee send Crummey notices to the beneficiaries is a complication of Crummey trusts not found in either Minors Act accounts or 2503(c) trusts. However, the comparative flexibility of the Crummey trust makes up for the added complexity. Suppose, for example, that a donor wishes to create a trust for the benefit of her grandchild and the donor is anxious for the child's parent to be sole trustee. As discussed above, the I.R.S. would likely argue that such a 2503(c) trust or Minors Act account would be included in the parent's estate if the parent were to die before termination of the trust or custodianship.[65] In contrast, a lawyer can prepare a Crummey trust to prevent the trustee/parent from using trust assets to discharge the parent's legal obligation of support. Thus, the assets will not be included in the trustee/parent's gross estate. There is the added advantage that the I.R.S. will not require the trustee/parent to send Crummey notices to herself.[66]

One minor downside arises if the trustee/parent dies during the window during which the power could be exercised. In this event, the I.R.S. will likely argue that the amount the beneficiary could have withdrawn is included in the trustee/parent's gross estate because the trustee/parent had the power to withdraw the gift and use it to satisfy her legal obligation of support.[67] Similarly, if the Crummey power-holder dies during the window when the power can be exercised, the property that could have been withdrawn will be included in her gross estate.[68] The lawyer cannot easily draft to avoid this possible inclusion because, to obtain the annual exclusion, the power to withdraw must be unlimited. The importance of this possible inclusion is limited, as the maximum amount included is $22,000 (if the donor is married and her spouse elects to split gifts). Furthermore, this is an issue only if the power-holder (or the trustee/parent of the power-holder) dies within the period of time for the exercise of the Crummey power, frequently 30 days following the gift.[69]

A final drawback of Crummey trusts is that for some period of time, frequently 30 days, after a donor makes a gift to the trust, the beneficiary has a power to withdraw his or her share of the gift. If the beneficiary is a minor, then the beneficiary's court-appointed guardian or parent should have the ability to exercise the power on the child's behalf.[70] In some situations, the donor may be uncomfortable giving the beneficiary (or the beneficiary's guardian) the right to withdraw contributions made to the trust. In this case, the client should not use a Crummey trust. Nevertheless, in the Crummey-trust context, the withdrawal power covers only the gift made to the trust at that time, which should never exceed the possible annual exclusion. In contrast, the withdrawal power in a 2503(c) trust allows the beneficiary to withdraw all of the assets held in the trust when he or she attains age 21.

Beneficiaries or their guardians frequently realize that the donor would prefer that the beneficiary not exercise the Crummey power—and in practice, trust beneficiaries rarely exercise their Crummey powers. The donor should not express the wish that the donees not exercise the Crummey power to the beneficiaries, especially in writing. The I.R.S. could use such a request to argue that the Crummey power was illusory and deny the annual exclusion for the gifts subject to the power.

## V. Generation-Skipping Transfer-Tax Issues

### A. Generation-Skipping Transfers

The federal generation-skipping transfer tax is distinct from the unified estate and gift tax. As a gross oversimplification, the generation-skipping transfer tax is imposed on transfers (either outright or in trust) to skip-persons. The donor's grandchildren and more remote descendants (and others) are skip-persons.[71] Similarly, a trust is a skip-person if all of the current beneficiaries are skip-persons.[72] Thus, for example, a trust exclusively for the benefit of the donor's several grandchildren would be a skip-person.

A transfer from the donor to a skip-person is a direct skip and is subject to the generation-skipping transfer tax.[73] Similarly, a transfer from a trust to a skip-person is a taxable distribution that is subject to the tax.[74] Lastly, a taxable termination occurs if some event (such as the death of a trust beneficiary) causes a trust to suddenly become a skip-person.[75]

The generation-skipping transfer tax is imposed at a flat rate equal to the highest marginal estate-tax rate.[76] Thus, the generation-skipping transfer-tax rate for 2002 is 50 percent.[77]

### B. Annual Exclusion Gifts as Generation-Skipping Transfers

If the beneficiary of an annual exclusion gift is the donor's grandchild (or other skip-person), the lawyer must be mindful of the potential generation-skipping transfer tax issues, in addition to ensuring that the gift is exempt from federal gift and estate tax.

For the most part, a gift that qualifies for the federal gift-tax annual exclusion has a zero inclusion ratio and is, therefore, exempt from the generation-skipping transfer tax.[78] If, however, the gift is made in trust, Section 2642(e)(2) provides that the gift will be generation-skipping transfer-tax exempt only if: (1) no trust income or principal may be paid to anyone other than the particular beneficiary, and (2) the trust assets will be included in the beneficiary's gross estate, if the beneficiary dies before termination of the trust.

### C. Minors Act Accounts and 2503(c) Trusts

Making an analogy of a Minors Act account to a trust, the account would meet the requirements of Section 2642(c)(2) because no distributions may be made to anyone other than the minor and, if the minor dies before reaching 21, the custodian must distribute property to the beneficiary's estate. Similarly, a 2503(c) trust will meet the requirements of Section 2642(c)(2) and will, therefore, be generation-skipping transfer-tax exempt.[79]

### D. Crummey Trusts

The issue is more difficult in the context of Crummey trusts. Specifically, a typical Crummey trust may not meet the requirements of Section 2642(c)(2). Thus, a gift to such a trust might be subject to the generation-skipping transfer tax, even though it is covered by the annual exclusion.

As mentioned, a lawyer can draft a Crummey trust to prevent the beneficiary's failure to exercise a $22,000 withdrawal power from being a taxable gift. In such a Crummey trust, only one beneficiary receives distributions from the trust, and the trust assets may be paid to the beneficiary's estate (or otherwise included in the beneficiary's gross estate) if he or she dies before termination of the trust. Fortunately, similar provisions would meet the requirements of Section 2642(c)(2). Thus, transfers to such a trust that are covered by the federal gift-tax annual exclusion will also be generation-skipping transfer-tax exempt.[80]

If the trust has more than one beneficiary or if the assets will not be included in the beneficiary's estate, then gifts to the trust will not be automatically exempt from generation-skipping transfer tax. If gifts to a Crummey trust are not automatically generation-skipping transfer tax exempt, then it may be wise to allocate a portion of the donor's generation-skipping transfer-tax exemption[81] to the trust, if grandchildren or other skip-persons are beneficiaries. This may not be a significant drawback if the client has no plans to otherwise make use of the generation-skipping transfer exemption and is willing to take the risk that no such plans will develop in the future. If substantial gifts that are potentially subject to generation-skipping transfer tax are likely, then the lawyer and the client must consider whether this is an efficient use of the generation-skipping transfer exemption.

## VI. Conclusion

The three methods discussed in this chapter allow a donor to make federal gift-tax-free transfers to a minor beneficiary. In addition, gifts to a Minors Act custodianship or a 2503(c) trust will always be generation-skipping transfer-tax exempt. Further, a lawyer can draft a Crummey trust so that gifts to it will be exempt from the generation-skipping transfer tax without the use of the donor's generation-skipping transfer exemption.

To some extent, these three methods fall on a spectrum. Minors Acts accounts are, administratively, the simplest of the three, but the donor has the least control over the terms governing the disposition of the property after she makes the gift. Crummey trusts, at the other end of the spectrum, allow far greater flexibility for the trust terms. With this flexibility comes greater administrative burdens, including the requirement of sending Crummey notices. Between Minors Act accounts and Crummey trusts, 2503(c) trusts allow for greater flexibility than custodianships, although not as much as Crummey trusts. Further, 2503(c) trusts are administratively simpler than Crummey trusts, although not as straightforward as Minors Act accounts.

If a donor plans to make large annual exclusion gifts to minors, the main concern will be the possibility that the minor will receive the assets outright at what the donor feels is an inappropriate age. In that case, a Minors Act account, which requires distribution of the custodial property to the minor at age 18 or 21, will be inappropriate. A 2503(c) trust that continues unless the beneficiary affirmatively elects to terminate it at age 21 may satisfy the donor. However, the donor must be made aware of the potential for the beneficiary to terminate the trust. Crummey trusts allow the donor to delay outright distribution until the beneficiary reaches a more suitable age, but the trust instrument must give the beneficiary (or his or her guardian) the temporary power to withdraw any contribution made to the trust, and the trustee must take on the added administrative difficulties in administering these powers.

Before employing any of these methods, the lawyer should discuss the disadvantages and advantages of each with the client. This discussion should involve the amount and type of property that the client plans to give because this will directly affect the selection. Regardless of the method chosen, the lawyer should not overlook the use of the federal gift-tax annual exclusion to make transfer-tax-free gifts for the benefit of a minor beneficiary. Use of any of these methods allows the client to make very substantial gifts free of federal gift tax and remove the amount of these gifts (and any future appreciation on them) from the client's estate. This can result in an enormous transfer tax savings.

## Endnotes

1. I.R.C. § 2503(b); Rev. Proc. 2001-59.
2. I.R.C. § 2513; Rev. Proc. 2001-59.
3. Pub. L. No. 97-34 § 441(a).
4. I.R.C. § 2503(b)(2).
5. Rev. Proc. 2001-59.
6. I.R.C. § 2210(a).
7. EGTRRA § 901.
8. Cf. I.R.C. § 2511(c). As discussed in more detail infra, EGTRRA tied the availability of the annual exclusion for gifts in trust to the income tax treatment of the trust. Id.
9. I.R.C. § 2503(b).
10. Treas. Reg. § 25.2503-3(b).
11. Rev. Rul. 59-357, 1959-2 C.B. 212; Rev. Rul. 56-86, 1956-1 C.B. 449.
12. UTMA § 1.
13. UGMA § 1(e).
14. UGMA § 4(d); UTMA § 14(a).
15. I.R.C. §§ 2036(a)(2), 2038; Rev. Rul. 70-348, 1970-2 C.B 193.
16. Gen. Couns. Mem. 37,840.
17. Treas. Reg. § 20.2041-1(c)(1).
18. I.R.C. § 2041.

19. UGMA § 2; UTMA § 9.

20. *See, e.g., In re* Levy, 412 N.Y.S.2d 285, 287 (Surr. Ct. Nassau Cty. 1978) (noting that the "paucity of cases" is indicative of the success of UGMA in creating a simple method for making gifts to minors).

21. *Id.*

22. Rev. Rul. 56-484, 1956-2 C.B. 23.

23. I.R.C. § 1(g).

24. I.R.C. § 1.

25. UGMA § 4(d); UTMA § 20; D.C. Stat. § 21-230 (age 18); La. R.S. 9:770 (age 18); N.Y. Est. Powers & Trusts Law §§ 7-6.20, 7-6.21 (generally age 21; age 18 under some circumstances) Pa. Stat. Ann. § 5320 (age 21). California's version of UTMA is unusual in that it allows the donor to specify that the custodian will hold the property until the beneficiary reaches age 25. Cal. Prob. Code § 3920.5.

26. I.R.C. § 2503(c)(1).

27. Treas. Reg. § 25.2503-4(b)(1).

28. *See, e.g.,* United States v. Mueller, 1969 WL 20748.

29. I.R.C. § 2503(c)(2)(B).

30. I.R.C. §§ 2033, 2041.

31. Treas. Reg. § 25.2503-4(b).

32. Treas. Reg. § 25.2503-4(b).

33. I.R.C. § 2503(c)(2)(A).

34. Treas. Reg. § 25.2503-4(b)(2).

35. Priv. Ltr. Rul. 8817037; *see also* Priv. Ltr. Rul. 8334071 (90 days).

36. Priv. Ltr. Rul. 9232013; Priv. Ltr. Rul. 9030005; Priv. Ltr. Rul. 8922062.

37. Rev. Rul. 81-7, 1981-1 C.B. 474; TAM 9532001.

38. I.R.C. §§ 2036, 2038; Rev. Rul. 59-357, 1959-2 C.B. 212.

39. I.R.C. § 2041; Treas. Reg. § 20.2041-1(c)(1).

40. Treas. Reg. § 25.2503-3(a).

41. Crummey v. Commissioner, 397 F.2d 82 (9th Cir. 1968).

42. *See, e.g.,* Priv. Ltr. Rul. 9232013, Priv. Ltr. Rul. 9030005, Priv. Ltr. Rul. 8922062.

43. Priv. Ltr. Rul. 8111123; Priv. Ltr. Rul. 7922107.

44. I.R.C. § 2513; Rev. Proc. 2001-59.

45. I.R.C. § 2514(e).

46. The unified credit, also known as the applicable exclusion amount, allows an individual to give away $1 million either during life or at death, as of calendar year 2002. I.R.C. § 2010.

47. I.R.C. § 2010(c); E.G.T.R.R.A. § 901.

48. Priv. Ltr. Rul. 8142061.

49. Priv. Ltr. Rul. 8517052; Priv. Ltr. Rul. 8229097.

50. Tech. Adv. Mem. 97-31-004; Tech. Adv. Mem. 96-28-004.

51. Kohlsaat, 73 T.C.M. 2732 (1997); Cristofani, 97 T.C. 74 (1991); see also Bradley E.S. Fogel, *The Emperor Does Not Need Clothes: The Expanding Use of "Naked" Crummey Withdrawal Powers to Obtain the Federal Gift Tax Annual Exclusion,* 72 TUL. L. REV. 555 (1998).

52. I.R.C. § 678(a)(1).

53. I.R.C. §§ 678(a)(2), 677, 674.

54. I.R.C. § 675(4). This power, or a myriad of others, would make the trust a grantor trust for income tax purposes. Of course, the lawyer must ensure that the power retained by the donor will not cause the trust to be included in her gross estate. I.R.C. §§ 2036-2038.

55. I.R.C. § 678(b); Priv. Ltr. Rul. 9141027.

56. I.R.C. § 2511(c).

I.R.C. § 2511(c), as originally enacted by EGTRRA, provided that a transfer in trust would be "a taxable gift under Section 2503" unless the trust was a grantor trust with respect to the donor. EGTRRA § 511(e).

In March 2002, "technical corrections" to Section 2511(c) changed that section to provide that a transfer in trust was a "transfer of property by gift" unless the trust is a grantor trust. Pub. L. 107-147, § 411(g) (March 9, 2002). Thus, although not beyond dispute, it seems that a transfer to a grantor trust is not treated as a gift (and is thus not taxable), regardless of whether it is a present interest. If the trust is not a grantor trust with respect to the donor, however, then transfers to it are treated as gifts. Presumably, such gifts could be offset by annual exclusions obtained through the use of Crummey powers. I.R.C. § 2503(b).

57. I.R.C. § 2511(c).

58. I.R.C. §§ 2503(b), 2511(c).

59. Rev. Rul. 81-7, 1981-1 C.B. 474; Tech. Adv. Mem. 95-32-001.

60. 397 F.2d at 88.

61. Rev. Rul. 81-7, 1981-1 C.B. 474; Tech. Adv. Mem. 95-32-001.

62. Priv. Ltr. Rul. 8143045.

63. Tech. Adv. Mem. 90-30-005.

64. I.R.C. § 2514(e).

65. Gen. Counsel Memo. 37840.

66. TAM 9030005.

67. I.R.C. § 2041.

68. *Id.*

69. This may also be an issue if the power exceeds the five-and-five limitation of Section 2514 and the power-holder has a continuing interest in or power over the trust assets. I.R.C. § 2041(a)(2).

70. Priv. Ltr. Rul. 8143045.

71. I.R.C. §§ 2613, 2651.

72. I.R.C. §§ 2613(a)(2), 2652(c).

A trust will also be a skip-person if there are no current beneficiaries and no distributors to non-skip-persons are ever possible. I.R.C. §§ 2613(a)(2)(B), 2652(c). Thus, for example, a trust that accumulates income for a number of years for eventual distribution to the donor's grandchildren would be a skip-person.

73. I.R.C. §§ 2611(a)(3), 2612(c).

74. I.R.C. §§ 2611(a)(1), 2612(b).

However, a transfer from a trust to a skip-person is a direct skip if the transfer is also subject to estate or gift tax at the time of the transfer. I.R.C. § 2612(b), 2612(c). Thus, for example, a transfer from a revocable trust to a skip-person is a direct skip.

75. I.R.C. §§ 2611(a)(2), 2612(a).

76. I.R.C. § 2614(a)(1).

77. I.R.C. § 2001(c).

78. I.R.C. § 2642(c)(1).

79. Priv. Ltr. Rul. 8334071.

80. I.R.C. § 2642(c)(2).

81. Every individual has a generation-skipping transfer-tax exemption that may be allocated, either during life or at death, to wholly or partially exempt transfers from the tax. Between 2002 and 2009 the generation-skipping transfer-tax exemption tracks the applicable credit amount in its slow progression from $1 million to $3.5 million. I.R.C. § 2631(c). Under current law, the generation-skipping transfer tax is repealed during 2010 only to be resurrected in 2011. I.R.C. § 2664; EGTRRA § 901. In 2011, the exemption will fall back to $1 million, plus an adjustment for inflation. I.R.C. § 2631.

# CHAPTER 10

# Estate Planning with Life Insurance Trusts

BRADLEY E.S. FOGEL

## I. Introduction

Life insurance trusts are the second-most-common estate-planning device, after bypass trusts. Moreover, because the transfer tax savings engendered by life insurance trusts are not limited by the unified credit, the potential savings are similarly unlimited. Indeed, by excluding the policy proceeds from the insured's gross estate, a life insurance trust can double the amount of policy proceeds enjoyed by the beneficiaries.[1]

Transfer tax savings are clearly the primary reason for creating life insurance trusts. There are, however, nontax advantages of holding a life insurance policy in trust. For example, the proceeds from life insurance held in a life insurance trust are generally not subject to a surviving spouse's right of election. In contrast, in some states and under the Uniform Probate Code, life insurance held by the decedent at the time of death is subject to the surviving spouse's right of election.[2] Other nontax advantages of having life insurance policy proceeds paid to a trust include flexibility, professional management, and spendthrift protection from the beneficiaries' creditors.

There are some disadvantages to setting up a life insurance trust. The primary disadvantage is that, in order to take advantage of the possible transfer tax benefits, the trust must be irrevocable. Thus, the insured must irrevocably designate the beneficiaries of the trust and, thereby, the policy. Moreover, the insured will need to part with the economic benefits in the policy, such as access to its cash-surrender value.[3] Additional disadvantages include the cost of setting up and the moderate complexity of maintaining a life insurance trust. Although both client and lawyer must consider these disadvantages, for many clients they pale in comparison to the possible transfer tax savings obtainable through an irrevocable life insurance trust.

Since the prime advantage of life insurance trusts is their transfer tax savings, their utility is quite sensitive to changes in the estate tax. The Economic Growth and Tax Relief Reconciliation Act of 2001 (EGTRRA) repealed the estate tax for decedents dying after December 31, 2009.[4] This repeal is itself repealed, and the estate tax thus reinstated, on December 31, 2010.[5] Legislative action to prevent this one-year repeal of the estate tax seems likely. It is, of course, unclear whether this legislative action will permanently repeal the federal estate tax, eliminate the temporary repeal, or follow another path.

Except for the one year that the estate tax is repealed (calendar year 2010), EGTRRA has made few changes that directly affect life insurance trusts. EGTRRA has, however, increased the applicable exclusion amount—the amount that can pass through an estate free of estate tax. The applicable exclusion amount is $1 million for 2002.[6] It slowly increases to $3.5 million in 2009 only to fall back to $1 million in 2011 when the estate tax is resurrected. The increase in the exclusion may make transfer tax planning irrelevant for some clients who would otherwise consider creating a life insurance trust. Because the increased exclusion is temporary, it seems wise to plan as if the exclusion amount were $1 million, unless an increase in the applicable exclusion amount is made permanent.

## II. Estate Taxation at the Death of the Insured

### A. Incidents of Ownership

Life insurance is included in the insured's gross estate if he or she possessed "incidents of ownership" in the policy at the time of death.[7] "Incidents of ownership" is a broad term that includes not only outright ownership of the life insurance policy, but also (for example) the right to change the beneficiary of the policy and the right to borrow against the policy or to use it as collateral for a loan.[8] To prevent the proceeds from a policy held by a life insurance trust from being included in the insured's estate, the trust must be drafted so that the insured has none of these powers in the policy, either individually or as trustee.[9] Therefore, the insured's control over, and rights to the economic benefit from, a policy held by a life insurance trust is greatly limited. For example, the insured may not have the power to designate the beneficiaries of the policy and should not be a trustee of his or her own life insurance trust.

### B. Payable to Executor

If the proceeds from a life insurance policy on the decedent's life are receivable by the executor of the decedent's estate, they will be included in the gross estate regardless of whether decedent held any incidents of ownership in the policy.[10] Even if the policy proceeds are not payable directly to the executor, they will be included in the decedent's gross estate if they are subject to a legally binding obligation to pay estate obligations.[11]

At first blush, this limitation seems to severely restrict the possible uses of life insurance held by a life insurance trust. This limitation can be circumvented, however, if the trust agreement provides that policy proceeds may be used for estate obligations. Specifically, the trustee should be given the discretionary power, instead of a legally binding obligation, to use policy proceeds to pay estate obligations, such as the estate tax.[12] This discretionary power will not by itself cause the policy proceeds to be included in the insured's gross estate. The policy proceeds actually paid pursuant to this discretionary authority may be included in the decedent's gross estate. Therefore, whenever possible, policy proceeds should be used to provide estate liquidity through loans made by the trust to the estate or the purchase by the trust of estate assets. Both the decedent's will and the life insurance trust should permit these transactions.

### C. Creation of the Trust and the Three-Year Rule

Once the insured has created the trust, the trustee should apply for the life insurance policy on the client's life. If the client, rather than the trustee, obtains the policy and then transfers it to the trustee, the policy proceeds will be included in the insured's gross estate if the insured does not survive the transfer by at least three years.[13]

Although it is advantageous to have the trustee purchase the policy, it will not be always be possible to do so. For example, the insured may own a policy at the time the trust is created. While one can avoid the reach of the three-year rule (Internal Revenue Code (I.R.C.) Section 2035) by surrendering the existing policy and having the trustee obtain a new policy,[14] this may not be economically efficient, or even possible, depending on the insured's health. In this case, the existing policy may be transferred to the trust in the hope that the insured will survive the transfer by the requisite three years.

The three-year rule does not apply to transfers for adequate and full consideration.[15] Thus, it is possible to avoid its reach if the insured sells the life insurance policy to a life insurance trust or to a beneficiary.[16] Although theoretically possible, this action is rife with hazards. Specifically, the value of the policy may be substantial, especially if the insured is ill. Moreover, the sale would be a transfer of the policy for value, which would engender adverse income tax consequences.[17] Further, if the insured created a trust, funded the trust, and then sold the policy to the trust, it seems possible that the transaction could be attacked as a step transaction.

### 1. Transfer of an Existing Policy

If an existing policy is transferred to a life insurance trust without adequate consideration, that transfer is a gift. The amount of the gift is the fair market value of the policy, which is the sale price of a comparable policy.[18] For example, the fair market value of a newly purchased policy is generally its purchase price.[19]

If sufficiently similar policies are not available, then it will be impossible to determine the purchase price of a comparable policy. In this case, the value of the policy is its interpolated terminal reserve plus the portion of the last-paid premium that covers the period subsequent to the gift.[20] In a nutshell, the interpolated terminal reserve of a policy is the amount that has been set aside, based on actuarial principles, on the insurer's books to satisfy its obligation. It should slightly exceed the cash surrender value of the policy.

If the insured is terminally ill, the value of the policy is based on the insured's life expectancy. Thus, the value of such a policy is approximately its face amount.[21] Regardless of how the value of the policy is determined, transfer of an existing policy to a trust is a gift. As detailed below, it may be possible to use Crummey withdrawal powers to obtain the federal gift-tax annual exclusions to offset part or all of the gift.

### 2. Group Term Policies

Another situation in which it will be necessary to transfer an existing policy to the trust, as opposed to having the trustee purchase the policy, is in the context of group term life insurance. Group term life insurance, which is provided by many employers, is frequently overlooked for inclusion in the insured's life insurance trust. In fact, since group term life insurance generally has no cash surrender value, the insured may be more willing to part with the economic benefits of the group term policy than a whole life policy. Therefore, group term is uniquely suited for life insurance trusts.

Although the insured may effectively cancel a typical group term policy by terminating current employment, the Internal Revenue Service (I.R.S.) has ruled that such possibility is not an incident of ownership.[22] Thus, by irrevocably transferring all of his or her rights in the group term policy to a properly drafted life insurance trust, the insured effectively parts with all incidents of ownership in the policy. As with the transfer of any existing life insurance policy, however, the policy proceeds will be included in the insured's gross estate if insured does not survive the transfer by at least three years.[23]

When the insured's employer pays the premiums on the group term policy it is an indirect gift by insured to the trust.[24] As in most life insurance trusts, in order to ensure that the federal gift-tax annual exclusion is available to offset these indirect gifts, the beneficiaries should be given Crummey withdrawal powers. Crummey powers require special care when the trust holds group term life insurance.

## III.  Life Insurance Premiums

### A.  Payment of Premiums by Donor

In many ways, life insurance trusts are merely a variation of the Crummey trusts described in Chapter 9 of this book. The essential difference is that in a life insurance trust, the trustee will presumably invest in life insurance on the donor's life.

Typically, the insured will pay the premiums on the life insurance held by the trust. Generally, the insured makes a gift to the trustee who will, in turn, use the gift to pay the policy premium. Alternatively, the insured may pay the premiums directly, which will also be a gift to the trust and, thus, the beneficiaries.[25] Since payment of premiums is not an incident of ownership in the policy, premium payment will not compromise the estate tax benefits of the trust.[26] Regardless, the insured's direct payment of the premiums makes the entire arrangement appear contrived. Moreover, if the insured pays the premiums directly, the formalities of the Crummey powers become more complicated. Therefore, the insured should pay the premiums through cash gifts to the trustee, rather than by direct payment to the insurer.

When the insured makes the transfer to the trust to pay the policy premiums, he or she is, of course, making a gift to the beneficiaries of the trust. These gifts will likely be future interests for purposes of the federal gift-tax annual exclusion[27]; thus, they will not qualify for the exclusion unless a method for obtaining it is found. If the transfers do not qualify for the annual exclusion, either some of the insured's unified credit (applicable credit amount) will be used or gift tax may be owed.

### B.  Crummey Powers

In order to obtain the annual exclusion for the gifts made to the trust, the beneficiaries of the trust are given rights—Crummey powers—to withdraw an aliquot share of the gift to the trust. This immediate, albeit temporary, right to withdraw the gift made to the trust makes the transfer a present interest, which qualifies for the federal gift-tax annual exclusion.[28] This is true even though the withdrawal power lapses.

A typical Crummey withdrawal power lapses 30 days after the gift is made to the trust. Although the I.R.S. has never explicitly so ruled, this seems to be the shortest period that will pass muster with it.[29] Courts have allowed annual exclusions based on Crummey powers that have lapsed after less than 30 days.[30] These cases do not, however, specifically address the time period.[31]

Although it may be possible to obtain the federal gift-tax annual exclusion through the use of a Crummey power that lapses after less than 30 days, little is gained by the shorter time period. Crummey powers are rarely exercised, regardless of the length of time the withdrawal power remains outstanding. Indeed, many lawyers draft Crummey powers that lapse 60 days or more after the gift.[32]

If the Crummey withdrawal power provisions of the trust agreement are not acceptable to the donor, it is possible to vary the terms of the withdrawal right in the instrument by which the donor makes the gift to the trustee. It may be wise to anticipate this possibility in the trust agreement. Such a variance might be appropriate if, for example, the withdrawal power provisions of the agreement fail to account for inflation adjustments in the annual exclusion, or to exclude a beneficiary who has demonstrated a propensity to exercise the withdrawal power.

### 1. Crummey Notices

No court has ever required that the beneficiary be given notice of their withdrawal right. Indeed, in *Crummey*, the Court noted that some of the beneficiaries were likely unaware of their rights.[33] Despite this observation, the annual exclusions were, of course, allowed. The I.R.S. has repeatedly ruled that the beneficiary must know of the existence of the withdrawal power.[34] It should be sufficient if the beneficiaries had actual knowledge of their withdrawal right.[35] However, the lack of written notice presents obvious difficulties in trying to prove the requisite knowledge. In practice, most lawyers instruct the trustee to send (or assist the trustee in sending) written notices, called Crummey notices, to the beneficiaries.

A Crummey notice should include the amount of the gift, the date the withdrawal power will lapse, and the extent of the beneficiary's power. It should be sent to the beneficiary. If the beneficiary is a minor, the notice should be sent to his or her court-appointed guardian, if any, or the natural guardian.[36] Crummey notices are commonly drafted to prompt the beneficiary to inform the trustee if the beneficiary chooses not to exercise his or her withdrawal power. This is frequently a mistake. Instead, the Crummey notice should instruct the beneficiary to do nothing if the wish is to allow the power to lapse.[37]

The nuances of Crummey powers seem bizarre to the average client. Particularly, Crummey notices seem like irrelevant technicalities, rather than acts that have significant tax ramifications.[38] Lay trustees who have not adhered to the Crummey notice requirements are common. The lawyer must stress the importance of these technicalities to the client and trustee.

### 2. Gift-Tax Consequences to Power-Holder

A Crummey withdrawal power is a general power of appointment for gift-tax purposes.[39] Thus, the lapse of a Crummey power is deemed a release of the power which, in turn, is a gift by the power-holder to the other beneficiaries of the trust.[40] However, a lapse is treated as a gift only to the extent it exceeds the greater of $5,000 or 5 percent of the trust principal.[41] Therefore, if a beneficiary allows a Crummey power restricted to the five-and-five amount to lapse, the lapse will not be deemed a gift and, therefore, no adverse gift-tax consequences to the power-holder ensue. The lapse of a power to withdraw a greater amount may be at least partially a taxable gift by the power-holder.

It is important to note that this five-and-five exclusion is available only if the Crummey withdrawal power lapses. If the beneficiary effectively releases the power, the five-and-five exclusion does not apply and the entire amount of the lapsed withdrawal right may be a taxable gift. To avoid this, the Crummey notice should instruct the beneficiary to simply do nothing if he or she does not wish to exercise the Crummey power. Indeed, it may be wise to provide in the trust agreement that an attempted release of the Crummey power is ineffective.

### 3. Annual Exclusion for Substantial Premiums

When a Crummey power is restricted by the five-and-five exclusion, the insured/donor will obtain an annual exclusion that is similarly limited. If the premium on the life insurance held by the trust is substantial, other methods must be found to ensure that the entire transfer by the insured to the trust is covered by the annual exclusion.

One possibility is to allow the beneficiaries (other than the donor's spouse[42]) to withdraw the full amount covered by the annual exclusion: $11,000 (as of calendar year 2002) or $22,000 if the donor splits the gift with his or her spouse.[43] This may engender adverse gift-tax consequences to the power-holder; however, it may be an acceptable cost. Crummey power-holders are frequently of a younger generation than the donor/insured, and efforts to minimize their estate tax may be wasted—especially considering the uncertain future of the federal estate tax and the possibility that the beneficiary's assets may never exceed the applicable exclusion amount.[44]

Another possibility is to draft the trust so that no individual other than the particular power-holder has an interest in his or her share of the trust. For example, if trust income and principal can be distributed only to the power-holder or power-holder's estate, then the lapse of the Crummey power cannot be a taxable gift by the power-holder for want of a donee.[45] This technique requires that each power-holder have a fully vested share in the trust, which may be inconsistent with the insured's estate plan. Further, the power-holder's share of the trust will be included in power-holder's gross estate at death.[46]

Even if there are other beneficiaries of the trust, if the beneficiary is given a power of appointment[47] over the trust assets, the lapse of the withdrawal power will not be a completed gift.[48] Thus, lapse of the power will not be a taxable gift.

A third option is the use of naked Crummey powers. Traditionally, only beneficiaries with relatively substantial interests in the trust were given Crummey powers. To obtain additional annual exclusions, trusts would sometimes be drafted so that individuals with minimal or no interest in the trust would also be given Crummey withdrawal powers. The I.R.S. has repeatedly attacked these arrangements as shams.[49] However, its efforts have been uniformly rebuffed by the courts.[50] Because it is the power-holders' immediate right to withdraw the contribution to the trust that creates the present interest, the I.R.S.'s arguments against naked Crummey powers are largely specious.[51] The I.R.S.'s demonstrated willingness to litigate this issue, however, should give the careful lawyer pause in recommending naked Crummey powers.

Another possible means of circumventing the five-and-five exclusion is the use of hanging Crummey powers. The donor's annual exclusion based on a single Crummey withdrawal power is, as of calendar year 2002, limited to $11,000 per year ($22,000 if the donor is married and the gift is split).[52] In contrast, adverse gift-tax consequences to the beneficiary ensue only if the withdrawal power exceeds the more modest five-and-five exclusion.[53] The crux of a hanging Crummey power is to allow the donor's annual exclusion to be determined by the more generous provisions of I.R.C. Section 2503 while limiting the lapse to merely the five-and-five amount.

A hanging Crummey power allows the beneficiary to withdraw the full amount of his or her aliquot share of a gift to the trust, up to the annual exclusion. However, the power lapses only to the extent covered by the five-and-five exclusion of I.R.C. Section

2514(e). The unlapsed portion hangs until the next year. Presumably, this hanging portion will lapse in later years when gifts are no longer made to the trust or when the value of the trust principal increases so that the 5-percent portion of the five-and-five exclusion allows for greater annual lapses.

Drafting hanging Crummey powers requires care. If the amount of the lapse is explicitly tied to the gift-tax ramifications to the power-holder, the gradual lapse will be disregarded for gift-tax purposes as a condition subsequent.[54] Instead, the amount of the lapse must be determined prospectively. For example, the power should lapse only to the extent of $5,000 or 5 percent of the trust principal. This should allow the power to lapse only to the extent such lapse is not a taxable gift without the provisions being disregarded as a condition subsequent.

### 4. *Crummey Powers and Group Term Life Insurance*

Special issues arise if the trust holds group term life insurance or if the insured pays the premiums directly. In these cases, the trustee may be unable to satisfy an exercised Crummey power if the trust holds only the insurance. If permitted by the terms of the policy, the trustee could satisfy an exercised Crummey power by assigning a fractional interest in the policy to the beneficiary. Alternatively, the trustee could either sell the policy and distribute the proceeds or distribute the entire policy to the beneficiary and attempt to recover the difference between the value of the policy and the exercised power from the beneficiary. Both options suffer from significant logistical difficulties and may be a transfer of the policy for value.[55] Having the insured initially fund the trust with a small amount of cash is a more palatable alternative. The trustee could hold this cash in reserve to satisfy an exercised Crummey power. In any event, upon hearing that a power has been exercised, the insured may decide to make an additional cash gift to the trust to enable the trustee to satisfy the power.

Crummey powers are rarely exercised. Thus, the difficulty in satisfying an exercised Crummey power may be more theoretical than practical. The power, however, must be legally enforceable in order for the donor to obtain the annual exclusion.[56] Ensuring that an exercised power could be satisfied will help defend against an argument that it is illusory. Further, although no rulings have turned on this issue, the I.R.S. has noted that the exclusion will be denied unless the trust holds sufficient assets that are reducible to cash so that an exercised power can be satisfied.[57]

### 5. *Crummey Powers after Estate Tax Repeal*

During the one-year repeal of the estate tax, gift tax consequences of a transfer to a trust are explicitly tied to income tax consequences. Specifically, during 2010, I.R.C. Section 2511(c) provides that a transfer in trust will be taxed as a "transfer of property by gift" unless the trust is a grantor trust,[58] for federal income tax purposes.[59] Thus, a transfer to a grantor trust would likely not be treated as a gift, regardless of whether a present interest is gifted and regardless of whether the beneficiary had a withdrawal power.[60] In contrast, a transfer to a non-grantor trust would be treated as a transfer of property by gift. Thus, such a transfer would potentially be subject to gift tax, unless the annual exclusion was available. Presumably, in this case, the annual exclusion could be obtained through the use of Crummey powers.

Life insurance trusts generally have little taxable income since they hold only the life insurance policies. The trust will, however, be a grantor trust to the extent that trust income is actually used to pay premiums on life insurance on the donor's life.[61] To the extent that the life insurance trust is a grantor trust, Section 2511(c) arguably implies that transfers to the trust will not be treated as gifts, regardless of whether Crummey powers are used. In contrast, if the trust is not a grantor trust, then the transfer to the trust to pay policy premiums will be treated as a gift. Thus, such transfer may be subject to gift tax unless the annual exclusion can be obtained, perhaps through the use of Crummey powers.

Section 2511(c) clearly has injected some uncertainty into this area. It is important to realize, however, that under current law 2511(c) is only effective for calendar year 2010. Indeed, the one year repeal of the estate tax for 2010, if made permanent, would render the issue largely moot by making transfer tax planning with life insurance trusts unnecessary.

## IV. Terms of a Typical Irrevocable Life Insurance Trust

There is great flexibility in selecting the terms of an irrevocable life insurance trust without compromising the tax advantages. For the most part, life insurance trusts tend to be categorized as either a single life or a joint and survivor (second-to-die) life insurance trust. A single-life life insurance trust is intended to hold insurance on the life of an individual insured. In contrast, a second-to-die life insurance trust typically holds life insurance upon the joint lives of husband and wife, that is, life insurance that pays upon the death of the survivor of both spouses.

Both single-life and joint-and-survivor life insurance trusts hold insubstantial assets, other than the life insurance policy, during the insured's life (insureds' lives). Thus, distributions during the insured's lifetime should be minimal. An exception, of course, is in the unlikely event of an exercised Crummey power.

During the insured's life (insureds' lives), it may be wise to give the trustee the discretionary power to distribute all trust assets to a beneficiary and, therefore, terminate the trust. For example, in a single-life trust, the trustee could be given the discretionary power to terminate the trust and distribute all assets to the insured's spouse. This allows the trust to be terminated if it becomes unnecessary. Terminating the trust might be desirable if, for example, some or all of the changes made by EGTRRA become permanent.

After the death of the insured(s), the trust will hold more substantial assets; specifically, the policy proceeds. At that time, depending on the decedent's estate plan, the assets could be held in further trust or distributed to the beneficiaries outright. In the case of a single-life trust, the insured's surviving spouse (if any) will likely be a beneficiary of the trust, even though the policy proceeds will not be subject to the surviving spouse's right of election.[62]

For the most part, the surviving spouse's interest in the trust can be as substantial as the insured/client desires, provided that the spouse does not have a general power of appointment over the trust assets. Since the assets held in the trust will pass to the beneficiaries without inclusion in the surviving spouse's gross estate, distributions to the surviving spouse should be limited to the extent consistent with the estate plan.

One possible means of limiting the assets distributed to the surviving spouse, while still ensuring that the proceeds are available, is through a five-and-five withdrawal power. Instead of requiring that income or principal be distributed to the surviving spouse, the surviving spouse may be given the power to withdraw the greater of $5,000 or 5 percent of the trust principal, per annum. As discussed in the Crummey context, to the extent the surviving spouse allows this power to lapse, the lapse will not be a taxable gift by the spouse (to the other trust beneficiaries) and the assets will remain in the trust.[63]

A beneficial provision in a single-life life insurance trust is a backup distribution that qualifies for the federal estate-tax marital deduction. The marital distribution would be made only if policy proceeds are included in the insured's gross estate. For example, if the insurance trust held a policy given to it by the insured, the trust agreement could provide that, if the insured does not survive the transfer by at least three years, policy proceeds are paid to the surviving spouse outright. In this case, the marital deduction would offset the inclusion of the policy proceeds in the insured's estate.[64] To the extent not expended, the assets will be included, of course, in the surviving spouse's gross estate upon his or her later death.[65]

## V. Generation-Skipping Transfer-Tax Issues

The generation-skipping transfer tax is a separate tax that is distinct from the estate and gift taxes. Although the generation-skipping transfer tax defies easy précis, it is imposed on transfers, in trust or outright, to the transferor's grandchildren, or more remote descendants (called "skip-persons").[66]

If the insured's grandchildren, or other skip-persons, are potential beneficiaries[67] (even contingent remainder beneficiaries) of the life insurance trust, then consideration must be given to the federal generation-skipping transfer tax. A possible generation-skipping transfer-tax trap awaits in a typical life insurance trust if the insured and insured's descendants do not die in the usual order. For example, assume a life insurance trust were to pay to the insured's issue, per stirpes, upon the death of the insured. If a child of the insured predeceases the insured, distributions may be made from the trust to skip-persons (that is, the deceased child's descendants).

Many similar transfers would not be subject to the generation-skipping transfer tax because of the predeceased ancestor rule.[68] This rule provides that a transfer to a grandchild, or more-remote decedent, is not a generation-skipping transfer if the transferor's descendant who was also the ascendant of the donee is deceased. However, the predeceased ancestor rule applies only if the ancestor is deceased at the time of the transfer.[69] In the case of a life insurance trust, the transfer occurs when gifts are made to the trust to pay premiums and as the Crummey powers lapse.[70] Because the transfer occurs before the distribution to the skip-person, payment to such a skip-person would be a generation-skipping transfer.[71] The unexpected generation-skipping transfer may require allocation of some (or all) of the transferor's generation-skipping transfer tax exemption.[72] If insufficient exemption is available, generation-skipping transfer tax may be due.

Moreover, complexity is created in the generation-skipping transfer-tax context because a typical life insurance trust may have more than one transferor. A typical life insurance trust is funded through the lapse of numerous Crummey powers. To the extent that the lapse is covered by the five-and-five exclusion of I.R.C. Section 2514(e), the insured/donor is the transferor.[73] If a portion of the lapse is not covered by the five-and-five exclusion of Section 2514(e), however, the power-holder will be the transferor of that portion. This is another reason why it may be best for all lapses of Crummey powers to be covered by the five-and-five exclusion—even, if necessary, through use of hanging or naked Crummey powers.

If the generation-skipping transfer tax is an issue, it may be best to ensure the trust is generation-skipping transfer-tax exempt. This will ensue if the transfers to the trust (for example, to pay premiums) are exempt. Transfers covered by the annual exclusion are, normally, exempt.[74] In the case of annual exclusions obtained through the use of Crummey powers, however, the gift is generation-skipping transfer-tax exempt only if: (1) during the beneficiary's lifetime, distributions may not be made to anyone other than that particular beneficiary, and (2) trust assets will be included in the beneficiary's gross estate if he or she dies prior to termination of the trust.[75] In a nutshell, this limitation requires that no person other than the particular power-holder have an interest in that particular power-holder's share of the trust. This is not true in a typical life insurance trust, so annual exclusion gifts to such a trust will not be exempt.

Beyond prohibiting distributions to skip-persons, perhaps the simplest generation-skipping transfer-tax planning is to create a separate share in the trust for the benefit of each power-holder. As long as no one other than that particular power-holder has an interest in that share of the trust, gifts to the trust subject to Crummey powers should be exempt.[76] Of course, the creation of a separate share for each beneficiary may be impractical or inconsistent with the overall estate plan.

Another possibility is the allocation of generation-skipping transfer-tax exemption to the trust. If allocated to a life insurance (or any) trust, it is better to create one trust that is fully subject to the generation-skipping transfer tax in which distributions to skip-persons are impossible or, at least, unlikely. A second, fully-exempt trust should make the desired distributions to the skip-persons.

## VI. Income Tax Issues

Generally, an irrevocable life insurance trust holds only the policy and the funds used to pay the premiums. Thus, the trust will have little, if any, taxable income. Because trust income is applied to pay premiums on life insurance on the grantor's life, I.R.C. Section 677(a) provides that any taxable income will be taxed to the grantor under the grantor trust rules.[77]

In contrast, Section 678(a) provides that trust income is taxed to the Crummey power-holder because the power-holder has to the power to vest trust corpus in herself. However, Section 678(b) provides that Section 678(a) does not apply if trust income would otherwise be taxed to the grantor. By its terms, Section 678(b) applies only to a power over income. In fact, a Crummey power is a power over trust principal. Despite this distinction, the I.R.S. has ruled that trust income is taxed to the grantor, rather than to the Crummey power-holder.[78] Upon the grantor's death, the trust, assuming that it continues, is taxed as a separate taxpayer.[79]

## VII. Conclusion

Life insurance trusts can greatly increase life insurance policy proceeds actually enjoyed by beneficiaries. Careful drafting can yield a life insurance trust consistent with a client's objectives and estate plan without compromising the transfer tax benefits. The lawyer should draft the trust to anticipate possible changes in the federal transfer tax system. Working together, the lawyer can help the client realize the benefits of one of the most powerful estate planning techniques.

## *Endnotes*

1. Based on a maximum federal estate-tax rate of 50 percent, for calendar year 2002. I.R.C. § 2001(c).

2. Unif. Prob. Code § 2-205(1)(iv); MINN. STAT. § 524.2-205(1)(iii). In many states, however, life insurance is not subject to a surviving spouse's right of election regardless of whether it is held in a life insurance trust, unless paid to the estate. *See, e.g.,* N.J. STAT. ANN. § 3B:8-5; MONT. CODE ANN. § 72-2-222(3)(c).

3. Treas Reg. § 20.2042-1(c)(2).

4. I.R.C. § 2210(a).

5. EGTRRA § 901.

6. I.R.C. § 2010.

7. I.R.C. § 2042(2).

8. Treas. Reg. § 20.2042-1(c)(2).

9. Treas. Reg. § 20.2042-1(c)(4). *Cf.* Rev. Rul. 84-179.

10. I.R.C. § 2042(1).

11. Treas. Reg. § 20.2042-1(b)(1).

12. Treas. Reg. § 20.2042-1(b)(1); Rev. Rul. 77-157; Priv. Ltr. Rul. 9748029.

13. I.R.C. § 2035(a).

14. Subject to the unlikely application of the step transaction doctrine.

15. I.R.C. § 2035.

16. I.R.C. § 2035(d).

17. I.R.C. § 101(a)(2).

18. Treas. Reg. § 25.2512-6(a).

19. Treas. Reg. § 25.2512-6(a), ex. (1).

20. Treas. Reg. §§ 25.2512-6(a), 25.2512-6(a), ex. (4).

21. Pritchard v. Commissioner, 4 T.C. 204 (1944).

22. Rev. Rul. 72-307.

23. I.R.C. § 2035(a).

24. Rev. Rul. 76-490. A gift to a trust is, of course, a gift to the beneficiaries of the trust.

25. Rev. Rul. 72-307.

26. I.R.C. § 2042.

27. Gifts of future interests do not qualify for the annual exclusion. I.R.C. § 2503(b). Gifts made in trust are, generally, at least partially future interests. Treas. Reg. § 25.2503-3(b). Thus, gifts to the trust to pay the premiums will not, in and of themselves, qualify for the annual exclusion.

28. Crummey v. Commissioner, 397 F.2d 82 (9th Cir. 1968).

29. Rev. Rul. 81-7; Priv. Ltr. Rul. 9232013; Priv. Ltr. Rul. 9030005; Priv. Ltr. Rul. 8922062; Priv. Ltr. Rul. 8022048.

  For example, in Tech. Adv. Mem. 91-31-008 the I.R.S. ruled that a 20-day period too severely restricted the beneficiary's possible exercise of the power.

  A few older private rulings seem to allow the exclusion even though the power lapsed in less than 30 days. *See, e.g.,* Priv. Ltr. Rul. 8111123 (ten days); Priv. Ltr. Rul. 7922107 (three days).

30. *Crummey,* 397 F.2d at 83 (power lapsed after 12 days); Cristofani V. Commissioner, 1991 T.C. 94 (power lapsed after 15 days).

31. *Id.*

32. *See, e.g.,* Priv. Ltr. Rul. 8022048.

33. 397 F.2d at 87–88.

34. Rev. Rul. 81-7; Tech. Adv. Mem. 9532001.

35. Holland v. Commissioner, 73 T.C.M. 3236 (1997).

36. Priv. Ltr. Rul. 8143045; Priv. Ltr. Rul. 8922062; Priv. Ltr. Rul. 8806063.

37. As discussed below, if the power-holder effectively releases the Crummey power then the benefit of the five-and-five rule is unavailable. I.R.C. § 2514(e). Thus, the power-holder will likely be deemed to have made a taxable gift of the entire amount he or she could have withdrawn.

38. In this respect, the layperson's opinion is, arguably, substantially more enlightened than the expert's.

39. I.R.C. § 2514(c).

40. I.R.C. §§ 2514(b), 2514(e).

41. I.R.C. § 2514(e).

42. Generally the donor's spouse is excluded because allowing the spouse to use his or her unified credit in this manner is likely an inefficient use of the credit. The reasons for disregarding this issue with respect to the donor's descendants, which are discussed in the main text, do not apply to the spouse.

43. I.R.C. §§ 2503(b), 2513; Rev. Proc. 2001-59.

44. I.R.C. § 2010; EGTRRA § 901.

Under current law, the applicable exclusion amount will vary greatly over the next several years prior to temporary estate tax repeal. Due to the uncertain nature of legislative action, it seems unwise to plan based on the one-year repeal of the estate tax or the temporary increases in the unified credit. It seems likely, however, that, at a minimum, some increase in the unified credit will be made permanent. Such an increase would, of course, increase the likelihood that the beneficiary's assets would never exceed the applicable exclusion amount.

45. Priv. Ltr. Rul. 8142061.

46. I.R.C. § 2041.

47. The power of appointment does not need to be a general power of appointment. The crucial point is that the power-holder retain a sufficient power over the beneficial enjoyment so that he or she retains dominion and control over the property. Treas. Reg. § 25.2511-2(b).

48. Priv. Ltr. Rul. 8517052; Priv. Ltr. Rul. 8229097.

49. Tech. Adv. Mem. 9731004; Tech. Adv. Mem. 9628004; Tech. Adv. Mem. 9045002.

50. See, e.g., Kohlsaat v. Commissioner, 73 T.C.M. 2732 (1997); Holland v. Commissioner, 73 T.C.M. 3236 (1997); Christofani v. Commissioner, 97 T.C. 74 (1991).

51. Bradley E.S. Fogel, The Emperor Does Not Need Clothes: The Expanding Use of "Naked" Crummey Withdrawal Powers to Obtain the Federal Gift Tax Annual Exclusion, 73 TUL. L. REV. 555 (1998).

52. I.R.C. §§ 2503(b), 2513; Rev. Proc. 2001-59.

53  I.R.C. § 2514(e).

54. Commissioner v. Proctor, 142 F.2d 824 (4th Cir. 1944); Tech. Adv. Mem. 8901004.

55. I.R.C. § 101.

Other difficulties include the need to determine the value of the policy.

56. Holland, 73 T.C.M. 3236 (1997).

57. Priv. Ltr. Rul. 8118051.

58. A "grantor trust" is a trust that is treated as owned by the grantor for federal income tax purposes. Thus, all trust income is reported by the grantor on her or his income tax return.

59. I.R.C. § 2511(c), as originally enacted by EGTRRA, provided that a transfer in trust would be "a taxable gift under Section 2503" unless the trust was a grantor trust with respect to the donor. EGTRRA § 511(e).

In March 2002, "technical corrections" to Section 2511(c) changed that section to provide that a transfer in trust was a "transfer of property by gift" unless the trust is a grantor trust. Pub. L. 107-147, § 411(g) (March 9, 2002). Thus, although not beyond dispute, it seems that a transfer to a grantor trust is not treated as a gift (and is thus not taxable), regardless of whether it is a present interest. If the trust is not a grantor trust with respect to the donor, however, then transfers to it are treated as gifts. Presumably, such gifts could be offset by annual exclusions obtained through the use of Crummey powers. I.R.C. § 2503(b).

60. This statement is not free from doubt. I.R.C. Section 2511(c) states that a transfer in trust is treated as a gift "unless" the trust is a grantor trust. As a matter of semantics, this is equivalent to a statement that if the trust is not a grantor trust, then the transfer is treated as a gift. Technically, Section 2511(c) is silent regarding a transfer to a grantor trust. Of course, a more informal interpretation of 2511(c) would interpret it to mean, inter alia, that a transfer to a grantor trust will not be treated as a transfer of property by gift. In any event, since Section 2511(c) does not even become effective until December 31, 2009 (and is then repealed on December 31, 2010) a precise exegesis of its provisions may be premature. EGTRRA § 901.

61. I.R.C. § 677(a); Rand v. Commissioner, 40 B.T.A. 233, 238-39, aff'd, 116 F.2d 929 (1941).

62. See, e.g., Mo. Rev. Stat. § 474.160; N.Y. Est. Pow. & Trusts Law § 5-1.1; Unif. Prob. Code § 2-205(1)(iv).

63. I.R.C. § 2514(e).

64. I.R.C. §§ 2035(a), 2056.

65. I.R.C. §§ 2033, 2044.

66. I.R.C. §§ 2611, 2612, 2613.

67. Although a trust can be a skip-person, the typical life insurance trust is not because the insured's spouse and/or children will likely have an interest in the trust. I.R.C. §§ 2613(a), 2652(c).

68. I.R.C. § 2651(e).

69. I.R.C. § 2651(e)(1).

70. The transfer occurs when the gift is subject to gift (or estate) tax upon the transferor. I.R.C. § 2651(e)(2). To the extent the lapse of a Crummey power is covered by the five-and-five exclusion, the donor is the transferor and the transfer occurs when the gift is made to the trust. *Id.;* Treas. Reg. 26.2652-1(a)(5), ex. (5). To the extent the lapse is not covered by the five-and-five rule, the power-holder is the transferor and the transfer occurs when the Crummey power lapses. I.R.C. § 2651(e)(2); Treas. Reg. § 26.2652-1(a)(5), ex. (5).

71. I.R.C. § 2612(b).

72. I.R.C. § 2642.

Every individual has a generation-skipping transfer-tax exemption, that, if properly allocated, can insulate transfers from the generation-skipping transfer tax. Between 2002 and 2009, the GST exemption tracks the applicable credit amount in its slow progression from $1 million to $3.5 million. I.R.C. § 2631(c). Under current law, the generation-skipping transfer tax is repealed during 2010 and then resurrected in 2011. I.R.C. § 2664; EGTRRA § 901. In 2011, the exemption will fall back to $1 million plus an adjustment for inflation. I.R.C. § 2631.

73. Treas. Reg. § 26.2652-1(a)(5), ex. (5); I.R.C. § 2652(a).

74. I.R.C. § 2642.

75. I.R.C. § 2642(c)(2).

76. I.R.C. § 2642(c)(2).

77. I.R.C. § 677(a); Rand, 40 B.T.A. at 233, 238-39 (1939).

78. Priv. Ltr. Rul. 9141027.

79. *Id.*

# CHAPTER 11

# Family Limited Partnerships

BRIAN T. WHITLOCK

## I. Introduction

Partnerships are one of the oldest forms of doing business around. They have existed both formally and informally since the time of creation. As a result of numerous developments over the past 15 years, the partnership represents the foundation of the hottest wealth transfer vehicle available: the family limited partnership.

## II. Background

There are two types of partnerships available under state law: general partnerships and limited partnerships. General partnerships may be informal (that is, a mutual understanding to cooperate or a handshake agreement) or formal (a written partnership agreement).

Limited partnerships require certain formalities under the law. These requirements include a written agreement, registration with state and county governmental authorities, and a partner residing within the state to accept notice. The members of the limited partnership can be individuals, corporations, foreign or domestic trusts, other partnerships, or combinations of any of these.

### A. Limited Partnerships: A Bad Reputation

For many people, the simple mention of the words "limited partnership" can recall horrible memories. In the 1970s and early 1980s, many tax shelter promoters used limited partnerships they controlled to bilk millions of unsuspecting investors of their hard-earned dollars. Investors purchased limited partnership interests that offered tax refunds in excess of their investment, and if the partnership made money, then they stood to reap huge returns. Too good to be true? It was.

Greed took over. Unsavory promoters set up questionable schemes, loaded them down with up-front fees and massive debt, and then dumped them in the laps of the limited partners. To add insult to injury, the Internal Revenue Service (I.R.S.) often disallowed the income tax refund claims of the investors and hit them with interest and penalties. Because of the introduction of passive activity loss limitation rules, limited partnerships and tax shelter schemes were abandoned wholesale after the 1986 Income Tax Act.

### B. Family Limited Partnerships: Sizzle

A family limited partnership (FLP) is simply a limited partnership that is controlled by members of a family. It bears no resemblance to the tax shelter partnerships of the past. There are no outsiders or promoters skimming the cream off of the investment.

The typical FLP consists of one or more general partners (who control management and investment decisions) and one or more limited partners (nonvoting or silent partners). Unlike irrevocable trusts and corporations, a limited partnership is a flexible tool that can be amended and adapted to meet the changing needs of a family.

Three developments have catapulted FLPs into the limelight as a family investment tool. First, since 1985, 49 of the 50 states have adopted the Revised Uniform Limited Partnership Act (RULPA) as their state law governing the formation and operation of limited partnerships.[1] Louisiana is the exception. RULPA put in place numerous provisions that protect the partnership from the claims of a limited partner's creditors. Adoption of this act effectively expanded the use of limited partnerships.

Second, a provision added to the Internal Revenue Code (I.R.C.) in 1990 specifically clarifies the gift and estate tax valuation rules governing the transfer of voting and nonvoting partnership interests.[2]

Third, in March 1993, the I.R.S. changed its long-standing opposition to valuation discounts on gifts of stock and partnership interests to members of the same family.[3]

These three changes, when taken together, have encouraged numerous families to embrace the FLP as a family investment-management vehicle and as a tool that can help minimize gift and estate taxes.

## III. How Do Family Limited Partnerships Work?

FLPs are very flexible and can aid in the management and transfer of almost any kind of asset: real estate, equipment, marketable securities, closely held businesses, and so forth.

### A. Family Asset Management

A practical example demonstrates the power of the family limited partnership:

John and Mary have accumulated various types of real estate (worth $6 million) during their lifetime in Illinois, Iowa, and Missouri. Their holdings include farmland, commercial rental property, resort property, and residential rental property. John and Mary collect the rents, keep their own books, and contract with third parties for the maintenance and repairs on the residential properties. The tenants of the other properties are responsible for all such items under triple-net leases. John and Mary have five children and 18 grandchildren spread throughout the country.

John and Mary have a number of concerns they wish to address:

- the preservation of the real estate values after their lifetimes through proper coordinated management and diversification of their real estate holdings over time in an orderly manner,

- minimization of potential conflicts among the children ensuring the financial well-being of their children and grandchildren, and
- reduction of their potential income and estate taxes.

A limited partnership consisting of only family members can be used to shift estate value and investment income free of transfer taxes from John and Mary to their children and grandchildren. Here is how it operates:

1. John and Mary prepare a written Limited Partnership Agreement. They create a general partnership interest, generally comprising less than 5 percent of the ownership; and a limited partnership interest, generally comprising more than 95 percent of the ownership.
2. John and Mary transfer the $6 million of real estate to the partnership in exchange for both the general and limited partnership interests.
3. John and Mary retain the general partnership interests for their lifetime while they gift the limited partnership interests over time directly to (or via a trust for the benefit of) their children and grandchildren.

   NOTE: Because the limited partnership units are unable to control investments or distributions, they are eligible for valuation discounts. These discounts will be discussed in greater detail in Part VI, but typically they reduce the value of the limited partnership 30 to 35 percent.

4. The general partners control the investment and management of the partnership assets. The general partners (John and Mary) must receive adequate compensation for any services that they personally render to the partnership.
5. John and Mary each make 23 gifts of $10,000 per child and grandchild for each year that they are alive. Each $10,000 gift is sheltered by the gift-tax annual exclusion. As a result, in years when John and Mary are alive, they can gift, free of transfer tax, up to $460,000 (23 x 2 x $10,000) of limited partnership interests to each of their children and grandchildren.

   NOTE: Assuming appropriate discounts, approximately 7 percent of the partnership can be gifted each year. If John and Mary also gift limited partnership interests equal in value to an amount that can be sheltered by their gift-tax credit equivalent amount ($1 million each in 2002), they can transfer nearly two-thirds of their partnership in the first year.

*The bottom line:* John and Mary can transfer $6 million of assets tax-free within a five-year period to their children and grandchildren. If the value of the real estate held by the partnership appreciates 4 percent over the next ten years, John and Mary will have been able to transfer $8.875 million of value to their family.

### B. How Is the Partnership Income Taxed?

A partnership pays no federal income tax, but it must file an annual information return (IRS Form 1065). The net income earned by a partnership is allocated by the partnership and reported to the partners (IRS Form 1065, Schedule K-1).

The net income, losses, and credits to each partner are reported on the respective individual income tax return. If the limited partners (children and grandchildren) are in lower income tax brackets than the general partners (parents) are, then less income tax is paid by the family as a whole.

### C. What Happens to the Income Accumulated in the Partnership?

The general partners (John and Mary) control the timing of cash and/or property distributions. Distributions reduce the capital accounts of each partner receiving cash and/or property. Distributions can be made on a non–pro rata basis at the discretion of the general partners to allow the limited partners to pay the income taxes on their partnership income, educational expenses, and/or any expenses the general partners deem appropriate. A general partner might even make distributions to a limited partner to help the limited partner pay for a wedding or purchase a home.

### D. When Does the Partnership End?

After the death of the general partners (John and Mary, in our example), the children can elect to continue or terminate the partnership.

If the limited partners elect to wind up the affairs of the partnership, they could sell some or all of the partnership assets and then distribute the remaining assets pro rata to the partners. Because the partnership is flexible, some individuals may take cash while others take an equal amount of real estate or other property.

## IV.  Some Basic Tax Facts about Partnerships

The rules regarding income taxation of partnerships are generally found beginning at I.R.C. Section 701.[4]

### A.  Creating the Partnership

In general, there is no income tax recognized upon initial contribution of cash or appreciated assets to a partnership.[5] However, if more than 80 percent of the assets consist of solely marketable securities (that is, stocks, bonds, and treasury securities), then the net capital gains are taxable.[6] Therefore, when forming a limited partnership, be sure to contribute significant property other than cash and securities, such as real estate.

### B.  Operating the Partnership

#### 1.  Income Taxation

Partnerships are not subject to federal income tax. Regardless of the distribution of cash to property, each item of income and/or loss flows through to the individual partner in accordance with the terms of the partnership agreement.[7]

#### 2.  Substantial Economic Effect

Non–pro rata allocations of income and loss must have a substantial economic effect upon the capital accounts of the partners. In other words, allocations of income and losses must be for a business purpose and actually increase or decrease the capital and obligations of the partners.[8]

## 3. Capital Accounts

Partnerships must maintain books and records that trace the relative investment of capital of each partner. This account is your capital account. Your capital account is increased by the tax cost of what you contribute to the partnership and your share of the partnership income. Your capital account is decreased by distributions of your share of partnership losses and by the tax cost of property distributed to you.

## 4. Example

Joe is a 5-percent limited partner in Jepco Family Partners. He originally contributed land to the partnership that cost him $10,000. In 2001, the partnership earned $10,000 from rent, interest, and dividends. Joe's 5-percent share of the income is $500. Joe's initial capital account increases from $10,000 to $10,500. In 2002, the partnership distributes $100 to Joe. His capital account is reduced to $10,400.

## 5. Service Partnerships

Partnership allocations of income must fairly compensate partners rendering services to the partnership before they allocate income to remaining partners. However, I.R.C. Section 701(e) makes it impossible to shift income of service partnerships (accounting, law, and medicine) to family members that are not actively involved in the partnership.[9]

## C. The Passive-Loss Rules

In 1986, Congress introduced the passive activity loss-limitation rules.[10] These rules state that losses from any investment in which you do not actively, continually, and materially participate cannot be used to offset any type of income except income from other such similar activities (excluding investments). Therefore, you cannot deduct passive losses from limited partnerships to offset nonpassive income, such as salary or interest. However, you can use such losses to offset income from similar passive activities. Warning: Review every partnership and S corporation in which you have an interest and which is likely to produce a loss. If you don't materially participate, you may have a loss subject to the passive loss rules.

Unused passive activity losses are carried forward indefinitely (but not carried back), generally to be applied against passive activity income in future years.

## 1. Real Estate

All real estate rental income/loss is treated as a passive activity, even if you participate in managing the property. One exception rescues you: If your adjusted gross income is less than $100,000, you can deduct up to $25,000 of losses as long as you actively participate in the rental activity and have at least a 10 percent ownership in it. For those earning over $100,000, the $25,000 loss amount is reduced by $504 for every $1 of income over $100,000.[11]

If you have other passive losses and are trying to offset them with passive income from a family partnership, be wary of I.R.S. regulations that may thwart you. One rule provides that net income from renting nondepreciable property (such as vacant land) will be recharacterized as nonpassive. Similarly, net income resulting from renting property to an activity in which you materially participate (such as your closely held corporation) will not be treated as passive income.[12]

### 2. Real Estate Professionals

There is an exception to the passive activity loss rules for taxpayers involved in real property trades or business. The 1993 Revenue Reconciliation Act included a provision that allows eligible taxpayers to deduct rental estate losses. Eligible taxpayers must meet all of the following requirements:

a. They must *materially participate* in the trade or business.
b. More than 50 percent of an individual's personal services during the tax year are performed in real property trades or businesses in which the individual materially participates.
c. A real property trade or business includes development, redevelopment, construction, reconstruction, acquisition, conversion, rental, operation, management, leasing, or brokerage trade or business.
d. The individual performs more than 750 hours of service during the year in the real property trade or businesses in which the individual materially participates.[13]

### D. Partnership Distributions

Distributions of cash and property are not taxable unless they are in excess of a partner's capital account. Certain distributions that are made during the first five years of the partnership are closely scrutinized in order to ensure they are not merely disguised sales of assets between partners.[14]

Distributions of cash and property that are made upon the liquidation or termination of a partner's interest are generally nontaxable. Exceptions exist for certain assets, such as inventory and accounts receivable, unless they are made on a pro rata basis.[15]

## V. Family Limited Partnerships: Asset-Management Vehicles

Consider the plight of Bill and Barbara Baker. Bill and Barbara have 13 children. They not only survived, but they prospered. The Bakers, now in their 70s, have built an estate in excess of $10 million through hard work, wise real estate investments, and careful management. Acting on the sound advice of their lawyer, Bill created a trust for each of their children, with Barbara as trustee, and gifted $20,000 per year to each trust. Each trust was now in excess of $100,000. In the aggregate, the trusts held assets equal in value to nearly $1.5 million, but individually they represented a mess. More specifically, Bill and Barbara were being overrun with paper: 13 different trust investment accounts, 13 different tax returns, and 13 brokerage statements and bank accounts. We joked about putting on an addition to their home to accommodate future filing cabinets and about how many accountants' children they must be putting through school with annual fees.

To simplify review of the investment account statements and to avoid having one child's trust either overperform or underperform the others, he invested them all alike—a surprising lack of diversification considering Barbara was the trustee of over $1.5 million of assets.

The solution to Bill and Barbara's paper woes is to create an FLP. The following subsections show how an FLP simplifies the Bakers' investment management.

## A. Consolidation of Assets

Each trust contributes its assets to the partnership in exchange for a small limited partnership interest. Bill and Barbara contribute real estate and investment assets of their own for a small general partnership interest, as well as additional limited partnership interests of their own.

## B. Consolidation of Management

Bill and Barbara, acting as general partners, continue to control the management and investment of the assets, but now inside of a single account. Bill and Barbara also control all distributions of partnership cash and property, and they can make distributions to each partner as needed without the limitation of trust standards.

## C. Reduction of Operating Expenses

The pooling of securities allows for reduced investment fees, avoidance of minimum account balances, and discounts available to large transactions. Also, pooling investments allows a family to attract a sophisticated money manager. The pooling of investments in rental real estate might allow a family to hire a full-time janitor or management company to monitor properties. Lower insurance premiums and real estate taxes may be available when dealing with multiple and/or continuous parcels of real estate. Vacant real estate can be developed more cost efficiently when planned as a whole and managed in orderly succession. Finally, the pooling of assets may allow Barbara, as trustee of the individual trusts, to terminate the trusts of the adult children and distribute the assets outright to a child when additional safeguards are no longer necessary. This method could eliminate the expense of preparing some of the trust income tax returns.

## D. Enhanced Flexibility in Operation

Compared to an irrevocable trust, a limited partnership agreement is a flexible document. If all partners (in a family partnership, all family members) agree, the partnership agreement may be amended or terminated. In contrast, an irrevocable trust generally may not be amended or terminated without participation by a court and possibly by a guardian ad litem.

## E. Enhanced Investment Flexibility

A family partnership agreement provides greater investment flexibility because of the operation of the business-judgment rule. The prudent-person rule, which applies to the trustees, is a stricter standard than the business-judgment rule, which is the standard that applies to managing partners of a partnership. Many business decisions that may be reasonable can violate the prudent-person rule (for example, the decision to develop a wildcat oil field). Many people want to protect—particularly from 20-20 hindsight—a family member who is responsible for making investment decisions. Unquestionably, it is easier to defend the family decision maker if the standard is the business-judgment rule, not the prudent-person rule.

## F.  Diversification of Investments

As a practical matter, Bill and Barbara are free to diversify investments under the common wrapper of the partnership without fear of having unequal results among each of the various trusts. The successes and failures will be spread pro rata among the limited partners.

## G.  Use of Modern Portfolio Theory of Investing

Trustees, particularly independent trustees, such as banks and professionals, are cautious in their investment choices because of their concern over treating either the income beneficiary or the remainder beneficiary unfairly. Income beneficiaries are entitled to dividend income and interest income; remainder beneficiaries are entitled to the appreciation in value of the trust portfolio. This division of returns may produce a conflict between the income beneficiary and the remainder beneficiary.

Most trustees are so afraid of being sued by either the income beneficiary or the remainder beneficiary that they are paralyzed and thus doomed to mediocre investment results.

Use of an FLP encourages the use of the modern portfolio theory of investing. The modern portfolio theory, or modern asset allocation theory, emphasizes that an investor should concentrate on obtaining the highest rate of return, consistent with the investor's tolerance for risk, from whatever source.

## H.  Protection of Assets from the Claims of Spouses

The statistics are clear and convincing. Marriages fail 50 percent of the time.[16] What are the Bakers' odds of avoiding divorce with 13 kids? One way to protect against some of the financial exposure of a failed marriage is through a prenuptial or postnuptial agreement, but many clients find these agreements distasteful. However, if the wealth of a client's child consists of limited partnership interests, that wealth can be protected from an award to a divorced spouse. Generally, jurisdictions do not award separate property to a divorced spouse. The partnership obviously provides a convenient means of segregating separate assets for each child of the client.

Even in the rare event that a divorce court awards part of a limited partnership interest to a divorced spouse, a partnership agreement may provide that involuntary transfers are subject to a partnership redemption right and that the limited interest will be bought at its fair market value. If the fair market value of the limited partnership interest is less than the value of the underlying assets, the child will have at least some protection if part of the partnership is awarded to the former spouse.

## I.  Protection of Assets from Future Creditors

Trusts and limited partnerships are both asset-protection tools. Neither tool can keep assets away from someone's existing creditors. Most self-settled trusts are just as incapable of forestalling future creditors. However, a limited partnership can be used to shelter a contributing limited partner from outside liabilities as well as protect the limited partner's assets from his or her future creditors.

Once a partner's personal assets are exhausted, a creditor can receive a charging order against the partner's limited partnership interest. In other words, the creditor steps into the shoes of the partner as an assignee. Yet, an assignee has almost no rights at all—no management rights, no voting rights, only distribution rights (the right to receive a pro rata share of distributions actually made). Because the general partner controls distributions and can accumulate income for a large number of valid business reasons, distributions can be severely limited. In addition, the family limited partnership agreement can provide that an involuntary transfer of a partnership interest to a creditor (or to any other third party) is not a permissible transfer and the transferred interest will be purchased by the partnership (or remaining partners) at its fair market value. The fair market value of a limited partnership interest frequently is much less than the value of the underlying assets; thus, the creditor is satisfied with an amount that allows the family assets to survive the creditor's charging order.

## J. Retention of Assets in the Family

Real estate and certain securities may have extraordinary value to your family as they do with the Bakers. Frequently, family partnerships are drafted with buy-sell provisions to help ensure that the properties remain in the family. If any family member attempts to assign his or her interest in the partnership to someone outside the family, the partnership agreement may provide that the other partners or the partnership may acquire the assigned interest on the same terms (or at its fair market value if the transfer is a gratuitous transfer).

## K. Avoidance of Family Disputes

The partnership agreement also serves as a means of limiting family disputes. A partnership agreement, as a contract, can be drafted to require settlement of disputes by arbitration. Arbitration is preferable to jury litigation for many clients. The fact-finder in business arbitration is an experienced businessperson. Also, the publicity that family disputes generate may produce an unfair advantage to the person who is suing. That publicity can be avoided through arbitration, particularly if there is a confidentiality provision in the partnership agreement.

Family disputes with little merit may be deterred by a family limited agreement that adopts the English rule. A family partnership agreement can provide that when a partner brings an unsuccessful arbitration action against the partnership management, the unsuccessful partner pays all arbitration costs. Such a provision should deter frivolous actions.

## L. Avoidance of Probate

A limited partnership provides an opportunity to avoid probate of the assets held by the partnership. Out-of-state real estate and assets held in foreign countries are considered intangible personal property when held in partnership. Probate only applies to the partnership interests, not the underlying property owned by the partnership. Probate of the partnership interests can also be avoided by using joint tenancy or living trusts.

## M. Support for Initiative and Entrepreneurship

The thought of transferring substantial wealth to children and grandchildren is usually accompanied by a fear regarding their ability to handle it. Unrestricted gifts, large amounts of current cash flow, and easy affluence may undermine personal initiative and destroy entrepreneurship. Use of a family limited partnership can limit cash flow by reinvesting significant portions of earnings in new investments and keeping a tight rein on assets. Progressive general partners may choose to use family partnerships as an opportunity to educate their children and grandchildren by allowing them to follow the investment of assets, and family partnerships foster entrepreneurship by involving children and grandchildren in the management of the family partnership.

## VI.  Leveraging through Valuation Discounts

If I put $1,000 in your hand (no strings attached), how much is that worth to you? Simple. It's worth $1,000. Why? Because you control it. Easy enough, right?

Now what if I give you 1 percent of a partnership that has $100,000 inside? Is it still worth $1,000? Probably not. Why? Control! If you have control, and you can cash in your 1 percent immediately, then it is worth $1,000; but if you cannot, then it is worth something less than $1,000. In other words, the gift of the partnership interest is subject to a valuation discount.

Numerous types of valuation discounts have been acknowledged by the courts. The most common discounts affecting partnerships are discounts for general lack of marketability and minority interest.

### A.  Lack of Marketability Discount

The lack of marketability discount arises from illiquidity. It takes more time and costs more to find a buyer for the partnership interest. The buyer will pay less knowing there will be a similar liquidity problem if he or she decides to sell the interest.

The I.R.S. acknowledges the concept of lack of marketability discount as a matter of law.[17] Empirical data support a substantial discount for illiquidity in valuing closely held corporations. Although this data generally focus on corporations, they remain a valuable source for developing the discount for a partnership interest.

The empirical data on discounts for marketability and illiquidity of corporate stock generally have found discounts of 30 to 40 percent from the mid-1960s to 1993.[18] Since the 1970s, numerous publicly traded limited partnerships have been offered through many brokerage firms. A secondary market has arisen in recent years that allows some of these partnerships to trade hands. It is not unusual for these public partnerships to trade at discounts of between 50 to 60 percent of their capital accounts.[19]

### B.  Minority Discount

The minority discount is recognized because the holder of a minority interest lacks management control, cannot direct the payment of dividends and executive compensations, and cannot compel a liquidation of an entity's assets.

Although most litigated valuation cases deal with minority interests in closely held corporations, the U.S. Tax Court has held that the concept is equally applicable to partnership interests. Limited partnership interests clearly lack control because they do not have (1) voting rights, (2) rights to cause a liquidation of the entity, and (3) any right to force distributions.[20]

In RULPA states, an assignee of a partnership interest is subject to substantial limitations. The assignee is not a limited partner unless elected to that status by the partnership. Thus, the assignee has even fewer rights than the limited partner. Under RULPA, an assignee has no right to withdraw or require the partnership to purchase his or her interest. There is simply no market for the assignee's interest in the partnership.[21]

### C. Minority Discounts and Intrafamily Transfers

For many years, the I.R.S. maintained that multiple transfers of minority interest units in a family business were to be valued as part of a block that controlled the business even though the actual interest transferred was a minority interest. Courts repeatedly rejected the I.R.S.'s position by holding that there is no presumption that family members necessarily act in concert.[22]

At long last, the I.R.S. relented, agreeing with the courts and ruling that a parent's transfer of five separate blocks of 20 percent of the common stock of his wholly owned family business to each of his five children should be valued separately as five minority interests rather that as part of a family block.[23]

### D. Discounts Exemplified

Let's look at an example of how marketability and minority discounts affect valuation:

Mike and Donna contribute $2 million of real estate and securities into a family partnership and receive a 2-percent general partnership interest and 98 percent in the form of limited partnership interests. The limited partnership interest has no voting rights and may not participate in management. The partnership agreement restricts the transfer of the partnership interests. As a result, the appraisers determine that a 35-percent discount for lack of marketability and minority interests is applicable. Without the discount, a 1-percent limited partnership interest would be worth $20,000 (1 percent of $2 million). However, after allowing for the discount, the same 1-percent limited partnership interest is worth only $13,000 ($20,000 minus 35 percent of $20,000).

In sum, the exact amount of the discount that a family partnership can use will depend upon not only the type of assets held by the partnership but also the limitations of local law.

### E. File Early and Often

If you plan to make significant transfers of limited partnership interests, then you should get a professional valuation of the limited partnership interests and file a U.S. Gift Tax Return (I.R.S. Form 709) that discloses the gift and how it was valued. Adequately disclosing the gift on the face of a timely filed U.S. Gift Tax Return prevents the I.R.S. from challenging the valuation after the three-year federal gift-tax statute of limitations has expired.

## VII. Hit the I.R.S. with Everything but the Kitchen Sink

Throughout this analysis, we have discussed strategies for using FLPs to overcome income and transfer taxes, to benefit from valuation discounts, to control assets, and to protect your family from outside creditors. Are FLPs loved by the I.R.S.? Naturally not. However, FLPs have been largely untouchable, so they remain a sound investment.

## A. I.R.S.-Resistant

For years, the "Infernal" Revenue Service has been pounding its chest and screaming from atop an ivory tower in an attempt to thwart practitioners from rescuing clients by engaging in discount strategies, particularly in the area of FLPs. However, these efforts have been largely unsuccessful.

### 1. Estate Tax

Prior to 2001, the only time the I.R.S. had been remotely successful in attacking FLPs was in the estate tax venue. In both *Schauerhamer*[24] and *Reichardt*,[25] the I.R.S. was successful in including FLP assets in the estate of the decedent under I.R.C. Section 2036(a)(1) because the deceased taxpayer had effectively retained control over the assets of the partnership. Operationally, the taxpayers failed to maintain the formalities of the partnership. Nothing changed after the assets were nominally transferred to the FLP, books and records were not maintained, and income found its way into the decedent's personal accounts. As a result, the Tax Court required that the value of the assets be included in the taxable estates of the deceased general partners.

### 2. Gift Tax

In the gift-tax arena, the Tax Court has considered a series of significant cases over the last two years. The cases represent significant support for using FLPs in the future. The Tax Court systematically rejected each of the theories that the I.R.S. has attempted to advance via rulings over the last future years. The Tax Court gift-tax cases have two common threads: (1) the Tax Court places great reliance on the written partnership document—so draft accordingly, and (2) the Tax Court places great reliance on state law to determine both partnership existence and the timing of gifted partnership interests.[26] In its rulings, the Tax Court is obviously trying to send a message to the I.R.S.: Stop trying to challenge FLPs merely on procedural grounds.

## B. Transfer Tactics

Having dispensed with litigation concerns and being fully armed with knowledge of FLPs, we are ready for battle. It's time to let loose with both barrels: Let the transfers begin!

### 1. Annual Exclusion Gifts of Limited Partnership Units

As we discussed earlier, you can make gifts of $10,000 per person per year tax-free ($20,000 if married). Gifts of limited partnership interests can be given directly to each donee (child, spouse, grandchild, and so forth) without loss of voting control. Warning: Be careful with in-laws; they can become outlaws. Consider making indirect gifts of the limited partnership interests to the donees by using trusts as the direct recipients of the gifts.

### 2. Use Your Full Credit Shelter Amount

In addition to the annual exclusion amounts, consider using up your entire gift-tax applicable exclusion amount. Effective January 1, 2002, you can transfer up to $1 million ($2 million if married) of limited partnership units, in addition to your annual exclusion amounts, without paying a gift tax.

### 3. Use Your Full Generation-Skipping Tax Exemption

Instead of making the gifts on the limited partnership interest outright to the donees, consider using your full generation-skipping transfer-tax exemption ($1.06 million in calendar 2001 for each spouse) by making indirect gifts of the limited partnership interests to a single trust that will benefit multiple current and future generations.

### 4. Gifts of Discount-Limited Partnership Units

By using the leveraging available to you through a discount-limited partnership, you can transfer the same amount and leverage it by an additional 30 to 50 percent, depending upon the available discounts. In other words, you can nearly double the amount of your tax-free transfers.

### 5. Freeze Partnership Interests

FLPs can also be combined with partnership estate freezes that comply with I.R.C. Chapter 14.[27] A freeze partnership typically has two classes of equity: common units and preferred units. In this arrangement, the older family members may transfer most of the future growth of the partnership through transfers of discounted-limited partnership interests while retaining frozen cumulative preferred general partner interests that control the partnership. As the partnership grows in value, the preferred interests held by the older family members will remain frozen in value, and all other growth will inure to the benefit of the junior family members holding the common-limited partnership interests.

Normally, the senior family members want to retain control (voting rights) and much of the income (such as preferred distributions), but they would prefer that the asset value not continue to escalate in their hands (and ultimately be taxed by as much as 55 percent, the highest estate tax rate). The freeze partnership accommodates these goals and thus is the preferable vehicle if the underlying assets are high in equity value *and* produce sufficient income to cover the cumulative preferred return. In order to be effective, the cumulative return must be paid out within four years or else a tax disaster occurs: compounding of gifts that will add to the transfer tax burden. Often a partial freeze, 50 percent of the units as preferred, can be structured to permit the senior family members to preserve capital, receive all the current income, and shift up to 100 percent of future growth to their heirs.

## C. EGTRRA

The passage of the Economic Growth and Tax Relief Reconciliation Act of 2001 (EGTRRA) brought higher applicable exclusion amounts for gift, estate, and generation-skipping transfer (GST) tax purposes. The applicable exclusion rose to $1 million for all three taxes on January 1, 2002. Although EGTRRA promises even higher limits for estate and GST taxes in the future and even a short-lived repeal in the year 2010, the gift tax remains as a backstop to the income tax system. Without a lifetime transfer tax, capital gains taxes could be circumvented. Assets with built-in gains could be transferred freely from the high-income-tax-bracket taxpayers to low-income-tax-bracket taxpayers. The low-bracket taxpayers could recognize the gain and transfer the proceeds back to the higher-bracket taxpayers. As a result, measuring the value of gifts will continue to be a major battlefield for practitioners and the I.R.S. for years to come.

## VIII.  Conclusion

FLPs are exceptional inter vivos gifting tools. They ease much of the uncertainty and discomfort that creates psychological obstacles to family gift-gifting. Cash and other liquid gifts make parents uneasy. Questions frequently arise. Will the gift be used and invested wisely? Will it be saved or wasted? Will it run the risk of being taken by in-laws, outlaws (future ex-spouses), or future creditors?

FLPs allow clients to make nonspendable gifts of property in the form of nonvoting limited partnership interests by removing many of the obstacles to giving. FLPs offer control, protection, and most importantly peace of mind. Limited partnerships allow clients to create the following safeguards:

- retain control over the investment and management of assets;
- allow for greater diversification of investments by centralizing ownership and management;
- provide a cost-efficient mechanism for managing securities (through lower investment advisory fees);
- provide centralized management and effective land use planning of real estate investments;
- retain control over the distribution of cash and property;
- protect assets from the claims of interlopers and creditors; and
- provide for the accumulation of income and new wealth for younger generations.

Above all, FLPs allow clients and their families tax dollars. The transfer of limited partnership interests will enable clients to make lifetime transfers of value that avoid gift and estate taxes, while allowing them to shift taxable income to younger family members in lower income tax brackets. Family limited partnerships can serve as the centerpiece of your clients' gifting strategy.

### Endnotes

1. REVISED UNIFORM LIMITED PARTNERSHIP ACT, as adopted by The National Conference of Commissioners on Uniform State Laws at its Annual Conference in Minneapolis, Minn. (Aug. 2–9, 1985).
2. I.R.C. § 2701(1986) (as amended).
3. Rev. Rul. 93-12, 1993-1 C.B. 202, I.R.B. 1993-7, 13 (Feb. 16, 1993).
4. I.R.C. § 701 (1986) (as amended).
5. I.R.C. § 721 (1986) (as amended).
6. I.R.C. § 721(b) (1986) (as amended).
7. I.R.C. § 702 (1986) (as amended).
8. I.R.C. § 704(a) (1986) (as amended).

9. I.R.C. § 704(e) (1986) (as amended).

10. I.R.C. § 469 (1986) (as amended).

11. I.R.C. § 469(i) (1986) (as amended).

12. Treas. Reg. § 1.1469-2T(f); Treas. Dec. 8175, Feb. 19, 1988, *amended by* Treas. Dec. 8253, May 11, 1989; Treas. Dec. 8290, Feb. 23, 1990; Treas. Dec. 8318, Nov. 16, 1990; Treas. Dec. 8417, May 11, 1992; Treas. Dec. 8477, Feb. 22, 1993; Treas. Dec. 8495, Nov. 3, 1993.

13. I.R.C. § 469(c)(7)(B) (1986) (as amended).

14. I.R.C. § 735(a) (1986) (as amended) (imposes a 5-year holding requirement on inventory); I.R.C. § 737(b) (1986) (as amended) (imposes a 7-year holding requirement in order to avoid gain on prerecognition gains).

15. I.R.C. § 731(a) (1986) (as amended).

16. Rose M. Kreider and Jason M. Fields, "Number, Timing and Duration of Marriages and Divorces: 1996", UNITED STATES CENSUS BUREAU CURRENT POPULATION REPORTS, Feb. 2002, at 18.

17. Rev. Rul. 93-12, *supra*.

18. SHANNON P. PRATT, BUSINESS VALUATION: DISCOUNTS AND PREMIUMS 80–83 (John Wiley and Sons, Inc. 2001).

19. 2000 Partnership Re-Sale Discount Study (Partnership Profiles, Inc., Dallas, 2000).

20. Estate of Jones v. Commissioner, 116 T.C. 11 (2001).

21. PRATT, supra n.17 at 281.

22. *Estate of McLendon*, 77 A.F.T.R. 2d 96-666 (5th Cir., 1995); Estate of Andrews v. Commissioner, 79 T.C. 938 (1982); United States v. Estate of Bright, 658 F.2d 999, (5th Cir., 1981).

23. Rev. Rul. 93-12, *supra;* Estate of Schauerhamer v. Commissioner, T.C. Memo 1997-242 (1997); Estate of Reichardt v. Commissioner, 114 T.C. 9 (2000).

24. Strangi v. Commissioner, 115 T.C. 478 (2000); Knight v. Commissioner, 115 T.C. 36 (2000); Shepherd v. Commissioner, 115 T.C. 30 (2000); Kerr v. Commissioner, 113 T.C. 449 (Dec. 23, 1999).

25. I.R.C. § 2701 (1986) (as amended).

26. 73 T.C.M. 2855 (1977).

27. 114 T.C. 144 (2000).

# CHAPTER 12

# Family Foundations: The Legacy Continues

STEPHEN A. FROST

## I. Introduction

A family foundation is an entity established, administered, and controlled by a family for charitable purposes. A family foundation may be created during the donor's lifetime or upon the donor's death. It may be a private foundation or a private-operating foundation. A private foundation is essentially a passive organization. It receives contributions and turns around and makes grants to charitable organizations or provides scholarships. A private-operating foundation actually carries on exempt activities such as operating a library or museum.

Although some families may wish to set up a private-operating foundation, most family foundations are private foundations. Therefore, the term "family foundation" is usually used in estate- and tax-planning circles to mean a private foundation established and controlled by a particular person or family. This chapter assumes that the family foundation will be a private foundation.

This chapter will discuss the purposes for establishing a family foundation, the mechanics of establishing and administering the foundation, and the tax issues related to the foundation.

## II. Purposes for Establishing a Family Foundation

### A. Nontax Reasons for Establishing a Family Foundation

The most obvious reason for establishing a family foundation is to accomplish the charitable intentions of the donor. Although the donor's charitable intentions are often implemented in tax-efficient ways, a family foundation without a true philanthropic grounding seldom makes sense.

Provided the applicable tax rules are followed, the foundation's donor can continue to maintain control of the assets transferred to the family foundation throughout the donor's lifetime. The donor can control the foundation's investments, the foundation's distributions, and the foundation's administration. Upon the donor's death and provided the donor desires such an outcome, the family can continue to maintain and control the foundation's assets (plus any contributions received from other family members) into the indefinite future. This issue is critical because control often constitutes the most important issue when considering the creation of a family foundation.

In addition to offering control, creating a family foundation allows an individual to establish a legacy that can endure indefinitely into the future. High-net-worth clients often find the prospect of establishing a philanthropic legacy an attractive goal. For example, an individual named Joe Smith may want to establish the Joe Smith Foundation to perpetuate his name and ensure that his memory is preserved into the future.

Finally, transferring assets to a family foundation allows a family to preserve and consolidate family assets. The most skilled and responsible managers and investors within the family can invest and husband the family's combined assets. Economies of scale, especially as to investing, can be achieved.

A foundation that is exempt under Section 501(c)(3) of the Internal Revenue Code of 1986 (I.R.C.), as amended, may own S corporation stock issued by a family corporation, but it will be subject to tax on the investment as if it were a corporation. Provided that its holdings are not too large and the investment is prudent, the foundation may hold S corporation stock for long periods of time. This allows for continued control of the stock within the family.

### B. Tax Reasons for Establishing a Family Foundation

Provided that the foundation is a charitable organization as defined under I.R.C. Section 501(c)(3), lifetime transfers to a family foundation are deductible for federal income tax purposes and are not subject to gift tax.

Investment income earned by the foundation is taxed at a de minimus rate for federal tax purposes and is exempt from taxation in most states. Depending on the circumstances, a foundation's purchases are also exempt from sales tax in most states.

Testamentary gifts to a family foundation are deductible from the decedent's gross estate for estate tax purposes. The estate tax savings may be quite significant. A donor may establish a family foundation upon his or her demise and initially fund the foundation with assets from the estate. Alternatively, a donor may choose to create a family foundation during his or her lifetime and make an additional contribution to the family foundation at death.

## III. Basic Structure of a Family Foundation

A family foundation can be established as a trust or as a not-for-profit corporation under state law. If a trust is used, the trust may be either inter vivos or testamentary. However the foundation is created, the mere creation of a foundation in accordance with state law does not automatically determine its income tax status under I.R.C. Section 501(c)(3). In other words, the creation and continuance of a foundation as an entity are a function of state law, and the creation and preservation of its special tax status are solely a function of federal tax law.

### A. Family Foundation Created by Trust under State Law

Creating a foundation with a trust is relatively simple. A trust that by its terms creates a family foundation must be in writing and contain sufficient charitable language to meet the standards under I.R.C. Section 501(c)(3). The trust must be viable under state law. The control of the trust is vested in the trustee and his or her successors. The administration of the trust must conform to the terms of trust agreement and applicable state trust law. The trustee has fiduciary obligations and is held to a high standard of care. The state in which the trust is created may require annual reporting to the attorney general or other state administrative body. The trust is a separate legal entity and must apply for its own federal identification number. The trust must file annual tax returns.

### B. Family Foundation in the Corporate Form under State Law

A family foundation can also be established by creating a not-for-profit corporation in accordance with state law. Each state has a not-for-profit corporation act or its equivalent. The corporation is established by filing Articles of Incorporation with the applicable secretary of state. The articles should specifically enumerate all of the charitable purposes of the corporation and should mirror the applicable statutory purposes listed in the relevant not-for-profit corporation act. The articles should also have an express provision dedicating the corporation's assets to an exempt purpose upon dissolution. The corporation should adopt and follow the bylaws. The corporation must file annual reports with the appropriate secretary of state.

If the foundation has members, which is unlikely, control may be retained by its members or by a board of directors. More commonly, the corporation has no members and control rests solely within the board of directors. If the corporation has no members, the bylaws will determine the succession of the board seats. State law may require a minimum number of directors, so it is important that the minimum number is initially provided for and all vacancies are promptly filled.

The corporation is a separate legal entity and must apply for its own federal identification number. The corporation must file annual tax returns.

## IV. Establishing Tax-Exempt Status under I.R.C. Section 501(c)(3)

A key reason for establishing a family foundation is to make charitable contributions to an entity controlled by the donor or the donor's family. Under federal tax law, charitable contributions are not deductible unless the organization is exempt from taxation under I.R.C. Section 501(c)(3).[1] An organization that believes that it is exempt from taxation under I.R.C. Section 501(c)(3) must file a determination letter request with the Internal Revenue Service (I.R.S.). Under I.R.C. Section 508(a), a foundation is not recognized as exempt from taxation until it notifies the I.R.S. that it is seeking exempt status. The request is filed using Form 1023.

### A. Foundation Must Meet Organizational and Operational Tests

In order for a family foundation to achieve and sustain tax-exempt status under I.R.C. Section 501(c)(3), the foundation must be organized and operated exclusively for one or more of the exempt purposes listed in Section 501(c)(3). If the foundation fails either the organizational or operational tests under Section 501(c)(3), it will not be considered tax-exempt.[2]

If the foundation desires to meet the organizational test, the Articles of Incorporation or the trust agreement must (1) limit the organization's purposes to one or more of the exempt purposes listed in I.R.C. Section 501(c)(3); (2) not expressly authorize the organization to engage in activities which do not further one or more exempt purposes except to an insubstantial degree; and (3) contain an express or implied provision dedicating the foundation's assets to an exempt purpose upon the dissolution of the organization.[3]

A foundation created as a trust must identify the class of charitable beneficiaries and limit distributions from the trust to solely those charitable beneficiaries.

In order to meet the operational test, a foundation must be operated exclusively for one or more exempt purposes.[4] The foundation is operated exclusively for exempt purposes if it engages primarily in activities that further its exempt purposes.[5] A foundation may participate in nonexempt activities only to an insubstantial degree.[6] Therefore, the trustee or the board of directors and the manager, if any, must always be able to identify what exempt purpose is advanced by any foundation activity. Whether the operational test is met is a question of fact. I.R.S. audits evaluate compliance with the operational test and may lead to revocation of the foundation's exempt status if the operational test is not met.

### B. Procedural Requirements for Securing Exempt Status

Filing Form 1023 with the I.R.S. constitutes the first step in applying for exempt status under I.R.C. Section 501(c)(3).[7] If Form 1023 is timely filed and the I.R.S. ultimately determines that the organization is exempt under Section 501(c)(3), the organization's exempt status relates back to the date that the organization was organized.[8] If Form 1023 is filed late, the organization's exempt status begins as of the filing date.[9]

Form 1023 is considered to be filed in a timely fashion if it is filed within 15 months after the entity was organized.[10] An automatic 12-month extension will be granted if the extension is filed within 15 months after the entity is organized.[11] In other words, an organization may have up to 27 months to file Form 1023 and have its exempt status relate back to the date that it was organized. Provided that it is an organization described in I.R.C. Section 501(c)(3) since its inception, the entity is considered organized on the date of its incorporation or the date that the trust was created.[12]

Once Form 1023 is filed, the I.R.S. has 120 days to rule on the taxpayer's request.[13] Quite often, the I.R.S. requests additional information from the taxpayer. As long as the taxpayer responds to such requests in a timely manner, the I.R.S.'s determination will continue to relate back to the date that the entity was organized. If the I.R.S. fails to rule within 120 days, the taxpayer can get declaratory judgment as relief.[14]

Each family foundation with annual contributions in excess of $10,000 per year must pay a $500 filing fee.[15] If the annual contributions are less than $10,000 per year, the filing fee is reduced to $150.[16]

## V. Maintaining the Organization's Tax-Exempt Status under I.R.C. Section 501(c)(3)

After the foundation receives a favorable determination letter from the I.R.S. as to its tax-exempt status under I.R.C. Section 501(c)(3), the foundation must be administered in accordance with federal tax laws or risk losing its tax-exempt status—potentially retroactively.

### A. Operational Test Must Be Met at All Times

All activities performed by the foundation must further the exempt purposes of the foundation.[17] Failure to meet the operational test may result in revocation of the foundation's tax-exempt status.

## B. Private Inurement Prohibited

In order to obtain or maintain the foundation's exempt status, no part of the organization's net earnings may inure in whole or in part to the benefit of any individual or private shareholder.[18] This rule is called the prohibition against private inurement. For example, private inurement may occur whenever the foundation pays unreasonable compensation for services or any compensation for services that are not actually rendered.[19] The organization must not be organized or operated for the benefit of private interests such as designated individuals, the donor, the donor's family, shareholders of the organization, or people controlled directly or indirectly by such interests.[20] The foundation must be operated exclusively to further a public rather than a private interest.[21]

## C. Political Activities Prohibited

Except as provided under I.R.C. Section 501(h), an organization engaging in substantial legislative activities is not operated primarily to further one or more exempt purposes, so it cannot be a charitable organization.[22] Furthermore, an organization may not carry on propaganda, influence specific legislation, or participate (directly or indirectly) in any political campaign for or against any candidate for public office and maintain its exempt status.[23]

## D. Record Keeping

The foundation must keep permanent books of account or records (including inventories) as are sufficient to establish the items of gross income, receipts, and disbursements, and to substantiate the information required for the annual information return (that is, Form 990PF).[24] The organization should maintain sufficient records to avoid the excise taxes that could be imposed on the organization, certain disqualified persons, and the organization manager.[25] The organization should keep sufficient records to identify all substantial contributors to the organization. A substantial contributor is anyone who contributes more than $5,000 in a tax year when that amount constitutes more than 2 percent of all contributions received in such year. (Once a party becomes a substantial contributor to an organization, that donor always remains a substantial contributor in future years—even if making no further contributions.) Keeping records from the inception of the organization protects against an I.R.S. attempt to revoke the organization's exempt status retroactively.

## E. Public Disclosure

A foundation is required to make its application for tax exemption, annual information returns, and certain other information available for public inspection.[26] A copy of the foundation's application for tax exemption must be maintained for public inspection at the organization's principal office (and certain regional offices) during business hours.[27] Certain materials, such as trade secrets, do not have to be disclosed.[28] The foundation does not have to disclose the application until the I.R.S. issues a favorable tax-exempt determination letter.[29] Requests for inspection may be made by mail or in person. The foundation may charge a reasonable fee (set by the government) for copying and mailing costs.[30] The foundation may require that the fees for copying and mailing be paid in advance.

Similar disclosure rules apply to tax returns filed with the I.R.S. annually.[31] However, a foundation does not have to divulge the names, addresses, and contributions of contributors (except other private foundations) to the public. Furthermore, the disclosure rules do not apply to Form 990-T, the form on which unrelated business income is reported.[32]

If a foundation fails to comply with public inspection provisions as to its application for exemption, it will be subject to a $20-per-day penalty.[33] If a foundation fails to comply with public inspection provisions as to an annual report, it will be subject to a $20-per-day penalty up to $10,000.[34] A willful failure to comply with I.R.C. Section 6104(d) regarding public inspection of an annual report or the application for exemption shall subject the foundation to a $5,000 penalty tax.[35]

### F. Revocation of Exempt Status

The I.R.S. may revoke a foundation's exempt status if the foundation fails to maintain such status.[36] The I.R.S. may revoke the foundation's exempt status retroactively if (a) a material fact was omitted or misstated on Form 1023 or (b) the organization was operated materially different than was originally represented in Form 1023.[37] If the foundation's activities and purposes were accurately described in Form 1023 and there has been no material change in the operations of the foundation, the foundation may rely on its exempt determination letter.

## VI. Income Taxation of the Family Foundation

### A. Tax Accounting

As a general rule, a foundation must follow all of the tax accounting rules regarding accounting periods and accounting methods just like other taxpayers must.[38] The accrual accounting method is required if the foundation has unrelated business income in excess of $5 million.

### B. Income Taxes on Income Earned by a Private Foundation

#### 1. Contributions

Contributions to a private foundation are not included in the foundation's investment income and, therefore, are not subject to taxation.[39] The foundation receives property with a carryover basis whenever the property is contributed to it during the donor's lifetime.[40] The foundation receives property with a stepped-up basis equal to its fair market value with respect to testamentary transfers.[41] Capital gains on contributed property are included in the foundation's investment income and are subject to taxation.

#### 2. Fund-Raising

The I.R.S. has issued Publication 1391 to instruct foundations on fund-raising matters. In addition to the publication, each foundation that intends to conduct fund-raisers should be familiar with Rev. Proc. 90-12 and Rev. Rul. 67-246. Because family foundations rely on donations from within the family, fund-raising usually does not constitute a primary concern.

Each state has its own laws regarding fund-raising. The foundation manager must become familiar with the requirements of the state in which the foundation operates in order to avoid engaging in fund-raising illegalities.

### 3. Excise Tax on Investment Income

A foundation does not pay federal income taxes. Instead, a 2-percent excise tax is imposed annually on all net investment income recognized during the taxable year unless the foundation is an exempt operating foundation.[42] (Private operating foundations are not subject to this excise tax.) The excise tax rate imposed under I.R.C. Section 4940 is reduced to 1 percent whenever the foundation meets certain distribution requirements.[43]

Net investment income equals (a) the foundation's gross investment income and capital gains less (b) ordinary and necessary expenses either related to the production or collection of the gross investment income or related to the management, conservation, or maintenance of property held for production of such income.[44]

### 4. Income Taxes Due on Unrelated Business-Taxable Income

A foundation may make a number of investments beyond marketable securities, including real estate interests, partnerships, and S corporations. If the foundation invests in an unrelated trade or business that is regularly carried on, it will have to pay tax on the income derived from such investments.

An unrelated trade or business means any trade or business whose conduct is not substantially related to the organization's exempt purposes.[45] (Certain activities are excepted from the definition of unrelated trade or business under I.R.C. Section 513(a)(1)–(3), but these are not generally relevant to a family foundation.) The need for income is not considered an exempt purpose under Section 513(a).

#### a. COMPUTATION

The foundation's unrelated business taxable income (UBTI), if any, is taxed as if the organization were a corporation.[46] The foundation must also pay estimated taxes on its UBTI as if it were a corporation.[47]

The foundation's UBTI for a given tax year equals (a) the gross income derived from any unrelated trade or business regularly carried on by the organization less (b) the allowable deductions (subject to certain modifications) that are directly connected with the carrying on of such trade or business.[48]

If the foundation is a partner in a partnership that regularly carries on an unrelated trade or business, the foundation's share of the partnership's income is considered unrelated business taxable income.[49] If the foundation is a shareholder in an S corporation that regularly carries on an unrelated trade or business, the foundation's share of the S corporation's income is considered unrelated business taxable income.[50]

#### b. EXCLUSIONS

In computing UBTI, the I.R.C. mandates certain modifications. Exclusions from UBTI include passive income items such as dividends, interest, annuities, non-debt-financed rental income, and royalties.[51] Gains and losses from the sale, exchange, or other disposition of non-debt-financed real property are also excluded from UBTI as long as the foundation is not a dealer.[52] Similarly, gains and losses from the sale, exchange, or other disposition of certain real property that is considered distressed are excluded from UBTI.[53]

## c. INCLUSIONS

I.R.C. modifications also require certain inclusion modifications. For example, a portion of rents related to debt-financed real property is included in UBTI.[54] A portion of gains or losses from the sale, exchange, or other disposition of debt-financed property is also included in UBTI.[55] Unless substantially all of the use of the real property is related to the foundation's exempt purposes, any income derived from real property that is held to produce income and with respect to which there is an acquisition indebtedness constitutes UBTI.

With respect to each parcel of real property, the portion of rents and/or gains to be included in UBTI equals the average acquisition indebtedness divided by the average adjusted basis of such property for the taxable year.[56] Deductions related to the property are also taken into account based on the same formula, but only straight-line depreciation is allowed.[57]

With regard to rents, average acquisition indebtedness means the average acquisition indebtedness for the taxable year.[58] With regard to gains or losses upon the sale, exchange, or other disposition of the property, average acquisition indebtedness means the highest amount of the acquisition indebtedness for the 12 months ending on the date of such sale, exchange, or other disposition.[59]

Acquisition indebtedness includes indebtedness incurred to acquire or improve real property.[60] Except for the ten years after acquiring real property by bequest or devise, any real property acquired subject to a mortgage or other lien will be considered subject to acquisition indebtedness.[61] Extending, renewing, or refinancing a debt is a continuation of the existing indebtedness to the extent that the indebtedness does not exceed the original debt.[62] To the extent that a debt is refinanced and the principal of the debt is increased, the increase is not acquisition indebtedness.[63]

## C. Excise Taxes on Private Foundations

Excise taxes are imposed on private foundations whenever certain acts are committed. These acts include self-dealing, holding excess business investments, failing to distribute income, jeopardizing charitable purpose, and making certain taxable expenditures.

### 1. Excise Tax Assessed on Self-Dealing

An excise tax is imposed on foundation managers as defined in section V.B.3. and disqualified persons for acts of self-dealing.[64] A foundation manager includes an officer, director, trustee, and anyone else who has the similar powers and responsibilities.[65]

A disqualified person is (a) a substantial contributor; (b) a foundation manager; (c) any party who owns (either directly or indirectly) more than 20 percent of a corporation, limited liability company, or a partnership that is substantial contributor or has more than a 20 percent beneficial interest in a trust that is substantial contributor; (d) a family member of a substantial contributor, a foundation manager, or a party described in (c) above, including the individual's spouse, ancestors, descendants, and spouses of descendants; (e) any corporation, limited liability company, or partnership owned (either directly or indirectly) by disqualified persons owning, in the aggregate, more than 35 percent of such corporation, limited liability company, or partnership; (f) any trust whose beneficial interests are owned (either directly or indirectly) by disqualified persons owning, in the aggregate, more than 35 percent of such beneficial interests; or (g) a government official.

a. SELF-DEALING

The sale or exchange of property may constitute self-dealing.[66] Transferring property without consideration is not self-dealing, unless the foundation assumes a debt or obligation related to the property transferred.[67] Leasing property between a private foundation and a disqualified person is generally self-dealing, but leasing property to a private foundation without charge is not self-dealing.[68] The foundation's payment of janitorial services, utilities, and maintenance costs is not self-dealing so long as such payments are not made to a disqualified person either directly or indirectly.[69] Lending money or providing credit between a private foundation and a disqualified person is self-dealing, but lending money to a foundation without interest or other charge is not self-dealing.[70] A disqualified person furnishing goods, services, or utilities to a foundation constitutes self-dealing unless such goods, services, or utilities are rendered without charge.[71] A foundation furnishing goods, services, or utilities to a disqualified person constitutes self-dealing unless (a) such goods, services, or utilities are functionally related to the foundation's charitable purpose, (b) such goods, services, or utilities are provided to the general public, and (c) the disqualified person pays the same rate as the general public.[72] Payment of compensation to a disqualified person is self-dealing unless the compensation (a) is paid for personal services that are reasonable and necessary to carry out the exempt purpose of the foundation and (b) is not excessive.[73] Allowing a disqualified person to use or benefit from foundation assets is self-dealing.[74] This includes a grant that satisfies a legal obligation of a disqualified person.[75] Payments to and contracting with a government official are self-dealing.[76] Mergers, liquidations, and similar organic corporate changes are not self-dealing.[77] Indemnifying a foundation manager for self-dealing taxes assessed against the foundation manager is self-dealing.[78] Future gifts, such as pledges, are not counted when determining self-dealing.[79]

b. THREE TIERS OF TAX

Three tiers of tax are imposed on foundation managers for self-dealing. First, any foundation manager who participates in self-dealing must pay an excise tax equal to 2.5 percent times the amount involved *each* tax year (or partial tax year) from the act to the date that it is corrected (or the excise tax is assessed or a deficiency notice is issued, whichever is earlier). The maximum that may be assessed is $10,000.[80] Second, if the self-dealing transaction is not corrected before the first-tier excise tax is assessed or a deficiency notice is issued, whichever is earlier, any foundation manager who participated in the self-dealing must pay an excise tax equal to 50 percent times the amount involved up to a maximum of $10,000.[81] For repeated violations or willful and flagrant violations, I.R.C. Section 6684 assesses a third-tier tax equal to the sum of the first-tier and second-tier taxes.

Three tiers of tax are also imposed on disqualified persons for self-dealing. First, any disqualified person who participates in self-dealing must pay an excise tax equal to 5 percent times the amount involved each tax year (or partial tax year) from the act to the date that it is corrected (or the excise tax is assessed or a deficiency notice is issued, whichever is earlier).[82] Second, if the self-dealing transaction is not corrected before the first-tier excise tax is assessed or a deficiency notice is issued, whichever is earlier, any disqualified person who participated in the self-dealing must pay an excise tax equal to 200 percent times the amount involved up to a maximum of $10,000.[83] For repeated violations or willful and flagrant violations, I.R.C. Section 6684 assesses a third-tier tax equal to the sum of the first-tier and second-tier taxes.

The excise taxes assessed under I.R.C. Section 4941 apply separately to each act of self-dealing. The liability for the excise tax is joint and several. Willful and repeated violations will result in involuntary termination of the foundation's tax-exempt status.


## 2. *Excise Tax on Excess Business Holdings*

The combined holdings of a private foundation and all disqualified persons in any corporation conducting a business that is not substantially related (aside from the need of the foundation for income or funds or the use it makes of the profits derived) to the exempt purposes of the foundation are limited to 20 percent of the voting stock of such corporation.[84] The combined holdings of a private foundation and all disqualified persons in any partnership or limited liability company conducting a business that is not substantially related (aside from the need of the foundation for income or funds or the use it makes of the profits derived) to the exempt purposes of the foundation are limited to 20 percent of the beneficial or profits interest in such business.[85] A foundation is not permitted to own any holdings in a sole proprietorship that is not substantially related to the exempt purposes of the foundation (aside from the need of the foundation for income or funds or the use it makes of the profits derived).[86] Any foundation that fails to follow these rules is subject to an excise tax equal to 5 percent of the value of the excess business holdings.[87] If the foundation then fails to divest its excess business holdings in a timely manner, the I.R.C. imposes an additional excise tax equal to 200 percent of the value of the excess business holdings.[88]


## 3. *Excise Taxes on Failure to Distribute Income*

A foundation must make qualifying distributions (in aggregate) equal to at least 5 percent of the average fair market value of its assets (other than those used or held for use in carrying out the foundation's exempt purposes) within 12 months after the end of each tax year.[89]

If a foundation fails to make a minimum distribution by the first day of the second succeeding tax year, the I.R.C. imposes a 15-percent excise tax on the foundation.[90] The excise tax is based on the amount that should have been distributed but was not.[91] If the minimum distribution is not made by the end on the second succeeding year, the I.R.C. imposes an additional excise tax equal to 100 percent of the undistributed income.[92]

A foundation that distributes more than the required minimum amount may carry over the excess to future years (up to five) for purposes of the minimum distribution calculations.[93]

For purposes of I.R.C. Section 4942, qualifying distributions include distributions to public charities and private operating foundations.[94] Distributions to private foundations also qualify provided that the donee then distributes the amount received to a public charity or private operating foundation within the next succeeding tax year.[95] Payments of reasonable and necessary administrative expenses qualify as distributions[96] as do amounts paid to acquire assets used (or held for use) directly to carry out the organization's exempt purposes.[97] Amounts set aside for future specific projects that further the organization's exempt purposes also qualify.[98]

This excise tax does not apply to private operating foundations.[99]

### 4. Excise Tax on Investments That Jeopardize Charitable Purpose

In order to curb imprudent investments by foundations, the I.R.C. imposes an excise tax on the foundation and the foundation manager whenever the foundation invests any amount in such a manner that jeopardizes the fulfillment of any of its exempt purposes.

The excise tax is to equal 5 percent of the amount so invested.[100] If the foundation fails to promptly remove the investment from jeopardy, the I.R.C. imposes an additional excise tax equal to 200 percent of the amount of the investment.[101]

Any time that a 5 percent tax is imposed on the foundation, the foundation manager is also taxed 5 percent of the amount invested unless manager participation was due to reasonable cause and was not willful.[102] If the foundation fails to promptly remove the investment from jeopardy, the foundation manager is subject to an additional excise tax equal to 5 percent of the amount invested unless the manager agreed to the timely removal of the investment from jeopardy.[103]

### 5. Taxable Expenditures

The I.R.C. imposes excise taxes on certain taxable expenditures as a way to dissuade foundations from using foundation assets to support certain activities, particularly political activities.

A taxable expenditure is defined in I.R.C. Section 4945(d) to mean any amount paid or incurred by a private foundation

1. to carry on propaganda or otherwise attempt to influence legislation;
2. to influence the outcome of any specific public election or to carry on (directly or indirectly) any voter registration drives (except as specifically provided in I.R.C. Section 4945(e));
3. as a grant to an individual for travel, study, or other similar purposes by such individual, unless certain requirements under I.R.C. Section 4945(g) are met;
4. as a grant to an organization that is not a public charity unless the granting foundation retains expenditure responsibility with respect to the grant; and
5. for any purpose other than a religious, charitable, scientific, literary, or educational purpose; to foster national or international amateur sports competition; or for the prevention of cruelty to children or animals.

Any foundation that makes a taxable expenditure is subject to an annual excise tax equal to 10 percent of the expenditure.[104] If the foundation fails to promptly correct the taxable expenditure, the I.R.C. imposes an additional excise tax equal to 100 percent of the expenditure on the foundation.[105] A third-tier penalty may be assessed under I.R.C. Sections 6684 and 507 for willful violations of I.R.C. Section 4945. A willful and flagrant violation may ultimately result in the termination of the foundation's exempt status and the imposition of a termination tax.

Any time that a foundation makes a taxable expenditure and the foundation manager agreed to the expenditure knowing that it was a taxable expenditure, the I.R.C. imposes an excise tax equal to 2.5 percent of the taxable expenditure on the foundation manager unless manager participation was due to reasonable cause and was not willful.[106] (With regard to any one taxable expenditure, the maximum amount of the first-tier tax imposed on a manager is $5,000.)[107] Whenever an additional excise tax equal to

100 percent of a taxable expenditure is imposed on the foundation because the foundation continued to make taxable expenditures, the I.R.C. also taxes the foundation manager 50 percent of the taxable expenditure unless the manager attempted to cancel the taxable expenditure.[108] (With regard to any one taxable expenditure, the maximum amount of the second-tier tax imposed on a manager is $10,000.)[109]

### D.  Tax Returns Filings

A private foundation is obliged to file annual income tax returns with the I.R.S. Form 990-PF must be filed on or before the 15th day of the fifth month following the end of the foundation's year.[110] For a foundation operating on the calendar year, this means that a federal tax return is due on May 15. If the foundation has unrelated business taxable income, Form 990-T must be filed on the same date.[111] Form 4720 must be filed on the same date if excise taxes are due and owing.[112] Tax payments are due with each return.

Foundations are obliged to file annual returns with individual states. In addition to state law requirements, annual filings with the states constitute a federal obligation as well.[113]

Annual returns filed with the I.R.S. are subject to public inspection.[114]

Any foundation that sells, exchanges, or otherwise disposes of certain property transferred to it within two years of receipt must file Form 8282 with the IRS.[115] The property subject to this rule is any property (other than marketable securities) with a claimed value in excess of $5,000 at the time of contribution.[116] Form 8282 must be filed within 125 days after the sale, exchange, or other disposition of the property.[117]

The I.R.C. assesses late filing penalties of $20 per day (up to $10,000) under I.R.C. Section 6652(c)(1)(A). There is an additional late filing penalty equal to 5 percent of the tax required to be shown on the return for each month or portion of a month that the return is late, up to a maximum of 25 percent.[118] There is also a late payment penalty equal to 0.5 percent of the tax due for each month or portion of a month that the final payment is late, up to a maximum of 25 percent.[119] The I.R.C. assesses interest on late payments under I.R.C. Section 6601.

For estimated tax purposes, a foundation is treated like a corporation.[120] Hence, a foundation must pay estimated taxes on its investment income quarterly. Failing to make estimated payments in a timely fashion results in the assessment of penalties under I.R.C. Section 6655. For a foundation operating on a calendar year, estimated tax payments are due on May 15, June 15, September 15, and December 15. A foundation may use the same estimated tax-safe harbors as a corporation to avoid estimated tax underpayment penalties. A foundation is also subject to the large corporation rules for estimated tax purposes.

The I.R.C. obligates a foundation to pay payroll taxes and file miscellaneous tax returns such as payroll tax returns (such as Forms 940, 941, and W-3) and information returns (such as Forms W-2 and 1099).

## VII.  Income Taxation Associated with Contributions

A primary reason for establishing a private foundation during the donor's lifetime is to take advantage of the charitable income tax deduction associated with such transfers. Although the foundation may make grants to other charitable organizations over several years or decades, the donor will get a current income tax deduction in the year of the contribution.

## A.  Income Tax Deduction for Contributions Made to Private Foundations

Contributions to a private foundation are tax-deductible to the donor. (See I.R.C. Section 170.) However, there are limitations applicable to such charitable deductions. The type of property contributed to a private foundation has a significant impact on the amount of the donor's charitable deduction. Cash contributions to a private foundation are tax-deductible in full.[121] Contributions of marketable stock that is eligible for long-term capital gains, that is, qualified appreciated stock, may be deducted based on the fair market value of the stock.[122] (Because this rule also applies to loss property, it is wiser to sell loss property, utilize the long-term capital loss on the donor's individual tax return, and contribute the sales proceeds to the private foundation.) Personal property, nonmarketable stock, and short-term marketable stock are deductible only to the extent of the donor's basis, which is usually cost.[123]

Because of the amazing increase in stock values over the last decade, many people own significantly appreciated stock. Provided that this stock is traded on an exchange and is eligible for long-term treatment, contributions of appreciated stock to a private foundation will maximize the income tax benefits to the donor. Not only will the donor be able to utilize a charitable deduction equal to the fair market value of the stock, the foundation will only be subject to a 2-percent excise tax (1 percent in some circumstances) on the sale of the stock. In other words, the tax on the capital gain is reduced from 20 percent to 2 percent (1 percent in some circumstances). Everyone, except the government, appears to benefit.

## B.  Limits on Income Tax Deductibility

Although the amount of the charitable contribution may not be limited, the timing of the deduction may be limited. Contributions of cash and nonappreciated property are, in aggregate, deductible up to 30 percent of the donor's contribution base, that is, the donor's adjusted gross income without considering any net operating loss carryback.[124] Capital asset contributions that are eligible for long-term treatment are, in aggregate, deductible up to 20 percent of the donor's contribution base.[125] Ordinary income items and capital asset contributions that are eligible for short-term treatment are, in aggregate, deductible up to 30 percent of the donor's contribution base.[126] Any charitable contributions that exceed these limits may be carried forward for up to five years.[127]

## C.  Reporting of Noncash Contributions

A donor must report contributions of property (other than cash), including marketable stock, worth more than $500 on the donor's individual income tax return for the year in which the transfer occurred.[128] The donor must attach Form 8283 to his individual income tax return and give details related to the property transferred to the foundation.[129]

An appraisal attached to the donor's income tax return must accompany any contribution of property with a claimed value more than $5,000 and which is not traded on an established exchange.[130]

## D.  Contemporaneous Written Acknowledgment

A contemporaneous acknowledgment issued by the foundation must accompany any contribution of cash and/or property with a good faith estimate of value in excess of

$250.[131] If the donor fails to secure such an acknowledgment, the contributions may be denied on audit. Therefore, the foundation should always acknowledge every contribution in writing as a matter of course.

If the foundation files a tax return that reports all of the information that would have been reported on acknowledgment, the donor may still receive his deduction.[132]

## VIII.  *Estate and Gift Taxation Associated with Contributions*

### A.  Estate Taxes

Testamentary transfers to charitable organizations, including private foundations, are unlimited for estate tax purposes.[133] In other words, a taxpayer who leaves an entire estate to a private foundation avoids the imposition of the federal estate tax. The types and amounts of property contributed to a private foundation are irrelevant.[134] A private foundation may receive a specific bequest, a percentage of the estate, a formulaic amount, a contingent bequest, or a residual interest. A private foundation may also take as a contingent beneficiary should a noncharitable beneficiary timely execute and file a disclaimer.

### B.  Gift Taxes

Gifts to charity are not subject to gift tax.[135] Indeed, gifts to a charity (including a private foundation) in excess of the annual exclusion amount under I.R.C. Section 2503 are not subject to the I.R.C. Section 6019 gift-tax return filing requirements as long as the donor transferred his or her entire interest in the property and the transfer qualifies for the gift-tax charitable deduction under I.R.C. Section 2522.[136]

## IX.  *Termination of a Family Foundation*

I.R.C. Section 507 controls the termination of foundations. Two types of terminations create taxable events. First, a foundation may voluntarily terminate its exempt status under I.R.C. Section 507(a)(1). Second, the I.R.S. may terminate a foundation's exempt status if there have been either willful repeated acts (or failures to act) or a willful and flagrant act (or failure to act), giving rise to a penalty tax under I.R.C. Section 6864.[137] If a foundation's exempt status is voluntarily or involuntarily terminated, a termination tax is imposed on the foundation equal to the lesser of (a) the aggregate tax benefit enjoyed by the foundation throughout its existence, or (b) the value of its net assets.[138]

A foundation may terminate tax-free in one of several ways:

1. It may distribute all of its net assets to certain public charities that have been in existence for a continuous period of at least 60 calendar months immediately preceding the distribution.[139]
2. It may operate the foundation as a public charity for at least 60 months and then terminate.[140]
3. It may transfer all of its assets to another private foundation and then voluntarily terminate the foundation.[141] (The transferor will be required to exercise expenditure authority with respect to transfers made to the transferee private foundation.)

4. It may merge the foundation into another private foundation in good status.[142] The transferee foundation is not treated as a newly created organization and, therefore, acquires all of the distributing foundation's tax benefits.[143]

## X. Conclusion

A family foundation offers a number of attractive tax and nontax advantages for clients with sufficient assets and charitable inclinations. Every practitioner should become familiar with the many advantages associated with a private foundation. Every practitioner should also remain cognizant of the potential pitfalls inherent in the administration of a private foundation. Each private foundation may become a bountiful garden, but it must always be a well-tended one.

### *Endnotes*

1. *See* I.R.C. § 170 (1986).
2. Treas. Reg. § 1.501(c)(3)-1(a)(1).
3. I.R.C. § 508(e); Treas. Reg. § 1.501(c)(3)-1(b)(1)-(4).
4. Treas. Reg. § 1.501(c)(3)-1(c)(1).
5. *Id.*
6. *Id.*
7. Treas. Reg. § 1.508-1(a)(2).
8. I.R.C. § 508(a) (1986); Treas. Reg. §§ 1.508-1(a)(2)(i), 301.9100-2.
9. I.R.C. § 508(a)(2).
10. Treas. Reg. § 1.508-1(a)(2)(i).
11. Treas. Reg. § 301.9100-2.
12. Treas. Reg. § 1.508-1(a)(2)(iii).
13. I.R.C. § 7428(b)(2) (1986).
14. *Id.*
15. I.R.S. Form 8718.
16. *Id.*
17. Treas. Reg. § 1.501(c)(3)-1(c)(1).
18. Treas. Reg. § 1.501(c)(3)-1(c).
19. *See* Rev. Rul. 73-126, 1973-1 C.B. 220.
20. Treas. Reg. § 1.501(c)(3)-1(d)(1)(ii).
21. *Id.*
22. Treas. Reg. § 1.501(c)(3)-1(c)(3)(i).
23. Treas. Reg. § 1.501(c)(3)-1(c)(3).
24. I.R.C. § 6001 (1986); Treas. Reg. § 1.6001-1(a).
25. Rev. Rul. 56-304, 1956-2 C.B. 306.
26. I.R.C. § 6104.
27. I.R.C. § 6104(d)(1).
28. I.R.C. § 6104(a)(1)(D).
29. Treas. Reg. § 301.6104(d)-1(b)(3)(iii)(A).
30. I.R.C. § 6104(d)(1)(B) (1986); Treas. Reg. § 301.6104(d)-1(d)(3).
31. I.R.C. § 6104(b).
32. Treas. Reg. § 301.6104(d)-1(b)(4)(ii).
33. I.R.C. § 6652(c)(1)(D).
34. I.R.C. § 6652(c)(1)(C).
35. I.R.C. § 6685 (1986).
36. Rev. Proc. 90-27, 1990-1 C.B. 514.

37. *Id.*
38. Treas. Reg. § 1.511-3(c).
39. I.R.C. § 102.
40. I.R.C. § 1015.
41. I.R.C. § 1014 (1986).
42. I.R.C. § 4940(a), (c).
43. I.R.C. § 4940(e).
44. I.R.C. § 4940(c).
45. I.R.C. § 513(a).
46. I.R.C. § 511(a) (1986).
47. I.R.C. § 6655(g)(3).
48. I.R.C. § 512(a).
49. I.R.C. § 512(c).
50. I.R.C. § 512(e) (1986).
51. I.R.C. §§ 512(b)(1), (2).
52. I.R.C. § 512(b)(5).
53. I.R.C. § 512(b)(16).
54. I.R.C. § 512(b)(3).
55. *Id.*
56. I.R.C. § 514(a) (1986).
57. I.R.C. § 514(a)(2).
58. I.R.C. § 514(c)(7).
59. *Id.*
60. I.R.C. § 514(c)(1).
61. I.R.C. § 514(c)(2) (1986).
62. I.R.C. § 514(c)(3); Treas. Reg. § 1.514(c)-1(c).
63. Treas. Reg. § 1.514(c)-1(c)(3).
64. I.R.C. § 4941.
65. *Id.*
66. *Id.*
67. I.R.C. § 4941(d) (1986).
68. *Id.*
69. *Id.*
70. *Id.*
71. *Id.*
72. *Id.*
73. *Id.*
74. *Id.*
75. *Id.*
76. *Id.*
77. *Id.*
78. *Id.*
79. *Id.*
80. I.R.C. § 4941 (1986).
81. *Id.*
82. *Id.*
83. *Id.*
84. I.R.C. § 4943 (1986); Treas. Reg. § 53.4943-1.
85. Treas. Reg. § 53.4943-1.
86. *Id.*
87. I.R.C. § 4943(a).
88. I.R.C. § 4943(b) (1986).
89. I.R.C. §§ 4942(a), (e).
90. I.R.C. § 4942(a).

91. *Id.*
92. I.R.C. § 4942(b).
93. I.R.C. § 4942(i) (1986).
94. I.R.C. § 4942(g).
95. I.R.C. § 4942(g)(3).
96. I.R.C. § 4942(g)(1)(A).
97. I.R.C. § 4942(g)(1)(B).
98. I.R.C. § 4942(g)(2) (1986).
99. I.R.C. §§ 4942(a), (j)(3).
100. I.R.C. § 4944(a)(1).
101. I.R.C. § 4944(b)(1).
102. I.R.C. § 4944(a)(2).
103. I.R.C. § 4944(b)(2) (1986).
104. I.R.C. § 4945(a)(1).
105. I.R.C. § 4945(b)(1).
106. I.R.C. § 4945(a)(2).
107. I.R.C. § 4945(c)(2).
108. I.R.C. § 4945(b)(2) (1986).
109. I.R.C. § 4945(c)(2).
110. I.R.C. § 6072(e); Treas. Reg. § 1.6033-2(e).
111. I.R.C. § 6072(e).
112. I.R.S. Form 4720, Instructions.
113. *See* I.R.C. § 6033(c) (1986).
114. I.R.C. § 6104(b).
115. I.R.C. § 6050L(a).
116. I.R.C. § 6050L(b).
117. Treas. Reg. §§ 1.6050L-1(f).
118. I.R.C. § 6651(a)(1) (1986).
119. I.R.C. § 6651(a)(2)(A).
120. I.R.C. § 6655(g)(3).
121. I.R.C. § 170.
122. I.R.C. §§ 170(e)(1)(B)(ii), (e)(5).
123. I.R.C. § 170(e)(1) (1986).
124. I.R.C. §§ 170(b)(1)(B), (D).
125. I.R.C. §§ 170(b)(1)(C), (D).
126. *Id.*
127. I.R.C. § 170(d); Treas. Reg. § 1.170A-10.
128. Treas. Reg. § 1.170A-13 (1986).
129. *Id.*
130. *Id.*
131. I.R.C. § 170(f)(8); Treas. Reg. § 1.170A-13.
132. I.R.C. § 170(f)(8)(D).
133. I.R.C. § 2055 (1986).
134. *Id.*
135. I.R.C. § 2522.
136. Taxpayer Relief Act of 1997, Pub. L. No. 105-34, § 1301, 111 Stat. 788 (1997).
137. I.R.C. § 507(a)(2)(A).
138. I.R.C. § 507(c) (1986).
139. I.R.C. § 507(b)(1)(A).
140. I.R.C. § 507(b)(1)(B).
141. I.R.C. § 507(b); Priv. Ltr. Rul. 9326062 (April 9, 1993).
142. I.R.C. § 507(b)(1).
143. I.R.C. § 507(b)(2) (1986).

# CHAPTER 13

# Qualified Personal Residence Trusts

CARMELA T. MONTESANO

## I. Introduction

In order to minimize transfer taxes, taxpayers should consider the use of a qualified personal residence trust (QPRT). A QPRT is an irrevocable trust (that is, a trust that is not amendable or revocable) to which a taxpayer transfers title on his or her principal residence or vacation residence for a specified number of years (fixed term), during which the taxpayer retains the full right to use and occupy the residence. If, at any time prior to the expiration of the fixed term, the residence is sold, the trust may either hold the after-tax proceeds in a separate account (in which event the taxpayer's interest in the trust will be converted into an annuity for the remainder of the fixed term) or a replacement residence (if the purchase of such residence occurs within a two-year qualifying period).

Upon the expiration of the fixed term, the trustee may either distribute the trust property, outright and free of trust, to the remainder beneficiaries (who are typically the taxpayer's children, grandchildren, or other lineal descendants selected by the taxpayer); or retain the trust property in further trust for the benefit of such beneficiaries, upon such terms and conditions as the taxpayer may determine in the governing trust instrument.

The taxpayer may continue to reside in the residence upon the expiration of the fixed term if the taxpayer rents the residence from the remainder beneficiaries at its fair market rental value. Alternatively, the taxpayer has the option of leaving the residence and finding a new one.

## II. Overview of Federal Estate, Gift, and Income Tax Consequences upon Transfer of Residence to QPRT

### A. Federal Estate Tax Consequences

The key tax advantage in establishing a QPRT is that if the taxpayer survives the fixed term, the entire fair market value of the trust property escapes inclusion in the taxpayer's gross estate. If the taxpayer does not survive the fixed term, the entire fair market value of the trust property is includable in the taxpayer's gross estate. However, this result is no worse than if the taxpayer had not established a QPRT and had simply continued to own the residence, either individually or as a joint tenant with another. Because of the danger of estate tax inclusion, estate planners typically recommend that the fixed term for the trust be equal to or shorter than the taxpayer's life expectancy.

## B. Federal Gift-Tax Consequences

Another key tax advantage in establishing a QPRT is that upon transfer, the taxpayer will be treated under federal gift-tax law as having made a taxable gift of the residence to the trust in an amount equal only to the present value of the remainder interest in the residence. In other words, the value of the gift is not the fair market value of the property at the time of the transfer, but rather a significantly discounted value.

This discounted value is determined by reference to Internal Revenue Service (I.R.S.) actuarial tables, the fair market value of the residence at the time of transfer (as determined by an independent qualified appraisal), and the taxpayer's actuarial age at the time of the transfer. In determining the amount of the discount, the I.R.S. applies an interest factor, which changes each month. For example, the appropriate applicable federal rate for transfers occurring in November 2001 was 5.0 percent and the appropriate applicable federal rate for transfers occurring in December 2001 was 4.8 percent.

In addition, the amount of the taxable gift may be further reduced for federal gift tax purposes if the taxpayer retains a reversionary interest in the QPRT in the event that such taxpayer dies prior to the expiration of the fixed term. For example, if the taxpayer dies prior to the expiration of the fixed term, the governing trust instrument may require that the residence reverts back to the taxpayer's estate or vests the taxpayer with a contingent general power of appointment over the trust property. Because of the statistical probability that the taxpayer may die prior to the expiration of the fixed term and that the trust property may actually revert to the taxpayer's estate or be subject to the taxpayer's contingent general power of appointment, the amount of the taxable gift deemed made under federal gift tax law upon the initial transfer of the residence to the QPRT is further reduced.

There is one additional way taxpayers may minimize their federal gift tax burden. Married taxpayers may hold title to their homes as tenants in common. Each taxpayer may then establish a QPRT using this fractional interest, which is typically accorded significant valuation discounts. Such discounts are determined by qualified independent appraisers at the time the property is transferred to the QPRT and may range generally from 10 percent to 40 percent depending upon the specific facts and circumstances regarding the property and the partial interest owned by the taxpayer therein.

A taxpayer may use the taxpayer's unused applicable credit amount ($1 million in calendar year 2002) to offset any gift tax the establishment of a QPRT may generate. In many instances, this will make the establishment of a QPRT gift-tax–free.

## C. Federal Income Tax Consequences

No federal income tax consequences ensue from the establishment of a QPRT. Because all QPRT income is paid to the taxpayer (in the form of the retained use of the residence), the QPRT is considered to be a grantor trust for federal income tax purposes with respect to the retained income portion of the trust.[1] In addition, if the value of the taxpayer's reversionary interest in the QPRT exceeds 5 percent of the value of the trust at its inception, the QPRT will also be a grantor trust for federal income tax purposes with respect to the principal of the trust.[2]

Grantor trust status is desirable for federal income tax purposes because, as such, the taxpayer is taxed on any income realized by the trust during the fixed term, including any capital gain on the sale of the residence, which is not otherwise excludible. Tax payments that may arise serve to further reduce the taxpayer's gross estate for federal estate-tax purposes. Under certain circumstances, grantor trust status may be obtained by the taxpayer even after the expiration of the fixed term by the incorporation of certain technical provisions into the governing trust instrument.

## III. Example Illustrating Federal Gift and Estate-Tax Consequences upon Transfer of Residence to QPRT

Assume a taxpayer, age 62, holds title to a residence valued at $1.4 million. Assume further that the taxpayer transfers title on the residence to a QPRT in November 2001 (at which time the appropriate applicable federal rate is 5 percent, with a 15-year fixed term (which is approximately two-thirds of such taxpayer's adjusted life expectancy)[3] and a reversionary interest therein if she should die during the fixed term.

Based upon the appropriate I.R.S. tables, the value of the interest retained by the taxpayer (in the form of the retained use of the residence during the fixed term) is $635,670 and the value of the reversionary interest retained by the taxpayer is $317,044, for an aggregate retained value by the taxpayer in the residence during the fixed term of $952,714. Thus, the value of the taxable gift upon transfer of the residence to the QPRT for federal gift-tax purposes is $447,286 ($1.4 million minus $952,714). Hence, while the fair market value of the asset transferred by the taxpayer to the QPRT is $1.4 million, for federal gift-tax purposes the value is not $1.4 million, but rather the significantly reduced value of $447,286.

If the taxpayer survives the fixed term and the residence appreciates at the rate of 4 percent per year, the fair market value of the residence upon the expiration of the fixed term will be $2,521,321. If the taxpayer should die immediately after the expiration of the fixed term, no portion of the $2,521,321 value will be included in her gross estate for federal estate-tax purposes.

The federal transfer tax savings upon the transfer of a residence to a QPRT are dramatic and would be even more so in this example if (1) the fixed term was greater than 15 years, (2) the fair market value of the property appreciated at a rate of greater than 4 percent per year, and/or (3) the property interest transferred to the QPRT was an undivided 50 percent ownership interest in the residence held by the taxpayer as a tenant in common (thus entitling her to an up-front valuation discount in an amount ranging approximately from 10 to 40 percent).

## IV. Statutory and Regulatory Basis for Establishment of QPRT

### A. Statutory and Regulatory Provisions

In general, special valuation rules are provided in Section 2702 of the Internal Revenue Code (I.R.C.) of 1986, as amended, with regard to transfers of interests in trust to, or for the benefit of, a member of the transferor's family. Under such rules, the value of any such trust interest that is retained by the transferor (or any applicable family member) is zero, unless certain rules apply.

An exception to such valuation rules is provided for in I.R.C. Section 2702(a)(3)(A)(ii) with regard to any transfer "if such transfer involves the transfer of an interest in trust all the property in which consists of a residence to be used as a personal residence by persons holding term interests in such trust." To implement this statutory provision, the regulations promulgated under I.R.C. Section 2702 allow for the creation of a QPRT. Stringent requirements are provided in Treas. Reg. Section 25.2702-5 regarding the establishment, administration, and disposition of a QPRT.

### B. Regulatory Provisions Required to Establish Valid QPRT

The provisions in the QPRT must meet each of the requirements specified in the regulations, and such provisions must by their terms continue in effect during the entire QPRT existence.[4] The terms of a QPRT must include, for example, the following:

- A requirement that any income of the QPRT be distributed to the termholder not less frequently than annually.[5]
- A provision prohibiting the QPRT from making distributions of corpus to any beneficiary other than the transferor prior to the expiration of the retained term interest.[6]
- A provision prohibiting the QPRT from holding any asset other than one residence to be used or held for use as a personal residence of the termholder, with detailed exceptions being allowed under the regulations for certain additions of cash, improvements, sales proceeds, insurance, and insurance proceeds.[7]
- A provision prohibiting the QPRT from containing a "commutation" power (or prepayment of the termholder's interest).[8]
- Incorporation of certain provisions into the QPRT regarding the cessation of use of the property as a personal residence[9] and the disposition of QPRT assets upon cessation as a personal residence trust.[10]
- A provision prohibiting the QPRT from selling or transferring the residence, directly or indirectly, to the grantor, the grantor's spouse, or an entity controlled by the grantor or the grantor's spouse during the retained term interest of the QPRT, or at any time after the retained term interest that the QPRT is a grantor trust.[11]

While these requirements are highly technically detailed, they are concisely delineated in the regulations. This helps the taxpayer in that a properly drafted QPRT that incorporates all such requirements should be accepted by the I.R.S. as valid. This certainty enhances the viability of the QPRT as an estate-planning technique.

## V. Additional Considerations

### A. Regulatory Provisions and I.R.S. Rulings Regarding Personal Residence

#### 1. QPRT May Hold Only One Personal Residence of Taxpayer

In order to constitute a valid QPRT, the governing instrument must prohibit the trust from holding during the fixed term any asset other than one residence to be used or held for use as a personal residence of the termholder, with detailed exceptions being allowed under the regulations for certain additions of cash, improvements, sales proceeds, insurance, and insurance proceeds.[12] Under these rules, a QPRT may hold only one personal residence of the taxpayer. For these purposes, the term "personal residence" means[13] (1) the principal residence of the termholder (within the meaning of former I.R.C. Section 1034, regarding the nonrecognition of gain upon sale of a principal residence);[14] (2) one other residence of the termholder (within the meaning of I.R.C. Section 280(d)(1) but without regard to Section 280A(d)(2));[15] or (3) an undivided fractional interest in either.[16]

The determination that a residence constitutes a principal residence of the termholder (within the meaning of former I.R.C. Section 1034) is based upon all of the relevant facts and circumstances.[17] Property used by the taxpayer as his or her principal residence may include a single-family dwelling, a houseboat, a house trailer, and stock held by a tenant-stockholder in a cooperative housing corporation (as those terms are defined in I.R.C. Sections 216(b)(1) and (2)), if the dwelling which the taxpayer is entitled to occupy as such stockholder is used by such taxpayer as his or her principal residence.[18] It may also include a condominium.[19]

The determination that a residence constitutes one other residence of the termholder is made with regard to I.R.C. Section 280(d)(1) but without regard to Section 280A(d)(2).[20] Under Section 280A(d)(1), a taxpayer is deemed to use a dwelling unit during the taxable year as a residence if he or she uses such unit (or portion thereof) for personal purposes for a number of days that exceeds the greater of fourteen days or 10 percent of the number of days during such year for which such unit is rented at a fair rental. For these purposes, the term "dwelling unit" includes a house, apartment, condominium, mobile home, boat, or similar property, which provides basic living accommodations such as sleeping space, toilet, and cooking facilities.[21] A unit will not be treated as rented at a fair rental for any day for which it is used for personal purposes.[22] Hence, the residence transferred to a QPRT may be a vacation residence or may be a residence rented for a portion of the year, as long as such rental does not prevent the taxpayer from meeting the personal-use requirements set forth under I.R.C. Section 280A(d)(1).[23]

A residence is a personal residence only if its primary use is as a residence of the termholder when occupied by the termholder.[24] The principal residence of the termholder will meet these requirements even if a portion of the residence is used (1) as an office in the home within the meaning of I.R.C. Section 280A(c)(1)[25] or (2) in providing day care services within the meaning of Section 280A(c)(4),[26] provided that in all events such use is secondary to use of the residence as a residence.[27] A residence is not used primarily as a residence if it is used to provide transient lodging, and substantial services are provided in connection with the provision of lodging (such as a hotel or a bed-and-breakfast).[28]

Critical to the determination that a residence is a qualifying residence for QPRT purposes is that the residence is used or held for use as a personal residence of the termholder.[29] A residence is held for use as a personal residence of the termholder as long as the residence is not occupied by any other person (other than the spouse or a dependent of the termholder) and is available at all times for use by the termholder as a personal residence.[30] This latter held-for-use test will prevent the loss of QPRT status when the termholder moves to a nursing home or other health care facility after the creation of the QPRT.[31]

The fact that a residence is subject to a mortgage does not affect its status as a personal residence.[32]

The term "personal residence" does not extend to include personal property (such as household furnishings).[33]

### 2. *Personal Residence May Include Appurtenant Structures and Adjacent Land*

A personal residence may include appurtenant structures used by the termholder for residential purposes and adjacent land not in excess of that which is reasonably appropriate for residential purposes (taking into account the residence's size and location).[34] The determination as to what is reasonably appropriate for residential purposes will be made by the I.R.S. in a private letter ruling if requested by a taxpayer. Numerous such rulings have been issued by the IRS.

Interestingly, multiple parcels of land with diverse structures may constitute a single residence for these purposes.[35] Critical to such determinations is typically the manner in which such properties are reflected on the tax maps, the manner in which such properties have been historically used by the taxpayer, and how the size of such properties compares with similar properties in the same area.

### 3. *Illustrative I.R.S. Rulings*

The I.R.S. has approved residence status in a host of private letter rulings. The following sample rulings illustrate some of the IRS's determinations:

- Property consisting of x acres of land that is improved by a single-family dwelling, a barn, a small shed, and a garage constitutes a personal residence.[36]
- Property consisting of x acres of land that is improved by a residence, a small shed, and a small caretaker's facility is a personal residence.[37]
- Property consisting of x acres of land that includes a taxpayer's vacation home, a detached garage with an apartment above the garage where a maintenance person lives rent-free for a portion of the year, a one-bedroom cabin with a loft, a tennis court, and a Jacuzzi with an outdoor shower constitutes a personal residence.[38]
- Property consisting of an 8.7-acre main lot, a one-seventh undivided interest in a 16.7-acre woodland preserve, and easements granting rights of access, improved by a taxpayer's vacation house and guest house that did not include a separate kitchen and is not rented out by the taxpayer, is a personal residence.[39]
- A certain parcel of land improved by a main house, a carport, a pier and boat dock, and a small guest house constitutes a personal residence.[40]
- A parcel of property that includes a large single-family dwelling, a swimming pool, a caretaker residence, a garage, a small barn or stable, and a fenced pasture is a personal residence.[41]

## B.  Two-Trust Limit Per Grantor

In general, a taxpayer may establish two QPRTs.[42] Trusts holding fractional interests in the same residence are treated as one trust.[43]

## C.  Selection of Fixed Term

There are no hard-and-fast rules in connection with a taxpayer selecting a fixed term. The longer the term selected by the taxpayer, the lower the amount of the taxable gift. However, in order to achieve the desired transfer-tax consequences upon establishing a QPRT, the objective clearly is to select a fixed term that the taxpayer will survive, based upon the information available to the taxpayer immediately prior to the execution of the QPRT. Assuming the taxpayer is essentially in good health, a general rule of thumb is to select a fixed term slightly shorter than the taxpayer's actuarial life span.

In light of the Economic Growth and Tax Relief Reconciliation Act of 2001, Public L. No. 107-16, signed into law by President George W. Bush on June 6, 2001 (EGTRRA), the taxpayer must also take into account that there may be no federal estate tax after 2009. That being the case, most practitioners will have the fixed term lapse prior to that date unless the taxpayer instructs otherwise, presumably under the assumption that the federal estate tax will remain in place.

## D. Selection of Trustee

The taxpayer may serve as the initial trustee of the QPRT, subject to certain technical limitations that must be set forth in the governing trust instrument. For example, if the taxpayer serves as trustee, the taxpayer may not have a power that would (1) result in the transfer of the residence to the QPRT being incomplete in whole or in part for federal gift-tax purposes, (2) enlarge the beneficial interest of any beneficiary under the governing instrument, or (3) shift any beneficial interest thereunder as between beneficiaries.

## E. Continued Possession of Residence after Expiration of Fixed Term

If the taxpayer wishes to continue to reside in the residence after the expiration of the fixed term, the taxpayer may rent the residence from the remainder beneficiaries for its fair market rental value. Rental payments are essentially an opportunity for the taxpayer to make tax-free gifts to the taxpayer's remainder beneficiaries in the form of rent after the expiration of the fixed term. In order to achieve the desired tax effects, such rental arrangements should not, however, be prearranged by the parties either prior to, or simultaneously upon, the execution of the QPRT.

## F. Title Insurance Considerations

Title insurance considerations affecting the transfer of a residence to a QPRT should also be considered at this time. Without appropriate planning, the title insurance coverage of a residence transferred to a QPRT may be lost. The typical title insurance policy is not assignable. Coverage does not continue generally for the transferor after transfers of the property (except, possibly, for deed warranties) and does not typically include a transferee in its definition of insured, even in an instance such as this where the transferee is a trust of which the named insured is the settlor (creator), current beneficiary, and perhaps even the initial trustee. Hence, prior to transferring the residence to a QPRT, the taxpayer should inquire into the possible effect of the transfer on the property's title insurance coverage. In some circumstances, title insurance coverage may be preserved at a nominal cost or by acquiring a new title insurance premium.

## G. General Effect of EGTRRA on QPRTs

The EGTRRA significantly alters the federal transfer tax system, reducing rates, increasing exemptions, and temporarily repealing the estate tax in 2010. The salient aspects of the EGTRRA call into doubt the continued utility of QPRTs. Yet, QPRTs will remain a viable estate-planning tool for taxpayers and practitioners alike who believe that the federal estate tax will ultimately persist.

## VI. Conclusion

QPRTs have proven to be an effective estate-planning technique. Scores of taxpayers have significantly reduced the size of their estates via their use of QPRTs. Over the next ten years, QPRTs may not prove as useful. However, if the estate tax is not repealed, QPRTs will retain their stature as an important estate-planning vehicle.

### Endnotes

1. I.R.C. § 677(a).

2. I.R.C. § 673(a).

3. In this example, the taxpayer's life expectancy is approximately 19 years and her adjusted life expectancy is approximately 22 years. To compute her life expectancy, Table 90CM, mortality table, was used. This table is an I.R.S. mortality table used for determining the federal gift- and estate-tax values of various component interests in property for dates after June 30, 1999. Because the table is used to value both life interests and remainder interests, it is basically neutral, neither favoring nor discriminating against one component interest (for example, a life interest) over another (for example, a remainder interest). Consequently, life expectancy and probability statistics based on the table are more representative of the population as a whole. It is also a unisex table, which means that the mortality statistics were designed to reflect the experience of both males and females.

4. Treas. Reg. § 25.2702-5(c)(1).

5. Treas. Reg. § 25.2702-5(c)(3), captioned "Income Of The Trust."

6. Treas. Reg. § 25.2702-5(c)(4), captioned "Distributions From The Trust To Other Persons."

7. Treas. Reg. § 25.2702-5(c)(5)(i).

8. Treas. Reg. § 25.2702-5(c)(6), captioned "Commutation."

9. Treas. Reg. § 25.2702-5(c)(7), captioned "Cessation Of Use As A Personal Residence."

10. Treas. Reg. § 25.2702-5(c)(8), captioned "Disposition Of Trust Assets On Cessation As Personal Residence Trust."

11. Treas. Reg. § 25.2702-5(c)(9), captioned "Sale Of Residence To Grantor, Grantor's Spouse, Or Entity Controlled By Grantor Or Grantor's Spouse."

12. Treas. Reg. § 25.2702-5(c)(5)(i).

13. Treas. Reg. § 25.2702-5(c)(2)(i).

14. Treas. Reg. § 25.2702-5(c)(2)(i)(A). Cf. Public L. No. 105-34, §312(a), (b). I.R.C. § 1034, captioned "Rollover Of Gain On Sale Of Principal Residence," was repealed (after the publication of the regulations under I.R.C. § 2702) by the Taxpayer Relief Act of 1997.

15. Treas. Reg. § 25.2702-5(c)(2)(i)(B).

16. Treas. Reg. § 25.2702-5(c)(2)(i)(C).

17. Treas. Reg. § 1.1034-1(c)(3)(i). This regulatory provision provides, in relevant part, as follows:

Whether or not property is used by the taxpayer as his residence, and whether or not property is used by the taxpayer as his principal residence (in the case of a taxpayer using more than one property as a residence), depends upon all the facts and circumstances in each case, including the good faith of the taxpayer. The mere fact that property is, or has been, rented is not determinative that such property is not used by the taxpayer as his principal residence. For example, if the taxpayer purchases his new residence before he sells his old residence, the fact that he temporarily rents out the new residence during the period before he vacates the old residence may not, in the light of all the facts and circumstances in the case, prevent the new residence from being considered as property used by the taxpayer as his principal residence.

18. Treas. Reg. § 1.1034-1(c)(3)(i). See also Priv. Ltr. Rul. 94-48-035 (December 2, 1994) (I.R.S. ruled that a personal residence includes shares of stock in a cooperative apartment); Priv. Ltr. Rul. 1999-25-027 (March

25, 1999) (I.R.S. ruled that if a cooperative association does not permit the transfer of stock to a QPRT, the tax-payer's beneficial interest in the cooperative stock and lease qualifies as an interest in a personal residence).

19. Rev. Rul. 64-31, 1964-1 C.B. 300.

20. I.R.C. § 280A(d)(2) provides that a taxpayer will be deemed to have used a dwelling unit for personal purposes for a day if, for any part of such day, the unit is used (i) for personal purposes by the taxpayer or any other person who has an interest in such unit, or by any member of the family (as defined in I.R.C. § 267(c)(4)) of the taxpayer or such other person; (ii) by any individual who uses the unit under an arrangement that enables the taxpayer to use some other dwelling unit (whether or not a rental is charged for the use of such other unit); or (iii) by any individual (other than an employee with respect to whose use I.R.C. § 119 applies), unless for such day the dwelling unit is rented for a rental that, under the facts and circumstances, is fair rental. As Treas. Reg. § 25.2702-5(c)(2)(i)(B) expressly negates the application of I.R.C. § 280A(d)(2), actual use of the residence by the taxpayer for the stated period of time set forth in I.R.C. § 280A(d)(1) is required.

21. I.R.C. § 280A(f)(1)(A); Prop. Treas. Reg. § 1.280A-1(c)(1).

22. I.R.C. § 280A(d)(1)(B).

23. *See, e.g.,* Priv. Ltr. Rul. 2001-17-021 (January 25, 2001). In this ruling, the taxpayer inherited property that he used as a vacation home, except for two months of the year when he leased the property for fair market rental on a short-term basis. The taxpayer provided no services in connection with the rental and represented that his annual personal use of the property exceeded the greater of 14 days or 10 percent of the number of days the property was leased. Based upon the facts submitted, the I.R.S. ruled that the property constituted a personal residence within the meaning of I.R.C. § 2702(a)(3)(A)(ii) and Treas. Reg. § 25.2702-5(c)(2). *See also* Priv. Ltr. Rul. 2001-26-026 (April 2, 2001); Treas. Reg. § 25.2702-5(d), example 2.

24. Treas. Reg. § 25.2702-5(c)(2)(iii), captioned "Use Of Residence."

25. I.R.C. § 280A(c)(1), captioned "Certain Business Use," applies generally to any portion of a dwelling unit that is exclusively used on a regular basis (i) as the principal place of business for any trade or business of the taxpayer; (ii) as a place of business that is used by patients, clients, or customers in meeting or dealing with the taxpayer in the normal course of his trade or business; or (iii) in the case of a separate structure that is not attached to the dwelling unit, in connection with the taxpayer's trade or business.

26. I.R.C. § 280A(c)(4), captioned "Use In Providing Day Care Services," applies generally to any portion of a dwelling unit used on a regular basis in the taxpayer's trade or business of providing day care for children, for individuals who have attained age 65, or for individuals who are physically or mentally incapable of caring for themselves.

27. Treas. Reg. § 25.2702-5(c)(2)(iii).

28. *Id.*

29. Treas. Reg. § 25.2702-5(c)(5)(i).

30. Treas. Reg. § 25.2702-5(c)(7)(i).

31. *See, e.g.,* Treas. Reg. § 25.2702-5(d), example 5:

T transfers a personal residence to a trust that meets the requirements of a qualified personal residence trust, retaining a term interest in the trust for 10 years. During the period of T's retained term interest, T is forced for health reasons to move to a nursing home. T's spouse continues to occupy the residence. If the residence is available at all times for T's use as a residence during the term (without regard to T's ability to actually use the residence), the residence continues to be held for T's use and the trust does not cease to be a qualified personal residence trust. The residence would cease to be held for use as a personal residence of T if the trustee rented the residence to an unrelated party, because the residence would no longer be available for T's use at all times.

32. Treas. Reg. § 25.2702-5(c)(2)(ii), captioned "Additional Property."

33. *Id.*

34. *Id.*

35. *See, e.g.,* Priv. Ltr. Rul. 97-05-017 (January 31, 1997); Priv. Ltr. Rul 97-01-046.

36. Priv. Ltr. Rul. 2001-26-026 (April 2, 2001). In this ruling, the taxpayer represented that she used the property as a vacation home and that her annual personal use thereof exceeded the requirements set forth in I.R.C. § 280A(d)(1). The I.R.S. determined that other residential parcels in proximity to the property generally

contained a similar amount of acreage and that the improvements on the property were consistent with other residential properties in the community.

37. Priv. Ltr. Rul. 2001-21-015 (February 14, 2001). The I.R.S. found that the property is comparable in size to other adjoining and nearby residential properties and concluded, thus, that such property is not in excess of that which is reasonably appropriate for residential purposes.

38. Priv. Ltr. Rul. 2001-09-017 (November 27, 2000).

39. Priv. Ltr. Rul. 2001-12-018 (December 15, 2000).

40. Priv. Ltr. Rul. 1999-08-032 (November 30, 1998).

41. Priv. Ltr. Rul. 1999-16-030 (January 22, 1999).

42. Treas. Reg. § 25.2702-5(a)(1), providing, in part, that a trust of which the termholder is the grantor that otherwise meets the requirements of a QPRT is not a QPRT if, at the time of transfer, the termholder of the trust already holds term interests in two trusts that are QPRTs of which the termholder was the grantor.

43. *Id.*

# CHAPTER 14

# Grantor-Retained Annuity Trusts and Grantor-Retained Unitrusts

ZEB LAW

## I. Introduction

Grantor-Retained Annuity Trusts (GRATs) and Grantor-Retained Unitrusts (GRUTs) (herein, GRATs and GRUTs will collectively be referred to as GRTs) are sophisticated estate-planning trusts into which the trust's settlor (grantor) transfers property. In exchange, the grantor generally reserves a right to receive an annuity from the trust for a term of years, after which the remaining assets in the trust are generally distributed to the grantor's heirs. In the case of a grantor-retained annuity trust, the grantor generally receives a fixed annuity. In the case of a grantor-retained unitrust, the grantor retains the right to receive a variable annuity based on a fixed percentage of the trust's assets.

## II. Overview

This chapter summarizes how GRAT and GRUT techniques can be used as part of an effective estate plan. GRTs are irrevocable trusts into which the grantor transfers property and retains a predetermined annuity (or unitrust) interest. The annuity is normally paid out over a term of years[1] (fixed term[2]). After the expiration of the fixed term, the trust's assets are eventually distributed to the grantor's heirs.

### A. Procedure

Procedurally, the GRT is normally drafted, signed, and then funded. During the drafting stage, the grantor (with the help of the practitioner) selects the key aspects of the trust, such as the annuity percentage, the length of the fixed term, and the disposition of the trust's assets. The grantor then ordinarily funds the GRT by making a contribution the trust. The value of the gift is equal to the fair market value of the contributed property less the value of the retained annuity interest or unitrust interest. Put differently, the value of the gift is equal to the present value of the remainder interest.[3] The property transferred to the trust is excluded from the estate of the grantor if the grantor outlives the fixed term.[4]

## B. Freezing

How do GRTs work? GRTs freeze the value of the assets transferred into the GRT. This is because the GRT technique represents the grantor exchanging one or more assets (trust assets) for a fixed or variable annuity for a term of years (annuity). If the grantor outlives the GRT's fixed term, the value of the grantor's estate (for estate-tax purposes) is frozen at the present value of the annuity only. With proper planning (such as by funding the GRT with highly appreciating trust assets), this can establish an instant estate-tax savings potential. The following example illustrates the freeze concept:

Assume Grantor owns commercial real estate worth $1 million that generates positive rental cash flow of $100,000 per year. Grantor expects the real estate to double in value in ten years. Grantor puts the property into a ten-year GRAT, retaining a right to receive $100,000 per year for ten years. Assuming Grantor survives the ten-year term, the property held in the GRAT will be excluded from Grantor's estate. For federal gift-tax purposes, the grantor makes a present gift of approximately $275,560 (the present value of the remainder interest, assuming an applicable federal rate (AFR)[5] of 5.6 percent).[6] Assuming the value of the real estate subsequently doubles, the grantor has removed a $2-million asset from his estate at a gift-tax cost of only $275,560.[7]

*Planning Note:* Because the AFR is the basis for determining the present value of the annuity, GRATs are generally considered most useful when the trust assets are expected to appreciate in value more quickly than the AFR. Because the annuity of a GRAT is fixed, the ability of a GRAT to leverage the benefit of the appreciation in asset value is better than that of a GRUT.[8]

## C. Discounting

Contributions to GRTs are often made at substantial discounts. As a general rule, discounting the value of the asset transferred to the GRT enhances the ability to transfer the asset to the grantor's heirs at a reduced tax cost. For example, where appropriate, the grantor should seek to obtain a low, but reasonable, value for the underlying property being transferred into the trust. It is often worth consulting with several valuation experts prior to finalizing an asset transfer into a GRT. In certain cases, a well-reasoned appraisal alone can lead to substantial tax savings.

Sometimes, the grantor will transfer the asset to a business entity (such as a partnership or limited-liability company) prior to the transfer of the entity interest to the GRT. For example, transferring an asset to an entity may be an appropriate way to transfer only a portion of an asset (such as real estate) to the GRT while allowing the grantor to retain the other portion. Transferring a business entity interest can also lead to a valuation discount that results in tax savings.[9] The following example identifies the advantage of discount planning:

Assume that, for liability protection, the commercial real estate referenced in the prior example is transferred to a limited liability company (L.L.C.). Working with a qualified appraiser, the practitioner determines that a 99-percent ownership interest in the L.L.C. is worth only $800,000 (A 20-percent marketability discount is fairly common with respect to closely held business interests.). Assuming there is still sufficient cash flow to pay an annuity of $100,000, a GRAT with a 12.5-percent annuity may be selected. At an applicable federal rate of 5.6 percent, this contribution would result in a $75,560 gift. Transferring the real estate into a limited-liability company significantly reduces the value of the gift.

## III. Background

In the Omnibus Budget Reconciliation Act,[10] Congress added Chapter 14 of the Internal Revenue Code (I.R.C) of 1986, as amended. This chapter, entitled "Special Valuation," introduced I.R.C. Section 2702, which provides the current statutory basis for GRATs and GRUTs. Today, many of the rules regarding these two trusts are contained in the Treasury Regulations under this I.R.C. section.

Congress enacted Chapter 14 (I.R.C. Sections 2701–2704) to impose greater consistency in the valuation-planning area. Chapter 14 provides that when a transferor conveys a partial property interest to a family member while simultaneously retaining an interest in the same property, the value of the retained interest is zero. In such cases, for gift-tax purposes, the value of the transferred interest is equal to the value of the entire property.

Chapter 14 carves out certain exceptions to this general rule. Under these exceptions, the value of the retained interest is taken into account in measuring the value of the gifted interest. These exceptions are set forth in I.R.C. Section 2702, which authorizes property transfers to GRATs and GRUTs. In order to qualify as a GRT, several requirements must be met.

## IV. GRT Requirements

GRTs must be drafted to conform to three separate sets of tax rules: (1) those set forth under I.R.C. Section 2702; (2) the "grantor trust" rules under subpart E (I.R.C. Sections 671–679); and (3) the applicable transfer tax rules.

### A. I.R.C. Section 2702 Rules

The GRT rules are set forth under I.R.C. Section 2702. This section provides that, in connection with all property transfers to a trust in which the grantor retains any interest in the trust, the value of the gift will equal 100 percent of the value of the property transferred, unless the retained interest is a qualified interest and unless the other requirements in Section 2702 are met. I.R.C. Section 2702(b) defines a "qualified interest" as an interest consisting of a right to receive fixed amounts payable not less frequently than annually (a qualified fixed annuity), or any interest that is calculated as a fixed percentage of the fair market value of the property, payable annually (a qualified unitrust payment).[11]

For example, grantor desires to contribute $1 million cash to an irrevocable trust, retain an income interest therein for a number of years, and then have the balance of trust property pass to the grantor's heirs. Under I.R.C. Section 2702, the grantor has three options:

1. Grantor retains the right to receive all of the income of the trust for ten years. Because the retained interest is *not* a qualified interest, the amount of the gift equals 100 percent of the value of the property transferred or $1 million.
2. Grantor retains the right to receive $100,000 per year from the trust. The retained interest is a qualified annuity and, therefore, constitutes a qualified annuity interest (assuming all of the other requirements of I.R.C. Section 2702 are met). Assuming an AFR of 5 percent, the amount of the gift would be $252,330.

3. Grantor retains the right to receive 10 percent of the value of the trust's assets per year for ten years. The retained interest is a qualified annuity and, therefore, constitutes a qualified-unitrust interest (assuming all of the other requirements of I.R.C. Section 2702 are met). Assuming an AFR of 5 percent, the amount of the gift would be $385,593.

## B. Grantor Trust Rules

The grantor trust rules of I.R.C. Sections 671–679 treat trusts containing certain characteristics as disregarded entities for income tax purposes. All income or losses generated by such trusts are reportable on the grantor's individual income tax return.

Any trust in which the grantor retains an income interest is treated as a grantor trust. Because I.R.C. Section 2702 requires the grantor to retain a qualified interest, which must be either a qualified annuity or a qualified unitrust interest, GRTs are normally taxable as grantor trusts under I.R.C. Section 671 during the fixed term.

Grantor trust status normally provides the grantor with better tax results than nongrantor trust status. If, for example, there is insufficient income to pay the GRT's annuity, the trustee can simply distribute an asset from the GRT to the grantor to satisfy the annuity obligation without triggering capital gains tax.[12] If the GRT were not a grantor trust during the fixed term, then the payment of an asset to satisfy the pecuniary annuity obligation would trigger income tax.[13]

GRTs should often be drafted to maintain grantor trust status after the expiration of the fixed term. One way to do so would be to grant a nonadverse trustee the power to add beneficiaries.[14] By maintaining grantor trust status after the expiration of the fixed term, the grantor continues to be responsible for paying income tax on the GRT's earnings. In paying the income tax on the GRT's earnings, the grantor effectively makes a free additional gift to the remainder beneficiaries in the amount of the taxes paid.[15] The following example illustrates the benefits of grantor trust status:

Assume a grantor in the 40-percent income tax bracket establishes a ten-year GRAT funded with $1 million that pays a $50,000 annuity to the grantor. Assume further that the GRAT invests the $1 million and earns $90,000 in taxable income in the first year.

If the GRAT were *not* a grantor trust, the GRAT would pay $16,000 of income tax on the $40,000 of undistributed trust income ($90,000 taxable income less the $50,000 annuity).[16] At the beginning of the second year, the GRAT would have $1.024 million ($1 million plus $90,000 income minus $50,000 distribution and $16,000 tax payment).

If the GRAT were a grantor trust, the grantor would bear the entire income tax on the GRAT's earnings. At the beginning of the second year, the trust would have $1.04 million ($1 million plus $90,000 earnings minus $50,000 distribution). Compare this amount to the $1.024 million in the first example (involving a nongrantor trust). The grantor trust status results in an additional $16,000 being made available to eventually distribute to the trust's beneficiaries.

## C. Transfer-Tax Issues

### 1. Gift-Tax Issues

In transferring property to a GRAT or GRUT, a grantor bifurcates property ownership into an income interest and a remainder interest. The grantor retains the income interest and transfers the remainder interest.

The completed gift requires the filing of a gift-tax return.[17] The amount of the gift can be roughly calculated by subtracting the present value of the annuity interest from the value of the entire property transferred to the GRT. The annuity interest is determined by an annuity factor under rules set forth in I.R.C. Section 7520. This annuity factor is partially based on the actuarial mortality of the grantor. [18]

Because the property is gifted to the GRT, the trust's beneficiaries will receive a carryover tax basis in the contributed trust property.[19]

### 2. Estate-Tax Issues

The Internal Revenue Service (I.R.S.) position is that the entire value of the trust property is included in the grantor's estate if the grantor dies during the fixed term.[20] If the I.R.S. position were to withstand judicial scrutiny, the grantor may serve as GRT trustee during the fixed term without any downside risk. Nonetheless, the terms of a GRT should provide that if the grantor were to die prematurely (that is, during the fixed term), the GRT's assets should be distributed to the grantor's surviving spouse (thus qualifying for the unlimited marital deduction) or should be otherwise made available to help alleviate the resulting estate tax.

Assuming the grantor survives the fixed term, the GRT must be drafted to keep the trust assets from being includable in the grantor's estate for estate-tax purposes. In other words, the grantor cannot retain any powers over the trust (or the trust's assets) that would cause inclusion of the trust assets for purposes of the estate tax.

### 3. Generation-Skipping Tax Issues

The I.R.C. imposes a second layer of tax on generation-skipping transfers. This tax applies to transfers made to skip-persons. These are essentially people who are two or more generations younger than the grantor (that is, starting with the grantor's grandchildren). Taxpayers may shelter transfers to skip-persons by allocating generation-skipping tax exemption (currently up to $1.06 million) to the applicable transfer.[21]

GRTs are not considered effective generation-skipping vehicles. This is because I.R.C. Section 2631 specifies that the generation-skipping tax exemption cannot be allocated during the fixed term of the GRT.

GST exemption can be allocated to a GRT upon the expiration of the fixed term. However, any such allocation of GST exemption is measured against the value of the GRT's assets as of the date of the allocation (that is, the full value of the GRT's assets upon the expiration of the fixed term). Oftentimes, it is preferential to use GST exemption allocation for transfers to other types of trusts (such as generation-skipping or dynasty trusts).

## V. Ancillary Issues

### A. Selection of Trustee

In order to secure the estate-tax advantages of GRT planning, the grantor may only serve as trustee during the GRT's fixed term. Upon the expiration of the GRT's fixed term, neither the grantor nor the grantor's spouse should serve as trustee.[22] Instead, the grantor should select a trust beneficiary (or an independent party whom the grantor trusts) to fulfill the terms of the GRT.

## B. Term of GRT

The grantor must select the fixed term length of the annuity. The term is established as part of the trust instrument, and because the trust is irrevocable, the term cannot be changed. Although there is no hard-and-fast rule in selecting the length of a GRT's fixed term, the grantor will want to choose one that he or she is reasonably likely to survive.

By using a high-enough payout percentage, and a long-enough term, it is possible to eliminate the gift made in transferring property to a GRAT (but not to a GRUT). In other words, a transfer of property to such a trust would not result in any gift taxes because the value of the gift would be zero. This technique is known as the Zeroed-Out GRAT. Assume, for example, grantor sets up a GRAT with a 23.855-percent payment and a five-year fixed term. Assuming the applicable federal rate is 5.6 percent, the value of the gift would be approximately zero. This is because the value of the retained interest equals the value of the property contributed to the trust. Therefore, there is no taxable gift.

The longer the fixed term of the GRT is, the smaller the gift will be—because the longer term reduces the present value of the remainder interest to the heirs. This must be balanced with the consideration that the longer the term, the greater the risk that the grantor will die during the term (negating the benefit of excluding the property held in trust from the grantor's estate). As a practical matter, practitioners usually select a term in which the grantor has a fairly high likelihood of surviving and often will dissuade a client in poor health from considering GRT utilization.

## C. Dispositive Provisions upon Expiration of Fixed Term

The practitioner should review with the client the various dispositive alternatives available if the grantor outlives the fixed term of the GRT. Sometimes, the GRT property passes outright to the grantor's heirs. Other times, it is held in further trust.

## D. Other Drafting Considerations

In order to qualify as a GRT, the following items must be accounted for under the I.R.C.:

1. The trust must not include the power to commute (pay off) the annuity during the GRT's fixed term.[23] In other words, the trust cannot simply make a lump-sum payment of all remaining annuity amounts for the grantor.
2. The trust may not be modifiable for tax reasons after it is formed.[24]
3. A GRAT (but not a GRUT) must prohibit additional contributions to the trust once it is initially funded.[25] If further contributions are desired, the grantor should consider the use of a GRUT or the establishment of a new GRAT.

## VI. Conclusion

Since the enactment of I.R.C. Section 2702, GRTs have provided a statutorily authorized estate-planning vehicle that, when properly used, can lead to substantial transfer tax savings. GRTs combine the benefits of several different areas of estate planning, including estate freezing, discount planning, and leveraging the use of the grantor's unified credit amount.

The Economic Growth and Tax Relief Reconciliation Act of 2001 (EGTRRA) gradually reduces estate-tax rates through 2009, repeals the estate tax in 2010, and then reinstates it in 2011 at today's estate-tax rates. Practitioners should discuss the EGTRRA provisions with their clients to determine their impact on the client's estate plan. However, until the estate tax is permanently repealed—and keeping in mind that the U.S. estate tax has been "permanently" repealed in the past, only to be reinstated—GRTs will continue to serve as a useful tool for estate planners.

## Endnotes

1. Treas. Reg. § 25.2702-3(b)(1), (c)(1). The annuity can be for the lifetime of the grantor, but, as will be noted below, the term is almost invariably set up for a fixed number of years for estate-tax reasons. The annuity must be paid (note that this does not include a mere right of withdrawal; the annuity must actually be paid) on an annual or more frequent basis (for example, monthly, quarterly, and so forth). The payment may be made after the close of the taxable year but must be made on or before the due date of the return (without regard to extensions).

2. Treas. Reg. § 25-2702-3(d)(3) (ruling that the fixed term is selected at the formation of the GRT).

3. Note that the Tax Relief Act added I.R.C. § 2511(c) so that transfers to grantor trusts made after 2009 will generally be deemed to constitute incomplete gifts for transfer-tax purposes. It has been noted that this does not mean that all transfers to all grantor trusts after 2009 will automatically be exempt from gift tax; a gift to such a trust would be considered incomplete if the trust is treated as a grantor trust in its entirety as to the grantor (or the grantor's spouse). GRATs and GRUTs are generally drafted so that the grantor is treated as the owner of the trust in its entirety; therefore, it appears that transfers to GRATs or GRUTs after 2009 will not trigger gift tax until the term of the GRAT expires (at which point, the grantor is typically no longer treated as the owner of the trust under I.R.C. § 677).

4. If the grantor dies during the GRT's term, the assets of the GRAT or GRUT are includible in the grantor's estate. *See infra* text accompanying endnote 20.

5. *See* I.R.C. § 2702(a)(2)(B). The applicable federal rate for GRATs and GRUTs is the I.R.C. § 7520 rate.

6. Rev. Rul. 2001-49, 2001-41 I.R.B. 312 (representing the I.R.C. § 7520 rate for the month of October 2001).

7. GRT planning often tries to freeze the value of the remainder interest (which represents the value of the asset(s) being transferred to the GRT's beneficiaries) to a value below the grantor's available unified credit amount (which as of this writing shelters up to $1 million of asset transfers from gift or estate tax over a taxpayer's lifetime). In doing so, the client can make a gift without triggering any out-of-pocket payment of gift tax.

8. *See, e.g.,* Jonathan G. Blattmachr and Georgiana J. Slade, *Partial Interests—GRATs, GRUTS, and QPRTs* (Section 2702), 836 T.M. 41 (noting that a GRUT annuity simply increases each year as the value of the trust assets increase).

9. *See, e.g.,* Howard Zaritsky, Tax Planning for Family Wealth Transfers, ¶ 9.08 (Warren, Gorham & Lamont 3rd ed.).

10. Pub. L. No. 101-508.

11. *See* Treas. Reg. § 25.2702-3(b)(1)(iii) (pointing out that the trust can provide for an amount in excess of a qualified annuity amount to be paid to the grantor; the grantor will simply not receive the benefit of the reduced gift valuation in connection with such excess).

12. Rev. Rul. 85-13, 1985-1 C.B. 184.

13. I.R.C. §§ 643(e), 663(a).

14. This would make the trust a grantor trust under I.R.C. § 674(a).

15. *See, e.g.,* Jonathan G. Blattmachr and Georgiana J. Slade, *Partial Interests—GRATs, GRUTS, and QPRTs* (Section 2702), 836 T.M. 38. The I.R.S. has not formally approved of this free additional gift. The I.R.S. seems to prefer trusts that provide a tax reimbursement provision, whereby the trust is obligated to reimburse the grantor the "additional" tax paid by the grantor in excess of the taxes arising from the annuity amount. This is noted from I.R.S. pronouncements that it will not rule unless the trust contains such a provision (or a provision that the grantor will receive the greater of the annuity amount or the trust's actual

income). The authors of this portfolio point out, properly, that the I.R.S. has no basis under Code § 2702 or the regulations thereunder to support this position.

16. The $16,000 represents 40 percent of the trust's taxable income, which, for this purpose, is measured by starting with the $90,000 overall taxable income for the trust and deducting $50,000 as a distribution of income to a beneficiary as permitted under I.R.C. § 661.

17. Note that a gift-tax return will be required in all instances when the gift to a GRT has any value (that is, in all instances other than a zeroed-out GRAT).

18. The exact amount of the gift can be calculated using a number of software packages. Such software packages include Number Cruncher (visited May 24, 2002) http://www.leimberg.com; Crescendo (visited May 24, 2002) http://www.crescendosoft.com; and CCH's Viewplan (visited May 24, 2002) http://cch.com.

19. I.R.C. § 1015. This should be considered one of the primary disadvantages of a GRT, and the tax consequences should be compared to simply waiting until death to transfer assets with a stepped-up basis. In a community property state, the planner should also consider the consequences of simply waiting for the first spouse to die (thereby generating a stepped-up basis in all community assets under I.R.C. § 1014(b)(6)) before setting up the GRT.

20. The I.R.S. bases its position on I.R.C. §§ 2036 and 2039. Treas. Reg. § 20.2036-1(a) provides that when a grantor retains a right to receive income, the corresponding portion of the trust is includible in the grantor's estate. Treas. Reg. § 20.2039-1(b)(1) provides that where a taxpayer receives an annuity or other payment, the value received by any beneficiary under the contract shall be includable in the estate of the taxpayer. The I.R.S. has taken this position in private letter rulings and, most recently, in field service advice 200036012.

21. I.R.C. § 2631.

22. If the grantor is the trustee of the trust and has any right to adjust the timing or amount received by any beneficiary under the trust, the assets of the trust will be includible in the estate of the grantor under I.R.C. § 2036.

23. Technically, if a GRT (let's say, a GRAT) is set up with a taxable gift, the gift is reported on Form 706, and, as applicable, the grantor's unified credit amount (currently $1 million) is used to reduce the out-of-pocket gift tax expense. If the grantor dies during the GRAT's term, all of the then-existing unified credit would be used on the grantor's Form 709. In other words, the grantor does not "lose" the unified credit—the grantor simply does not get the benefit (if any) of removing from his or her estate the excess of the income/growth on the assets in the GRAT over the I.R.C. § 7520 rate.

24. Treas. Reg. § 25.2702-3(d)(4).

25. T.A.M. 97-17-008.

# CHAPTER 15

# Use of the Self-Canceling Installment Note and the Private Annuity in Estate Planning

DAVE L. CORNFELD
JAY A. SOLED
HERBERT L. ZUCKERMAN

## I. Introduction

If a lawyer has prospered and invested wisely, there may come a time when he or she may wish to reduce transfer taxes by assigning estate assets to a younger generation at minimal transfer-tax expense, while retaining an income stream for a term of years or for life. Suppose the lawyer is already engaged in an annual gift-giving program, has created irrevocable insurance trusts, and has a will that makes maximum use of the unified credit, the generation-skipping transfer-tax exemption, and the marital deduction. Are there any less-traditional techniques for furthering estate-planning objectives by reducing death and transfer taxes?

This chapter explores the opportunity to use two devices, the self-canceling installment note (SCIN) and the private annuity. The goal of both is to transfer appreciating assets out of a taxable estate at little or no transfer tax and, at the same time, to provide an income stream for retirement.

## II. The Basics

### A. SCIN

In an ordinary installment sale that is not self-canceling, the buyer purchases property using a note calling for periodic payments that are not dependent upon the seller surviving the note's term. The buyer (or maker of the note) satisfies his or her obligation under the note when it is paid in full. Should the seller die before the note is fully paid, the seller's estate (or successors, heirs, and assigns) is, of course, entitled to the note and the payments made thereon. On the seller's estate tax return, the present value of the remaining installment payments would be fully included in the seller's gross estate and would be exposed to estate tax (in 2002, the rate was as high as 50 percent).

If there is a cancellation feature in the installment note by which the maker of the note is relieved of further liability upon the seller's death, the United States Tax Court in *Estate of Moss v. Commissioner* [1] has ruled that there is no fair market value of the note

211

for transfer-tax purposes. It ceases to have any value at the moment of the seller's death because there are no monies due to the seller, the seller's estate, or the seller's heirs. It is this cancellation feature that unlocks estate-planning opportunities.

A SCIN obligates a buyer to make payments for the shorter of the payment term or the seller's life. As long as the fixed payment term is less than the life expectancy of the seller at the time of the sale, the transaction will be characterized as an installment sale with a contingent sales price. In the Internal Revenue Service's (I.R.S.'s) view, if the fixed payment term is longer than the seller's life expectancy at the time of the sale, the structure cannot be a SCIN; instead, it will be characterized as a private annuity.[2]

The cancellation feature is of obvious value to the buyer. Negotiating this feature into the note enhances the deal, but it represents a potentially taxable transfer by the seller to the buyer. Because the seller wants to avoid making a taxable gift to the buyer, seller must charge the buyer a premium for the note's cancellation feature. This premium is necessary to reflect seller's additional risk in possibly failing to recoup the full fair market value of the item sold in the event that seller dies before receiving all payments. In the absence of a premium (either in a higher sales price, higher interest rate, or both), the I.R.S. could and probably would contend that seller has engaged in a part sale/part gift with the buyer at the time of the exchange.

Determining the exact amount of the premium seller should charge can be a complicated task. It depends on seller's age and the actuarial likelihood that seller will survive the note's maturity. As noted, the premium itself can be reflected in an upward adjustment of the purchase price, the interest rate charged, or a combination of both. The services of an actuary or specially designed computer software can be invaluable in determining the premium.

In order to use the normal mortality tables in calculating the premium, it is important that the seller not be terminally ill at the time of the sale.[3] In the recent case of *Estate of Costanza v. Commissioner*,[4] the tax court found the SCIN transaction to result in gift tax because at the closing of the transaction, the taxpayer had been diagnosed with heart disease requiring bypass surgery, and he died some four months later.

When the seller is not terminally ill (defined as having a 50-percent probability that seller will die within one year) but is in poor health and not likely to live to mortality table life expectancy, the use of a SCIN may well result in estate-tax savings. The mortality tables prescribed under I.R.C. Section 7520 are unisex and based on the 1990 census. The unisex feature will prove favorable to men and unfavorable to women. New tables based on the 2000 census will probably not be available before May 2009.

On the other hand, if the seller is in excellent health and is likely to outlive the proposed term of the note, the use of an installment note sale without any contingency may be preferable. If the seller actually outlives the term, it will result in transferring future appreciation to the buyer with lower total payments to the seller.

It is important that the parties handle the transaction in a manner that clearly establishes the date of the sale. All required payments should be made in a timely fashion.

## B. Private Annuity

In a commercial setting, one can purchase an annuity from an insurance company that will pay proceeds to the annuitant during his or her lifetime. Assuming it is a straight annuity and not a term-certain or a refund annuity, the annuity is extinguished at the annuitant's death and is not includable in the annuitant's gross estate.

The tax treatment of a private annuity corresponds with that of a commercial annuity. The twist with a private annuity is that the annuity is not issued by an organization that normally issues annuities. Instead, in a typical case, a member of one's family purchases property from an elder member, issuing in return a note or other undertaking in the form of an annuity obligation.

As with the case of a SCIN, the seller of property to a family member in return for an annuity has to be alert to the possibility of the transaction being treated as a direct or indirect gift. In the SCIN situation, a premium for the self-canceling feature must be exacted in order to avoid a taxable gift; however, in the private annuity context, the present value of the future annuity payments must equal the fair market value of the property transferred on the date of sale. If the present value of the annuity is less than the fair market value of the property, then the seller has made a taxable gift at the time of transfer equal to this difference. To illustrate, suppose a 65-year-old mother with a life expectancy of 20 years under the I.R.S.'s mortality tables transfers a painting with a fair market value of $100,000 to her son for a $10,000 annual annuity. If the present value of the annuity is $97,500, then the mother has made a taxable gift to her son of $2,500, the difference between $100,000 and $97,500.

## III. *Advantages and Disadvantages*

Assuming the seller has sold property to a member of the younger generation of the family in return for a SCIN or private annuity, the advantages to the seller and seller's estate are obvious. First and most important, seller has removed the transferred property (and its subsequent appreciation) from seller's taxable estate; under no circumstances will the property sold be subject to estate tax. Second, seller will receive a fixed sum of money for a term of years (in the case of SCIN) or for the remainder of seller's life (in the case of a private annuity), obviously facilitating or enriching seller's retirement. Finally, because the buyer is presumably a family member, the property transferred remains under family control, opening the opportunity for the younger generation to manage the property while seller is still available to render sage advice.

However, the disadvantages of SCINs and private annuities cannot be ignored. First, in the case of a SCIN, should the seller survive the entire term of the note, there may be minimal estate-tax savings in light of the seller's recoupment of the entire purchase price of the property sold and the SCIN premium. Likewise, in the case of the private annuity, should the superannuated transferor/seller outlive his or her life expectancy, the buyer will pay more than originally anticipated. Second, in both the SCIN and private-annuity contexts, to the extent that the seller cannot consume the installment or annuity payments, seller's taxable estate will correspondingly grow. Third, the buyer may have a difficult time making installment or annuity payments, especially if the property itself is an asset such as undeveloped land that does not produce income. If the buyer defaults in the case of a private annuity, the seller's only recourse is to sue for recovery as an unsecured creditor—because of the tax law requirement that a private annuity be unsecured. Finally, there are consequences to both a SCIN and a private annuity if the seller dies prematurely. For a SCIN, the unrealized gain, if any, on the property sold must be included on the seller's estate income tax return; for the private annuity, though there is no inclusion of the unrealized gain on the seller's estate income tax return, the buyer's tax basis is reduced from fair market value on the date of sale to the amount of the annuity payments to date.

## IV. Income Tax Consequences

Aside from the gift- and estate-tax consequences of a SCIN or a private annuity, both the buyer and the seller should also consider the income tax implications of both of these estate-planning techniques.

### A. SCIN

#### 1. Income Tax Consequences for the Seller

Because a SCIN meets the requirements of being an installment note, the seller may use the installment method to report income. Under the installment method, each principal payment the seller receives (in addition to interest payments, which are subject to tax as ordinary income) must be separated into two components: (1) return of basis and (2) gain (capital gain if the property sold is a capital asset).

This bifurcation process is accomplished by first determining the gross profit ratio, which is equal to the seller's gain (the difference between the sales price less adjusted basis) over the sales price. This ratio is then multiplied by each payment to determine the taxable gain. The difference between the payment and the taxable gain represents the seller's nontaxable return of basis.

The I.R.S. takes the position that on the seller's death, any deferred gain on the sale of the property must be included on the seller's estate's initial income tax return.[5]

#### 2. Income Tax Consequences for the Buyer

The buyer includes the face amount of the note as buyer's basis in the purchased property, which is not adjusted even if the seller dies before the note's maturity. In addition, the interest portion of the SCIN payment is deductible, subject to normal deductibility limitations under the Internal Revenue Code (I.R.C.) (for example, if the purchased property is investment in nature, the buyer must have sufficient investment income to use the interest expense).

### B. Private Annuity

#### 1. Income Tax Consequences for the Seller

In general, transferring property in exchange for a private annuity of equal value does not trigger immediate income tax consequences. This deferral of tax, however, does not mean its elimination: each annuity payment must be broken into three components: (1) a return of basis of the property transferred, (2) capital gain, and (3) annuity income.

To calculate the return-of-basis portion of an annual annuity payment, the seller must determine the exclusion ratio. This ratio is equal to the seller's investment in the contract (the seller's adjusted basis in the property transferred) divided by the expected return (annual annuity payments multiplied by the seller's life expectancy). Once determined, each annuity payment is multiplied by this ratio, and the resulting product is the seller's nontaxable return of basis.

To calculate the capital gain portion of an annual annuity payment, the seller divides the gain attributable to the transfer (the difference between the present value of the private annuity contract and the seller's adjusted basis in the property) by the buyer's life expectancy in years at the time of transfer. This portion of each payment will be subject to capital gain rather than ordinary income tax rates, assuming the property sold is a capital asset or is treated as a capital asset (for example, I.R.C. Section 1231 property). Finally, in order to calculate the ordinary annuity income portion, the seller simply subtracts the sum of the return-of-basis component and the capital gain component from the annuity payment.

When and if seller recovers all of seller's basis and capital gain by attaining seller's life expectancy (determined at the time of the initial property transfer), then both of these components of the annuity payment are merged and become ordinary annuity income. On the other hand, if the seller dies prematurely, the decedent is entitled to a loss on his final income tax return for the unrecovered basis in the private annuity contract.

### 2. Income Tax Consequences for the Buyer

The buyer receives a basis in the purchased property equal to its fair market value (assuming the present value of the annuity does not reflect any donative element). Once total payments exceed fair market value, the buyer's basis will increase, thereafter corresponding to each additional annuity payment. Conversely, should the seller die before this break-even point (where payments equal the fair market value of the property), the buyer's basis will be reduced to the accumulation of annuity payments to date, less any depreciation deductions taken with respect to the property. If the buyer resells the property prior to the death of the annuitant, the buyer recognizes gain or loss based on the facts known at the time of sale. However, additional gain or loss will be recognized when the annuitant dies.

In contrast to a SCIN arrangement, the buyer may not deduct any portion of his or her annuity payment as an interest expense.

## V. Comparison

An example illustrates the mechanics of a SCIN and a private annuity. Suppose a father, age 75, with a life expectancy of 12$^1$/$_2$ years (as determined under I.R.S. actuarial tables), purchased an unimproved tract of land as an investment in 1995 for $200,000. It is currently worth $500,000 and the I.R.C. Section 7520 interest rate is 7 percent. Suppose further that the father has already exhausted his unified credit in the form of large taxable gifts, and he now wishes to transfer his investment real estate to his daughter. He wishes to do so because he anticipates that the property will greatly appreciate over the course of the next few years, and he does not want the property to be includable in his gross estate. He can opt to use either a SCIN or a private annuity to accomplish all of his goals.

### A. SCIN (Principal Premium Method)

With the aid of a computer software program or an actuary, the father is able to determine that the SCIN premium principal amount (reflecting the cancellation feature in the note) for semiannual payments over a ten-year term is $121,580. He transfers title to the property to his daughter, who, in return, gives her father a SCIN with a ten-year term containing a semiannual principal payment schedule of $31,079 and a face value of $621,580. Assume further that the SCIN bears interest of 7.0 percent payable semiannually (an amount, using the I.R.S. monthly tables, that will not be considered below market and, consequently, will not create a gift-tax situation).

The gross profit ratio is 67.824 percent: the amount of gain ($421,580, which is $621,580 less $200,000) over the purchase price ($621,580). Therefore, $21,079 of each semiannual payment ( 67.824 percent of the $31,079 semiannual payment) is subject to capital gains tax on the father's income tax return, and the remaining $10,000 ($31,079 less $21,079) constitutes a nontaxable return of the father's basis. The 7.0-percent interest payment the father receives is subject to tax as ordinary income on the father's income tax return (for example, for the first semiannual payment, the outstanding balance of the note generates $21,755 of taxable income ($621,580 times 3.5 percent)).

Meanwhile, during the SCIN term, the daughter can deduct her interest payments as investment interest expense (subject to I.R.C. limitations), and her basis in the real estate would equal $621,580.

## B.  Alternative SCIN (Interest Premium Method)

If the parties wish, the transaction may be structured to increase the interest rate and eliminate any principal premium. In such a case, the principal of the note would be $500,000 resulting in a $25,000 semiannual principal payment. However, the interest rate must be increased to 12.477 percent per year. While principal payments will be $12,158 smaller each year, the increased interest rate will cause the total payments to be greater if death occurs prior to year eight. If death occurs after year seven, the total principal and interest payments will be smaller if the interest payment premium method is used. Any decision as to which method to use should also take into account the income tax consequences discussed above. If death occurs earlier, the full capital gains tax must still be paid under the position of the I.R.S., but no further interest will be payable subject to income tax.

## C.  Private Annuity

Given the father's age and the current applicable federal interest rate (which we assume to be 7 percent), one can use tables provided by the I.R.S. to determine that the semiannual annuity payment is $36,049. This annuity in conjunction with the father's life expectancy produces an overall expected return of $901,225. The exclusion ratio is 22.192 percent: the father's investment ($200,000) over the expected return ($901,225). This means $8,000 (22.192 percent of $36,049) of every annuity payment represents the father's nontaxable return of basis. The capital gain portion of each semiannual annuity payment is $12,000: the gain on the sale of the property ($300,000) over the father's expected life span ($12\frac{1}{2}$ years). The remaining $16,049 represents annuity income and is subject to tax as ordinary income. Should the father live beyond age $87\frac{1}{2}$, all additional payments would be subject to tax as ordinary income; on the other hand, should the father not attain age $87\frac{1}{2}$, his executors could take a loss for his unrecovered basis in the annuity contract on his final income tax return.

During the father's life, the daughter is precluded from deducting any portion of the annuity payment as an interest expense. Her initial basis in the property is equal to $500,000, but it would be subject to an upward or downward adjustment based upon the entire amount of annuity payments actually made at the time of her father's death.

## D.  Concise Fact Illustrations

Figures 15.1 and 15.2 offer concise illustrations of the use of a SCIN or a private annuity, given the facts at hand.

**FIGURE 15.1**

Sale of Investment Real Estate in Return for SCIN versus Private Annuity

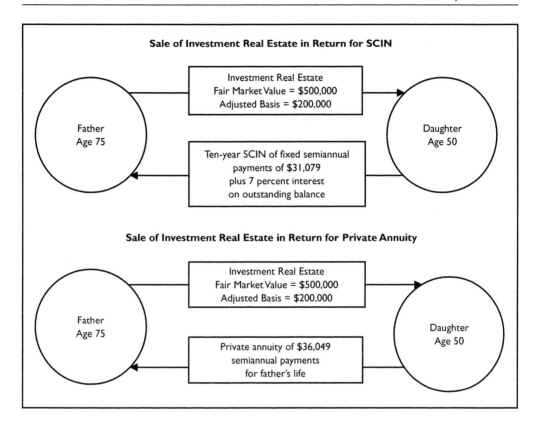

### E. Dramatic Savings Illustrated

The tax savings realized through a SCIN or a private annuity can be substantial. In the examples just cited, suppose (1) that the father were to die in an accident one year after the date of sale and (2) that the investment real estate appreciated in that same year by 20 percent, to a fair market value of $600,000. In the case of a SCIN, the father is able to rid his estate of a $600,000 asset and receives in return payments totaling $104,581 (two $31,079 installment payments plus 7-percent interest on the unpaid balances), netting him an estate-tax savings of $247,710 (the difference between $600,000 and $104,581 times an assumed effective estate-tax rate of 50 percent). On the father's final income tax return, his executors would report $42,423 in interest and $42,158 of capital gain with respect to the two payments received. In addition, the father's executors would report $379,422 of capital gain on the estate's initial income tax return.

In the case of a private annuity, the savings are even more dramatic: the father is able to rid his estate of the same $600,000 asset and receives in return payments totaling $72,098, netting him an estate-tax savings of $263,951 (the difference between $600,000 and $72,098 times an assumed effective estate-tax rate of 50 percent). On the father's final income tax return, his executors would report $24,000 of capital gain plus $35,987.84 in ordinary income. The estate-tax savings will be further enhanced if (1) the

**FIGURE 15.2**

Summary of Use of SCIN versus Private Annuity

| Father | | | | Daughter | |
|---|---|---|---|---|---|
| Income Tax | | | | | |
| Each Year During Life | Upon Death | Estate Tax | Gift Tax | Payments | Adjusted Tax Basis |
| SCIN $42,158 capital gain plus 7-percent interest on outstanding balance | Remaining untaxed gain Includable on (Estate and Trust Income Tax Return) Form 1041 | 0 | 0 | Interest portion would be deductible (subject to some limitations) | $621,581 (full face value of note) plus any improvements made and less any depreciation deductions |
| PRIVATE ANNUITY $24,000 capital gain, $32,098 ordinary income, and $16,000 nontaxable for 12.5 years. Thereafter, the entire annuity is taxable as ordinary income | | 0 | 0 | Use after-tax dollars, none of which are deductible | $500,000 plus any improvements made and less any depreciation deductions; if actual payments exceed this amount, excess is added to basis; at father's death, the daughter's basis equals the total payments made |

father consumes the installment or annuity payments made to him by his daughter and/or (2) the investment real estate appreciates further in value.

## VI. Conclusion

Unlike grantor-retained income trusts, grantor-retained annuity trusts, and grantor-retained unitrusts (discussed in Chapter 14), which depend on the longevity of the client, both the SCIN and the private annuity work most advantageously for the individual who is in ill or poor health and who is not expected to survive normal life span. (The I.R.S. has ruled, however, that the valuation and actuarial tables necessary to implement SCINs and private annuities may *not* be used when the individual has a terminal illness.) When there is no terminal illness, the advantage of a SCIN or a private annuity is that death annuls all obligations for future payments; the installment or annuity obligation is deemed valueless, and therefore, not includable on the seller's estate tax return.

If the seller surprisingly regains health or just "hangs on," though, a SCIN or a private annuity is less advantageous. The seller's longer-than-expected life means the buyer remains obligated to make payments well beyond the anticipated installment or annuity time period. At the same time, the seller's taxable estate grows correspondingly, waiting for the day of reckoning when it will ultimately be subject to estate tax. Consideration of such disadvantages weighed against the obvious advantages of SCINs and private annuities is a necessary part of thorough estate planning.

## Endnotes

1. Estate of Moss v. Commissioner, 74 T.C. 1239 (1980).
2. *See* Rev. Rul. 86-72, 1986-1 C.B. 253; Gen. Couns. Mem. 39,503 (May 19, 1980).
3. *See* Treas. Reg. § 25.7520-3(b)(3)(1995).
4. Estate of Costanza v. Commissioner, 81 T.C.M. (CCH) 1693 (2001).
5. *See* Rev. Rul. 86-72, 1986-1 C.B. 253; Estate of Frane v. Commissioner, 998 F.2d 567 (8th Cir. 1993).

# CHAPTER 16

# Durable Powers of Attorney and Advance Directives

ANDREW H. HOOK

## I. Introduction

Several years ago, Howard Zaritsky asked me to present a paper on Durable Powers of Attorney (DPAs) at the Virginia Advanced Estate Planning and Administration Seminar. I was flattered; however, I was also troubled. What was I going to say to some of the nation's leading elder law and trusts and estates lawyers about a document that many lawyers consider a simple form? After much consideration, I decided to title my presentation "Durable Powers of Attorney—They Are Not Forms!" The themes of my presentation were that (1) a DPA is a powerful legal instrument that requires the time and attention of a lawyer to draft properly, and (2) agents need the assistance of lawyers to properly exercise the authority a DPA grants. The presentation paper grew to 125 pages. Since that presentation, I have written extensively on the topic and given numerous presentations about DPAs. My objective was to demonstrate to the legal profession that DPAs are powerful legal instruments that should be customized to meet the needs of the individual clients. Let me reiterate: They are not forms! Most clients should include customized DPAs as part of their estate and elder-law planning. This planning advice extends to advance directives (living wills and/or medical powers of attorney) as well.

## II. What Is Durable Power of Attorney?

The DPA is a written instrument by which one person, the principal, appoints another person(s) as his or her agent(s). Although agency law is derived from English common law, the DPA is a relatively recent legal tool. Historically, an agency relationship terminates on the death or incapacity of the principal. Therefore, agency law did not provide an alternative to the use of a guardianship or conservatorship.

Frankly, the public views guardianships and conservatorships with the same fear and dislike that it views probate. Therefore, the legal profession has sought practical alternatives. The DPA has become the primary alternative.

Between 1954 and 1987, all of the states and the District of Columbia enacted statutes that permit a principal to create an agency that survives the principal's incapacity. These statutes provide that the agency relationship will survive the principal's incapacity if the DPA expressly states such. A power of attorney that survives the principal's incapacity or disability is referred to as "durable."

## III. Why Are DPAs a Popular Disability Planning Technique?

The DPA has become a popular management technique for incapacitated persons. Why? First, a DPA is relatively quick and easy to implement. A client can implement a DPA by the execution of a single instrument. Second, a DPA does not require the transfer of title of the principal's assets to the agent. Third, the principal's grant of authority to the agent can be quite broad and drafted to meet the client's needs. A guardian or conservator can act only as authorized by the applicable state statute. For example, in many states the guardian or conservator cannot make gifts or undertake Medicaid planning without court approval. Fourth, the client can pick the agent and craft the terms of the agency to his or her wishes. Fifth, a DPA is a relatively inexpensive plan to prepare and implement.

### A. How Do Guardianships and Conservatorships Rate as Management Tools?

Traditionally, guardianships and conservatorships have been the tools used for the management of an incapacitated person's affairs. A guardian is a person appointed by a court to make personal decisions for an incapacitated person. A conservator is a person appointed by a court to make financial decisions for an incapacitated person. These judicial proceedings are designed to protect the interests of the incapacitated person; however, they have drawbacks that the public finds unpalatable. First, they are relatively time-consuming. For example, the initial appointment process in southeast Virginia can easily take six weeks or more. This process will include meetings with the lawyers and the guardian ad litem, and hearings before a court. Thereafter, the guardian or conservator must prepare and file regular public reports with the court. Most of my clients who serve as guardians or conservators and the families of incapacitated persons find the process burdensome. Second, these proceedings are relatively expensive with lawyer's fees, filing fees, and premiums on surety bonds. However, the use of guardianships and conservatorships will remain necessary when the client does not have the capacity to implement an alternative plan, third parties refuse to accept the authority of the client's agent, or the client's family challenges the authority or actions of the client's agent.

### B. How Do Joint Bank Accounts Rate as Management Tools?

As an alternative to conservatorship or guardianship, many people use a jointly owned bank account for the management of the incapacitated person's affairs. While a joint bank account can be helpful, it is an incomplete plan at best. For example, the co-owner of the account has no authority to sign tax returns, withdraw funds from an IRA, contract for care, or sell real property. Therefore, the joint bank account is an inadequate management technique for most incapacitated persons.

### C. How Do Revocable Living Trusts Rate as Management Tools?

Another planning technique is a revocable living trust. The trustee or successor trustee of the trust typically has the authority to manage the trust assets and distribute them in accordance with the terms of the trust agreement. This technique, too, has limitations and drawbacks. First, the trustee is authorized to manage only the assets that the grantor has transferred to the trust. Therefore, the grantor must spend time and money to transfer the assets to the trust. Second, there are assets that the grantor can't transfer to the trust, and therefore, the trustee will have no authority to manage them. For example, a grantor is not allowed to transfer ownership of a retirement plan account, such as an IRA. Third, many aspects of the incapacitated person's affairs are decisions outside the scope of the management of trust assets, for example, the grantor's living arrangements. A revocable living trust can be a valuable part of a disability plan, but it is normally accompanied by a DPA to provide for the management of the grantor's affairs outside the scope of the management of the trust assets.

## IV. Are DPAs Simple Legal Forms?

### A. What Is the Historical Incidence of DPA Cases?

Some lawyers draft DPAs as forms because their state DPA statute provides for a form DPA. Yet, just as there is no single form will or trust agreement that is appropriate for all clients, there is no single form DPA that is appropriate for every client. Even in states with a statutory DPA form, the lawyer should customize it or prepare a customized DPA to address the particular needs of the client and the client's family.[1] Lawyers frequently tell me that they use the statutory DPA because third parties will not accept other DPAs. This has not been my experience. I have found that third parties and agents prefer DPAs that expressly address the extent of the agent's authority and the relationship between the principal, agent, and third parties.

DPA statutes are relatively short and provide few default rules. Therefore, it is frequently necessary to refer to the common law of agency concerning the interpretation and use of DPAs. I purchased the *Restatement (Second) of Agency,* a massive legal work written in 1959, five years after the first DPA statute. Although it has been supplemented, I was struck by how little case law concerning DPAs there was. Why? Because DPAs are relatively new legal instruments. All 50 states did not have a DPA statute until 1987. Additionally, until all 50 states had DPA statutes and third parties became familiar with them, many lawyers did not advise their clients to plan for the management of their affairs using DPAs.

### B. Why Has the Incidence of DPA Cases Increased?

Since my first presentation on DPAs in 1999, I have noticed more and more cases involving DPAs. Why? More usage of DPAs combined with a lack of customization has led to many questionable interpretations of DPAs.

DPA use has increased for several reasons. Although modern medicine has lengthened our life expectancy by reducing deaths from acute illness, many clients will suffer extended periods of incapacity during their lengthened lifetimes from chronic conditions, such as Alzheimer's disease. These clients need DPAs to manage their affairs. Furthermore, after all 50 states adopted DPA statutes, lawyers began to recommend their use.

The problem is that many lawyers drafting those DPAs merely use a simple form. Many lawyers do not customize DPAs to meet their client's needs. Every client is given the same power of attorney. The only customization is the name of the principal and the name of the agent(s). These same lawyers will draft a ten-or-more-page revocable trust agreement for the management of a client's assets, but devote only a page or two to a DPA that grants the agent much broader authority than is granted to the trustee. When a principal becomes incapacitated, the principal's children and other family members frequently disagree about the management of the principal's affairs. Litigation follows. Specific directions in a customized DPA will often deter such action.

## V. What Issues Should a Lawyer Address in Drafting a DPA?

A lawyer drafting a DPA should address each of the following issues:

- Does the principal have the capacity to execute the DPA?
- What law will apply to the DPA?
- Who should be named as the agent?
- Who will be named as the successor agent?
- What is the effective date of the agent's authority?
- What authority should be granted to the agent?
- Should the DPA place any limitations on the agent's authority?
- Should the DPA give the agent instructions concerning the exercise of authority?
- How shall the relationship between the agent, principal, and third parties be defined?

My tax management portfolio on DPAs[2] includes a flowchart providing a decision tree for addressing these issues and drafting the DPA. A DPA drafted using the decision tree will frequently consist of five or more pages. The failure to adequately address each of these issues in the preparation of the DPA materially increases the likelihood of problems in the implementation of the client's disability plan.

### A.  Does the Principal Have the Capacity to Execute a DPA?

Clients frequently ask their lawyers to prepare DPAs for people with mental impairments. This request raises the practical problem of determining if the principal has the requisite mental capacity to execute the DPA.

The lawyer should start with the legal presumption that all adults have legal capacity. When the principal has a serious mental impairment, the lawyer must determine if the principal has the capacity to consent to the creation of a consensual fiduciary relationship and the delegation of authority to the agent.[3] The lawyer should meet with the principal in private outside of the presence of family members and the proposed agent. The lawyer must determine whether the principal understands that (1) lawyer is authorizing an agent to act for principal, and (2) principal will be legally bound by the agent's actions.

When the client is mentally impaired but the lawyer ultimately determines that the principal has the requisite capacity, I recommend that two disinterested people witness the principal's signature. The witnesses should prepare a file memo concerning the client's capacity.

When the lawyer is seriously concerned about the principal's capacity, the lawyer should seek consent to discuss the principal's capacity with the principal's physician and other caregivers. The lawyer obtains, for a file, the physician and caregiver's written opinions concerning the principal's capacity.

A physical impairment will rarely preclude the use of a DPA. The principal must be capable of communicating consent to the creation of the fiduciary relationship with the agent, the delegation of authority to the agent, and the execution of the DPA on the principal's behalf. This consent may be communicated by signals, such as blinking of the eyes or hand squeezes. Once again, the execution of the DPA should be witnessed by two disinterested people who prepare a memo for the file about the principal's capacity and understanding of the DPA.

### B. What Law Will Apply to the DPA?

Generally, the laws of the state in which the DPA is executed determine its validity. The law of the state where the agent is acting determines the validity of the agent's actions.[4] All 50 states and the District of Columbia have DPA statutes. These DPA statutes differ in many material respects, particularly concerning requirements for form and execution. When the applicable DPA statute is silent, the common-law agency rules apply. On occasion, the DPA must be recorded in various public records. All 50 states and the District of Columbia have statutes and regulations concerning the format and execution requirements for recording documents.

Federal law imposes additional rules. DPAs for military personnel are exempt from state form, substance, and recording rules and must be treated as if they complied with applicable state law.[5] The U.S. Office of Personnel Management (OPM) and the Social Security Administration (SSA) do not recognize DPAs.[6] The OPM and SSA appoint representative payees to receive a beneficiary's funds. The Internal Revenue Code (I.R.C.) and applicable regulations govern the appointment of an agent to inspect tax returns, sign tax returns, negotiate checks for tax refunds, and represent the taxpayer before the I.R.S.[7]

We live in a mobile society. I recommend that you draft a client's DPA to comply with the laws of the states in which the client resides and owns substantial property. If you are unfamiliar with the laws of another state, then you should retain counsel in that state. When you review a client's estate plan, you should ensure that the client's DPA complies with the laws of all states in which the principal owns residential property. The client may have acquired other residences or property after the preparation of the DPA.

### C. Who Should Be Named as the Agent(s)?

A significant advantage of a DPA over a guardianship or conservatorship is that the principal can choose his or her own agent(s). Frequently, the principal will be in a much better position than a judge to do so.

### 1. What Factors Should Be Considered?

The selection of the agents will be the most important, and often the most difficult, decision the principal must make. Whom should the principal select as an agent? As a general rule, any person may serve as an agent,[8] including a resident of another state or country. A corporation, partnership, or other entity may also act as an agent.

The lawyer should guide the principal in carefully considering who will serve as the agent(s). The lawyer should note that the principal's spouse or oldest child will not always be the best choice. The following factors should be considered:

- Is the person trustworthy?
- Is the person willing to serve?
- Does the person have good judgment?
- Does the person have financial and investment expertise?
- Does the person have the time to serve?
- Does the person have any conflicts of interest?
- Does the person live close to the principal?
- If the person is the principal's spouse, is there a risk of divorce or separation?
- If the person is one of the principal's children, is there a risk of family friction?

## 2. Are Multiple Agents Acceptable?

The principal may authorize more than one person to act as agents. When the principal has multiple children, the lawyer should recommend that the principal consider appointing several of his children as multiple agents to avoid family friction, self-serving decisions, and litigation.

When the principal appoints multiple agents, the DPA should expressly state whether the agents may act independently or whether they must act jointly. The DPA should also provide a mechanism for the resolution of disputes among the agents. I frequently recommend that the DPA provide for arbitration and name the arbiter. "If my agents cannot agree on a decision or action under this DPA, then the dispute shall be resolved by arbitration carried out under the rules of the _____[State]_____ Uniform Arbitration Act by a single arbitrator, who shall be _____[Name of Arbitrator]_____ if he or she is available."[9] In my experience, the mere existence of the arbitration mechanism (or perhaps the avoidance of arbiter's fees) encourages the agents to discuss issues and resolve differences of opinion among themselves.

## 3. Who Will Be Named as the Successor Agent(s)?

While a court may appoint a successor trustee of a trust if no trustee is currently serving, a court has no jurisdiction to appoint a successor agent under a DPA. If there is no agent, then the DPA is terminated. Therefore, a lawyer should counsel the principal to appoint one or more successor agents if the primary agent is unable or unwilling to serve. The principal may also authorize the agent to appoint successor agents and subagents.[10]

When the DPA provides for the appointment of successor agents, how will third parties determine when the successor agent is authorized to act? One solution is to have the DPA specify that a successor agent is authorized to act only with a requisite certificate.

## 4. What Is the Effective Date of the Agent's Authority?

A DPA that is unconditional is effective immediately upon execution by the principal (an immediately effective DPA).

## *VI. Other DPA Options*

Principals can also create springing DPAs, hybrid DPAs, or escrowed DPAs. The effective date of the agent's authority differs with each of these choices.

### A. What Is a Springing DPA?

Many state statutes expressly authorize the creation of DPAs that become effective upon the occurrence of a future event, such as the disability or incapacity of the principal (springing DPAs).

Other states are silent concerning the creation of springing DPAs. Can you create a springing DPA in a state with a DPA statute that doesn't mention springing DPAs? The Texas Court of Appeals held that a springing DPA executed before the Texas Code expressly authorized springing DPAs was valid. The court could not find any current cases prohibiting the creation of a future agency relationship. At least one state, Florida, expressly prohibits springing DPAs.[11]

When the authority granted by the DPA is dependent on a future event, it is important to carefully define the triggering event:

> The authority granted to my agent shall be exercisable only on my incapacity. For the purposes of this DPA, my incapacity shall mean that I am unable to manage my financial affairs due to a mental or cognitive impairment. My incapacity shall be evidenced by the written opinion of a physician, who has personally examined me, that I am unable to manage my financial affairs.

### B. What Is a Hybrid DPA?

It is possible to draft a DPA that is immediately effective for the primary agent but conditioned on the principal's incapacity for the successor agent (a hybrid DPA). Married couples frequently use hybrid DPAs to grant immediately effective authority to the spouse, but they condition the authority of the successor agent (say, a child) both on the incapacity of the principal and also on the death or incapacity of the primary agent.

### C. What Are Other Alternatives to the Springing DPA?

Clients who are reluctant to grant the agent immediate authority to act have two additional alternatives to a springing DPA. First, the principal can execute an immediately effective DPA but place it in escrow with a third party. The third party should be instructed in a written escrow agreement to deliver the DPA to the agent only upon the occurrence of a specified event, for example, the principal's incapacity. Second, the principal can retain the originals of the DPA and all copies. The agent is advised of the existence of the DPA and its location. This arrangement runs the risk that the agency relationship will not be created because if the principal fails to deliver the DPA, the principal did not consent to the agent acting on his or her behalf. At a minimum, the principal should advise the agent of the existence of the DPA and provide the agent with access to the originals of the DPA.

## D. What Type of DPA Should One Choose?

Should a DPA be immediately effective, springing, or escrowed? There is no one answer that is appropriate for all clients. The principal should choose the type of DPA after a thorough discussion of the relevant factors with the lawyer. There are several factors to consider:

- The immediately effective DPA is easier to use than a springing DPA because it is unnecessary for the agent to prove the occurrence of the triggering event/ condition each time he or she exercises his or her authority.
- The springing DPA and escrowed DPA provide a measure of protection against the premature use of the DPA.
- The escrowed DPA arrangement is more difficult to establish because it requires that a third party agree to serve as the escrow agent.
- Some lawyers fear that third parties may not accept a springing DPA as readily as an immediately effective DPA. Many lawyers who draft springing DPAs, however, report otherwise.

I recommend that the power of attorney expressly state the principal's intent concerning the effective date. For example, the DPA should state: "I intend to create an immediately effective general Durable Power of Attorney," or "I intend to create a springing general Durable Power of Attorney."

## E. What Authority Should Be Granted to the Agent(s)?

What can a principal authorize an agent to do? A principal may authorize an agent to perform any act "unless public policy or an agreement with another requires personal performance."[12] The courts have defined nondelegability narrowly.[13] The following acts generally are held to be nondelegable:

- marriage or divorce;
- voting in a public election;
- executing, amending, or revoking a will.[14]

A DPA can either be a special DPA, a general DPA, or a limited DPA. A general DPA is a grant of broad authority. A limited DPA places limitations on the agent's authority, for example, a grant of authority for a limited period of time. A special DPA is a grant of authority to undertake specific acts. I recommend that the DPA clearly state the principal's intention as to the type of authority being granted to the agent: For example, "I intend to create a general DPA," or "I intend to create a special DPA."

## F. When Should One Choose a General DPA?

The lawyer should recommend a general DPA when the client is seeking an alternative to the use of a guardianship or conservatorship if the client becomes incapacitated. In these cases, the client grants his or her agent very broad and general authority similar to the authority granted to a conservator.

### 1. Should a General DPA Be All-Inclusive?

Can the general DPA simply state that the principal grants the agent the authority to perform any delegable act that the principal could personally perform? No. DPAs are strictly construed and generally held to grant only the authority that is clearly delineated.[15] The courts generally discount or discard all-embracing expressions of authority.[16] Therefore, a lawyer should include within the DPA a list of authority to be granted to the agent. To prevent the list from becoming unnecessarily long or inappropriate, the lawyer should customize the list of authority to meet the particular needs of the client.

### 2. How Does One Craft a General DPA to Replace a Guardianship?

In order for the DPA to be an effective alternative to a guardianship, it should expressly authorize the agent to manage and provide for the principal's care and custody. For example, the DPA should authorize the agent to do the following:

- establish the principal's residence in an assisted living facility or nursing home,
- provide for the principal's travel or transportation,
- provide for the care and disposition of the principal's pets and animals,
- arrange for the principal's funeral and burial,
- hire caregivers and geriatric-care managers,
- provide for recreation and companionship, and
- store or dispose of the principal's tangible personal property, such as the principal's automobiles, furniture, and appliances.

### 3. Does a General DPA Empower an Agent Regarding a Trust?

Generally, a principal cannot authorize an agent to make a will that disposes of principal's assets at principal's death. A trust agreement is frequently used as a will substitute. However, without express statutory or case law, it is not clear that a principal may authorize an agent to create a trust that disposes of principal's assets at the principal's death.

Some state DPA statutes provide that a principal may expressly authorize an agent to create and fund a trust on the principal's behalf;[17] however, these statutes do not specifically state that the principal can authorize the agent to create a trust that disposes of the principal's assets at the principal's death. It is clear that a principal can expressly authorize an agent to make a gift of the principal's assets, and the disposition of the trust assets at the principal's death is a gift of a future interest in property. Therefore, the principal should be able to expressly authorize an agent to create and fund a trust that disposes of the principal's assets at the principal's death.

## G. When Should One Choose a Special DPA?

A lawyer should consider recommending a special DPA when the principal needs to deal with specific property, such as a professional practice, or the agent needs to take specific acts, such as representation of the principal before a governmental body. A special power of attorney can authorize a grandparent to care for and to consent to medical treatment of the principal's minor child while the child is in the grandparent's care; it can also authorize a neighbor or friend to seek veterinary treatment for the principal's pet while the principal is on vacation or incapacitated. In other cases, it is prudent to recommend use of a special DPA for real property transactions, securities transactions, or Medicaid planning.

## H.  When Should One Choose a Limited DPA?

When drafting a DPA, the lawyer should ask the principal if he/she wants to impose any limitations on the authority of the agent(s). There is no one boilerplate list of instructions and limitations to include in every DPA. Each principal will have a different set of desires and goals. The lawyer drafting the DPA should ascertain those desires and goals and draft the DPA to conform to them.

For example, if the principal is authorizing a person to care for her minor child while she is out of town, the principal may want to place a limitation on the duration of the authority. Principals who have designated their spouses as their agents may wish to terminate the agent's authority in the event of a divorce. If the principal has executed a special DPA for the management of a particular asset, such as a professional practice, then the principal should limit the agent's authority concerning the professional practice in the general DPA. Furthermore, some principals may want to expressly limit the agent's investment authority.

To avoid adverse estate and gift-tax consequences, the lawyer drafting a DPA should consider recommending several limitations on the agent's authority. When the agent is authorized to make gifts to him- or herself, limitations on that authority will preclude an attempt by the I.R.S. to treat that authority as a general power of appointment.[18]

## I.  When Should One Choose a Combination of Different Powers of Attorney?

On other occasions a combination of different powers of attorney will be appropriate. For example, the principal may grant one agent a special DPA and another agent a limited, general DPA. A client who has a professional practice that requires a professional license to manage may grant a special DPA to a colleague to manage the practice and a limited, general DPA to a family member to manage all of his remaining assets and affairs.

The I.R.S. has not asserted that a DPA authorizing an agent to make gifts to himself is a general power of appointment for estate and gift-tax purposes. There is, however, considerable uncertainty on this point. A power to dispose of property is a general power of appointment if the holder of the power can self-appoint the property or satisfy holder's debts.[19] The power is not a general power of appointment if it is exercisable only with the consent of the creator of the power.[20]

Some lawyers assert that the DPA is not a general power of appointment because the principal's power of revocation of the DPA is analogous to a power exercisable only with the consent of the creator of the power.[21] Other lawyers argue that the agent's fiduciary duties to the principal preclude the DPA from being considered a general power of appointment. Still others argue that the I.R.S. will not treat a DPA as a general power of appointment because it would be too easy for a principal to designate the principal's spouse as an agent under a DPA and obtain a step-up in basis for the principal's property upon the spouse's death. In light of this uncertainty, it is prudent to impose limitations on the agent's authority to make gifts where estate or gift taxes are a concern to the agent.[22]

These limitations should not necessarily be included in every DPA. For clients interested in Medicaid planning, these limitations may preclude some gifting strategies and the transfer of countable resources to a community spouse to fund his or her Community Spouse Resource Allowance.[23] When the principal owns insurance on the life of the agent, the lawyer should consider recommending that the DPA not grant the agent any authority with respect to the policy in order to avoid granting the agent any incidents of ownership in the policy.[24] As the federal estate-tax-applicable exemption amount increases, the number of times that these limitations will be advisable will consequently decrease.

### J. Should a DPA Contain Special Instructions?

When drafting a DPA, the lawyer should ask the principal if he or she wants to give the agent(s) instructions concerning the exercise of the grant of authority. For example, a principal may want to give the agent instructions not to sell particular assets. Another principal may want to instruct the agent that the principal wishes to reside in her home as long as it is possible, even if it is more expensive than facility care.

## VII. How Should the Relationship among the Agent(s), Principal, and Third Parties Be Defined?

### A. What Are an Agent's Duties to the Principal?

The agent under a DPA is a fiduciary with respect to the matters within the scope of the agency.[25] As a fiduciary, the agent owes the following duties to the principal:

- duty of care and skill,
- duty to keep and render accounts,
- duty to act only as authorized,
- duty of loyalty,
- duty to avoid conflicts of interest, and
- duty to keep the agent's property and the principal's property separate.

Most principals will name a close family member or friend as their agent. Therefore, the lawyer should discuss with the principal whether one or more of these duties should be expressly waived or modified in the DPA. For example, it is very common for spouses to own property jointly. If the principal names his or her spouse as the agent, the principal may not want to require that the spouse sever the joint ownership of every asset that they own jointly in order to comply with the duty not to commingle assets. In these cases, the DPA should authorize commingling. In other cases, the principal may wish to authorize the agent to make gifts to the agent or to purchase the principal's property. Therefore, the DPA should expressly authorize self-dealing. In still other cases, the principal may not want to hold the agent liable for errors or require that the agent comply with the Prudent Investor Act (PIA). When this is the case, the DPA should exonerate the agent for simple negligence or waive compliance with the PIA.

### B. Does the Agent Have the Obligation to Act on the Principal's Behalf?

Generally, agency law imposes an obligation upon the agent to act only (1) based on the agent's express agreement to act, or (2) based on promissory estoppel.[26] When the principal does not intend that the agent be obligated to act on the principal's behalf, the DPA should expressly state that the agent is not obligated to act and appoint a successor agent if the agent fails to act. When the principal intends that the agent will be obligated to act, then the agent should expressly agree within the DPA to act on the principal's behalf.

## C. What Duties Does a Principal Owe an Agent?

The principal owes the duty to (1) compensate the agent and (2) reimburse the agent for expenses incurred in the course of the agency. When a family member is serving as the agent, however, compensation may cause disputes or controversies among members of the principal's family. The lawyer should discuss with the principal whether compensation should be paid to the agent and, if so, how the compensation should be determined. Such decisions should be expressly set out in the DPA.

## D. What Duties Does an Agent Owe a Third Party?

If the principal is incapacitated and unable to supervise the agent, the principal's family will be interested in monitoring the agent's actions. Generally, the family will have no right to information and the agent will have no authority to provide the information. However, if the family has no information, they will think the worst and litigation is possible. Additionally, the agent's conduct and performance will likely be improved, if scrutinized. Therefore, the principal should consider requiring the agent to provide information to certain members of the principal's family either on a periodic basis or upon request. These family members could be authorized to remove the agent and appoint a successor agent. In other cases, such as when the principal's spouse is serving as the agent, the principal may wish to expressly state that the agent has no obligation to provide anyone with information.

## VIII. How Will the Principal's Health-Care Decisions Be Made If the Principal Is Incapacitated?

Our common law has long recognized that each of us has the right to decide what medical care to accept or refuse. In *Cruzan v. Director, Missouri Department of Health,*[27] the U.S. Supreme Court decided that (1) the right to refuse medical treatment is a liberty interest protected by the Fourteenth Amendment to the U.S. Constitution, but (2) the states could require clear and convincing evidence of the patient's intentions before treatment was withdrawn. The U.S. Supreme Court has also held that there is no constitutional right (1) to physician-assisted suicide or (2) to commit suicide.[28]

A competent adult may express his or her decisions concerning medical treatment. An incapacitated person is not able to exercise this right. Because this right is meaningless unless it can be exercised, the courts have permitted a surrogate to exercise the patient's rights.[29] The surrogate may be a court, guardian, family, or person selected by the patient.

It is important for the lawyer to assist the client in exercising medical treatment rights and selecting a surrogate to make health-care decisions. This planning is especially important should the client's family disagree about the treatment. Depending on the state in which the client resides, the legal authority will be created in a living will, health-care power of attorney, or an advance directive. The term "advance directive" is used nationally since it is the term used in the federal Patient Self-Determination Act[30] and the Uniform Health-Care Decisions Act.[31]

There are two types of advance directives: living wills and health-care powers of attorney.

## A. Living Will

A living will gives instructions concerning the client's medical treatment if the client becomes terminally ill or is in a persistent vegetative state and is unable to communicate his health-care instructions. All 50 states have living will statutes, and most of them provide a model form. The format and execution requirements of these statutes vary from state to state. A state has no obligation to require compliance with a living will that is executed in another state and that does not comply with its requirements. Some states, however, recognize living wills that are valid in the states where they were executed. Even if the living will does not meet the requirements of local law, it is evidence of the client's intent.

## B. Health-Care Power of Attorney

Most states permit a client to create a health-care power of attorney that authorizes an agent to make medical decisions if the principal is unable to make such decisions. A major distinction between a living will and a health-care power of attorney is that the power of attorney can be used for a broad range of medical decision-making while the living will is restricted to decisions concerning dying. Here, too, the states impose different format and execution requirements. Most state statutes contain optional-form health-care powers of attorney. Clients frequently sign both living wills and health-care powers of attorney. The living will gives instructions concerning the client's care if the client is dying, and the medical power of attorney authorizes an agent to make health-care decisions in less serious situations.

Recent tax legislation, which substantially increases the amount that one may exempt for estate taxation, has made the client's decision-making about whether to use a living will or medical power of attorney more difficult. A living will directs the withholding of or termination of life support if the client is in a terminally ill or a persistent vegetative state. However, phased increases in the estate and GST unified credit, phased decreases in marginal estate and GST tax rates, repeal of the estate and GST tax in 2010, and the sunset provision may result in significant financial differences if the client survives until the next year. Therefore, some clients may wish to use a medical power of attorney that authorizes the agent to consider the client's desire to reduce estate and GST taxes.

## C. Making Health-Care Decisions

As part of the client's estate or elder-law planning, the lawyer should consult with the client about how the client's health-care decisions will be made if the client is unable to make them. The client should exercise the right to provide for health-care decisions in a customized advance directive. After a thorough discussion, the lawyer should assist the client in drafting and executing the documents necessary to implement the client's plan. The advance directive should, at a minimum, address the following:

- Does the client want to authorize the withdrawal or withholding of life-sustaining care, or does the client want the maximum care available?
- Does the client want to include nutrition and hydration in the care that can be withdrawn or withheld?

- Does the client have any known medical conditions, and, if so, what care does the client want provided for these conditions?
- The names, addresses, and telephone numbers of the client's surrogate decision makers and their successors.

## IX. Conclusion

DPAs and advance directives are not commodity legal services or simple forms. They are powerful legal documents. After a thorough interview with the client, a lawyer should customize these documents to meet the client's needs and goals. In order to efficiently draft customized DPAs and advance directives, the lawyer should develop or use powerful drafting systems.[32] The lawyer should charge a fee to prepare DPAs and advance directives based on the effort required. Even with a document assembly system, it can require about two hours for the lawyer to interview the client, draft the DPA and advance directive, and supervise their execution. After an explanation of the benefits of a customized DPA and advance directive, clients are willing to pay the cost associated with customized instruments.

### Endnotes

1. *But cf.* MINN. STAT. §523.23(3) (prohibiting modification of the statutory form). Minnesota is the only state, to my knowledge, that prohibits statutory-form changes. Most state DPA statutes that provide for a DPA statutory form permit customization of the statutory form.

2. Andrew H. Hook, 859 T.M., Durable Powers of Attorney, B-1301

3. *See* RESTATEMENT (SECOND) OF AGENCY § 20.

4. RESTATEMENT (SECOND) ON CONFLICT OF LAWS §§291–292(1971).

5. *See* 10 U.S.C. §§ 1044b(a) and (c).

6. Social Security Administration Publication No. 05-10076, *A Guide For Representative Payees* (1997); letter from the Office of Personnel Management (August 6, 1998) (on file with author).

7. *See* I.R.C. § 6103(e)(6) and § 6012(b)(2); Treas. Reg. §§ 1.6012-1(a)(5), 1.601.502.

8. *See* RESTATEMENT (SECOND) OF AGENCY § 21.

9. Andrew H. Hook, 859 T.M., Durable Powers of Attorney, A-19.

10. RESTATEMENT (SECOND) OF AGENCY § 77.

11. FLA. STAT. ANN § 709.08(1).

12. RESTATEMENT (SECOND) OF AGENCY § 17.

13. First Union Nat'l Bank of Virginia v. Thomas, 37 Va. Cir. 35, 40 (1995).

14. *But see* WASH. REV. CODE §11.94.050 (providing that an agent shall not have the authority, unless specifically provided in the DPA, to make, amend, or revoke a will). By implication, a principal can expressly authorize these acts.

15. Kunewa v. Joshua, 83 Haw. 65 (1996); Muller v. Bank of Am., 28 Kan. App. 2d 136 (2000); King v. Bankerd, 303 Md. 98 (1985).

16. RESTATEMENT (SECOND) OF AGENCY §§ 34, 37.

17. *See* MO. REV. STAT. § 404.710(6)(2); CAL. PROB. CODE §4264(c); WASH. REV. CODE § 11.94.050.

18. Reg. § 20.2041-1(b) provides that a power of appointment includes all powers that are in substance and effect powers of appointment regardless of the nomenclature used in creating them.

19. I.R.C. §§ 2041, 2514.

20. Reg. § 25.2514-3(b)(1).

21. There is authority, however, that the power to revoke is not the equivalent of consent. *See* G.C.M. 37428.

22. For example, consider (1) prohibiting gifts to the agent, the agent's creditors, or the agent's estate, or to discharge the agent's debts; (2) limit gifts to the agent by the five-and-five power exception; or (3) limit gifts to the agent by an ascertainable standard.

23. 42 U.S.C.S. § 1396r-5(f). The Community Spouse Resource Allowance (CRSA) is the amount of countable resources that a community spouse may retain while qualifying the institutionalized spouse for Medicaid assistance for the payment of nursing-home care. The assets funding the CSRA must be titled in the name of the community spouse.

24. I.R.C. § 2042 (including in a decedent's estate any life insurance on the decedent's life over which the decedent held an incidence of ownership).

25. RESTATEMENT (SECOND) OF AGENCY § 13.

26. RESTATEMENT (SECOND) OF AGENCY § 377.

27. 497 U.S. 261 (1990).

28. Washington v. Glucksberg, 521 U.S. 702 (1997); Vacco v. Quill, 521 U.S. 793 (1997).

29. Cruzan v. Dir. of Mo. Dept. of Health, 497 U.S. 261 (1990); *In re Quinlan,* 70 N.J. 10 (1976).

30. 42 U.S.C. §1395cc(f).

31. Drafted by the National Conference of Commissioners on Uniform Laws. Final Act 1993.

32. For examples of drafting systems *see* Thomas Begley, Jr. & Andrew H. Hook, R.I.A., Representing the Elderly or Disabled Client, and Andrew H. Hook, 859 T.M., Durable Powers of Attorney.

# PART III

## *Testamentary Deposition*

# CHAPTER 17

# Wills

SUZANNE L. SHIER
REBECCA WALLENFELSZ

## I. Introduction

A will is the instrument by which a person makes a disposition of his or her property to take effect after his death; by its nature, a will is amendable and revocable during a person's lifetime. The property of a person who dies with a valid will (testate) is disposed of in accordance with the will. The property of a person who dies without a valid will (intestate) is disposed of in accordance with the governing state law of descent and distribution to his or her heirs at law.

There are many advantages to having a valid will. A will permits the maker (testator) to provide for the payment of debts and expenses, to determine who will receive testator's property and in what shares, to provide for distributions to minor beneficiaries, to provide for guardians for minor children, to choose the personal representative (referred to in some jurisdictions as the executor) of testator's estate, and to provide for the powers of the personal representative. In addition, a will can provide for estate tax and generation-skipping transfer (GST) tax planning.

A will applies to a testator's property subject to probate administration, but not to property that is not subject to probate administration. Property subject to probate administration includes property owned by a testator individually, property owned by a testator as a tenant in common with others, a testator's interest in community property, and any property made payable to a testator's estate. There are many types of property that are not subject to probate administration, including: joint tenancy with right of survivorship property; tenancy by the entirety property; property held in trust; and property subject to disposition pursuant to a beneficiary designation, such as life insurance, individual retirement accounts, qualified plans, and annuities. Because a will does not determine the disposition of all types of property, it is important to coordinate the provisions of a will with a testator's other estate planning documents, including any trust or insurance or retirement account beneficiary designations.

A will may be used alone or in conjunction with a revocable trust. A revocable trust is not a substitute for a will. If a revocable trust is used, a simple will should direct the disposition of probate property to the trust at death.

The following discussion is an overview of the basics of drafting a will, testamentary capacity, execution requirements, revocation and modification of a will, and safeguarding a will. Only general principles are discussed because state law governs the testate disposition and the intestate succession of property.[1] Thus, in each particular case, it will be necessary to determine the rules and requirements of the governing state law.

## II. Drafting a Will

The first step in drafting a will is interviewing the testator to determine the testator's intentions with respect to the disposition of testator's property, the extent of the property, how title to the property is held, and any special needs or circumstances. Practitioners typically use a form of estate-planning questionnaire for this purpose.

A will should revoke all prior wills and include provision with respect to domicile; family relationships; payment of expenses; debts and taxes the disposition of assets; and the designation of fiduciaries.

### A. Name and Domicile of Testator

A will should state the name of the testator. If the testator is known by more than one name, the will should note the other name(s). Stating the testator's domicile in the will is helpful in determining the validity of the will. A will is typically valid if executed in conformity with the law of the testator's domicile at the time of execution. An international will executed in conformance with the Uniform International Wills Act[2] satisfies state law execution requirements in jurisdictions that have adopted the Uniform International Wills Act.

### B. Identification of Family Members

Identifying family members in a will is helpful. Naming the testator's spouse and children or a recital of the absence of either in the will may help to resolve disputes regarding marriage or paternity after the testator dies. Specific provision should be made to include children born to or adopted by the testator after the will is executed. In many jurisdictions, children of a testator born after the execution of a will are entitled to their intestate share of the testator's estate unless the will provides for them or specifically disinherits them.[3] If a testator intends to disinherit any child, he should expressly state such intention in the will.

### C. Expenses, Debts, and Taxes

A will should provide for the payment of expenses, debts, and taxes. How expenses, debts, and taxes will be paid and from what sources directly affects the ultimate disposition of assets among the beneficiaries under the will. Thus, the often-overlooked provisions of a will regarding payment of expenses, debts, and taxes are actually dispositive in nature, not just administrative. The importance of these provisions cannot be overemphasized.

#### 1. Expenses

The principal issue regarding payment of administration expenses is apportionment. State law may or may not provide for the apportionment of administration expenses between probate and nonprobate property. When a will provides for the payment of administration expenses, the provisions of the will control. Wills often provide for the payment of probate and nonprobate property expenses from the residue of the probate estate. Providing for payment from the residue of the probate estate may simplify the administration of the estate, but other options may be desirable if there are significant nonprobate assets.

A will may also provide for the payment of funeral expenses. However, it is not advisable to provide for organ donations or funeral or burial arrangements in a will because the will may not be readily accessible at the time of death. Organ donations may be made under a separate instrument. The testator should discuss funeral and burial arrangements with his or her family during testator's lifetime.

### 2. Debts

A will customarily provides for the payment of a testator's debts. The absence of a provision providing for the payment of debts will not preclude the payment of properly filed claims against a testator's estate. Conversely, the presence of a direction to pay debts will not compel the payment of claims not properly filed.[4] In the case of debts secured by real estate, the devisee typically takes the real estate subject to the mortgage. If a testator intends that the executor pay the mortgage, the will should provide for payment. Proceeds from a life insurance policy typically pay for any loans on the life insurance. If a testator intends that the executor pay an insurance loan, the will should provide for payment.

### 3. Taxes

The primary issues regarding the payment of estate, inheritance, and GST taxes are apportionment and reimbursement. In the absence of state law directing otherwise, under common law the tax burden falls on the residuary estate with no apportionment among probate and nonprobate assets (outside apportionment) or among dispositions under the will (inside apportionment).[5] Similarly, the Internal Revenue Code of 1986, as amended (I.R.C.), calls for (1) payment of the federal estate tax from the residuary estate absent a contrary provision in the testator's will or state law, and (2) imposes on the personal representative the initial obligation to pay the entire federal estate tax levied on a decedent's gross estate (whether probate or nonprobate property) even though certain assets constituting the gross estate for federal estate tax purposes may not be in the personal representative's possession or control.[6] The I.R.C., however, provides for reimbursement to the estate for federal estate tax on insurance proceeds, power of appointment property, qualified terminable interest property (QTIP) and transfers with retained interest under I.R.C. Section 2036.[7] The federal GST tax contains its own apportionment provisions under I.R.C. Section 2603.

Many decisions must be made regarding tax apportionment and reimbursement, and when there are multiple estate-planning documents, such as a will and revocable trust, the tax payment provisions of all instruments must be coordinated. One common approach is to provide for payment from the residue generally, subject to apportionment for power of appointment property and assets held in QTIP trust. Another is to provide for payment from the residue, subject to reimbursement for life insurance, power of appointment property, QTIP, and transfers with a retained interest under I.R.C. Section 2036.

## D. Dispositive Provisions

A will should effectively dispose of all of a testator's property subject to probate administration. The dispositive provisions of a will include any desired specific gifts, disposition of tangible personal property generally, exercise of any testamentary powers of appointment, and disposition of the residue of the estate. There are a number of special considerations regarding the dispositive provisions of a will.

### 1. Specific Gifts and Disinheritance

In all of the dispositive provisions, a will should clearly identify the property being disposed and the intended beneficiaries. It is advisable to state each beneficiary's full name and beneficiary's relationship to the testator. In the case of charitable gifts, special care should be used in properly identifying the charity and the charitable purpose of the gift.

All of the dispositive provisions of a will should also provide for situations in which the beneficiary does not survive the testator. Under common law, if a testamentary gift was made to an individual who did not survive the testator, the gift would lapse and pass along with the residuary estate.[8] To avoid this result, many states have antilapse statutes, the provisions of which vary substantially. For example, an antilapse statute may provide that a testamentary gift to a testator's child who predeceases the testator will pass to the deceased child's descendants. In order to avoid any uncertainty as to the disposition of a testamentary gift in the event a designated beneficiary does not survive the testator, it is advisable to condition gifts on a beneficiary's being alive at the time of the testator's death and to provide for any desired alternative disposition if a designated beneficiary is not living.

A testator may choose to disinherit or significantly limit the inheritance of certain descendants and heirs. No-contest provisions are commonly used in conjunction with any disinheritance to discourage contest of the will. Under a typical no-contest provision, a contesting beneficiary loses any interest he or she would otherwise receive under the will if he contests the will. Thus, a testator should give the anticipated contestant some interest of more than nominal value, which would be lost upon contest.

### 2. Tangible Personal Property and Tax Considerations

A will should provide for the disposition of tangible personal property separately from the disposition of the residue to avoid having income from the estate attributed to the recipients of tangible personal property for income tax purposes. Under I.R.C. Section 663, distributions (regardless of whether the distributions are cash or in-kind) to residuary beneficiaries during the administration of an estate will cause income of an estate to be taxable to them. However, the distribution of gifts of specific property or specific sums of money does not cause income of an estate to become taxable to the beneficiaries.

### 3. Testamentary Powers of Appointment

If a testator is the donee of any testamentary powers of appointment, the testator and the drafting lawyer should determine whether to exercise such powers under the testator's will, considering the tax consequences of any exercise. Any exercise of a power of appointment should clearly identify the instrument creating the power and the power itself and should conform to any requirements under the granting instrument.

### 4. *Residue of the Estate*

A residuary clause is the final dispositive provision of a will. It must be drafted in light of the other provisions of the will and should avoid any property passing intestate. In order to avoid the inadvertent exercise of a power of appointment under a residuary clause, the residuary clause should specifically exclude any property over which the testator has a power of appointment. For example, a will may provide that "All the residue of my estate, including all lapsed gifts hereunder (but excluding any property over which I have any power of appointment), I give to ____." Distribution may be outright or held in trust.

Class gifts to descendants are commonly used in residuary clauses to take into account the birth and death of descendants after a will is executed and prior to the testator's death. When making a gift to a class, the will should clearly designate the class, the time(s) for determining membership in the class, and the shares class members take. For example, a will may provide for distribution of the residue to the testator's spouse, if living at the time of the testator's death, otherwise to the testator's descendants then living, per stirpes and not per capita. The drafting lawyer must determine who will be included in the designated class under the governing state law and how the residue will be divided among the class under the language used in the will.

### 5. *Special Considerations*

Some additional issues to consider regarding dispositive provisions include incorporation by reference, community property, renunciation, and disclaimer.

### a. INCORPORATION BY REFERENCE

In many jurisdictions an extraneous document, such as a list of tangible personal property, may be incorporated in a will by reference whether or not the document is executed with the formalities of a will, *provided* the document referred to is described with sufficient detail and was in existence at the time the will was executed. Several states have enacted statutes with respect to the incorporation of extrinsic documents in a will by reference.[9] Although the incorporation of extrinsic documents, particularly lists of tangible personal property, may be convenient, such documents should always conform to the requirements of the governing state law. It is generally advisable to provide for the disposition of any items of particular value under a will, using a codicil instead of a list where changes are made to avoid any uncertainties.

### b. RENUNCIATION OR DISCLAIMER

Renunciation or disclaimer may modify a testator's intended estate disposition. A surviving spouse may renounce a testator's will and take that share of the estate provided for by state statute in lieu of surviving spouse's interest under the will. Furthermore, any beneficiary may choose to disclaim beneficiary's own interest under a will. The effect of disclaimer is to treat the beneficiary as having predeceased the testator.

### c. COMMUNITY PROPERTY

Community property laws of the various community property jurisdictions differ so special planning is required.[10] A testator may only dispose of testator's separate property and his or her half of community property by will.

### E. The Fiduciary and Fiduciary Powers

Another important aspect of drafting a will is the selection of fiduciaries. A testator can appoint four types of fiduciaries by his will: a guardian of the person of minor children, a guardian of the estate of minor children, a testamentary trustee, and a personal representative of the estate. The guardian of the person is responsible for the custody and personal care of the minor. The guardian of the estate is responsible for the management and care of the property belonging to the minor. The testamentary trustee is responsible for the management of estate assets given to the trustee and the administration of the trust under the terms of the will. The personal representative is responsible for the collection and distribution of all probate assets and the payment of the estate expenses. A will can waive bond for any of the foregoing fiduciaries.

#### 1. Selecting the Fiduciary

For the drafting lawyer, the main consideration in the fiduciary selection process is the state law requirements. Generally, a fiduciary must be 18 years of age, a resident of the United States and of sound mind or not adjudged disabled. Some states prohibit convicted felons from acting as a fiduciary.[11] In addition, there may be state residency requirements or special qualification rules for nonresident fiduciaries under state law. Except for a guardian of the person, a corporate entity, such as a bank or trust company, can normally act as a fiduciary.

A lawyer may act as a fiduciary at the request of a client. The Model Code of Professional Responsibility prohibits lawyers from consciously influencing a client to name the lawyer as fiduciary.[12] However, there is no prohibition against a lawyer acting as a fiduciary when so requested by a client. Nonetheless, some states prohibit a lawyer from receiving compensation both as a lawyer and as a fiduciary.

If a named fiduciary is not a corporation, the will should name at least one alternate fiduciary if the first-named fiduciary is unable to act. If a testator does not want to select an alternate fiduciary or does not have an alternate in mind, the will should give the named fiduciary the power to select a successor.

#### 2. Clarifying Fiduciary Powers

A fiduciary is typically given numerous powers by state statute. Nevertheless, there should be a recitation of the fiduciary's powers in the will. As a general rule, it is best to specify the powers the fiduciary has, even if they duplicate a state statute since the testator may reside in a different state at the time of death and that state may have more restrictive powers, or the statutory powers may change. In addition, particular assets in an estate may require a fiduciary to have additional powers.

There are several general powers that a will should give a fiduciary. First, a will should give the fiduciary the power to hire agents, managers, brokers, accountants, lawyers, and so forth, for the administration of the estate and/or trust. Second, a will should give the fiduciary the power to control, sell, mortgage or pledge, and lease estate property. Third, a will should give the fiduciary the power to designate an ancillary fiduciary if the named fiduciary cannot act in another jurisdiction.

Several specific powers that may be given in a will are often not covered by state law. First, a will may give the fiduciary the power to manage or dispose of environmentally hazardous property. Second, although fiduciaries are generally prohibited from self-dealing (that is, they cannot purchase assets in the estate or trust, lend money to the estate or trust or have business dealings with the estate or trust), a will may specifically give the fiduciary this ability. Third, if a testator holds a business interest, whether a sole proprietorship, partnership, limited liability company, or closely held corporation, the will should include a provision to allow the fiduciary to continue the business. State statutes often limit a fiduciary's power to continue a decedent's business, if the issue is addressed at all, particularly in the case of a personal representative. Therefore, if a testator wishes a business to be continued, it becomes vitally important to give the fiduciary express authority to continue the business; in such cases, the will should also address fiduciary liability issues.[13]

## III. Drafting Testamentary Trusts

Trusts may be created during life (intervivos) or under a will (testamentary). When no intervivos trust has been established, the will may create a testamentary trust to provide for minor beneficiaries, or estate tax and GST tax planning.

### A. Minor Beneficiaries

When there are minor beneficiaries, a testamentary trust may be used to avoid the necessity of property guardianship and to defer asset distribution beyond the age of majority. Distribution may also be spread over a number of years. Often a testamentary trust for children will be administered as a single trust for support and education of the children until the youngest child completes his education and will then be split into separate trusts for each child. Each child's trust would then be administered for the benefit of that child and that child's descendants, and would often give withdrawal rights to the child when the child attains various ages.

### B. Estate-Tax Planning

Testamentary trusts can defer and minimize estate taxes. The marginal federal estate-tax rate under the Economic Growth and Tax Relief Reconciliation Act of 2001 (EGTRRA) is 55 percent in 2001 and is scheduled to decrease gradually to 45 percent by 2007. The I.R.C. provides unlimited marital and charitable deductions. It also provides for an estate-tax exemption. The exemption amount under EGTRRA is $675,000 in 2001; $1.0 million in 2002 and 2003; $1.5 million in 2004 and 2005; $2.0 million in 2006, 2007 and 2008; and, $3.5 million in 2009.[14] Under EGTRRA the estate tax is repealed in 2010 but, absent a change in the law, will be reinstated in 2011 with a 55-percent marginal tax rate and a $1-million estate tax exemption. Because of changes in the tax law, all tax planning with respect to the use of testamentary trusts will require regular review to assure that any planning continues to conform to the intentions of the testator and applicable law.

In the case of a married couple, the estate-tax planning objectives typically include deferring tax until the death of the surviving spouse by use of the unlimited marital deduction and fully utilizing each spouse's estate tax exemption.

### 1. Unlimited Marital Deductions

The unlimited marital deduction is available for outright transfers and certain transfers in trust to or for the benefit of a surviving spouse who is a U.S. citizen. Transfers in trust for the benefit of a spouse who is not a U.S. citizen also qualify for the federal estate-tax deduction if the trust satisfies the requirements of a qualified domestic trust (QDOT) under the I.R.C.

a. U.S. CITIZEN SPOUSE

The most frequently used types of trusts to qualify for the federal estate tax marital deduction in the case of a U.S. citizen spouse are the general power of appointment trust and the QTIP trust. In order to qualify for the federal estate tax marital deduction as a general power of appointment trust, the trust must provide that the spouse is entitled to all income from the trust payable at least annually for life, and the spouse must have the power to appoint the trust to herself or her estate. The power must be exercisable by the spouse alone and in all events. At the spouse's death, a general power of appointment trust will be included in the spouse's gross estate for federal estate tax purposes. In order to qualify for the federal estate tax deduction as a QTIP trust:

(1) The trust must pay the entire net income to the spouse at least annually for life;
(2) No person may have the power to appoint any part of the trust to any person other than the surviving spouse; and
(3) An election must be made to qualify the trust as a QTIP on the testator's federal estate tax return. A partial election may also be made for a QTIP trust.

At the surviving spouse's death, the spouse's gross estate will include, for federal estate-tax purposes, the principal of the elected portion of a QTIP trust and the undistributed income between the last distribution date and the date of the spouse's death.[15] With either a general power of appointment trust or a QTIP trust, the spouse may receive discretionary distributions of trust principal. Under EGTRRA, following the repeal of the estate tax in 2010, QTIP trusts will qualify for a special basis step-up, but general power of appointment trusts will not qualify for the basis step-up.

b. NON–U.S. CITIZEN SPOUSE

In the case of a spouse who is not a U.S. citizen, a QDOT may preserve the unlimited federal estate-tax marital deduction. There are many technical requirements for a QDOT under the I.R.C., including the requirement that principal distributions from a QDOT, other than a hardship distribution, are subject to withholding of the QDOT estate tax and the trust must include provisions securing the collection of the QDOT estate tax.[16]

c. METHODS FOR FUNDING

Marital trusts are usually funded on the basis of a pecuniary amount or a fractional share. In the case of a pecuniary amount, the marital trust is expressed as a dollar amount equal to the maximum marital deduction. Funding a pecuniary trust with items of income in respect of a decedent, such as retirement accounts, will cause the current recognition of income. In the case of a fractional share, the marital trust is expressed as a fraction of the trust equal to the maximum marital deduction. Funding a fractional share trust with items of income in respect of a decedent will not cause the current recognition of income. Thus, use of a fractional share trust should be considered when items of income in respect of a decedent constitute a significant part of the assets that will fund the trust.

## 2. *Spousal Estate-Tax Exemption*

In the case of a married couple, if the testator's entire estate passes to the surviving spouse, the benefit of the testator's estate-tax exemption will be lost. To fully utilize each spouse's estate-tax exemption, a will can establish a QTIP marital trust, under which a partial QTIP election may be made. If a partial QTIP election is made, the surviving spouse's gross estate will not include the nonelected portion from federal estate tax purposes.

Another way to fully utilize each spouse's estate tax exemption is to establish a credit shelter trust. The surviving spouse may be a beneficiary of a credit shelter trust, but the surviving spouse's interests in the trust must be limited to avoid inclusion of the trust in the surviving spouse's estate. The spouse may receive the net income from a credit shelter trust and discretionary trust principal. In addition, the spouse may have the annual right to withdraw the greater of $5,000 or 5 percent of the aggregate value of a credit shelter trust and a limited intervivos and testamentary power of appointment over a credit shelter trust. The spouse may also be the trustee of a credit shelter trust, provided all discretionary distributions to the spouse are subject to an ascertainable standard and no discretionary distributions are made to discharge any legal obligation of support of the spouse. The spouse may not have an unlimited right to withdraw the principal of a credit shelter trust or the power to appoint the trust principal to him- or herself, spouse's estate, or creditors of same.

## 3. *GST Tax Planning*

Testamentary trusts may also utilize a testator's GST tax exemption. A married couple may use a testamentary trust to fully utilize both spouses' GST tax exemptions, resulting in significant transfer tax savings.

The GST tax is a tax on transfers to beneficiaries in the second or more remote generation. The GST tax rate is the highest marginal federal estate-tax rate. The GST tax exemption under EGTRRA is $1.06 million in 2001, $1.1 million in 2002 and 2003, $1.5 million in 2004 and 2005, $2.0 million in 2006, 2007, and 2008 and $3.5 million in 2009.[17] The GST tax is repealed in 2010 but, absent a change in the law, the GST tax will be reinstated in 2011 with a 55 percent rate and a $1-million exemption, adjusted for inflation.

Planning to utilize the GST tax exemption is complex, particularly in the case of a married couple, and there are numerous planning alternatives. In its simplest form, a GST testamentary plan sets aside an amount equal to the available GST tax exemption in a trust (exempt trust) for the benefit of multiple generations of beneficiaries. The interests of the beneficiaries in the trust are limited so as to avoid federal estate taxes at the death of a beneficiary. A GST exempt trust may be administered free of estate or GST tax for the length of any applicable perpetuities period. A married couple must use a QTIP marital trust to fully utilize the first deceased spouse's GST exemption in years when the estate tax exemption is less than the GST tax exemption, and make an election to treat the first decedent as the transferor of the QTIP trust for GST tax purposes.

# IV. *Execution Requirements of Wills*

All states require certain formalities for the execution of a will. Generally, a will must be in writing, signed, and witnessed. Certain states make allowances for holographic wills (wills written wholly in the handwriting of the testator but not witnessed)[18] and nuncupative wills (oral dispositions of personal property).[19]

## A. Signature

The first formal requirement for execution is that a will be in writing and signed by the testator or by someone in the presence of and at the direction of the testator. What constitutes a sufficient signature to a will depends largely on state law and the facts and circumstances of each case. Typically, an incomplete signature, use of a nickname, or a misspelling does not render a signature inadequate. Courts have also accepted a signature made with the assistance of another person. In some cases, a testator's use of engraving, die, or rubber stamp; typewriting; or other mark intended to indicate a signature has been accepted.[20] When a testator will have difficulty executing a will, the best practice is to look at local law to determine if a will may be signed by another person at the direction of and in the presence of the testator. If local law permits another person to so sign, this method of signature is preferable to an unintelligible mark or stamp by the testator or having another person assist the testator in signing the will. Although many states allow a signature to appear anyplace on a will, some states require the signature to appear at the end of a will or following the dispositive provisions of a will.

## B. Witnesses

State law varies as to whether a testator must sign the will in the presence of the witnesses or merely acknowledge signing the will, and whether the witnesses must sign in the presence of the testator and/or the presence of each other.[21] Therefore, it is a good practice to have a testator sign the will in the presence of the witnesses and to have the witnesses sign in the presence of the testator and the other witnesses. There is no requirement that the witnesses read the will or that they know its contents.

State law varies as to the number and competency of the witnesses. Two or three witnesses are usually required. Witnesses must be competent to testify as to the validity of the will and its execution.[22] The problem of witness competency is generally related to whether the witness has an interest in the estate. An interested witness is one who receives a benefit from the estate. An interested witness may not testify at the probate of the will, or he or she must give up interest in the estate in order to testify.

### 1. Publication

Some states require publication of the will.[23] Publication is the act of or statement by the testator to the witnesses that the document is testator's will. The testator should tell the witnesses that the document is his or her will and request the witnesses to sign the will.

### 2. Attestation and Self-Proving Affidavits

All states require attestation in some form. Attestation is the act of witnessing the actual execution of an instrument or signing one's name as a witness to the fact that the document was executed. The attestation clause is the paragraph following a will's dispositive provisions and preceding the witnesses' signatures. The attestation clause recites the facts required for the legal execution of the will: the statutory requirements for valid execution. Furthermore, the attestation clause should reflect any special circumstances present at the execution of the will. When the testator receives assistance in signing the will, has another sign for him or her, or has specifically acknowledged knowing the contents of the will or needed it read or explained, the attestation clause should specify this information.

In addition to the attestation clause, a will may also include a self-proving affidavit. The purpose of the self-proving affidavit is to admit the will to probate without the necessity of producing the witnesses to testify. In some states, an attestation clause is sufficient to make a will self-proving without an additional affidavit. A self-proving affidavit should be prepared and signed at the time a will is witnessed,[24] but it may be signed when a will is produced for admission to probate. A self-proving affidavit states the facts that establish the genuineness of the will, the validity of its execution, the competency of the testator to execute a will, and the lack of restraint or undue influence. Like the attestation clause, the self-proving affidavit should reflect any unique facts, such as signature by a third party, assistance from a third party, blindness, illiteracy, inability to understand English, pertinent provisions of the will being read to the testator, or the testator's acknowledgment that the contents of the will were understood.

A number of states have statutory forms for the attestation clause and self-proving affidavit.

## C. Testamentary Capacity and Testator's Volition

Testamentary capacity is the requisite capacity to make a will. The capacity required is typically sound mind and memory. This standard requires that the testator knows or has the mental capacity to understand: (1) that the document being signed is a will; (2) the contents of the will, in general; (3) the nature and extent of testator's property generally; and (4) the natural objects of testator's bounty (family, friends, and so forth). The testator's knowledge of the will's contents does not require the testator to know the meaning of the technical terms or legal phraseology in the will. When a testator is blind, illiterate, or does not understand English, the relevant portions of the will should be read to or translated for the testator.[25] The testator should tell the witnesses that the contents of the will are known and understood.

Capacity must exist at the time a will is executed. Even when a testator suffers from delusions or is irrational, forgetful, or senile, the testator may have lucid moments in which he or she is fully capable of executing a will. The law usually presumes that the testator had capacity if the will was properly executed and attested.

In addition to capacity, a testator must freely express desires in the will. Fraud, duress, coercion, undue influence, or compulsion will invalidate a will. Although these forms of improper conduct can be exerted upon any person, regardless of age or health, they are much more likely to occur when a testator is elderly or infirm. As a result, questions of fraud and undue influence often involve questions of testamentary capacity. However, a testator can have capacity and still be subjected to undue influence, fraud, or coercion.

Fraud occurs when there is any trick, deception, or artifice by which the testator is circumvented, cheated, or deceived as to the disposition of his property. Duress or coercion exists when one person, by the unlawful act of another, is induced to perform some act under circumstances that deprive the person of the exercise of his free will. Duress or coercion occurs when the testator is prevented from exercising testator's free will by force or by threats of harm to testator or those close to him or her.

Undue influence is defined in a variety of ways. Most simply, it is influence exerted upon the testator that causes testator to make a disposition of his property that is not a free and voluntary act. The influencer has substituted his or her will for the will of the testator in the disposition of assets. What constitutes undue influence is dependent on the facts and circumstances of each case.

If the person exercising the influence over the testator is in a fiduciary relationship with the testator and the influence is directly connected with the execution of a will that benefits the fiduciary or the fiduciary's family, the law will presume that the influence is undue. A fiduciary relationship can occur by reason of law, as between lawyer and client or principal and agent, or by nature of a close relationship whereby one party trusts and relies on the judgment and knowledge of another. Because of the presumption of undue influence, a lawyer should not draft a will in which the lawyer or lawyer's family members are beneficiaries, unless the will is for a family member and the lawyer is a natural object of the testator's bounty. If a testator wishes to benefit a lawyer or a lawyer's family and the testator is not closely related to the lawyer, a lawyer in another law firm should draft the will. The fact that a lawyer or confidential friend drafts a will and is named the personal representative or trustee under the will typically does not raise the presumption of undue influence.

A lawyer has an ethical obligation to ensure that a testator has capacity to sign the will and is signing the will of testator's own volition. A lawyer should not proceed unless he is satisfied in these matters.[26]

## V. Revocation and Modification of Wills

A will can be revoked by a variety of acts, either intentional or unintentional. Most states provide by statute that a will is revoked by a subsequent will or codicil declaring the revocation.[27] A codicil is an addition to or a modification of an existing will. Any form of a letter or writing can operate as a codicil if it is executed with the same formalities as required for a will. As such, a codicil can function as a republication and re-execution of a will and, therefore, may cure a defect in the execution of the original will. Codicils are generally read together with the will to express the testator's intent. Because a codicil will revoke a will only to the extent its terms are inconsistent with the will, the codicil should specifically state if a particular provision is intended to replace (substitute for) a provision in the will or if a provision is intended to be in addition to the provisions in the will.

In some states a subsequent will automatically revokes the prior will. In other states, the revocation must be expressly stated to effectively revoke the prior will; otherwise, the subsequent will revokes only the portion of the prior will that is inconsistent with the new will. Therefore, a will should always expressly revoke all prior wills.

Under common law, if a testator has written several wills and the last will is revoked, the prior will is revived if it has been preserved.[28] A number of states require the re-execution and republication of a prior will in order to revive the prior will.[29] Often, however, if a will is only partially revoked by an instrument that is itself later revoked, the revoked part of the will is revived and takes effect as if there had been no revocation. For example, when a codicil revokes a bequest in a will and the codicil is later revoked, the bequest in the will is revived.

When a testator cancels or destroys a will with the intent of making a new one immediately and as a substitute for the revoked will, but a new will is not made or fails to be effective, the revoked will may be brought back. Under the doctrine of dependent relative revocation, there is a presumption that the testator prefers the old will to intestacy so the old instrument is admitted to probate in the absence of evidence overcoming the presumption (and assuming that the contents of the old will can be proved).[30]

Revocation is tricky when the testator writes on the will or otherwise tries to change the disposition of his estate on the face of the will rather than executing a codicil or new will. When a testator strikes out a provision, changes an amount or description of a bequest, changes the name of a beneficiary or tries to write a new bequest or devise, the changes are ignored and the will is probated according to its original terms. An addition to a will or an alternation or deletion of a will does not revoke the provisions of the will and is of no effect unless the testator, after making the changes, signs the will and has the will attested in the manner prescribed by law. However, when a testator has obliterated part of the will, a court may find that the testator revoked the entire will since the testator can revoke a will by burning, canceling, tearing, or obliterating the will, or directing another to do so in testator's presence.[31] Lawyers should caution the testator to prepare a new will or codicil rather than making any changes on the face of the original will.

As a general rule, if a testator marries after the execution of a will, the marriage will not revoke the will. However, the dissolution or invalidity of a marriage will often revoke any legacies to the former spouse and nomination of the former spouse as a fiduciary.[32] The birth of a child or adoption of a child after the execution of a will can modify a will as to the after-born child's intestate share of the estate, unless the will provided for after-born children.

## VI. Safeguarding the Will

The lawyer should keep copies of all versions of a will in case proof is later needed as to the terms of a will or a prior will becomes effective at the revocation of the subsequent will. A testator should execute only one copy of testator's will. If more than one original will is signed and one of these signed copies cannot be produced, there is a presumption that the will has been revoked. In addition, having only one original will may prevent the testator from defacing the original or prevent a disgruntled heir from destroying a copy. Some states provide for the filing of an original will with the court until the death of the testator to prevent such problems.[33] In the absence of such a filing, the testator should keep the original in a safety deposit box, with his or her lawyer, or with the designated corporate fiduciary.

Although there has been some criticism of the practice of having the lawyer who drafted the will keep the original, there should not be any impropriety in such an act if the lawyer does not induce the client to do so. If the lawyer retains the will, the lawyer must have a plan to ensure that the will is filed with the appropriate probate court at the death of the testator or ultimately delivered to the testator at the lawyer's death or retirement. When a lawyer who is a solo practitioner dies, the lawyer's family and estate must see to the distribution of the will either to the testator or to a new lawyer.

## VII. Conclusion

With a properly drafted and executed will a testator can provide for the orderly administration of the estate by the fiduciaries of testator's choice; the distribution of assets to the beneficiaries of testator's choice, and the minimization and deferral of estate and GST taxes. Absent a will, the court will appoint fiduciaries according to a statutory preference under state law, assets will be distributed to heirs, as determined under state law, and there will be limited estate and GST tax planning alternatives. Thus, it is advisable to make a will and to review and update the will on a regular basis.

## *Endnotes*

1. Although the focus of this chapter is on a general understanding of wills and how to draft them, the authors relied on Illinois law where a discussion of specific state law was applicable. Always consult the local law of your jurisdiction to determine the state law requirements for drafting and executing a will.

2. The Uniform International Wills Act is part of the Uniform Probate Code, UNIF. PROB. CODE § 2-1001, §§ 2-1001–2-1010, 8 PT. 1 U.L.A. 467 (1998) (hereinafter referred to as U.P.C.).

3. *See* 755 ILCS 5/4-10.

4. *See* 755 ILCS 5/18-12 (imposing six-month limitations on all claims not filed with the executor or the probate court after notice is published); U.P.C. §3-801(b) (barring all claims not properly filed with executor or court after four months).

5. *See* Jeffrey N. Pennell, *Tax Payment Provisions and Equitable Apportionment*, SF79 ALI-ABA 401, 414-15 (2001). Many states have enacted apportionment statutes to provide apportionment of estate taxes between probate and nonprobate assets. *See also* UNIF. ESTATE TAX APPORT. ACT, 8A U.L.A. 331 (1993).

6. I.R.C. § 2002.

7. *See* I.R.C. §§ 2205–2207B.

8. This common law rule has been adopted by state statute. *See* 755 ILCS 5/4-11(c), U.P.C. § 2-606(a).

9. U.P.C. § 2-510.

10. *See* Paul N. Frimmer, *Will Drafting for Community Property*, 185 PLI/EST. 95 (1985).

11. *See* 755 ILCS 5/6-13.

12. MODEL CODE OF PROFESSIONAL RESPONSIBILITY Canon 5-6 (1980).

13. *See* Boone Schwartzel, *Continuing a Decedent's Business: Selected Creditors' Rights and Fiduciary Liability Issues*, 26 REAL PROP. & TR. J. 775 (1992).

14. I.R.C. § 2010.

15. I.R.C. § 2044.

16. *See* I.R.C. § 2056A.

17. I.R.C. § 2631.

18. *See* N.Y. EPTL § 3-2.2.

19. The few states that allow oral wills typically place restrictions on the circumstances when an oral will is permitted, such as last sickness or emergency. *See, e.g.,* KAN. STAT. ANN. § 59-608; OHIO REV. CODE § 2107.60; TEX. PROB. CODE §§ 64, 65.

20. ANNOTATION, *Validity of Will Signed by Testator's Mark, Stamp, or Symbol, or Partial or Abbreviated Signature*, 98 A.L.R.2d 841.

21. *See* 755 ILCS 5/4-3, U.P.C. §2-203; TEX. PROB. CODE §59, CAL. PROB. CODE §6110(c).

22. ANNOTATION, *Competency of Interested Witness to Testify to Signature or Handwriting of Deceased*, 13 A.L.R.3d 404. *See, e.g.,* 755 ILCS 5/4-6, TEX. PROB. CODE §61.

23. *See* N.Y. EPTL § 3-2.1(a)(3),(4). Publication is generally not required in the absence of a statutory requirement. ANNOTATION, *Sufficiency of Publication of Will*, 60 A.L.R.2d 124.

24. A properly executed self-proving affidavit may serve to cure any defects in the execution of the will. *See* Christopher Vaeth, *Proper Execution of Self-Proving Affidavit as Validating or Otherwise Curing Defect in Execution of Will Itself*, 1 A.L.R.5th 965.

25. ANNOTATION, *Wills: Testator's Illiteracy or Lack of Knowledge of Language in Which Will is Written as Affecting Its Validity*, 37 A.L.R.3d 889.

26. *See* Joseph T. Bockrath, *Attorney's Negligence in Connection with Estate, Will or Succession Matters*, 55 A.L.R.3d 977.

27. *See* 755 ILCS 5/4-7, U.P.C. §2-507 (a)(1).

28. 79 AM. JR. 2D *Wills* §§ 688–693.

29. *See* 755 ILCS 5/4-7(c).

30. 79 *Wills* AM. JR. 2d §§ 536–569.

31. *See Estate of Helgert*, 139 N.W.2d 81 (Wis. 1966) (writing on will held to revoke whole will). For a discussion of acts that can revoke a will, *see* 79 AM. JR. 2D *Wills* §§ 547–562.

32. Daniel E. Feld, *Divorce or Annulment as Affecting Will Previouxsly Executed By Husband or Wife*, 71 A.L.R.3d 1297.

33. *See* COLO. REV. STAT. §15-11-515; DE. STAT. tit. 12 §2513; N.C. GEN. STAT. ANN. §31-11; OK. STAT. ANN. Tit. 84 §83.

# CHAPTER 18

# The Living (Revocable) Trust:
# An Estate-Planning Tool

SARAH M. LINSLEY*

## I. Introduction

The fundamental consideration when instituting a new estate plan or revising an old estate plan is whether a living (revocable) trust is the appropriate principal dispositive vehicle for the plan. To make this determination, understanding the benefits of having a living trust and, just as importantly, those estate-planning goals a living trust can and cannot accomplish is critical.

## II. The Living Trust as a Primary Estate-Plan Vehicle

A trust is a legal instrument designating one or more individuals or a qualified corporation to act as trustees to receive and hold legal title to property and to administer such property in accordance with the terms of the instrument. Furthermore, a trust must identify one or more persons or entities with a beneficial interest in the property held in trust. A living trust is a trust that is created by an individual (the settlor) during the individual's lifetime and that is revocable by the individual prior to his or her death. Although the individual is often the initial trustee of the trust, the individual may appoint another individual or corporate fiduciary as trustee or as cotrustee with the individual.

The purpose of a living trust is to provide a vehicle for the administration of assets during the individual's lifetime and to direct distribution of those assets at his or her death. An unfunded living trust is a living trust which, either by design or inadvertence, is not funded at the time it is created. A funded living trust is one that is funded with assets over which the trustee then has effective control.

### A. Unfunded Living Trust

An unfunded living trust is a flexible vehicle. It can be funded by the individual settlor at any time during the individual's life. If the individual becomes disabled, it may be

---

*With special thanks to my partner, Thomas A. Polachek, the author of "Living (Revocable) Trusts for the Retiring Attorney" (1998).

particularly useful to fund the living trust in order to manage the individual's assets without having to rely upon a durable power of attorney. While an agent under a durable power of attorney may be equally capable of managing assets for a principal, funding a living trust in the event of a principal's disability has the added benefits of consolidating assets, allowing the trustee to exercise the specific powers granted under the trust instrument, and effectively putting into place the trustee succession provisions applicable in the living trust. Further, financial institutions are often reluctant to honor powers of attorney.

Many living trusts remain unfunded at an individual's death, but, under a will, the individual's assets pour over to the trust at death. Although it may appear that an individual would be as well off having only a will and no trust, there are certain benefits to creating a living trust.

First, unlike a will, a living trust is not a public record. Therefore, the dispositive plan incorporated into the trust will remain private. Although the simple pour-over will that is a companion to a living trust will be a public document, the only dispositive information included in the will is a direction that all assets of the estate are to be distributed at death to the individual's living trust and administered as provided therein.

Second, with a living trust and pour-over will, the trustee of the trust is the primary beneficiary of the estate. In many jurisdictions, this will substantially reduce the paperwork required in order to settle the probate estate, particularly if many beneficiaries ultimately share trust assets.

### B. Funded Living Trust

In order for a living trust to be fully funded, an individual must have transferred all assets titled in the individual's own name to the trust during his or her life. The trust will not control assets that pass by joint tenancy, beneficiary designations, payable on death accounts, or the like unless the trust is designated as beneficiary of these assets. Many living trusts are partially, rather than fully, funded. Notwithstanding one's best efforts to title assets in the name of the trust, it is commonplace to find at settlor's death title to some assets that were missed or acquired in settlor's own name after the creation of the trust. Settlor's pour-over will passes these assets to the trust upon his or her death.

Aside from inadvertence, another reason for partial funding in this manner is the avoidance of ancillary probate administration. If settlor owns real estate, including working interests in oil or gas wells out of settlor's domiciliary state, the transfer of these assets to a living trust can avoid the necessity of ancillary probate administration in those jurisdictions where title is held. Although there may be benefits to having a probate estate in a decedent's domiciliary state, there are no benefits to ancillary administration.

## III. Funding a Living Trust

The process of funding a living trust compels an individual to identify assets, examine how those assets are titled, and effectively transfer assets into the name of the trust. In planning for a husband and wife, this process often requires the severing of joint tenancy between husband and wife and the transfer of assets either in equal shares into the husband's trust and the wife's trust, or with select assets going to the husband's trust and others to the wife's trust.

## A. Assets Appropriate to Transfer

Care should be taken in the process of retitling the assets. Consider the following examples:

1. Many married couples own their residence as joint tenants. The tenancy may need to be severed and the property transferred either to one spouse's trust or one-half to each trust as tenants in common. The terms of the living trust should be clear about the surviving spouse's right to use the residence (or the share of the residence) owned by the trust of the first to die. The trust should allow the surviving spouse the rent-free use of the residence. Also, the trust should allocate to the surviving spouse the obligation to pay interest on any mortgage as well as any real estate taxes to assure that the surviving spouse will be entitled to these deductions for income tax purposes.

2. Any mortgage on a residence should be reviewed prior to the transfer of a residence to determine whether there is an acceleration-on-transfer clause. Despite the provisions of the Garn-St. Germain Depository Institutions Act of 1982,[1] regarding federal preemption of certain due-on-sale clauses, it may be advisable to obtain a comfort letter from the mortgage lender prior to effecting the transfer to a revocable trust.

3. A bill of sale can be used to transfer personal property to a living trust. A bill of sale should transfer after-acquired personal property as well.

4. Stocks and bonds held in certificate form must be transferred through the appropriate transfer agents. The transfer of certificated shares to a brokerage account in the name of the trust could significantly reduce the post-mortem administrative time and cost.

5. Brokerage, bank, mutual fund, and money market accounts should be retitled in the name of the trustee of the living trust. Depending on the institutions' procedures, this may be merely a change in the name on the account or it may require the creation of a new account.

6. Insurance policies and other assets transferred by beneficiary designations (IRAs, pension and profit-sharing plans, and so forth) should be reviewed and, if appropriate, changed. The trust will control disposition of these assets at death only if the trust is named as beneficiary. If a trust is the beneficiary of an IRA or qualified plan, the trustee must strictly comply with required distribution rules applicable to IRAs and qualified plans.

7. Working and royalty interests in oil and gas wells should be transferred. Even if the individual elects not to fully fund the living trust, these interests should be transferred if the interests are located out of the state of the decedent's domicile in order to avoid ancillary probate administration.

8. Safe-deposit box rental agreements should be changed to the trustee's name to assure that cash, bearer bonds, and other unregistered property held in the safe deposit box are considered trust property.

## B. Assets Inappropriate to Transfer

Certain assets may be inappropriate to transfer and special care should be taken. Consider the following examples:

1. Closely held business interests, partnership interests, and the like may be subject to restrictions that demand compliance in order to transfer the interests.
2. A living trust is a permissible shareholder of an S corporation as long as the requirements of I.R.C. Section 1361(c)(2) are met for two years after the grantor's death. An estate is not subject to this two-year limitation. The two-year limitation may force the trustee of a living trust to make an early distribution.
3. Generally, property generating passive activity losses (frequently rental or real property) should not be used to fund a living trust.[2]
4. When real property subject to potential environmental cleanup liability is held in a living trust, the trust fiduciary or beneficiaries may not be eligible for inheritance defense against liability that would otherwise be allowable to an individual who acquired the property by inheritance or bequest.[3]
5. An IRA should *not* be transferred into the name of a revocable trust. IRAs must be held in the name of the individual. An inappropriate transfer could cause the IRA to cease being an IRA, thereby accelerating income taxes on the assets held therein. If the trust is the intended beneficiary of the IRA, the beneficiary designation for the IRA should designate the trustee of the living trust.
6. In a jurisdiction that allows spouses to hold title to a personal residence as tenants by the entirety, it may be preferable for spouses to do so, rather than holding title in either or both spouses' living trusts. Only creditors of both tenants by the entirety can attach property held by the entirety. In contrast, a creditor of a joint tenant may attach that tenant's interest and compel a partition and sale.

## IV.  Points to Consider Regarding Living Trusts

There are advantages and some shortcomings when using a living trust instead of a will as one's primary estate-planning vehicle. It is important to consider these issues when choosing among them.

### A.  Shortcomings

#### 1.  Will Considerations

Even with a fully funded living trust, an individual should execute a simple pour-over will to ensure that any assets owned by the individual are transferred to the trust at the individual's death to be distributed as part of the individual's overall estate plan.

Additionally, at least two circumstances should compel an individual to execute a will. First, if the individual has minor children, the individual should execute a will so that a guardian of the minor children may be appointed. In this circumstance, it may be necessary to admit the will to probate to confirm the appointment of the designated guardian. Second, when an individual is granted a testamentary power of appointment over a spouse's or other individual's trust, the power typically may be exercised only by will. To the extent that an individual has testamentarily exercised a power of appointment, it may be necessary to admit the individual's will to probate to confirm the validity of the appointment.

#### 2.  Elective-Share Considerations

For some couples, another consideration in using a living trust is the fact that in some jurisdictions, use of a living trust defeats the surviving spouse's elective share. In other jurisdictions, a surviving spouse has the right to receive an elective share of the deceased spouse's augmented estate, including all assets held in the deceased spouse's living trust.[4] Given the significance of this issue, married couples who are funding living trusts should understand what effect, if any, the funding has on their spousal rights.

### 3. Protective State-Statute Considerations

One shortcoming of living trusts is that protective state statutes that apply to wills may not apply to them. In most jurisdictions there are statutes that specifically address questions about antilapse issues in the context of a will, including automatic revocation of will provisions for the benefit of a spouse in the event of dissolution of marriage, automatic provision for an after-born child, and the automatic acceleration of an interest in the event of a disclaimer. It is not clear, however, whether these statutory provisions apply to a living trust. A state may or may not have a corresponding statute that applies to trusts. For this reason, it is critical that the law of the applicable jurisdiction be reviewed. To be safe, each of these issues should be addressed specifically in the trust document.

## B. Advantages

### 1. Contestation Considerations

A living trust may make it more difficult to contest the disposition of the decedent's (settlor's) assets. Reported cases tend to address the questions of undue influence or competency with no real distinction between the execution of a will and a living trust. A settlor's/trustee's continuing active management of trust assets would tend to dispute claims of incompetency, assuming that the management is carried out in a competent manner. More importantly, in probate, disgruntled heirs need to intervene only in the probate proceeding; with a living trust, the putative beneficiary may first have to institute a court proceeding even to learn the terms of the trust.

### 2. Claims Considerations

Having a probate estate, rather than having a fully funded revocable trust not subject to probate, may have certain advantages. A probate estate is generally subject to a substantially shorter period during which creditors may file claims against the estate. This shorter claims period may be a particularly attractive feature of probate for professionals such as physicians, lawyers, or other individuals for whom claims may be a significant issue.

### 3. Qualified Plan Considerations

A properly drafted trust is a more flexible beneficiary than an estate for a qualified plan interest. An estate is not a qualified beneficiary for purposes of Internal Revenue Code (I.R.C.) Section 401(a)(9) required minimum distribution rules. Therefore, if an estate is named a beneficiary and distributions had not commenced prior to the participant's death, the general rule mandates that distributions after the participant's death be completed by the end of the calendar year that includes the fifth anniversary of the participant's death (the five-year rule). If distributions had commenced prior to the participant's death, the remaining payments would be required to be made over the deceased participant's life expectancy immediately prior to distribution. If, instead, a trust is designated as beneficiary, distributions after death generally may take into account the life expectancy of the trust beneficiary regardless of whether or not distributions had commenced prior to the participant's death.

## V.  Postmortem Administration of a Living Trust

In many jurisdictions, probate is not the burden it once was due to the advent of informal administration. Informal probate administration usually requires the preparation of fairly standard pleadings and an initial court appearance; then, shortly prior to closing the estate, the preparation of a fairly simple inventory and account and one additional court appearance. (If informal probate administration has been elected, the inventory and account may not be a part of the public record.) As with a probate administration, the postmortem administration of a living trust will require the preparation of an inventory and account, but no court appearance is required.

The greatest amount of time spent on usual postmortem administration of a will relates to:

1. the identification of assets (an inventory);
2. the collection of third-party beneficiary payments;
3. the valuation of assets;
4. the allocation of assets to fund bequests;
5. investment review and possible sales;
6. the preparation and filing of the decedent's final income tax returns;
7. postmortem income tax planning matters and the preparation of fiduciary income tax returns;
8. the preparation and filing of federal and state estate or inheritance tax returns, if required; and
9. the reregistration of assets in the name of the personal representative or successor trustee and, again, in the name of the beneficiaries when distributed.

Substantially all of these activities and services are also required even though a properly drafted, fully funded, and operating living trust is in effect.

Probate administration will delay the distribution of assets. Frequently, assets are retained in a probate administration for two years or more, primarily because of the potential for a federal estate-tax audit. Fiduciaries are thus reluctant to distribute the entire estate until the federal estate tax return has either been audited or approved with a closing letter. Prudence dictates that an individual acting as a trustee of a postmortem living trust should adopt a similar course of conduct.

## VI.  Income Tax Considerations

A living trust is a grantor trust, and, as such, it is not a separate taxpayer from the settlor of the trust. As long as the settlor is the trustee or a cotrustee of the trust, the trust will use the settlor's social security number as its tax identification number. The trust will not file a separate income tax return; and all items of income, deductions, and credits will be reported on a settlor's personal return.

If the settlor of a living trust is neither the sole trustee nor a cotrustee of the trust, a living trust is still a grantor trust, but the third-party trustee must obtain a taxpayer identification number for the trust and file annual fiduciary income tax returns for the trust. Even though a fiduciary income tax return is filed, all items of income, deductions, and credits will still be reported on the settlor's personal tax return because of the living trust's grantor trust status. In addition, Treasury Form 56 (Notice Concerning Fiduciary Relationship) must be filed with the Internal Revenue Service (IRS). If a taxpayer identification number is obtained, the number should be used for all brokerage, bank, and other accounts in the name of the trust, rather than the grantor's social security number.

I.R.C. Section 121 provides for a $250,000 exclusion of gain ($500,000 for married persons filing a joint return) on the sale of a principal residence once every two years if the taxpayer (1) owned the residence and (2) used it as a principal residence for a period aggregating at least two years during the five-year period prior to the sale date. Ownership by a living trust should satisfy the ownership requirement.

During the settlor's lifetime, a living trust does not have any income tax consequences to the settlor. However, some tax implications do arise after the grantor's death. Consider, for example, the following:

- A trust has an income tax exemption of either $300 (complex trust) or $100 (simple trust). An estate has an exemption of $600.
- An estate may elect a fiscal or calendar year accounting period. A trust must use a calendar year.
- When an estate funds a pecuniary gift in-kind, the estate will recognize gain or loss to the extent the assets used have appreciated or depreciated in value from the date of death (or the alternate valuation date, if applicable) to the date of funding. When a trust funds a pecuniary gift in-kind, it will recognize gain, but it will not be allowed to offset losses against those gains as the losses are disallowed under I.R.C. Section 267 as a transaction between related parties. It is thus critical for the trustee to keep this rule in mind when funding pecuniary gifts since it may be necessary to sell loss assets rather than using them to fund a pecuniary gift.

Under I.R.C. Section 645 (2001), an executor and trustee may file an election to treat a revocable trust postmortem as part of the decedent's probate estate for income tax purposes. This provision eliminates the need to file two income tax returns even though the estate and trust are separate legal entities. In the event no executor is appointed by the applicable probate court, the trustee may make the election. There are specific time requirements for making the election. Once the election is made, it is irrevocable. Therefore, it is incumbent upon the executor and the trustee to determine whether the advantages of maintaining two taxpayers outweigh the advantages of filing such an election. Consider the following examples:

- Estates do not have to make estimated tax payments for taxable years ending within two years of the decedent's death.[5] A living trust postmortem now qualifies for the application of this rule if specific requirements are met.
- A separate-share rule has applied to postmortem trusts under I.R.C. Section 663(c) for determination of distributable net income for income tax purposes. This rule now extends to estates as well.
- A living trust postmortem has been able to take advantage of the sixty-five-day distribution rule under I.R.C. Section 663(b) (2001), which permits the trustee to assess the taxable income of the trust during the sixty-five-day period beginning after the end of the tax year, and, if appropriate, distribute additional amounts to beneficiaries that carry income out to beneficiaries for trust income tax purposes for the preceding year. This rule now extends to estates.

Some distinctions continue to apply. Consider the following:

- I.R.C. Section 194 provides for deductions of up to $10,000, amortized over a seven-year period, for costs incurred in a taxable year for forestation or refor-estation of timber property. This deduction is allowed to estates but is expressly denied to trusts. (If an election is made under I.R.C. Section 645(a) to treat the trust as being part of the decedent's estate for income tax purposes, the benefit of this election can be obtained for trust property.)
- In absence of a probate administration, a trustee is deemed to be a statutory executor and liable for the payment of federal estate tax with respect to property and the trust. While a personal representative (executor) may obtain a discharge from personal liability of the payment of federal estate taxes, this relief is not available to the postmortem trustee.

## VII.  Estate-Tax Issues

A living trust does not itself save state or federal estate taxes at the death of the settlor of the trust. Assets in the trust are treated as the settlor's assets and are included in the settlor's taxable estate.

A living trust often incorporates estate-tax-planning provisions that may save estate taxes at the death of the settlor's spouse and/or children. This type of planning also can be accomplished through a well-drafted will.

Thus, it is a myth that a living trust saves estate taxes that would otherwise be due if the living trust had not been created.

## VIII.  Joint Living Trusts

Joint living trusts are beyond the scope of this chapter. They are the vehicle of choice in some community property jurisdictions. A joint trust is typically designed to preserve the step-up in basis at death of 100 percent of community property interests owned by the community (husband and wife) and to assure full utilization of the applicable exemption amount allowable to both spouses. Lawyers in noncommunity property jurisdictions without experience with joint trusts should proceed with extreme caution if undertaking to draft a joint trust for themselves or for clients. They should not take this approach if the thought is that one trust is less expensive or less complicated than two trusts.[6]

## IX. Conclusion

A living trust can be an integral part of an estate plan and a very effective primary document in an individual's estate plan. A well-drafted living trust can cause an estate plan to be more effectively implemented during life and after death than a plan under a will that takes effect only at death. Nonetheless, absent a careful estate-planning effort, executing a living trust, particularly a standard form, will not have a material effect on the disposition of one's assets, will not save death taxes, and will not significantly reduce postmortem administration costs. In fact, using a standard form living trust can create many problems, and, certainly for clients whose net worth is in excess of the unified credit equivalent, can result in the incurrence of otherwise avoidable taxes. Before implementation of any estate plan, first consider an individual's objectives for the transfer of wealth, both during life and at death, and the transfer-tax implications of implementing these objectives. Only then should the decision be made whether a living trust, funded or unfunded, is the appropriate primary dispositive document.

## Endnotes

1. 12 U.S.C.A., § 1701j-3 (2000).
2. I.R.C. § 469(i).
3. 42 U.S.C.A. § 9601(35)(A)(iii) (2000).
4. *See* Unif. Probate Code § 2-202 (1975)
5. I.R.C. § 6654.
6. Roy Adams & Thomas Abendroth, *The Joint Trust: Are You Saving Anything Other Than Paper?*, Tr. & Est., August 9, 1992, at 39.

# CHAPTER 19

# Joint Accounts: Dangers and Alternatives

RICHARD V. WELLMAN

## I. Introduction

This chapter is about joint accounts in banks (credit unions and Savings and Loans (S&Ls) are included in the term "banks"); some risks and problems of joint accounts; and safer alternatives.

A joint account is an account (checking, savings, Certificate of Deposit (CD), money market, and the like) in a bank naming two or more persons as owners, such as an account payable to John Smith and Mary Smith. Many people do not realize that joint accounts invite misunderstandings and disputes that can be avoided by use of other common deposit arrangements or a power of attorney. The following case illustrates the point:

> Mary, an elderly, single person, had a bank account in her own name. She had a will also, giving her entire estate to her five nieces and nephews. Some years after signing the will, she decided that Amanda, a niece who lived in Mary's town, should be able to help her with account business; and so she asked the bank to add Amanda's name to the account. The bank offered a joint account form that Mary and Amanda signed. Some time later, Mary sold her residence and deposited the proceeds in the account pending decision on another investment. Unfortunately, Mary died unexpectedly, and Amanda became the survivor and apparent owner of the entire account.

The case raises many questions. Why did Mary establish the joint account? Would she have deposited the proceeds from the property sale in the account if she had known that Amanda could claim the account balance despite the provisions in Mary's will? Is it possible that Mary only wanted a dual-signature arrangement on her account to enable Amanda to help Mary with financial matters if she became disabled? Was Mary aware that ownership was involved in her simple request that Amanda's name be added to her account? Did Mary merely accept the form offered by the bank without knowing about the legalities involved? Indeed, was Mary aware that the bank offered other arrangements that would have authorized Amanda to draw on the account without having ownership rights? How can these important questions be answered now that Mary is gone?

Cases like this can invite bitter feelings, litigation, and results that are unsatisfactory to everyone.

## II. Available Information?

Unfortunately, useful information about joint accounts and other multiple-name account forms is scarce. Banking companies typically respond to customer questions about these accounts by use of computer menus or other lists of choices, and by offering complex contract forms for customer inspection. New-accounts personnel are often warned against giving advice to customers about their account choices or responding to questions about ownership between persons named on these accounts. This is wise bank policy because bank personnel may lack the training and experience needed to advise customers about the complex legal relationships that accompany accounts bearing more than one person's name.

This chapter seeks to increase general understanding of multiple-name deposit accounts. The goal is to equip readers with information needed to enable them to choose the type of multiple-name account best suited to their circumstances and purposes. Better understanding of available forms should reduce post-death disputes among depositors' survivors over checking, savings, and CD balances in accounts bearing more than one name.

## III. The Joint Account

Joint accounts naming two or more individuals as account owners are the oldest, most familiar, and most troublesome type of multiple-name account. Each owner has full control of the account without regard to whose money was deposited in the account or whether the other owner is alive or deceased, competent or incompetent, or agrees or disagrees with the purpose of a withdrawal. Ownership as between those named on the account is a matter with which the bank has no concern (other than as a possible witness). Indeed, ownership is important only when one person withdraws money from a joint account in excess of sums he or she deposited *and the other person objects.*

If the joint account paperwork includes a survivorship provision (which may or may not be obvious from the title), the death of one owner causes that person's ownership interest to pass by survivorship to the other owner (except, perhaps, in Louisiana, where survivorship among co-owners has not been recognized as of this writing). This transfer at death occurs outside the probate process even though the question of survivorship may require a court determination (see section V, subsection B). For now, simply note that each joint account owner has the power to withdraw from the account before or after the death of any other owner even if survivorship is not part of the deposit contract. One who withdraws more than his or her ownership interest will owe the excess to the other owner or that owner's estate, but enforcement of this right may require litigation. A bank may decline a withdrawal request by one owner if it is asked by another owner or that owner's estate to prevent the withdrawal, but the bank is not required to do so.

## IV. Advantages of Joint Accounts

The joint account is an all-purpose financial management tool that serves several objectives.

## A. Probate Avoidance

If survivorship is part of the joint account—it normally is, but not always—an owner's interest in the account balance at death passes outside probate to the surviving owner(s). Survivorship normally cannot be prevented by the decedent's will because a will controls probate assets only and a deceased owner's interest in a joint account is not part of the decedent's probate estate when survivorship applies.

Avoiding probate does *not* mean avoidance of federal and state taxes on transfers of property at death. This benefit only avoids any cost or delay of probate, which can be minimal.

## B. Access on Co-owner's Incompetence or Disability

The funds in a joint account are not frozen when an owner loses the ability to handle banking matters. No durable power of attorney or guardianship is necessary to access the funds in a joint account if a co-depositor is willing and able to transact with the bank.

## C. Financial Partnership

Happily married couples and others in comparable personal relationships often want to commingle funds because commingling overrides doubts about who owns what and reflects the trust they have in each other. A joint account suits these people because each is willing to risk any loss caused by the other's activities and wants the entire account to belong to the other in the event of death.

# V. Dangers of Joint Accounts

Joint accounts also involve risks that lead well-informed advisors to recommend other alternatives that offer the same benefits with reduced risks. These alternatives are described following elaboration about the perils of joint accounts.

## A. Risk of Loss

Either joint account owner may withdraw the entire balance and wrongfully refuse to repay the other what is rightfully due. Even if a depositor's trust in the other person is not misplaced, joint deposit paperwork routinely enables the bank or other creditors to seize the entire account balance to recover money owed by either owner. For example, Aunt Mary's money in the case described earlier could have been taken from the joint account by the bank to repay itself on an earlier or a later bank loan to Amanda even though Mary knew nothing about the loan and was unaware of the deposit contract provision putting her money at risk. Amanda would be obligated to repay Mary the amount taken to pay Amanda's debt, but Amanda may not be solvent. This risk may be acceptable to couples who expect to share financial rewards and risks, but it may be terrifying to others.

## B. Questionable Survivorship

Some joint account forms do not mention the survivorship feature that (except, perhaps, in Louisiana) avoids probate when an owner dies. Examples include an account payable to "A or B," an account payable to "A and B as joint tenants," and an account payable to "A and B."

In Texas and a few other states, if no express mention of survivorship appears in the deposit contract, a joint account deposit creates a tenants-in-common account, which is an arrangement without survivorship. In most other states, the opposite rule applies and survivorship is considered a part of a joint account unless the deposit contract specifies that the depositors are tenants in common, or otherwise expressly rejects survivorship.

If survivorship is not a part of the joint account, an owner's death is likely to precipitate a squabble between the surviving owner and the probate estate of the decedent over the size of each person's share. These disputes are difficult to resolve unless careful records of each owner's deposits and withdrawals are available.

There also is the significant risk (illustrated by our Mary and Amanda case) of survivorship rights that were unintended and attributable to depositor confusion. Thousands of court cases have litigated postdeath disputes involving survivorship rights in joint accounts. The theory usually urged in these cases is that the deceased person was unaware of the survivorship feature and opened the joint account solely to authorize an assistant to access the account in case of emergency or disability.

## VI.  Alternative Account Forms and Features

Given the uncertainties and risks apparent in joint accounts, lawyers should discuss with their clients alternative account forms that offer joint account advantages but avoid joint account risks.

Joint accounts serve to (1) assure access to funds in spite of a depositor's loss of capacity, (2) transfer the account balance at death via the survivorship right to avoid probate, and (3) permit full commingling of funds by people in close relationships who trust each other. Years ago, people who wanted only some of these features had to choose between all or none because the joint account was the only multiple-name account offered.

The good news is that most banking companies now offer alternatives to the joint account that meet the needs of most people interested in less than all of a conventional joint account's features. One is an account that designates a beneficiary(ies) who is only entitled to balances in the account at the depositor's death. The other is a single owner account that designates a depositor's agent; this agent has authority to withdraw for the depositor, but the agent has no personal beneficial interest in account balances immediately or at the depositor's death.

### A.  Death-Beneficiary-Only Account

Two account forms enable a depositor to retain sole ownership and control of an account that designates another to receive the account by a nonprobate transfer at the depositor's death. One is known as a pay on death (p.o.d.) account. A p.o.d. account title would appear as "John Q. Owens, p.o.d. Nancy Owens." The other, called a trust account or Totten trust, is an account in the name of the depositor who is described as trustee for, or as holding in trust for, the person named as beneficiary. A trust account title would appear as "John Q. Owens, trustee for Nancy Owens."

Both forms create what is called a death-beneficiary-only account, which has the following characteristics:

1. The owner (John Q. Owens) has sole ownership and control of the account.
2. Nancy Owens (whether named as "p.o.d. Nancy Owens" or as beneficiary in a trust account) becomes the new owner of the account if she survives the owner (John).
3. Nancy usually will not have to sign the bank form establishing the account, and she may or may not be aware of the account.
4. The owner (John) can close the account by withdrawing all money from it, and the beneficiary's (Nancy's) consent is not needed.
5. The bank should not be counted upon to notify a beneficiary of this death benefit. The owner should tell the beneficiary about the arrangement or leave information about it in a writing (for example, a will or letter) to be read after death in order to enable the beneficiary to apply to the bank for the proceeds.

A death-beneficiary-only account acts like a will, giving the death beneficiary whatever is in the account at the death of the owner. It differs from a will in that (a) it need not be probated; (b) it generally cannot be revoked by a later will; and (c) can be nullified only by closing the account or by signing another (new) account agreement.

In most states, divorce alone revokes a will's gifts to the former spouse by operation of law (meaning automatically and whether or not that result is intended by the people involved). This revocation-by-divorce rule generally does not extend to a death-beneficiary-only account by revoking a former spouse's right as death beneficiary of such an account. Some court decisions, however, recognize that the trust account form, but not the p.o.d. form, may be affected by a will, and a few recent statutes recognize explicit language in a will as effective to alter any account death benefit.

Despite these possible uncertainties, a death-beneficiary-only account is preferable to a joint account as a method of transferring money at death without probate. Unlike the joint account, the death-beneficiary-only account can serve no other purpose but to make a transfer at death; there can be no confusion about the owner's purpose, as was suggested in our Aunt Mary–Amanda case described earlier. An attack on a death-beneficiary-only account by the deceased owner's heirs should fail unless the decedent lacked capacity to understand the deposit transaction or was wrongfully misled or coerced in selecting the death benefit form.

A death beneficiary designation can be added to a joint account with survivorship. For example, a married couple might want a joint and survivor account and also want to provide that at the death of the survivor of the couple, the account should go to their children. As in the example of John and Nancy Owens, the account could be set up in this fashion:

> Payable to John Q. Owens and Nancy Owens, and the survivor of them, and upon the death of the survivor, p.o.d. to their children, Mary Owen and Mickey Owen, surviving them in equal shares (or in whatever proportion John and Nancy prefer).

The wording may change with particular banks and even may be in the form of a trust; payable to John Q. Owens and Nancy Owens, and the survivor, in trust for Mary Owen and Mickey Owen. Either way, the death beneficiary takes nothing until both John and Nancy die. (The survivor of the two original owners is the sole owner following the first death and is free to change the death benefit.)

## B.  Convenience or Agency Account

Some people may want a single or joint owner account with access by another person who is not an owner but is authorized to act as the owner's agent or assistant. This type of account offers the convenience of dual access, but it avoids the risk of loss to the assistant's creditors and avoids any survivorship benefit for the assistant.

One form serving this purpose is a single or multiple-person account that designates an additional authorized signatory who may sign withdrawals on behalf of the owner-depositor. Another form serving the same purpose describes the assistant as the owner's agent, or as authorized by the owner's power of attorney. Some banks refer to accounts in either of these forms as convenience accounts. This chapter refers to all of these forms as agency accounts.

On occasion a bank may insist on receiving an accompanying durable power of attorney document before opening an agency account. More commonly, power-of-attorney language will be included in account paperwork signed when the account is opened or simply implied from describing the assistant as an agent or otherwise authorized to act on behalf of the account owner.

Authority to access an owner's account as the owner's agent or additional authorized signatory ends when the bank receives written notice of the agency's revocation or the depositor's death. As a practical matter, banks rarely enforce an account agent's responsibility to the owner. Banks accept these arrangements only because they are protected by the account contract in recognizing the agent's withdrawal power as unconditional.

Most banks will recognize that the same person may be designated as the depositor's agent *and* as a death beneficiary. For example, an account might be designated:

Payable to Randolph Jones. Additional authorized signatory:

Randolph Jones II; p.o.d. Richard and Randolph Jones II.

This form offers the advantages of (1) dual access by one son without risk of loss to the son's creditors during the father's life and (2) a nonprobate transfer at the father's death to two sons, there being no need to favor the son who acted as the father's agent.

## VII.  A Statutory Form Aiding Account Selection

A model state statute known as the Uniform Multiple Person Accounts Act—designed for enactment by all states—encourages banking institutions to offer depositors a menu of available multiple-name accounts. This menu is reprinted in Figure 19.1 as a further illustration of the text. As a step toward informing depositors of their account options, people should urge their banks to adopt this national form.

## VIII.  Conclusion

This chapter will help you ask the right questions when you consider a multiple-name account or wish to discuss the topic with your advisors. Keep a copy handy with your account information for future reference, or pass it along to others with a need to know this important information.

**FIGURE 19.1**

Uniform Single- or Multiple-Party Account Form

---

**UNIFORM SINGLE- OR MULTIPLE-PARTY ACCOUNT FORM**

PARTIES [Name One or More Parties]:

_____     _____

OWNERSHIP [Select One And Initial]:

_____ SINGLE-PARTY ACCOUNT

_____ MULTIPLE-PARTY ACCOUNT

Parties own account in proportion to net contributions unless there is clear and convincing evidence of a different intent.

RIGHTS AT DEATH [Select One And Initial]:

_____ SINGLE-PARTY ACCOUNT

At death of party, ownership passes as part of party's estate.

_____ SINGLE-PARTY ACCOUNT WITH POD DESIGNATION

[Name One Or More Beneficiaries]:

_____     _____

At death of party, ownership passes to POD beneficiaries and is not part of party's estate.

_____ MULTIPLE-PARTY ACCOUNT WITH RIGHT OF SURVIVORSHIP

At death of party, ownership passes to surviving parties.

_____ MULTIPLE-PARTY ACCOUNT WITH RIGHT OF SURVIVORSHIP AND POD DESIGNATION

[Name One Or More Beneficiaries]:

_____     _____

At death of last surviving party, ownership passes to POD beneficiaries and is not part of last surviving party's estate.

_____ MULTIPLE-PARTY ACCOUNT WITHOUT RIGHT OF SURVIVORSHIP

At death of party, deceased party's ownership passes as part of deceased party's estate.

AGENCY (POWER OF ATTORNEY) DESIGNATION [Optional]

Agents may make account transactions for parties but have no ownership or rights at death unless named as POD beneficiaries.

[To Add Agency Designation To Account, Name One or More Agents]:

_____     _____

[Select One And Initial]:

_____ AGENCY DESIGNATION SURVIVES DISABILITY OR INCAPACITY OF PARTIES

_____ AGENCY DESIGNATION TERMINATES ON DISABILITY OR INCA-PACITY OF PARTIES

# CHAPTER 20

# Jointly Owned Property

ROBERT T. DANFORTH

## I. Introduction

This chapter discusses the estate-planning implications of holding jointly owned property, defined for our purposes as any interest in property in which there is a right of survivorship. Thus, the chapter considers ownership interests in joint tenancies and tenancies by the entirety, as well as contractual arrangements having a survivorship feature, such as joint bank accounts. The chapter begins with a description of the property-law attributes of joint ownership arrangements. Next, the chapter describes the estate- and gift-tax consequences of creating and transferring joint ownership arrangements. The chapter concludes by discussing the principal tax and nontax estate-planning considerations associated with jointly owned property.

## II. Types and Attributes of Jointly Owned Property

The ownership arrangements discussed in this chapter all involve concurrent interests in property—that is, interests enjoyed at the same time by multiple owners. The arrangements also share the common characteristic of a right of survivorship—the death of one concurrent owner extinguishes his or her interest in the property in favor of the surviving co-owner or co-owners. Unlike many other property interests, the deceased co-owner's interest is not a part of his or her estate for purposes of estate administration, so the interest does not pass by testate or intestate succession. Instead, the deceased owner's interest passes by operation of law, and the surviving co-owners become the new owners of the decedent's interest as of the date of his or her death. The chapter does not consider the other principal form of concurrent ownership, the tenancy in common, which lacks the survivorship attribute of the other ownership arrangements under consideration.

Here we are concerned with three principal types of joint ownership arrangements: joint tenancies, tenancies by the entirety, and contractual arrangements (such as joint bank accounts) having a right of survivorship.

### A. Joint Tenancies

A joint tenancy is a form of concurrent ownership of property in which each owner has an equal, undivided interest in the whole and holds a right of survivorship with respect to the interests held by the other co-owners. A joint tenancy can be formed between or among any two or more persons, typically by the co-owners accepting a transfer of property in which the instrument of title expressly establishes a right of survivorship.

An essential feature of the joint tenancy is that any joint tenant can convey his or her interest to another and, by so doing, sever the survivorship attribute associated with the transferred interest. Consider, for example, a joint tenancy among A, B, and C. A transfers his interest to D. Following the transfer, D has a one-third tenancy in common interest with B and C, who hold their two-thirds interest as joint tenants with each other. If, following the transfer from A to D, C dies, B will become the owner of C's interest by right of survivorship and thus will be a two-thirds tenant in common with D. In the more usual case involving two joint tenants, A and B each have a one-half interest in the property. At the death of B, A becomes the sole owner of the property.

### B.  Tenancies by the Entirety

A tenancy by the entirety is a concurrent ownership arrangement involving only a husband and wife, each holding a one-half undivided interest in the whole. Tenancies by the entirety are not recognized in all states. The tenancy by the entirety resembles the joint tenancy in that each co-owner has a right of survivorship with respect to the other co-owner's interest.

The principal distinction between a joint tenancy and a tenancy by the entirety is that an interest in a tenancy by the entirety cannot be transferred by the unilateral act of one co-owner; both owners must consent to such a transfer. Thus an interest in a tenancy by the entirety generally cannot be reached by the creditors of one co-owner. This rule applies both to claims that might arise voluntarily (thus, for example, one spouse cannot encumber the property without the other's consent) and to claims that might arise involuntarily (a judgment creditor of one spouse, therefore, cannot obtain a lien against the property). Note, however, that creditors to which both spouses are liable can reach the spouses' interests in the property.

### C.  Contractual Arrangements

Certain contractual arrangements, such as joint bank and brokerage accounts, share the survivorship attribute of joint tenancies. A joint account is established through a signed agreement with a bank or brokerage house, in which the co-account owners are described as holding their interests with rights of survivorship. In general, either co-owner can withdraw any portion of the account assets without the consent of the other co-owner, although this depends on the terms of the contractual arrangement. At the death of the first co-owner to die, his or her interest is extinguished in favor of the remaining owner or owners, just as in the case of the joint tenancy. A joint bank or brokerage account is not a true joint tenancy, because each account holder does not necessarily own an equal interest in the whole account—the relative interests of the co-owners in general depend on their relative contributions to the account and whether a contributing co-owner intended to make a gift to any other owner.

## III.  Estate and Gift Taxation of Jointly Held Property

This portion of the chapter summarizes the principal rules governing the estate and gift taxation of jointly held property; it also briefly considers some income tax basis rules associated with transfers of jointly held property, as well as the estate- and gift-tax consequences of disclaiming jointly held interests.

## A. Gift Taxation

The creation of a joint ownership arrangement may constitute a taxable transfer for gift-tax purposes. The amount of the gift depends on the value of the property and whether the donor retains any interest in the property. Consider the following example:

> A father (F) transfers his farm, worth $1 million, to his daughter (D) and D's husband (H), who take title as joint tenants. F has made a $500,000 gift to each of D and H. Because the joint tenancy can be severed unilaterally by either joint tenant, a portion of each gift qualifies for the gift-tax annual exclusion.

Compare the results of the following:

> F transfers the $1-million farm to himself and D as joint tenants. F has made a $500,000 gift to D, and again a portion of the gift qualifies for the gift-tax annual exclusion.

As illustrated by the following example, the identity of the donee can also affect the gift-tax consequences:

> F from the previous example transfers the farm to himself and his wife (W), and they take title as tenants by the entirety. Any gift from F to W is offset by an equal gift-tax marital deduction. Thus, the transfer is not subject to gift tax.

This example assumes that W is a U.S. citizen; in general, transfers to noncitizen spouses do not qualify for the marital deduction.

Transfers involving tenancies by the entirety can create difficult valuation questions. Consider the following example:

> F transfers a $20,000 painting to his daughter (D) and her husband (H), who take title as tenants by the entirety. Under state law, the tenancy cannot be severed unilaterally by either co-owner. The value of the interest received by D and H is thus determined actuarially, by taking into account their relative life expectancies. If D is younger than H, she is actuarially more likely to survive H and thus become the sole owner of the property; accordingly, D's interest is worth more than H's interest. For an example of this type of actuarial calculation, see Priv. Ltr. Rul. 87-46-026.

In this example, F will be surprised to discover that not all of his $20,000 transfer qualifies for the gift-tax annual exclusion; the gift to D fails to qualify to the extent that the value of her interest exceeds $10,000.

Taxable gifts can also occur in connection with joint purchases, as illustrated by the following example:

> A brother (B) and his sister (S) purchase a house at the beach for $300,000, taking title as joint tenants. B furnishes $100,000 of the purchase price, and S furnishes $200,000. Because the joint tenancy rules grant B and S equal, undivided interests, S has a made a $50,000 gift to B. A portion of the gift qualifies for the gift-tax annual exclusion.

In most circumstances a transfer or acquisition of property in joint tenancy will constitute a completed taxable gift. In the case of joint bank and brokerage accounts, however, a transfer of assets into the account is generally not a completed gift:

> A mother (M) transfers $20,000 into a joint bank account established in the names of herself and her son (S). Under the terms of the account, either co-owner can withdraw all or any portion of the funds at any time. The creation of the account does not constitute a completed gift from M to S, because M could at any time revest title to the assets in herself.

In the case of a joint account, a completed gift occurs at the time of a withdrawal by the noncontributing co-owner:

> With M's permission, S withdraws $5,000 from the account, which S uses to purchase himself an automobile. The $5,000 withdrawal constitutes a completed gift from M to S. The gift qualifies for the gift-tax annual exclusion.

Note, however, that whether a gift occurs depends on the purposes for which account assets are used:

> S writes a $1,000 check on the joint account to make the monthly mortgage payment on M's house. The negotiation of the check constitutes a gift to no one.

If both account owners have contributed to the account, whether a gift occurs depends on the circumstances, such as whether the co-owners make use of the account in proportion to their contributions:

> A sister (S) and her brother (B) create a joint brokerage account, each contributing $50,000 in cash, for a total of $100,000. Over the course of five years the account doubles in value to $200,000. S and B decide to transfer the account assets into equal separate accounts in their individual names. No gift occurs upon the transfer. If instead S and B transfer assets worth $175,000 into a separate account for S and assets worth $25,000 into a separate account for B, B has made a $75,000 gift to S, a portion of which qualifies for the annual exclusion.

As a general rule, the donee of a gift takes the income tax basis of the donor. With respect to transfers involving jointly held property, the donee's basis depends in part on whether the donor retains an interest in the property:

> A mother (M) owns commercial real estate worth $1 million with an adjusted basis of $400,000. M transfers the property to herself and her daughter (D), taking title as joint tenants. D's interest in the property is worth $500,000, with an adjusted basis of $200,000.

In the preceding example, if title were placed in D's name alone, her adjusted basis would be $400,000. In each case, under I.R.C. Section 1015(d)(6), D's basis would be increased by the gift-taxes, if any, paid by M attributable to the appreciated portion of the value of the gifted property.

## B. Estate Taxation

Estate taxation of jointly owned property is controlled by I.R.C. Section 2040, which establishes three different sets of rules:

- If all of the co-owners acquired their interests by gift or inheritance, under I.R.C. Section 2040(a) the amount includable in the deceased co-owner's estate is the value of the property divided by the number of co-owners.
- If the co-owners are spouses, the property is generally treated as a qualified joint interest, described in I.R.C. Section 2040(b), under which the amount includable in the deceased co-owner's estate is one-half of the value of the property. This special rule does not apply if the surviving spouse is not a U.S. citizen.
- In all other cases, under I.R.C. Section 2040(a) the entire value of the property is includable in the deceased co-owner's estate, except to the extent that the decedent's personal representative can establish that the surviving co-owner or co-owners contributed toward the acquisition or improvement of the property.

In the case of property acquired by gift or inheritance, a simple rule applies: each owner is treated as having made a proportionate contribution to the acquisition of the property:

> Following the death of their widowed mother, A, B, and C inherited their mother's residence. Under state law, they took title as joint tenants. At the death of A survived by B and C, one-third of the value of the residence is includable in A's estate. At B's subsequent death survived by C, one-half of the value of the property is includable in B's estate.

The following example illustrates a typical joint ownership arrangement between spouses:

> In 1990, a wife (W) furnishes all of the consideration ($200,000) to acquire a farm, to which she took title in the names of herself and her husband (H) as tenants by the entirety. In 2005, when the farm is worth $350,000, H dies survived by W. One-half of the value of the property—or $175,000—is includable in H's estate for estate-tax purposes.

In the case of jointly owned property between spouses, the amount includable will generally be offset by a marital deduction of an equal amount (assuming that the surviving spouse is a U.S. citizen). Thus, in the preceding example, H's estate would be entitled to a $175,000 estate-tax marital deduction.

The final rule, sometimes referred to as the consideration-furnished test, may be illustrated as follows:

> A brother (B) and his sister (S) acquire a house at the beach worth $500,000, B contributing $300,000 and S contributing $200,000. At S's death survived by B, the house has increased in value to $900,000. Because S's personal representative can establish that B contributed three-fifths of the acquisition cost, only two-fifths of the value of the property ($360,000) is includable in S's estate. If B had died first, three-fifths of the value ($540,000) would be includable in his estate.

Note that a proportionate amount is includable in either co-owner's estate irrespective of any gift-tax consequences to B or S upon acquisition of the property. Thus, even though acquisition of the house likely constituted a taxable gift from B to S, that fact has no bearing on the amount includable at S's death or, conversely, at B's death.

In the preceding example, the consideration furnished by each co-owner is easily determined. The consideration-furnished test becomes more complicated if the owners make improvements to the property, if one owner pays a disproportionate share of a mortgage, if income from property is reinvested, and so forth. Under these circumstances, establishing the proper amount includable at the first co-owner's death requires clear, detailed records of each owner's contributions to the property.

Under I.R.C. Section 1014, property includable in a decedent's estate generally receives an income tax basis equal to its fair market value. In the case of spousal joint ownership arrangements, the practical effect of I.R.C. Section 2040(b) is to determine not the incidence of estate taxation (because the amount includable will usually be off-set by a marital deduction), but the basis of the property following the death of the first spouse to die. To illustrate the point, consider the following extension of the preceding example:

> Following H's death in 2005, W sells the farm for $350,000. Her income tax basis for purposes of determining capital gains is established by combining the basis for the one-half share she held before H's death ($100,000) and the basis for the one-half share she received as a result of H's death ($175,000), for a total basis of $275,000. Thus, the sale of the $350,000 farm produces a capital gain of $75,000.

Changing the example somewhat illustrates that, under some circumstances, the special rule for spousal joint tenancies creates an income tax disadvantage for the surviving spouse:

> In the preceding example, assume that W dies in 2005 survived by H and that H then sells the farm for $350,000. As in the preceding example, H's basis is $275,000, and the sale produces a capital gain of $75,000. If the consideration-furnished test had applied, however, all of the property would have been includable in W's estate, H's basis would have been $350,000, and the sale would have produced no capital gain.

In limited circumstances, surviving spouses (such as H in our last example) have successfully argued, under the authority of *United States v. Gallenstein*, 975 F.2d 286 (6th Cir. 1992), that the consideration-furnished test, not Section 2040(b), applies to jointly held property. This argument is available only with respect to certain jointly held property acquired before January 1, 1977. In circumstances to which the *Gallenstein* rule applies, the surviving spouse has an incentive to establish that the deceased spouse furnished all consideration in acquiring the property. Causing a larger amount to be includable for estate-tax purposes does not disadvantage the surviving spouse, because the entire interest passing to the surviving spouse will qualify for the estate-tax marital deduction.

The same advantages of the consideration-furnished test can also arise in cases involving nonspousal joint tenancies:

> A sister (S) and her brother (B) purchase a house at the beach for $200,000, taking title as joint tenants. B furnishes all of the consideration. At B's death sur-

vived by S, the house is worth $300,000. B's only other substantial asset is a brokerage account in his own name worth $100,000. It is to S's advantage to establish that B furnished all consideration in acquiring the house. If the entire value of the house is includable in B's estate, S will take a $300,000 basis in the property. Including the entire value of the house in B's estate causes no estate-tax disadvantage, because B's estate is worth less than the amount that triggers imposition of estate tax.

## C. Disclaimers

Under certain circumstances a beneficiary may wish to disclaim his or her interest in an estate. To be effective for gift and estate-tax purposes, a disclaimer must satisfy the qualified disclaimer requirements of I.R.C. Section 2518. Special rules apply to disclaimers of jointly held property, described briefly in the paragraphs that follow.

As a general rule, a surviving joint tenant or tenant by the entirety can make a qualified disclaimer of the proportionate interest deemed transferred at the death of the deceased co-owner, which in most cases is one-half of the value of the property. To illustrate the point, consider the following variation of the preceding example:

> B furnishes all the consideration for the purchase of a house at the beach, to which title is taken in B and S's names as joint tenants. At B's death survived by S, S makes a qualified disclaimer of her survivorship interest. Under the disclaimer regulations, this amount is deemed to be one-half of the property, notwithstanding that the consideration-furnished test would cause the entire value of the property to be includable in B's estate. Following the disclaimer, one-half of the property is owned by S—this is the same interest that she held during B's lifetime. The other half passes by testate or intestate succession as part of B's estate.

Suppose S dies first? In that case, a disclaimer by B changes the amount includable in S's estate:

> At S's death survived by B, B makes a qualified disclaimer of his one-half survivorship interest. Following the disclaimer, B holds the one-half interest that he owned during S's lifetime. The disclaimed portion passes by testate or intestate succession as part of S's estate. Because B furnished all of the consideration for the property, no portion of the property is includable in S's estate under I.R.C. Section 2040(a). One-half of the property is, however, includable is S's estate by virtue of I.R.C. Section 2033, which applies generally to the assets that constitute a decedent's probate estate.

The general rule that a surviving cotenant can disclaim a one-half interest in the property also applies to tenancies by the entirety (assuming that the spouse who survives is a United States citizen):

> A husband (H) and his wife (W) purchase a residence in 1995, H furnishing all of the consideration. At H's death in 2005 survived by W, W makes a qualified disclaimer of her one-half survivorship interest. Following the disclaimer, W holds the same one-half interest that she held during H's lifetime. As a result of the disclaimer, the disclaimed portion passes as part of H's probate estate.

A special disclaimer rule applies in the case of most joint bank and brokerage accounts. If amounts contributed by a co-owner could at any time be withdrawn without the other co-owners' consent, the amount that can be disclaimed corresponds to the amount contributed by the deceased co-owner:

> A mother (M) places $20,000 in a joint bank account in the names of herself and her daughter (D). Either M or D can withdraw funds from the account at any time. Following M's death, D is entitled to disclaim up to 100 percent of the account. To the extent D disclaims, the disclaimed assets will form part of M's probate estate.

This special rule for joint accounts may create a planning opportunity for a surviving spouse:

> A wife (W) and her husband (H), both U.S. citizens, have a brokerage account holding assets worth $1 million with an income tax basis of $50,000. W furnished all of the consideration in acquiring the account assets. At W's death survived by H, H should take advantage of the joint account disclaimer rules and disclaim 100 percent of the account. The result for estate-tax purposes is that 100 percent of the account is includable in W's estate under I.R.C. Section 2033. The account accordingly receives a new basis of $1 million.

Of course, H in this example should disclaim only if doing so is consistent with his other financial and estate-planning objectives.

## IV.  Planning Considerations

Joint ownership of property is a simple means of avoiding estate administration: the decedent's interest passes automatically to the surviving co-owner(s) without passing as part of the decedent's probate estate. Thus, holding property jointly with others can simplify (or even eliminate the need for) estate administration, saving the survivors both time and money. Joint ownership arrangements afford survivors immediate access to the decedent's property, which can be particularly advantageous in the case of bank accounts and other highly liquid assets that the survivors may need to support themselves. Jointly owned property may also be sheltered from creditors' claims, both claims against the joint owner during his or her lifetime (in the case of tenancies by the entirety) and claims against the joint owner's estate (in the case of both joint tenancies and tenancies by the entirety). In some jurisdictions, jointly owned property can be used to avoid a surviving spouse's elective share claim. Joint property may also be treated more favorably than other types of property for purposes of state inheritance taxes. There are also significant psychological incentives for holding joint property, particularly in the case of joint ownership between spouses, for whom jointly owned property expresses the idea of a partnership and reinforces a sense of family harmony.

Joint bank and brokerage accounts may also afford certain conveniences during the co-owners' lifetimes. Consider the following illustration:

> A mother (M) wishes for her only child (C) to be able from time to time to pay M's bills, and she also intends to leave most of her estate to C at her death. Accordingly, M opens a joint checking account in her and C's names. The agreement with the bank permits each account owner to write checks on the account. The arrangement thus allows C to write checks on M's behalf when-

ever it is inconvenient for M to do so herself. At M's death survived by C, the
assets remaining in the account pass to C.

Note that this arrangement would be less likely to comport with W's wishes if C were
not W's only child. Under those circumstances, a more appropriate vehicle would probably be an agency account, which would allow C to draw checks, but the assets of
which would not pass to C at M's death. Instead, the remaining account assets would
pass as part of M's estate, presumably in equal shares to C and his siblings.

Estate planners often suggest that their married clients not hold all of their assets
as joint tenants or as tenants by the entirety. Consider the following example:

> A wife (W) and her husband (H) hold substantially all of their assets in a joint
> brokerage account, having a value of approximately $2 million. W and H's
> wills provide that, at the death of the first of them to die, the amount that can
> pass tax-free by virtue of the estate-tax applicable exclusion (as of 2002, $1
> million) will pass into a trust for the benefit of the surviving spouse, with the
> trust structured to be excluded from the spouse's estate at his or her subse-
> quent death. Following W's death in 2002 survived by H, the brokerage
> account assets pass by right of survivorship directly to H, and the trust for H's
> benefit is never funded. At H's death one year later, his estate is worth $2 mil-
> lion. The estate tax at his death is $435,000.

If the brokerage account had been held by W and H as tenants in common (with no
right of survivorship), W's one-half interest in the account would have passed into the
trust for H's benefit. At H's death in 2003, the only asset includable in his estate would
be his one-half interest in the account. The estate-tax applicable exclusion would shelter all $1 million of his assets from estate taxes.

Married persons who jointly own highly appreciated property may wish to terminate their joint ownership for a different reason:

> A husband (H) and his wife (W) own a $200,000 joint brokerage account, their
> only substantial asset. The account has a basis of approximately $15,000. H is
> 83 and in failing health, and W is 69 and in good health. H and W may wish
> to transfer the entire account into H's name for purposes of obtaining a new
> income tax basis at H's death. As a general rule, this planning technique is
> effective only if H survives the transfer by at least one year.

A final planning consideration is to recognize that, although joint property passes
at death outside of the probate estate, for several reasons holding jointly owned property does not eliminate the need for a will. First, the survivorship feature of jointly
owned property is irrelevant at the death of the last co-owner to die—he or she owns
the property outright and thus must have a will to direct its disposition. Second, many
who think they own all of their property jointly in fact have some property in their separate names. Finally, joint owners can die simultaneously, in which case a proportionate share of the property will pass under each joint owner's will.

## V. Conclusion

As described in this chapter, all three types of jointly owned property—joint tenancies,
tenancies by the entirety, and survivorship contractual arrangements—afford a simple
means of avoiding estate administration: jointly owned property passes by operation of

law to the surviving joint owner(s) and thus does not form part of the probate estate. Nevertheless, as discussed more fully above, holding property jointly is not appropriate in all circumstances, and owning joint property does not obviate the need for a will. Transfers of property into joint ownership arrangements can trigger gift taxation and, although joint property is not part of the estate for estate administration purposes, it *is* part of the estate for estate-tax purposes. These and other considerations must inform decisions about whether and when to enter into joint ownership arrangements.

# CHAPTER 21

# Estate Planning Malpractice and Ethical Issues

ISABEL MIRANDA

## I. Introduction

Estate planning is a complex area with ever-changing tax laws and implications that affect families for generations. With the enactment of the Economic Growth and Tax Relief Reconciliation Act of 2001 (EGTRRA), the issues have become more muddied as we struggle to determine whether we must draft as we have done in the past, or whether we vary our approach and plan for the eventual repeal of the estate tax in 2010 and its subsequent reinstatement in 2011.

There are quantum ethical issues confronting estate planners, and case law is replete with examples of lawyer liability for conflicts of interest and malpractice. Thus, we will identify potential conflicts of interest and other potential ethical traps as well as analyze the standard of care necessary in order to avoid or minimize potential liability for malpractice.

Circumspection and caution are the watchwords in estate planning. Failure to pay attention to detail, to remain current, or to meet clients' particular needs can result in professional ruin.

## II. Guidance

Upon admission to the bar of a particular jurisdiction, a lawyer becomes subject to that state's laws regulating professional conduct, and civil and criminal sanctions for non-compliance.[1] Most states have a regulatory code, promulgated by its highest court, which controls lawyer conduct. These codes are mostly based on two lawyer codes (published by the American Bar Association (ABA)), which differ in substantive areas: the Model Code of Professional Responsibility (Model Code) and the Model Rules of Professional Conduct (Model Rules). It is, therefore, critical to research the rules in your particular jurisdiction and to be cognizant of the differences in each state's rules if you are admitted in multiple jurisdictions. The purpose of these codes is mainly to establish mandatory standards for lawyers' conduct. They are not exclusive, however, and other rules affecting lawyers are also found in statutes, case law, and court rules.[2]

The highest courts in most states have ruled that it is within their purview to regulate lawyers' conduct. Many go as far as to state that this power is exclusive to the judicial branch.[3] Federal courts have followed this line of reasoning and have also enacted lawyer codes, which control lawyer conduct in the federal courts.

Bar associations, too, are active participants in regulating lawyers and exemplify the principle of self-regulation in a profession. Bar associations often offer lawyers advice on ethical issues and issue opinions for lawyers who periodically find themselves in ethical dilemmas.

## III. Ethical Considerations

Lawyers must be aware of various ethical considerations: conflicts of interests, unauthorized practice of law, and unreasonable legal fees. Ethical violations can result in payment of damages, loss of license, and/or malpractice.

### A. Conflicts of Interest

If the number of cases is any indication of the importance of a topic, then certainly conflicts of interest are of fundamental importance. On a daily basis one can read slip opinions in legal journals across the country citing lawyers with ethical gaffes founded in conflicts. The most common cases revolve around (1) representing clients with divergent interests and (2) self-dealing.

#### 1. Representing Multiple Clients Generally

The conflicts we encounter most frequently in the estate planning practice are those involving the dual representation of spouses. However, there are traps for the unwary practitioner everywhere in representing members of a family, their closely held businesses, and their charitable organizations.

The lawyer codes[4] establish a clear prohibition against representing parties when there would be a substantial risk that the representation would be materially or adversely affected by the lawyer's own interest, or by the lawyer's duty to another client or to a third party.[5] The genesis of the rule lies in the lawyer's duty of undivided loyalty to a client.

In order to represent parties who have a potential conflict, the lawyer must obtain informed consent from both parties.[6] Informed consent requires disclosure of the material aspects in which the representation could adversely affect each party and requires an affirmative response from each party. Silence from either party is not acquiescence.[7] Clients should sign a waiver and consent form to be kept in each client's file. The existence of the conflict should be determined by the facts the lawyer knows or should have known at the time of the engagement.[8]

#### a. MULTIPLE CLIENTS: REPRESENTING BOTH SPOUSES

Lawyers can represent both spouses either jointly or separately. This determination is one that the lawyer should help the couple make at their initial meeting and it should form the basis for the engagement letter with the parties.[9]

A typical scenario involves a husband and wife visiting the lawyer's office to consult on the preparation of their estate plan; they generally agree on the plan, are eager to proceed, and do not wish to engage separate counsel as they consider such a needless expense. In a joint representation like this, the couple is treated as a unit, and there are no confidences withheld from either spouse.

In theory, the representation may be separate; however, in practice, the situation will become untenable for the lawyer who has information that is adverse to one side. The states are split in their approach to this dilemma: some require disclosure,[10] some allow the lawyer to use his or her discretion,[11] and others allow confidentiality to remain.[12]

Although representing spouses in and of itself does not create a conflict, conflicts may arise during the course of the representation. In a society with divorce rates hovering at 50 percent, estate planners often encounter couples who have had multiple marriages and children from these marriages. During the course of representing both spouses, it may become apparent that the spouses do not share a vision for the transfer of wealth to their family. In states like New York, where spouses have a right to elect against a will that does not provide them with a minimum percentage of the estate as an outright disposition, estate planning can become a sensitive topic for couples who have former spouses and progeny from former marriages. Other conflicts may arise when one spouse is aware of certain facts, and the other spouse is ignorant of this information.

Conflicts can be overcome if both spouses, after being fully informed of their options, agree to a resolution and thereafter, sign a waiver and consent form. For lawyers who choose to represent both spouses, it is critical to have a standard operating procedure in place from the beginning of the engagement to address potential conflicts.

### b. MULTIPLE CLIENTS: REPRESENTING PARENT AND CHILD

Conflicts between parents and their children arise in several ways. Parents overreach regarding the children's assets, usually in an attempt to protect them from themselves. Sometimes parents use assets held in trust or custodial accounts to defray obligations that the courts find to be a support obligation of the parents.[13] In other cases, children overreach regarding parent's assets. In these instances, siblings often accuse a caretaking child of misusing or misappropriating funds from the infirm or incompetent parent.[14]

If the lawyer currently represents one party, informed consent must be obtained from both parties for dual representation. If a consenting party is under a disability (either because of minority or infirmity), the lawyer must not undertake the representation, as the consent will not be valid because of lack of capacity.[15]

Even after obtaining consent, the lawyer must be sensitive to the clients' wishes. For example, may a child be present at the meeting between the lawyer and the parent? The parent, preferably outside of the child's presence, must make this decision.

The source of payment of the legal fee is not dispositive in defining the duties of the lawyer.[16] In cases where the child is paying the parent's legal fees, it is especially important for the lawyer to proceed in every detail with the understanding that the duty is owed to the parent.

### c. MULTIPLE CLIENTS: TESTATOR AND REFERRAL SOURCES

It has long been common practice for estate-planning lawyers to have business relationships with accountants, insurance professionals, and bankers who can be a good source of client referrals. The ethical trap occurs when the referral source recommends the client for estate planning with the understanding that the client will use the referrer's products or services.[17] The lawyer is then placed in the position of vetting the product.[18] Again, the best practice is to have a standard operating procedure, which involves a frank discussion with the client and an examination of all of the client's available alternatives, including the referrer's services.

In addition, law firms often are designated as outside counsel to bank trust departments, which also may refer clients to the firm on occasion. The conflict in this instance is more obvious, and the rules of undivided loyalty that bar representing clients with adverse interests will apply.

### d. MULTIPLE CLIENTS: TESTATOR AND FAMILY BUSINESS

In light of the current popularity of family limited partnerships and limited liability companies for tax savings and asset management, cases involving a client and a controlled business are more prevalent than ever.

The seminal case on this issue is *Estate of Halas*,[19] in which the law firm represented the testator (one of the owners of the National Football League Chicago Bears franchise), the team itself, and the testator's father (executor and trustee, as well a co-owner of the team), individually. The beneficiaries of the estate objected to a corporate reorganization that left them with fewer rights and less control than they had previously, and the court agreed that the firm was representing too many diverse interests.

In *Griva v. Davison*[20] the law firm represented a family limited partnership as well as some of the family members individually. When a dispute erupted among family members, the firm, which kept the corporate records, refused to share them with the family members they did not represent. The court focused on the firm's fiduciary duty to all family members who participated in the family limited partnership and found that the firm had too many conflicting representations.

Practice Tip: In creating family limited partnerships for clients and their families, consider separate counsel for the new entity.

### e. MULTIPLE CLIENTS: FIDUCIARIES AND BENEFICIARIES

Conflicts in this area occur when a fiduciary has hired the drafting lawyer to represent him, but heirs or beneficiaries of the estate or trust believe that the lawyer represents their interests. The various jurisdictions disagree on the right approach,[21] and this topic is not addressed here. However, the answer to the threshold issue of whom the lawyer represents is important because it drives duty of care, privilege, and confidentiality.

### 2. Multiple Roles

Lawyers who have multiple roles in connection with a client will likely stretch ethical limitations. Regulatory bodies will perceive such lawyers as self-dealing.

### a. MULTIPLE ROLES: LAWYER AS BENEFICIARY

The lawyer codes[22] strongly warn against accepting gifts from clients. Accordingly, it is never wise for a lawyer to draft a document in which he or she is named as beneficiary unless the lawyer is the natural object of the testator's bounty. Even in those cases, the lawyer must not be treated more favorably than the lawyer's coheirs.[23] Lawyers who draft instruments that benefit them are frequently sanctioned for overreaching.[24]

In New York, the leading case is *Matter of Putnam*,[25] which stated that a client who wishes to benefit his lawyer should have the will drafted by another lawyer. The New York Bar Association has opined that a lawyer must either resign as counsel or refuse the bequest.[26] In California, lawyers are prohibited from receiving donative transfers under instruments they draft.[27]

Courts have also held that a lawyer who drafts a document benefiting himself must explain the circumstances. Absent an explanation, the jury may be permitted to draw an inference of undue influence, placing on the lawyer the burden of showing that the gift or bequest was willingly made. If the lawyer is unable to rebut the inference, the disposition is denied.[28] Courts have also found that the evidence of undue influence may be circumstantial and need not be shown by direct proof.[29]

### b. MULTIPLE ROLES: DRAFTER AS FIDUCIARY

Historically, the nature of the trust and estate practice was such that, as a matter of course, lawyers served as fiduciary for families they represented. This was accepted as common practice in an era when the lawyers did not charge an hourly rate for the preparation of the estate plan and the expectation was that the fees and commissions for serving as fiduciary and counsel for the estate would compensate for the foregone fees.

As law firms grew and the nature of the profession became more focused on the economics of the practice, departments in the law firms were judged by current revenues and not on future potential. Lawyers began to charge an hourly rate for estate planning, and the courts started to review the lawyers' nominations as fiduciary with a sharper lens. The Model Code in EC 5-6 provides that a lawyer should not "influence a client to name him executor, trustee or lawyer." Although the Model Rules are silent on the fiduciary issue, the commentary to Rule 1.7 (b) states that lawyers should not encourage clients to nominate them as fiduciary for personal pecuniary gain.

In New York, the seminal case in point is *Matter of Weinstock*,[30] which held that the relationship between the client and the drafting lawyer imposed on the lawyer a "special obligation of both full disclosure and fair dealing." The court found this standard breached when the drafting lawyer nominated himself as fiduciary. The court found constructive fraud and disallowed the appointment of the lawyer as fiduciary. Following the *Weinstock* decision, the courts in numerous cases focused on ensuring that lawyers were not unduly influencing clients in the selection of a fiduciary.[31] As a result of these decisions, the New York legislature addressed the issue by requiring an affidavit to be signed by the testator acknowledging the financial impact of the fiduciary appointment. Absent such affidavit, the lawyer-fiduciary is limited to one-half of the statutory commission.[32]

Practice Tip: It is critical to describe the roles of the executor and counsel for the estate to the client so that he fully understands them. It is also important to explain the usual fees in the jurisdiction for these services.

### c. MULTIPLE ROLES: DRAFTER AS FIDUCIARY AND AS COUNSEL FOR THE FIDUCIARY

The key concern at the heart of this discussion lies in the compensation of the lawyer as both fiduciary and as counsel, the double-dipping issue.[33] The law is clear that the scrivener's designation as counsel for the estate in the instrument is not binding, since the executor has the right to choose counsel for the estate. In addition, the engagement of the lawyer for the executor can be perceived as lacking independent judgment when the lawyer, who is also acting as executor, self-hires as counsel. Although the reasons for doing so are many, usually concerning administrative convenience and efficiency, courts have often looked askance at this practice.[34]

The courts have been particularly skeptical if the lawyer is allowed a fee as fiduciary as well as a legal fee for the representation. In order to curtail this practice, some states have limited the lawyers' ability to receive double compensation.[35] California takes this approach, disallowing dual compensation unless the will specifically provides for it,[36] and prohibiting lawyers from serving in a dual capacity except in instances where there is prior court approval.[37] Other states also proscribe the practice by limiting fees to the lawyer.[38] On the other hand, many states have no prohibition against this practice, and the courts are left to examine and regulate dual fees on a case-by-case basis.

### B. Unauthorized Practice of Law

A lawyer cannot practice in a state without having been duly admitted nor may a lawyer assist a nonlawyer to practice law. This issue is of import in estate planning because clients often own property in different jurisdictions. The extent to which a lawyer may practice across state lines is fact-driven.[39] The issues the courts often considered are whether the client (1) is a regular client, (2) is from the lawyer's home state, and (3) maintains substantial contacts with the lawyer's home state.[40]

### C. Legal Fees in Trusts and Estates

The lawyer codes require legal fees to be reasonable, and the burden is on the lawyer to show that the fee is reasonable.[41] The courts have long held that the following factors are critical in determining lawyers' fees: time and labor expended, the difficulty of the questions raised, the skill required in handling the matter, the lawyer's experience and reputation, the amount involved, the results obtained for the client, the contingency or certainty of compensation, the fee customarily charged in the locality, the time constraints involved, the nature and length of the relationship with the client, and the responsibility involved.[42]

The courts in most jurisdictions have zealously guarded their discretion to set and award legal fees.[43] Most states require that lawyers obtain court approval prior to receiving payment during probate.[44] The courts traditionally award fees only when the services are perceived to be in the interest of the estate, so in cases where the courts do not see a benefit accruing to the estate, no fee has been allowed.[45] Fiduciaries have been reimbursed for litigation expenses absent a showing of bad faith,[46] especially in cases where the will is ambiguous and calls for interpretation.[47]

Courts have not been sympathetic to legal bills that include routine office expenses such as disbursements and they have found postage, local transportation, fax, telephone, and other office overhead to be nonreimbursable.[48] In addition, time spent on preparing the legal bill is not considered billable time.[49]

Practice Tip: It is good practice to enter into a retainer agreement that fully describes the lawyer's hourly rate and how time will be billed. However, it is wise to remember that the courts are not bound by the agreement if it is found to be unreasonable.

## IV. Malpractice

Malpractice occurs when a lawyer fails to meet his duty of care. To prove legal malpractice, the plaintiff must prove the following four elements: (1) the existence of a lawyer-client relationship creating a duty of care on the lawyer, (2) a breach of that duty by the lawyer, (3) the breach was the proximate cause of the injury, and (4) damages.[50] A plaintiff's inability to prove each of these elements will prevent recovery of damages.

## A.  Lawyer-Client Relationship and Duty of Care

The relationship between a lawyer and the client is voluntary and arises when the lawyer and the client agree on the representation. The law recognizes a lawyer's duty to the client arising out of the lawyer's agreement to represent the client and render the service, and the client's justifiable reliance on that agreement. The existence of a legal duty of care in a particular case is a question of law to be determined by the court.[51] Absent the existence of a duty by the lawyer to the plaintiff, there can be no cause of action for malpractice. Lawyers are well-advised to have an engagement letter with the client detailing the scope of the representation because courts have recognized that lawyers may circumscribe their role by the terms of the engagement letter.[52]

Section 1.1 of the Model Rules requires competent representation, and it is generally understood that the lawyer must attempt to fulfill the client's lawful, defined objectives.

At the end of the representation, the lawyer's duty diminishes and includes only minimal duties, such as confidentiality and record keeping. However, breach of even these de minimus duties may also lead to a cause of action in malpractice.[53]

It is important for estate planners to document the end of the representation in order to limit any ongoing responsibility to the client. This will protect the lawyer from a duty to inform the client of changes in the law that would affect the estate plan. In some jurisdictions, California, for example, retention by the lawyer of the original will has been seen as evidence of a continuation of the lawyer-client relationship.

Practice Tip: In order to avoid continuing liability, it is wise to send a formal letter ending the estate planning assignment when delivering the documents and the final bill to the client.

## B.  Standard of Care

A lawyer must perform services with the same degree of skill and care that other members of the profession use in similar circumstances; therefore, the standard is that of a reasonably prudent lawyer.[54] This differs from the "reasonable-person standard in that a lawyer is not normally held liable for errors in judgment. Accordingly, a lawyer who acts in good faith will not be found negligent unless the mistake arose from ignorance of well-established law.[55]

The standard of care for estate planners has been broadly interpreted. Some courts have found the finer points of federal estate-tax law or fiduciary law to be beyond the reasonable understanding of regular practitioners;[56] most courts; however, have not.[57]

Courts will hold lawyers who present themselves as experts or specialists or who have specific professional designations to a higher standard of care.[58] Specialists will be held to the standard of care that they actually possess, based on their particular experience.[59] When a matter would normally be handled by a specialist, some courts have found a duty to refer the case.[60]

Estate planners often work with members of other disciplines in constructing an effective and thorough plan for sophisticated clients who have complicated estates. In light of the continuing discussion within the ABA of multidisciplinary practice, it is of some concern that a lawyer will be held liable for engaging a nonlawyer without the client's prior approval and, even having obtained the client's approval, might be held responsible for supervising the nonlawyer's work.

The most common areas where courts have found that estate planners have breached their duty of care are (1) errors in drafting, (2) improper execution of the document, and (3) failure to properly address transfer-tax issues.

### 1. Errors in Drafting/Scrivener Error

There are many instances when lawyers failed to draft their clients' wills and trusts in a proper fashion, frustrating the intent of the testator or grantor. Liability has resulted when the lawyer has inadvertently forgotten a residuary clause,[61] misdescribed property,[62] or omitted intended beneficiaries. Whatever the case, courts have shown little tolerance or patience for lawyers involved in these situations.

### 2. Improper Execution

Failure to comply with statutory requirements for the execution of testamentary documents is a common mistake leading to lawyer malpractice. For example, lawyers have been found liable when the intended beneficiary serves as one of the necessary witnesses or when there is an insufficient number of witnesses.[63]

### 3. Transfer-Tax Assessments

Transfer taxes can exact a heavy toll on estates that are improperly planned. Indeed, one of the primary reasons clients turn to professionals is to minimize the burden of these taxes. That being the case, courts have held lawyers liable for errors in misapplying or misconstruing the tax implications of the estate plan.[64]

## C. Causation

A plaintiff must prove causation; that is, but for the lawyer's negligence, no loss would have occurred.[65] In the area of estate planning, this is often not hard to do: an intended beneficiary receives nothing under the will, the will cannot be probated because it lacks the statutory requirements for execution, or there is an Internal Revenue Service (I.R.S.) transfer tax assessment because the lawyer conveyed the decedent's assets to a trust that did not qualify for the estate-tax marital deduction.

## D. Damages

The usual damages allowed for negligence seek to place the plaintiff in the same position plaintiff would have been but for the lawyer's mistake. Accordingly, the awards represent either recovery of the bequest the beneficiary would have received or the cost of curing the mistake.[66] Put differently, in order to recover in the area of estate planning, the plaintiff must show having received less than the testator intended.

The states are split regarding whether legal fees are recoverable. California allows recovery of legal fees incurred in instituting or defending a case as the direct result of the defendant's tort;[67] however, the majority rule is that lawyer's fees are not recoverable in instituting a malpractice action.[68] The courts have normally allowed the estate to recover the legal fee paid by the decedent for the lawyer's services or the cost of the litigation against the estate instituted by disgruntled beneficiaries.[69]

# *V. Defenses to Malpractice*

The most common defenses against malpractice used by lawyers are the statute of limitations and duty of care or privity (that is, I owe a duty of care but not to this person, who is not my client).

## A. Statute of Limitations

In estate planning, drafting and other errors are often not discovered until long after the lawyer has finished rendering services.[70] Despite the long passage of time, courts have not triggered the running of the statute of limitations until the client discovers[71] or could have reasonably discovered the negligence.[72]

## B. Privity

Foremost in the arsenal of lawyers' defenses against malpractice has been the privity defense because, historically, lawyers were held negligent only when a lawyer-client relationship existed. This often left putative beneficiaries with no redress. This defense has mostly fallen by the wayside as the majority of courts now impose liability to a nonclient third party when the testator engaged the lawyer with the intent of benefiting the nonclient.[73] On the other hand, several states, including New York, continue to adhere to the strict privity requirement.[74]

# *VI. Conclusion*

The best way of avoiding liability is to know the law and apply it carefully to each client's particular circumstance. If the fact pattern is very complicated, make sure that you confirm the facts with the client in writing and ensure that you have asked the client to provide you with a detailed list of assets and their nature, as well as a family tree including stepfamily and half-blood family members. An engagement letter describing a fee agreement and the exact duties you are undertaking is also recommended.

To avoid the commission of malpractice, make sure you do not fall below the standard of appropriate conduct and practice, engage in any conflicts without informed consent, or engage in the unauthorized practice of law. Such actions may result in a burdensome and embarrassing lawsuit or in disciplinary action by your state bar association.

## *Endnotes*

1. RESTATEMENT (THIRD) OF THE LAW GOVERNING LAWYERS § 1 (1998).

2. *See, e.g.,* N.Y. SURR. CT. PROC. ACT § 2307-(a); N.Y. UNIFORM CT., RULES FOR SURR. CT. § 207.16.

3. RESTATEMENT (THIRD) OF THE LAW GOVERNING LAWYERS § 1 cmt. c (1998).

4. MODEL CODE OF PROFESSIONAL RESPONSIBILITY Canon 5 (1980); MODEL RULES OF PROFESSIONAL CONDUCT §§ 1.7-1.13 (1983).

5. RESTATEMENT (THIRD) OF THE LAW GOVERNING LAWYERS § 121 (1998).

6. *Id.*

7. RESTATEMENT (THIRD) OF THE LAW GOVERNING LAWYERS § 122 cmt. (c) (1998).

8. RESTATEMENT (THIRD) OF THE LAW GOVERNING LAWYERS § 121 (1998).

9. *See Engagement Letters: A Guide for Practitioners* (American College of Trust & Estate Counsel, 1999).

10. Ass'n of the Bar of the City of N.Y. Op. 1994-10.

11. A v. B v. Hill Wallach, 158 NJ 51 (N.J. Super. Ct. App. Div. 1999).

12. Fla. Bar Ass'n Op. 95-4.

13. *See* Cohen v. Cohen, 609 A.2d 57 (N.J. 1992); Weiss v. Weiss, 984 F.Supp. 675 (S.D.N.Y. 1997); Sutliff v. Sutliff, 489 A.2d 764 (Penn. 1985); Jimenez v. Lee, 274 Or. 457, 547 P.2d 126 (1976); Erdmann v. Erdmann, 226 N.W.2d 439 (Wis. 1975).

14. *See* First Tenn. Bank, N.A. v. Webb, 03A01-9801-CH-00011, 1998 WL 906709 (Tenn. Ct. App. Dec. 22, 1998).

15. RESTATEMENT (THIRD) OF THE LAW GOVERNING LAWYERS § 122 (1998).

16. MODEL RULES OF PROFESSIONAL CONDUCT § 1.8 (f) (1983).

17. *See, e.g.,* Ill. State Bar Ass'n. Op. 90-2.

18. MODEL CODE OF PROFESSIONAL RESPONSIBILITY DR 5-107 (b) (1980) (stating that a lawyer may not be influenced by the fiduciary who recommends or employs the lawyer to represent the client).

19. 512 N.E.2d 1276 (Ill. App. Ct. 1987).

20. 637 A.2d 830 (D.C. 1994).

21. *Matter of Scanlon,* 2 Misc.2d 65 (Surr. Ct. Kings County 1956) (lawyer represents the executor); NYSBA Comm. on Professional Ethics Op. 512 (lawyer represents the estate); Gump v. Wells Fargo Bank, 237 Cal. Rptr. 311 (1987) (lawyer represents the beneficiaries).

22. MODEL RULES OF PROFESSIONAL CONDUCT §1.8 (c) (1983), MODEL CODE OF PROFESSIONAL RESPONSIBILITY EC 5-5 (1980).

23. *See* State v. Collentine, 159 N.W.2d 50 (Wis. 1968).

24. *See* Iowa Comm. on Prof'l. Ethics and Conduct of State Bar Ass'n v. Behnke, 276 N.W.2d 838 (Iowa 1979); Office of Disciplinary Counsel v. Walker, 366 A.2d 563 (Penn. 1976).

25. 257 N.Y. 140.

26. N.Y. State Bar Ass'n Op. 356. *But see,* Disciplinary Bd. v. Amundson, 297 N.W.2d 433 (N.D. 1980).

27. CAL. PROB. CODE § 21350 (West 1990).

28. *See* Estate of Lawson, 428 N.Y.S.2d 106 (N.Y. App. Div. 1980).

29. *See In re Witt's Estate,* 245 P.197 (Cal. 1926); *Matter of Panek,* 667 N.Y.S.2d 177 (N.Y. App. Div. 1977).

30. 351 N.E.2d 647 (N.Y. 1976).

31. *See Matter of Laflin,* 491 N.Y.S.2d 35 (N.Y. App. Div. 1985); *Matter of Thron,* 530 N.Y.S.2d 951 (Surr. Ct. 1988); *Matter of Klenk,* 574 N.Y.S.2d 438 (Surr. Ct. 1991); *Matter of Harris,* 473 N.Y.S.2d 125 (Surr. Ct. 1984).

32. N.Y. SURR. CT. PROC. ACT §2307-a (McKinney's 1995).

33. For an in-depth discussion on this topic, *see* Spurgeon & Ciccarello, *The Lawyer in Other Fiduciary Roles: Policy and Ethical Considerations,* 62 FORDHAM L. REV. 1357.

34. *See Matter of Corya,* 563 N.Y.S.2d 581 (Surr Ct 1990).

35. *See* N.Y. SURR CT. PROC. ACT §2307-a (McKinney's 1995).

36. *See In re Estate of Thompson,* 328 P. 2d 1 (Cal. 1958).

37. CAL. PROB. CODE § 10804 (West 1990).

38. *See, e.g.,* MISS. CODE ANN. § 91-281(1992); MO. ANN. STAT § 473.153 (West 1992).

39. Estate of Condon v. McHenry, 65 Cal. App. 4th 1138 (1998).

40. RESTATEMENT (THIRD) OF THE LAW GOVERNING LAWYERS § 3 (1998).

41. MODEL CODE OF PROFESSIONAL RESPONSIBILITY DR 2-106(B) (1980); MODEL RULES OF PROFESSIONAL CONDUCT § 1.5 (1983).

42. *Matter of Freeman,* 311 N.E.2d 480 (N.Y. 1974).

43. *See Matter of Estate of Thomson,* 487 N.E.2d 1193 (Ill. 1986); Pekofsky v. Cohen, 1999 WL 144919 (N.Y. App. Div. 1st Dept.); Stortecky v. Mazzone, 650 N.E.2d 391 (N.Y. 1995).

44. *See, e.g.,* IOWA CODE ANN § 633.198 (1992); N.Y. SURR CT. PROC. ACT § 2111 (McKinney's 1996).

45. *See Matter of Estate of Dyniewicz,* 648 N.E.2d 1076 (Ill. 1995); *Matter of Graves,* 95 N.Y.S.2d 310 (Surr. Ct. 1950).

46. *In re Breault's Estate,* 211 N.E.2d 424 (Ill. 1965).

47. Landmark Trust Co. v. Aitken, 587 N.E.2d 1076 (Ill. 1992).

48. *See Matter of Livinston,* 180 Misc.2d 977 (Sup. Ct. Queens Cty. 1999); *Matter of Diamond,* 219 A.2d 717 (N.Y. App. Div. 2d Dept. 1995).

49. *Matter of Thron,* 530 N.Y.S.2d 951 (Surr. Ct. 1988).

50. *See* Estate of Fitzgerald v. Linnus, 765 A.2d 251 (N.J. Super. Ct. App. Div. 2001); Henkel v. Winn, 550 S.E.2d 577 (S.C. 2001).

51. Estate of Fitzgerald v. Linnus, 765 A.2d 251 (N.J. Super. Ct. App. Div. 2001).

52. *Id.*

53. RESTATEMENT (THIRD) OF THE LAW GOVERNING LAWYERS § 33 (1998).

54. *See* Neel v. Magana, Olney, Levy, et al., 491 P.2d 421 (Cal.1971); Theobald v. Byers, 13 Cal. Rptr 864 (Cal. App. 1961); Berman v. Rubin, 227 S.E.2d 802 (Ga. 1976); Feil v. Wishek, 193 N.W.2d 218 (N.D. 1971); Glenn v. Haynes, 66 S.E.2d 509 (Va. 1951).

55. Hughes v. Malone, 247 S.E.2d 107 (Ga. Ct. App. 1978); Blair v. Ing, 21 P.2d 345 (Haw. 2001); Vort v. Hollander, 607 A.2d 1339 (N.J. 1992).

56. Lucas v. Hamm, 368 U.S. 987 (1978).

57. Horne v. Peckham, 158 Cal. Rptr. 714 (Cal. App. 1979).

58. *In re BCI Pancake House, Inc.,* 270 B.R. 15 (Bkruptcy Del. 2001); Rhodes v. Batilla, 848 S.W.2d 833 (Tex.App. 1993); *see also Admissibility and Necessity of Expert Evidence as to Standards of Practice and Negligence in Malpractice Actions against Attorneys,* 14 A.L.R. 4th 170 § 3 (1982).

59. *Estate of Pew,* 655 A.2d 521 (Pa. Super. 1994).

60. Horne v. Peckham, 158 Cal. Rptr. 714 (Cal. App. 1979).

61. *See* Arnold v. Carmichael, 524 So. 2d 464 (Fla. 1988); Nedham v. Hamilton, 459 A.2d 1060 (D.C. 1983).

62. *See* Strangland v. Brock, 747 P.2d 464 (Wash. 1987).

63. *See* Schirmer v. Nethercutt, 288 P. 265 (Wash. 1930); Auric v. Continental Casualty Co., 331 N.W.2d 325 (Wis. 1983).

64. *See* Linck v. Barokas & Martin, 667 P.2d 171 (Alaska 1983); Horne v. Peckham, 158 Cal. Rptr. 714 (Cal. App. 1979); Bucquet v. Livingston, 129 Cal. Rptr. 714 (1979).

65. Hunt v. Foster, Waldeck, Lind, & Gries, Ltd., CX-98-39, 1998 WL 373276 (Minn. App. July 7, 1998).

66. Ramp v. St. Paul Fire and Marine Ins. Co., 269 So. 2d 239 (La. 1972).

67. *See* Sindell v. Gibson Dunn & Crutcher, 63 Cal. Rptr.2d 594 (1997).

68. Ramp v. St. Paul Fire and Marine Ins. Co., 269 So. 2d 239 (La. 1972).

69. *See* Estate of Newhoff, 435 N.Y.S.2d 632 (Surr. Ct. 1980).

70. Greene v. Greene, 436 N.E.2d 496 (N.Y. 1982).

71. *See* Heyer v. Flaig, 449 P.2d 161 (Cal. 1969); Russell v. Black, 9501, 1998 WL 760406, Oct. 27, 1998 (Mass. App. Div.); Murphy v. Housel & Housel, 955 P.2d 880 (Wyo. 1998).

72. Laird v. Blacker, 279 Cal. Rptr. 700 (Cal. App. 1991).

73. Johnson v. Sandler, Balkin, Hellman & Weinstein, P.C., 958 S.W.2d 42 (Mo. 1998).

74. Noble v. Bruce, 709 A.2d 1264 (Md. 1998); Deeb v. Johnson, 566 N.Y.S.2d 688 (App. Div. 1991); Brinkman v. Doughty, 748 N.E.2d 116 (Ohio 2000); Guest v. Cochran, 993 S.W.2d 397 (Tex. 1999).

# ABOUT THE EDITOR

JAY A. SOLED is a tenured professor at Rutgers University. He is admitted to practice in New Jersey, the U.S. District Court, District of New Jersey, and New York. He is a member of the American Bar Association and a columnist for its *Experience* magazine. A magna cum laude and Phi Beta Kappa graduate of Haverford College, he holds a Juris Doctor from University of Michigan School of Law, cum laude, and a Master of Laws in Taxation from the New York University School of Law where he was an editor of the *Tax Law Review*. He has published several law review articles that have appeared in the *Virginia Tax Law Review*, *Boston College Law Review*, *Notre Dame Law Review*, *The Brigham Young Law Review*, *The Connecticut Law Review*, *The Arizona Law Review*, *The American Journal of Tax Policy*, *The Tax Lawyer*, and *Real Property, Probate and Trust Law Journal*. In addition, Professor Soled has had several articles published in the *Journal of Taxation, Estate Planning, Experience, Tax Management Portfolio*, and the *New Jersey Law Journal*. Professor Soled has also written chapters in both *Estate Planning Techniques* (JK Lasser, 1994) and *New Jersey Inheritance Tax* (Gann Law Books, 1995). He has been quoted in *The New York Times, Wall Street Journal*, and the *LA Times*, and has appeared on CBS News and the Fox News Network.

# ABOUT THE CONTRIBUTORS

ALLAN C. BELL is a member of the New Jersey law firm Sills Cummis Radin Tischman Epstein & Gross, where he specializes in tax and financial planning. Mr. Bell received his B.A. magna cum laude from the University of Pennsylvania, his J.D. from Columbia University, and his LL.M. in Taxation from New York University. He has written and lectured extensively on estate planning and related tax matters.

SANTO BISIGNANO, JR., is a partner in the Dallas law firm Bisignano & Harrison, L.L.P, where he specializes in estate and tax planning. He received his B.A. and J.D. from the University of Notre Dame, and an M.B.A. from the University of Chicago. He is a Fellow of the American College of Trust and Estate Counsel and of the Texas State Bar Foundation. He is a frequent local, state, and national speaker on estate planning.

MICHAEL V. BOURLAND is the founding shareholder of the Fort Worth, Texas, law firm of Bourland, Wall & Wenzel, P.C. He focuses on estate and business planning and tax and probate law. Mr. Bourland received his B.A. and J.D. from Baylor University and an LL.M. in Taxation from the University of Miami, Florida. He is a Fellow of the American College of Trust and Estate Counsel and a guest lecturer in estate planning at several Texas law schools and institutes.

DAVE L. CORNFELD is Of Counsel to the law firm of Husch & Eppenberger, L.L.C., in St. Louis, Missouri, where he specializes in estate and tax planning. He received his J.D. from Washington University School of Law, where he was on the adjunct faculty in the graduate tax program.

ROBERT T. DANFORTH is Assistant Professor of Law at from Washington and Lee University School of Law. He received his J.D. with high honors at Duke University and is a member of the District of Columbia, North Carolina, and Virginia bars.

TOBY M. EISENBERG is an associate in the Dallas law firm Bisignano & Harrison, L.L.P, where he focuses on estate planning and probate matters. He received a J.D. from the University of Texas School of Law at Austin and an M.A. in Biblical Studies and Theology from Fuller Theological Seminary in Pasadena, California.

BRADLEY E.S. FOGEL is an Assistant Professor at Saint Louis University School of Law in St. Louis, Missouri, where he teaches estate and tax planning. He received his J.D. from Columbia University School of Law and an LL.M. in Taxation from the New York University School of Law.

JONATHAN BARRY FORMAN is a professor of law at the University of Oklahoma in Norman. He holds degrees in law, economics, and psychology. He is the author of numerous articles on Social Security, tax, and pension law. He is also a member of the Internal Revenue Service Advisory Committee on Tax-Exempt and Government Entities, and he recently served as an academic advisor to the Joint Committee on Taxation.

STEPHEN A. FROST is a lawyer at the Chicago firm Pedersen & Houpt, specializing in estate and tax planning. He received his J.D. from the University of Iowa Law School, where he also earned his C.P.A.

DAVID L. HIGGS is a member of Husch & Eppenberger, L.L.C., in Peoria, Illinois, where he specializes in tax, business, and estate planning. He received his J.D. summa cum laude from Southern Illinois University School of Law.

ANDREW H. HOOK is a Vice President of Oast & Hook, P.C., in Portsmouth, Virginia. Mr. Hook is certified as an Elder Law Attorney and is on the Board of Directors of the National Elder Law Foundation, the only ABA-accredited elder law certification program. He received his J.D. from the University of Virginia School of Law.

ZEB LAW is a member of the Irvine, California, law firm Coss Shreier & Law, where he specializes in estate tax planning. He received a J.D. from The American University, Washington College of Law and an LL.M. in Taxation from the Georgetown University Law Center.

SARAH M. LINSLEY is a partner at the Chicago office of Quarles & Brady, L.L.C., where she specializes in estate planning and employee benefits. She received her A.B. magna cum laude from Harvard College and her J.D. from Northwestern University.

STEPHEN P. MAGOWAN is a shareholder and director with Gravel and Shea, P.C., of Burlington, Vermont, where he specializes in employee benefits and estate planning. His most recent publication is *Probate and Administration of Decedent's Estates*, published by BNA as part of the Tax Management Portfolio series. He received his J.D. at Washington University, where he was a member of the Order of the Coif. His B.A. with highest honors is from Ohio University.

LOUIS A. MEZZULLO is a member of the law firm Mezzullo & Guare, P.L.C., in Richmond, Virginia, specializing in tax and estate planning. He is Adjunct Professor of Law at the T.C. Williams School of Law at the University of Richmond Law School. He is the author of *An Estate Planner's Guide to Qualified Retirement Plan Benefits, Third Edition* (American Bar Association, 2002).

ISABEL MIRANDA manages the estates and trust practice in the Teaneck, New Jersey, office of DeCotiis, FitzPatrick, Gluck & Cole, L.L.P. She received her J.D. from St. John's University School of Law, and a B.S. in Economics and Finance, cum laude, from Fordham University. She lectures on ethical issues for estate planning lawyers for the Practicing Law Institute.

CARMELA T. MONTESANO is in private practice in Head of the Harbor, New York, where she concentrates on estate and tax planning. She received her J.D. cum laude from Georgetown University Law Center and her B.A. magna cum laude from Fairfield University in Fairfield, Connecticut.

JEFFREY N. MYERS is a shareholder of the Fort Worth, Texas, law firm of Bourland, Wall & Wenzel, P.C., where he specializes in estate and tax planning. He received his J.D. from California Western School of Law in San Diego, and his LL.M. in Taxation from the University of San Diego.

SUZANNE L. SHIER is a partner in the Chicago law firm Chapman and Cutler, specializing in estate planning and trust administration. She received her J.D. from Loyola University of Chicago and her L.L.M. in Taxation from DePaul University.

REBECCA WALLENFELSZ is a lawyer in the Chicago law firm Chapman and Cutler, specializing in estate planning and trust administration. She received her J.D. cum laude from Loyola University of Chicago and her B.A. cum laude from the University of Notre Dame.

RICHARD V. WELLMAN is professor emeritus at the University of Georgia School of Law, where he taught trusts and estates. He received his J.D. from the University of Michigan, where he also had been professor of law.

BRIAN T. WHITLOCK is a partner in charge of wealth transfer services in the Chicago law firm Blackman Kallick Bartelstein, L.L.P. He received his J.D. with honors from IIT/Chicago-Kent College of Law, where he also earned his C.P.A.

HAROLD G. WREN has been Of Counsel to the law firm of Voyles & Johnson, P.S.C., Louisville, Kentucky. He holds his A.B. and LL.B. from Columbia, and his J.S.D. from Yale. After practicing with Wilkie Farr & Gallagher of New York, he entered academia, where he was Dean of three law schools and taught at four others. He is author of several books, including *Creative Estate Planning* (1970) and *Tax Aspects of Marital Dissolution* (2d ed. 1997). He is past-Chair of the Senior Lawyers Division of the ABA.

HERBERT L. ZUCKERMAN is a member of the law firm of Sills, Cummins, Radin, Tischman, Epstein & Gross, P.A., in Newark, New Jersey. He specializes in criminal tax fraud, tax controversies, estate planning, and corporate tax matters, and has lectured and written extensively on all four areas. He received his J.D. from Rutgers University and is a Fellow of the American College of Tax Counsel.

# TABLE OF CASES

# INDEX